Indonesia and the ASEAN
Free Trade Agreement

Indonesia and the ASEAN Free Trade Agreement

Nationalists and Regional Integration Strategy

ALEXANDER C. CHANDRA

LEXINGTON BOOKS

A division of
ROWMAN & LITTLEFIELD PUBLISHERS, INC.
Lanham • Boulder • New York • Toronto • Plymouth, UK

LEXINGTON BOOKS

A division of Rowman & Littlefield Publishers, Inc.
A wholly owned subsidary of The Rowman & Littlefield Publishing Group, Inc.
4501 Forbes Boulevard, Suite 200
Lanham, MD 20706

Estover Road
Plymouth PL6 7PY
United Kingdom

British Library Cataloguing in Publication Information Available

Library of Congress Cataloging-in-Publication Data

Chandra, Alexander C.
 Indonesia and the ASEAN free trade agreement : nationalists and regional integration
strategy / Alexander C. Chandra.
    p. cm.
 Includes bibliographical references and index.
 ISBN-13: 978-0-7391-1620-3 (cloth : alk. paper)
 ISBN-10: 0-7391-1620-7 (cloth : alk. paper)
 1. Free trade—Indonesia. 2. Indonesia—Commercial treaties. I. Title.
 HF2343.C53 2008
 382'.91509598—dc22   2007052932

Printed in the United States of America

♾™ The paper used in this publication meets the minimum requirements of American
National Standard for Information Sciences—Permanence of Paper for Printed Library
Materials, ANSI/NISO Z39.48–1992.

In memory of my parents, and for Kartini, and the future generations of an integrated Southeast Asia

Contents

Contents

List of Figures

List of Tables

List of Abbreviations

ABAC	ASEAN Business Advisory Council
ABMI	Asian Bond Market Initiative
AC	ASEAN Community
ACCICG	AFTA-CER CEP Implementation and Co-ordination Group
ACFTA	ASEAN-China Free Trade Agreement
ADB	Asian Development Bank
AEC	ASEAN Economic Community
AEM	ASEAN Economic Ministerial Meeting
AFMM	ASEAN Finance Minister Meeting
AFTA	ASEAN Free Trade Agreement/Area
AI	Amnesty International
AIA	ASEAN Investment Area
AIC	ASEAN Industrial Complementation
AICO	ASEAN Industrial Co-operation
AIELTF	ASEAN-India Economic Linkages Task Force
AIJV	ASEAN Industrial Joint Venture
AIP	ASEAN Industrial Project
ALADI	*Asociación Latinoamericana de Integración* (Association of Latin American Integration)
AMF	Asian Monetary Fund
AMM	ASEAN Ministerial Meeting
APA	ASEAN People's Assembly
APBN	*Anggaran Pendapatan Belanja Negara* (State's Budget)
APEC	Asia-Pacific Economic Co-operation
APINDO	*Asosiasi Pengusaha Indonesia* (Indonesian Entrepreneurs Association)
APT	ASEAN plus Three
ARF	ASEAN Regional Forum
ASA	Association of Southeast Asia
ASA	ASEAN Swap Arrangement
ASC	ASEAN Security Community
ASCC	ASEAN Socio-Cultural Community
ASCU	ASEAN Surveillance Coordinating Unit
ASEAN	Association of Southeast Asian Nations
ASEAN-CCI	ASEAN Chambers of Commerce and Industry
ASEAN-ISIS	ASEAN Institute of Strategic and International Studies

ASEAN-PTA	ASEAN Preferential Trading Arrangement
ASEM	Asia-Europe Meeting
ASP	ASEAN Surveillance Process
ASPAC	Asia and Pacific Council
ATF	ASEAN Tourism Forum
BAFTA	Baltic Free Trade Area
BAKIN	*Badan Koordinasi Intelijen Negara* (State Intelligence Co-ordinating Agency)
BAPPENAS	*Badan Perencanaan Pembangunan Nasional* (National Development Planning Agency)
BBC	Brand to Brand Complementation
BDNI	*Bank Dagang Negara Indonesia* (National Trading Bank of Indonesia)
BFTA	Bilateral Free Trade Agreement
BI	*Bank Indonesia* (Central Bank of Indonesia)
BIMP-EAGA	Brunei Darussalam, Indonesia, Malaysia, the Philippines East ASEAN Growth Area
BKPM	*Badan Koordinasi Penanaman Modal* (Investment Coordinating Board)
BOIT	Board of Investment of Thailand
BORSUMY	Borneo-Sumatra Company
BPPMA	*Badan Pertimbangan Penanaman Modal Asing* (Foreign Capital Investment Advisory Board)
BSA	Bilateral Swap Arrangement
CACM	Central American Common Market
CARICOM	Caribbean Community and Common Market
CEP	Closer Economic Partnership
CEPP	Comprehensive Economic Partnership Program
CEPT	Common Effective Preferential Tariff
CER	Closer Economic Relations
CET	Common External Tariffs
CGI	Consultative Group on Indonesia
CICP	Cambodian Institute for Co-operation and Peace
CIDES	Centre for Information and Development Studies
CMEA	Council of Mutual Economic Assistance (also known as COMECON)
COMESA	Common Market of Eastern and Southern Africa
CSIS	Centre for Strategic and International Studies
CSOs	Civil Society Organizations
CUSFTA	Canada-U.S. Free Trade Agreement
DEPPERINDAG	*Departemen Industri dan Perdagangan* (Ministry of Industry and Trade)
DOM	*Daerah Operasi Militer* (Military Operation Area)
DPOD	*Dewan Perimbangan Otonomi Daerah* (Fiscal Balance Committee of Provincial Autonomy)

DPR	*Dewan Perwakilan Rakyat* (People's Representative Assembly)
EAEC	East Asian Economic Caucus
EAEG	East Asian Economic Group
EAFTA	East Asian Free Trade Area
EAI	Enterprise for ASEAN Initiative
EAIA	East Asian Investment Area
EAMF	East Asian Monetary Fund
EASG	East Asian Study Group
EAVG	East Asian Vision Group
EC	European Community
ECAFE	Economic Commission for Asia and the Far East
ECLA	Economic Commission on Latin America
ECOWAS	Economic Community of West African States
ECSC	European Coal and Steel Community
EFTA	European Free Trade Association
EHP	Early Harvest Program
EU	European Union
FEP	Foreign Economic Policy
FNPBI	*Front Nasional Perjuangan Buruh Indonesia* (Front National for the Indonesian Labor Struggle)
FPTA	Full Preferential Trading Arrangement
FSPSI	*Federasi Serikat Pekerja Seluruh Indonesia* (Federation of Indonesian Workers Union)
FTA	Free Trade Area
FTAA	Free Trade Area of the Americas
GAM	*Gerakan Aceh Merdeka* (Aceh Freedom Movement)
GATT	General Agreement on Tariffs and Trade
GDR	German Democratic Republic
GOLKAR	*Golongan Karya* (Functional Group)
GSP	General System of Preferences
GT	Growth Triangle
HPA	Hanoi Plan of Action
HST	Hegemonic Stability Theory
IBRA	Indonesian Banking Restructuring Agency
ICMI	*Ikatan Cendikiawan Muslim Indonesia* (Association of Indonesian Muslim Intellectuals)
IEI	International Economic Integration
IGGI	Inter-Governmental Group on Indonesia
IIA	Initial Investment Approval
IIR	Institute for International Relations (Vietnam)
IJEPA	Indonesia-Japan Economic Partnership Agreement
IKINI	*Ikatan Importir Nasional Indonesia* (Indonesian National Association of Importers)
IMF	International Monetary Fund

IMT-GT	Indonesia, Malaysia, Thailand Growth Triangle
INDEF	Institute for Development of Economic and Finance
INFID	International NGO Forum on Indonesian Development
Internatio	*Internationale Credie en Handelsvereeniging* (International Credit and Trading Association)
IOs	International Organizations
IOCU	International Organization of Consumers Union
IPE	International Political Economy
IR	International Relations
ISDS	Institute for Strategic and Development Studies (Philippines)
ISI	Import Substitution Industry
ISI	Indonesian Survey Institute
ISIS	Institute for Strategic and International Studies (Singapore)
ISIS	Institute for Security and International Studies (Thailand)
ITWG	Interim Technical Working Group
JSE	Jakarta Stock Exchange
JSG	Joint Study Group
KADIN	*Kamar Dagang dan Industri Indonesia* (Indonesian Chambers of Commerce and Industry)
KLIK	*Kajian Layanan Informasi untuk Kedaulatan Rakyat* (Civic and Information Studies)
KOMNAS-HAM	*Komisi Nasional untuk Hak-Hak AsasiManusia* (National Commission for Human Rights)
KPPOD	*Komite Pemantauan Pelaksanaan Otonomi Daerah* (Regional Autonomy Watch)
KUKMI	*Kerukunan Usahawan Kecil dan Menengah Indonesia* (Indonesian Society for Small and Medium Scale Entrepreneurs)
LAFTA	Latin American Free Agreement/Area
LDCs	Least Developed Countries
LEAD	Leadership for Environmental and Development
LIPI	*Lembaga Ilmu Pengetahuan Indonesia* (Indonesian Institute for Sciences)
LoI	Letter of Intent
LSI	*Lembaga Survey Indonesia* (Indonesian Survey Circle)
Maphilindo	Malaysia, the Philippines, and Indonesia
MCEDSEA	Ministerial Conference on Economic Development in Southeast Asia
MERCOSUR	*Mercado Común del Sur* (Southern Cone Common Market Agreement)
MFA	Ministry of Foreign Affairs
MHA	Ministry of Home Affairs
MoC-SMEs	Ministry of Co-operative, Small and Medium Enterprises
MoF	Ministry of Finance

MoJ	Ministry of Justice
MoP	Margin of Preference
MoU	Memorandum of Understanding
MPR	*Majelis Permusyahwaratan Rakyat* (House of Representatives)
NAFTA	North American Free Trade Area/Agreement
NAM	Non-Aligned Movement
NEFOS	New Emerging Forces
Nekolim	Neo-colonialism, Colonialism, and Imperialism
NEP	New Economic Policy
NGOs	Non-Governmental Organizations
NIEs	Newly Industrialized Countries
NRA	New Regionalism Approach
NRT	New Regionalism Theory
OECD	Organization for Economic Co-operation and Development
OLDEFOS	Old Established Forces
OPEC	Organization of Petroleum Exporting Countries
OPSUS	*Operasi Khusus* (Special Operation)
OtDa	*Otonomi Daerah* (Provincial Autonomy)
PAN	*Partai Amanat Nasional* (National Mandate Party)
PANI	Pesticide Action Network Indonesia
PBB	*Partai Bulan Bintang* (Crescent Moon and Star Party)
PDI-P	*Partai Demokrasi Indonesia untuk Perjuangan* (Indonesia Democratic Party for Struggle)
PEC	Pacific Economic Co-operation
PEKSI	*Persatuan Eksportir Indonesia* (Union of Indonesian Exporters)
PERDA	*Peraturan Daerah* (Provincial Regulations)
PERTAMINA	*Perusahaan Pertambangan Minyak dan Gas Bumi Negara* (Indonesian Gas and Oil Company)
PIFs	Pacific Island Forums
PK	*Partai Keadilan* (Justice Party)
PKB	*Partai Kebangkitan Bangsa* (National Awakening Party)
PKI	*Partai Komunis Indonesia* (Indonesian Communist Party)
PPP	*Partai Persatuan Pembangunan* (United Development Party)
PPTA	Partial Preferential Trade Arrangement
PSI	*Partai Sosialis Indonesia* (Indonesian Socialist Party)
PTA	Preferential Trade Arrangement
PTPM	*Panitia Teknis Penanaman Modal* (Technical Committee on Investment)
PUPUK	*Perkumpulan untuk Peningkatan Usaha Kecil* (Association for the Advancement of Small Businesses)
REI	Regional Economic Integration
RIA	Regional Integration Arrangement
RIIA	Royal Institute of International Affairs

RIS	Regional Integration Strategy
Rp.	Rupiah (Indonesian currency)
RTAs	Regional Trade Agreements
RTIA	Regional Trade Investment Area
RUSI	Republic United States of Indonesia
SAARC	South Asian Association for Regional Co-operation
SACU	South African Custom Union
SAFTA	South Asian Free Trade Area
SAPA	Solidarity for Asian People's Advocacy
SAPTA	South Asian Preferential Trade Arrangement
SEACEN	Southeast Asian Central Banks
SEATO	Southeast Asian Treaty Organization
SEOM	Senior Official Meeting
SIIA	Singapore Institute of International Affairs
SIJORI	Singapore, Johor, Riau (Growth Triangle)
SL	Sensitive List
SMEs	Small and Medium Sized Enterprises
TAC	Treaty of Amity and Co-operation
TNCs	Transnational Corporations
UN	United Nations
UNCTAD	United Nations' Conference on Trade and Development
UNDP	United Nations' Development Program
UNISOSDEM	Uni-Social Democrat
UPC	Urban Poor Consortium
UUPD	*Undang-Undang Peraturan Daerah* (Provincial Government Act)
UUPKPD	*Undang-Undang Perimbangan Keuangan Pusat dan Daerah* (Financial Balance between Central and Provincial Governments Act)
WAC	Western African Community
WEC	West-East Corridor (Mekong Basin Growth Triangle)
WTO	World Trade Organization
YLKI	*Yayasan Lembaga Konsumen Indonesia* (Indonesian Consumers Organization)

Acknowledgments

This book is entirely dedicated to my parents, Irwan and Nila Chandra, who have made everything possible. There are simply no words that can be used to replace the love, care, and support they have provided throughout the making of this book and beyond. May you both rest in peace.

I would also like to express my deepest gratitude to Dr. Christopher M. Dent and Simon D. Lee for their contributions in providing valuable and continuous encouragement, patience, guidance, assistance, and constructive criticism during the making of this book. My gratitude also goes to an anonymous referee for his or her generous comments and constructive criticisms in the final stage of the book publication. In addition, Dr. Tim J. Huxley, Prof. Joern Dosch, and Dr. Eric Grove all have provided me with valuable insights and guidance either during the early or the final stage of the research process. Moreover, I would also like to thank all my respondents in Indonesia who participated in the research interviews. It was an extraordinary experience to listen to them and to their opinions and visions about the future of Indonesian nationalism and ASEAN regionalism. Any mistakes or omissions in the research and writing of this book are entirely mine.

I would also like to acknowledge the contributions made by other individuals who were very supportive and helpful throughout the making of this book. I should also express my gratitude to Andrea McNicoll for her editing and proofreading assistance throughout the time I spent on my higher education and beyond. The completion of this book also owes much to my dearest one, Kartini Isabelle Pouchous, who has provided me with continuous inspiration and encouragement, as well as extravagant, extensive, and endless personal support during the whole project. Finally, my sincere gratitude also goes to family (Ratnasari Alam, Keisha, Andrew, and Richard Chandra) and friends (Budi Sulistianingrum, Sandi Wijaya, and Lucky A. Lontoh, Lucky Adelova, and Anne Pouchous (thanks for providing me the opportunity to finish the final manuscript of the book in Brussels), as well as others in both Southeast Asia, particularly Indonesia, Europe, and other parts of the world whose names cannot be included in this limited space despite their support. It has been a privilege to make the acquaintance of all these individuals.

Chapter 1

Introduction

Regionalism and Nationalism: An Initial Comment

Nationalism and regionalism are two major phenomena that have emerged during the twentieth century and the early part of the twenty-first. These two trends, however, do not exist in isolation from other prevailing developments, such as the emergence of ethnonationalism and globalization. While many nation-states have surrendered part of their sovereignty, they still continue to promote nationalistic ideals as a means of protecting the interests of their citizens. The demise of the Cold War in the late 1980s further undermined the existence of nation-states through the rise of ethnonationalist movements throughout the world, demonstrated most notably by the breaking up of the former Soviet Union, and, to cite another example, the emergence of East Timor as the youngest nation to exist on earth. Ethnonationalist movements have also developed in other parts of the world, but have yet to achieve independence (i.e., in Quebec and the Chechen Republic). The concurrent emergence of these trends during the latter part of the twentieth century has thrown up some interesting contradictions within global structures. Global capitalism continues to expand in search of more profitable ways for the production and the distribution of goods and services, leading to a more internationalized world economy. At the same time, nationalist economic policies are also prevalent in both developing and developed countries as a way of countering the forces of globalization and regionalization. It is, therefore, possible to suggest that the world is becoming both a more integrated and a more fragmented place at the same time.

The emergence of regionalism, globalization, and ethnonationalism has, nevertheless, challenged the existence of the established nation-state system. However, contemporary studies of regionalism, particularly those that fall within the sphere of the *New Regionalism Approach (NRA)*, challenge the conventional argument that the relationship between these different concepts is contentious. Instead of focusing upon the competing nature of these divergent forces, theorists in this line of study emphasize the *commonality* and *complementarity* within the relationship between these different forces. It is argued that most states take a nationalistic stance as a response toward the changes that occur as a result of global capitalism (Horsman and Marshall 1995: x). Regionalism also emerges as a response to the urgent need to find new ways of confronting global forces. As a mechanism for the achievement of a new world order, regionalism is useful to combat the negative impact of globalism, to minimize excessive con-

1

trol and abuse by the state, to achieve a desirable world order goals, and to strengthen the regional structures of governance (Falk 1999: 64). To date, regionalism is a phenomenon that is spreading throughout the world, in both developed and developing countries, as can be seen in the recent institutionalization of many regional groupings in the world.

The pattern of the institutionalization of regional grouping at the global level is varied, and ranges from the highly institutionalized regionalism of Europe to the much looser form of regionalism seen in developing regions, such as Latin America, Africa, the Middle East, Southeast Asia, and the Asia-Pacific. This book focuses mainly on the Association of Southeast Asian Nations (ASEAN), a regional organization that is composed of ten countries, namely Indonesia, Thailand, Malaysia, the Philippines, Singapore, Brunei, Vietnam, Myanmar, Laos, and Cambodia. The region itself has been described as dynamic due to "a wide range of developmental settings and conditions both between and within states. These range from chaos and isolation . . . to high development of technological and trade-driven economic development" (Ulack and Leinbach 2000: 1). However, these diversities, coupled with strongly nationalistic foreign policies, have meant that the process of regionalization in the Southeast Asian region has progressed slowly. Specific attention within this book will be given to Indonesians' perspectives on their country's involvement in ASEAN, particularly in reference to the grouping's main integration mechanism, the ASEAN Free Trade Area/Agreement (AFTA). The rest of this chapter will be devoted to outlining recent trends in regionalism in the global economy, the objectives, and the contribution this book to the ongoing debate on the relationship between nationalism and regionalism, and the structure and organization of this book.

Recent Trends in Regionalism in the Global Economy

There has been an increase in the number of formal regional organizations in recent years, which suggests a proliferation of regionalism among countries in the world today. The World Trade Organization (WTO) (see figure 1.1.), for example, notes that the General Agreement on Tariff and Trade (GATT) identified the existence of 124 RTAs during the period 1948-1994. Since the creation of the WTO in 1995, about one hundred additional regional arrangements have been added to promote liberalization of both trade and services. To date, there are 250 RTAs, of which 196, or roughly 78.4 percent, were operational by early 2005, while the remaining fifty-four RTAs are still under negotiation. The majority of the existing RTAs are formed bilaterally, either as a custom union, free trade agreements, preferential agreements, or service agreements. There is now one bilateral custom union between two states and four between a regional grouping and a state. Furthermore, there are also eighty-one bilateral free trade agreements between two states and forty-nine BFTAs between a regional grouping and a state. In addition, there is one bilateral preferential arrangement between two states, and thirteen bilateral service agreements between two states with another thirteen between a regional grouping and a state. The majority, or twenty-five, of the existing bilateral service agreement are also part of bilateral free trade agreements deals. In total, there are now 162 bilateral trade agreements in operation, or about 64.8 percent of total RTAs. Thus, to a large extent, a large part of regionalism is new bilateralism (Lloyd 2002). By 2002, the total number of RTAs had increased to 250, showing an increase of 130 since the creation of the WTO. A WTO study (2000: 3) also suggests that by the end of 2005 the total number of RTAs could reach approximately three hundred if those RTAs presently at the planning or negotiation stage are put into operation.

Figure 1.1.
RTAs in Force by Date of Notification

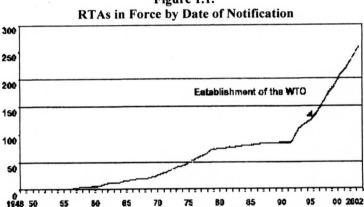

Source: WTO official web site (accessed 2006) at
http://www.wto.org/english/tratop_e/region_e/regfac_e.htm

Even with the increase in the number of RIAs, the European Union (EU) remains the most comprehensive regional grouping in the world today. It originated from the European Coal and Steel Community (ECSC), and has progressed toward the establishment of the Single Market in 1993, introducing euro notes and coins on the 1 January 2002. Apart from having gone through the enlargement process, the EU is also pursuing bilateral FTAs with non-European member countries (i.e., FTAs between the European Community (EC) and Morocco, EC and Israel, and between the European Free Trade Association (EFTA) and Israel).

During the first wave of integration, there was also an attempt among socialist states of Eastern Europe to form an RIA. The economies of Eastern Europe formed the Council for Mutual Economic Assistance (CMEA) in 1949, which sought to accelerate economic development and the establishment of a more rational division of labor among the socialist states of Eastern Europe (Robson 1987: 219). The grouping, which was also known as COMECON in the West, was composed of the Soviet Union, Bulgaria, Czechoslovakia, Hungary,

Poland, Romania, Albania, the German Democratic Republic (GDR), Cuba, Mongolia, and Vietnam as member countries. Initially, CMEA was only composed of Eastern European socialist states, but membership was expanded throughout the 1970s and 1980s to include non-Eastern European socialist states. Some non-socialist countries were also participated in this grouping. In 1976, for example, the CMEA also gave observer and co-operant status to Iraq and Mexico (Marer and Montias 1988). Over the years, however, the aim of the CMEA was to counter the rival Western European's European Community (EC) and the European Free Trade Association (EFTA). The CMEA, however, ceased to exist in 1991, largely as a result of internal conflict and divergent national interests among member countries.

In other regions, there are also examples of RIAs. In the Americas, for example, the North American Free Trade Agreement/Area (NAFTA) and the Southern Common Market Agreement (MERCOSUR—*Mercado Común del Sur*) have been the most significant ones to date. NAFTA was signed in 1992 as the formalization of the extensive economic ties among the United States, Canada, and Mexico (Evans and Newham 1998: 342). When it was signed, this trade agreement was considered as the most comprehensive economic integration project ever negotiated between a developing country and industrial countries (Mattli 1999: 179). Prior to the creation of NAFTA, there were also other forms of regional integration arrangements (RIAs) among North American countries. The first comprehensive one was the U.S.-Canada Auto Pact of 1965. In 1988 this RIA was transformed into the Canada-U.S. Free Trade Agreement (CUSFTA), which involved a total free trade agreement between the two countries. Many elements within the CUSFTA were later incorporated into the NAFTA agreement, while Mexico was asked to join the agreement.

Meanwhile, MERCOSUR was established in 1995 as the second most important trade bloc in the American continent. The creation of this regional grouping was initiated by two of the largest countries in Latin America, Brazil and Argentina, who wished to deepen their relationship after decades of mutual distrust between the two countries. Brazil and Argentina drafted twenty-four bilateral protocols that symbolized a new political and economic reality for these two Latin American countries. By 1991, Paraguay and Uruguay had asked to join the agreement, and, subsequently, the Treaty of Asuncion was signed on 26 March 1991, agreeing that the decision for the creation of a common market should be decided upon by 31 December 1994. Prior to the creation of MERCOSUR, there were several initiatives to create regional groupings in Latin America, which include Latin American Free Trade Area (LAFTA—1960) and the Association of Latin American Integration (ALADI—1980). Many of these initiatives, however, failed to succeed.

In Central America, there are also the Central American Common Market (CACM) and the Andean Group, which were established in 1960 and 1969 respectively. Recently, however, there have been efforts to unite the economies of the Western Hemisphere, which will incorporate member countries of both NAFTA and MERCOSUR as well as other older regional groupings, such as the

Andean Pact and the Central and Caribbean units (Phillips 2000: 288). This effort has materialized in the Free Trade Area of the Americas (FTAA), which was originated from a joint declaration made at the first Summit of the Americas that took place in Miami, in December 1994. The grouping will involve thirty-four countries in the region, all agreeing to a free trade area throughout the continent by 2005. To date, however, FTAA is still behind schedule due to increasing oppositions expressed by many civil society groups in both Latin America toward the possibility of increased the United States' domination over the Latin America economies.

Africa, however, has the largest number of RIAs in the world, although most of which are still in the form of preferential arrangements. Among these are the *Communaute Economique de L'Afrique de L'Ouest* (1974), the *Union Douaniere et Economique de L'Afrique* (1964), the *Communaute Economique des Pays de Grande Lacs* (1976), the *Communaute Economique des Etats de L'Afrique Centrale* (1983), the *Communaute Economique des Etats de L'Afrique Centrale* (1983), and the West African Community (WAC—1978). In South Africa, furthermore, there are three main regional organizations, which include the South African Custom Union (SACU—1969), the Southern African Development Co-ordination Conference (1980) and the Preferential Trade Area for East Africa (1981). In 1994, the Preferential Trade Area for East Africa was transformed into the Common Market of Eastern and Southern Africa (COMESA), which took the end objective to be a full common market (Odén 2000: 255).

A similar trend, however, was not reflected in Asia. The only comprehensive regional grouping in the region is ASEAN, which, at present, comprises all the Southeast Asian nations. Prior to the creation of ASEAN there were various different integration arrangements that existed among some Southeast Asian countries, but only in the very short-term. The first of these was the Association of Southeast Asia (ASA), which was created in 1961, composed of Thailand, the Philippines, and Malaysia as member countries. The second was Maphilindo, which was created in 1966, with member countries including Malaysia, the Philippines, and Indonesia. These two projects were mainly based on security issues, and sought to contain the spread of Communism in the region. The existence of both ASA and Maphilindo, however, was rather short owing to continuous conflicts among the member countries of each respective Association. A more recent regional integration scheme in Asia is the South Asian Association for Regional Cooperation (SAARC), formed in 1985 and consisting of Bangladesh, Bhutan, India, the Maldives, Nepal, Pakistan, and Sri Lanka. Despite other trade liberalization initiatives, SAARC is still the main tool that protects the political and security interests of South Asian countries. In 1993, member countries of SAARC agreed to form an ambitious regional trade agreement, the South Asian Preferential Trading Arrangement (SAPTA), which, subsequently, was put into effect in December 1995. The SAPTA was hoped to act as a stepping-stone to a more ambitious project to create the South Asian Free Trade Area (SAFTA) by the year 2000, or the latest by 2005 (Muni 2000: 125).

Nationalism as a New Domain in New Regionalism Approach Analysis

The global tendency toward regionalism started to re-emerge during the early 1990s. In light of increasing interest in regionalism, political scientists began to search for possible explanations for the proliferation of regionalism at the time. Aside from social constructivism, which had largely developed since the dismantling of the Cold War, a new theory was created to explain "the second wave of regional cooperation and integration" (Hettne 1999: 8). This approach was later called the New Regionalism Approach (NRA). Despite the increase proliferation of regionalism in the early 1990s, nationalism still plays significant role in determining the relationship among states. It is for this reason that the nexus between regionalism and nationalism deserves special attention. Although analyzes of nationalism in NRA analysis are not uncommon, there has been no specific explanation of the nature of the relationship between regionalism and nationalism in the literature of NRA (see, for example, Palmer 1991; Hettne 1999; Schulz et al. 2001). However, NRA's emphasis on the multidimensionality, heterogeneity, flexibility, and fluidity of regionalism today allows us to expand the current analysis of NRA beyond the regional-global nexus. With the increasing involvement of domestic actors in current international affairs, it is imperative to include the domestic domain in an analysis of the new regionalism. In the view of one of the main proponents of NRA, Hettne (1994: 1), the current "process of globalization and regionalization [can be] articulated within the same larger process of global structural change." This view, however, neglects the importance of the domestic domain in its analysis of regionalism. It is for this reason that the current analysis of NRA is expanded to argue that "regions and regionalization must be understood in a global perspective, as well as that in the interrelated global-regional-national-local levels" (Schulz et al. 2001a: 13-14). Regionalism is, indeed, a complex subject, and, as such, it should be treated in a multidisciplinary fashion, as there are no fixed definitions that can be attached to the term.

By the late 1990s, a more comprehensive approach was introduced to explain the global-regional-national-local nexus in NRA analysis to include the "world (global) system, interregional relation, the region, and the sub-national level" (Hettne 1999: 14-15). At the world (global) level, NRA analysis is concerned with the decline of the hegemonic powers, particularly in the context of the transformation from bipolarity to multipolarity. The emergence of a multipolar world order implies an increasing pattern of regionalism. At the interregional level, emphasis is placed upon the idea of action and response, or interaction that emerges between different regional groupings in the world. Moreover, this level of analysis also suggests a greater interdependency between different RIAs throughout the world. Furthermore, a regional level analysis stresses the process of homogenization in terms of culture, security, economic policies and political systems. More importantly, this level of analysis maintains that a region often constitutes arenas for both the competing and converging national interests of member countries. Finally, at the sub-national level, primary analysis is made of the argument that the process of regionalization is triggered by various forms of disintegration at the sub-national level.

One of NRA's major ideas that is useful to explain the relationship between regionalism and nationalism is the notion of the spontaneous process of regionalism, which primarily refers to the actors that are involved in the regionalization process (Hettne 1999: 9; Schulz et al. 2001a: 13). During the first wave of regionalism, there was a tendency for state actors to play a dominant role in determining the future of regional projects, including the process of institutionalization. This has not been the case with the second wave of regionalism, which is because of the overwhelming domestic and global issues that states now have to handle. It is for this reason that the "international community has had to come to accept the legitimacy and activity of several types of influential non-state actors" (Shaw 1994: 140) at both international and national levels. Since the second wave, non-state actors have begun to enter into the process of promoting regionalism. In the past, social actors, such as the religious community and transnational corporations (TNCs), have played an important role in informal transnational, if not regional, activities. Today, however, this role has been expanded to include new actors, such as non-governmental organizations (NGOs) and civil society organizations (CSOs), both of which are equally active in promoting greater interactions between citizens of different countries.[1] The regionalization process from within has been particularly evident in Southeast Asia in recent years. Apart from the recent expansion of a number of ASEAN-affiliated NGOs,[2] the launching of the ASEAN People's Assembly (APA)[3] and the ASEAN Civil Society Conference (ACSC)[4] since 2000 and 2005 respectively were examples of the push to include non-state actors in the regionalization process.

Another major feature of NRA analysis that is useful to explain the symbiotic nature of the relationship between regionalism and nationalism is the transition from protectionism, which was prevalent during the first wave of regionalism, to a more outward and more market-oriented form of regionalism (Palmer 1991; Bhalla and Bhalla 1997; Hettne 1999; Hettne and Söderbaum 2000). The recent intensification of global economic interactions has pushed countries to ease off on the high economic barriers that they used to impose in the past. Hence, the new regionalism has been generally characterized by an open economic system, which is being driven mainly by the markets and technology (Barry and Keith 1999). In fact, one of the main aims when the concept of new regionalism was launched was to avoid the kind of regionalization that would limit the scope for global economic liberalization (Odén 1999: 164). This more open world economic system is best illustrated in the recent World Bank (2001) report, which indicates that substantial cuts in tariffs levels have been made since the late 1980s or early 1990s.[5] It is, however, a matter of controversy as to whether an open economic system actually prevails in the global trading system today. In Ethier's (2001: 5) analysis, for example, since "a dramatic move to free trade between member [countries] is not central, the degree of liberalization is usually modest." Nevertheless, the tendency toward a more open or more market-oriented regionalism among most RIAs today suggests a shift of attitude among state and domestic actors in each RIA member country toward an increasing pattern of globalization and regionalization.

In the Southeast Asian context, one major fundamental shift that indicates the transformation away from the first wave of regionalism to the second wave of regionalism in the economic field is the region's pursuance of an open regionalism concept (Palmer 1991; Hallet and Braga 1994). However, unlike regionalism elsewhere in the world, the open regionalism concept in Southeast Asia has not been associated with advanced integration schemes, such as the common market, but cross-border investments and a flexible and a well-functioning financial system (Odén 1999: 161). The demise of the Cold War, in particular, had a definite impact on ASEAN countries, enabling them to expand their activities beyond the region. Among other factors, the intensification of regional economic trade, particularly since the early 1990s, has made it possible for ASEAN countries to enhance economic cooperation with countries beyond Southeast Asia. One example of this is the interest shown by ASEAN member countries to become involved in Asia-Pacific regionalism, under the auspices of the Asia-Pacific Economic Cooperation (APEC). A more recent example of the tendency of ASEAN member countries to pursue a more outward and open economic policy with external parties is their involvement in the ASEAN plus Three (APT) mechanism. To date, however, APT has been regarded with skepticism by the West since membership has included countries that should have been members of the failed East Asian Economic Caucus (EAEC), which was first proposed to safeguard the interests of East Asian countries in various multilateral negotiations (Leong 2000: 71). Beyond East Asia and the Asia-Pacific, ASEAN countries have also begun to rectify the weakness in their relations with the European Union (EU) by conducting closer bilateral efforts on both sides and by using the Asia-Europe Meeting (ASEM) as a framework for interregional cooperation (Dent 2001b: 25).[6] These examples suggest that the attitudes of Southeast Asian state and non-state actors today have transformed, and are more accommodating of the emerging patterns of regionalization and globalization.

More importantly, however, NRA's ability to explain the symbiotic nature of the relationship between nationalism and regionalism can be seen through the theory's emphasis upon the gradual transformation of a nation-state into a region-state (Hettne and Söderbaum 2000: 462-68). More comprehensively, both NRA theorists maintain that the new regionalism can be explained as a gradual transformation from nation-states into a regional space, regional society, regional community, and, finally, a region-state (refer to figure 1.2.) (Hettne and Söderbaum 2000: 462). These phases allow us to construct a general idea on how a region evolves into a more formalized institution, which is similar to the process of the formation of the nation-state system. At the *regional space* level, NRA analysis maintains that a region is composed of a group of people sharing

similar historical antecedents, cultures, and values.[7] It is at this level that regional actors and organizations conduct regional projects that will act as a basic
foundation for a more complex form of regionalism. Eventually, regional space
evolves into a *regional society* in which interaction between groups from two or
more different geographical locations within a region takes place. However,
interactions at this level tend to be minimal and largely informal. The process of
regionalization becomes more complex with the introduction of a *regional
community*, which implies the intensification of the interaction between those
groups in the different geographical locations. At this point of the regionalization process, the institutionalization of various domestic non-state actors, such as
the highly sophisticated traders and civil society groups, begins to take place.
Through either conscious or unconscious acts, these actors start to play various
roles in promoting regionalism. It is only within the *region-state* level that regionalism is finally institutionalized, and much of this is derived from a voluntary reaction toward the intensification of regional actors' interactions, rather than
an involuntary reaction, such as in the case when a state initiates regionalism.
Therefore, within the framework of NRA analysis, the institutionalization of a
regional grouping implies an evolutionary process from a nation-state to a region state.

Figure 1.2.
The Evolutionary Process of Regionalism

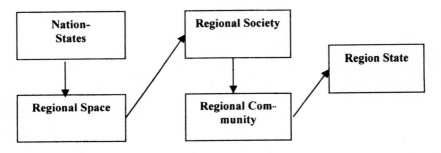

To sum up this analysis of NRA, it is important first of all to pinpoint some
of the main characteristics of the theory. The first characteristic is that NRA
attempts to be more critical and reflective than previous international relations
theories by drawing upon a more comprehensive range of social sciences
(Schulz et al. 2001c: 235). NRA, therefore, attempts to transcend the problem-
solving theory associated with the state-centric and rationalist epistemologies
(Schulz et al. 2001c: 235). As a result, the new regionalism can be characterized
as a more heterogeneous, comprehensive, multidimensional phenomenon, which
is concerned with the state, market, and social actors, and covers a whole range
of economic, cultural, political, security-related, and environmental aspects
(Murphy and Tooze 1991; Hettne 1995; Cox 1996; Hoogvelt 1997; Payne 1998;

Schulz et al. 2001a). This theory is particularly useful for studying the relationship between nationalism and regionalism primarily because of NRA's flexibility in comprehending the relationship between the two variables. The new patterns of regionalism do not necessarily imply a reduction of the nation-state's capacity, but can be seen as an extended form of nationalism. In this context, the nation-state is an entity that is given a specific function within larger global political structures (Hettne 1994: 36).

Objectives of the Book

The main objective of this book is to analyze the dynamics of the relationship between nationalism and regionalism. In this context, the author proposes his main hypothesis that *nationalism and regionalism stand in a symbiotic relationship to one another*. In the past, the relationship between these two ideologies has most often been characterized as contentious because the former has exhibited no more than offensive and aggressive policies toward regionalism (Breully 1985). Today, however, this has not been the case where the relationship between the two can sometimes be described as mutually reinforcing. In other words, nationalism and regionalism can stand in a symbiotic relationship to one another. Indeed, regionalism today should not always be understood as an alternative to nationalism, but more as a supplement to protect the role of the state in an interdependent world (Palmer 1991; Axline 1994). As mentioned earlier, to provide an empirical basis for this book, this book examines the case study of Indonesian nationalism and ASEAN regional integration, with specific reference to AFTA. Both Indonesia and ASEAN were chosen because, over the years, the former's development has been shaped by evidence of nationalism, and the latter a strong commitment toward regionalism.

Within the case study context, the book attempts to explore whether or not there is a shifting pattern of perceptions among Indonesian state and non-state actors[8] toward regionalism in Southeast Asia. Initially, the author assumed that in recent years a shift has taken place from a traditionally strong nationalistic attitude to a more outward-looking orientation that has manifested itself in opting for a stronger RIA in the Southeast Asian region. However, there are several related determining factors that emerged as motivations to shift the attitudes of Indonesian state and non-state actors to opt for regional strategy, which include the regional economic crisis of the late 1990s, the desire of Southeast Asian leaders to pursue a regional community formation, and, greater awareness among state and non-state actors of the positive contributions that a strengthened RIA may bring.

Firstly, the regional economic crisis has played a major role in opening the eyes of Indonesian domestic state and non-state actors about ASEAN regional integration. In contrast to the widely held assumption that ASEAN did little to deal with the regional economic crisis, I contend that this was not the case.

Among other things, delayed initiatives to eradicate the crisis came about largely as a result of the nature and structure of ASEAN as an organization whose decisions and actions are dependent upon the consent of member countries. It was only logical that ASEAN member countries' reactions toward the economic crisis were to concentrate on domestic problems first before initiating any regional attempts to face the economic crisis. More recently, ASEAN and several other Northeast Asian countries have become more aware of this problem and are instigating plans to minimize the possibility of a future crisis. Some of these initiatives include serious discussions on further institutional, economic, and financial cooperation, which can be seen in the new ASEAN plus Three (APT), an attempt to expand regionalism to include not only the ten Southeast Asian countries, but Japan, South Korea and China as well. As far as this particular initiative is concerned, discussions have included the possibility of the creation of an East Asian Free Trade Area (EAFTA) (Chung 2001: 397) and further financial cooperation under the 2000 Chiang Mai Initiative, and the 2003 Asian Bond Market Initiative (ABMI).[9] Some of these initiatives will be discussed further in Chapter 5.

Secondly, even long before the regional economic crisis began in 1997, there were intense discussions among academics and the ruling elites of various ASEAN countries to initiate a new level of regional community formation beyond AFTA. Some analysts have even noted the significant contribution of Chinese and Japanese economic networking to regional community formation in Southeast Asia, if not in East Asia (a region consisting of both Southeast and Northeast Asian countries) (Chung 2001: 407-12).[10] In recent years, both Japan and China have also been regarded as the center of "new Asian regionalism" (Katzenstein 2000: 359). However, significant moves toward the creation of a single regional community in the ASEAN region has been intensified following the emergence of the economic crisis of 1997. The economic crisis has, therefore, acted as a catalyst in advancing ideas of Western model of democracy in some ASEAN countries, which is particularly significant in Indonesia's case. Subsequently, the strengthening of the democratization process has led to the rapid development and expansion of the civil society movement in the region. Various domestic non-state actors have become both more interested and concerned with regional level issues as part of the deepening internationalization of their interests.

Thirdly, many Indonesian state and non-state actors are now increasingly aware that their countries' future development rests upon the strengthening of existing regionalism. The recent development of ASEAN has made a positive contribution in the form of confidence building measures (Sopiee 1986: 222), which were one of the Association's most significant objectives in the past. ASEAN, among other things, has increased the bargaining power of Southeast Asian countries in many international fora. Although there is limited evidence to suggest that ASEAN was able to bargain with various international institutions, such as the International Monetary Fund (IMF) and the World Bank during the economic crisis, ASEAN has the potential to carry out such tasks if member countries opt for greater and stronger cooperation. However, the question remains as to whether ASEAN will respond to a host of new regional challenges (Smith 2000a: 41). The emergence of an ethnonationalist movement, for example, has been a significant post-crisis concern among Indonesian state and non-state actors (Lay 2001). However, Indonesian state and non-state actors appear to hold the view that ASEAN has the potential to help Indonesian in resolving this domestic problem.

Although Indonesian state and non-state actors' attitudes toward ASEAN have become more positive in recent years, there are still some as yet unresolved issues which may hinder the development of further RIA in the region. One issue particularly worth stressing concerns the Association itself, which has become more exclusive in terms of its relations with the majority of the Southeast Asian population. The Association is still largely an elitist executive club for regional Foreign Ministers, if not leaders, whose decisions at the regional level do not necessarily correspond with the actual demands of the majority of the Southeast Asian population (Chandra 2004). There are, for example, many Indonesian non-state actors (particularly NGOs and CSOs) who believe that the implementation of AFTA is not feasible due to the Association's long-standing cardinal principle of *non-interference*.[11] The perpetuation of this principle could continue to be a major obstacle to greater economic cooperation, leading to bureaucratic dilemmas during the exchange of economic information among the member countries. Secondly, further RIA attempts will also face challenges from external forces. These include particularly the West's fear that strengthened Southeast and East Asian regionalism might jeopardize the future of the WTO's multilateralism (Higgot 2000: 256-59). The third major issue that may prevent a more open attitude among Indonesian state and non-state actors toward ASEAN regional integration is the fragmentation of the Indonesian state that has occurred as a result of strengthening ethnonationalist movements in various parts of the country.

The above issues may have implications for the formation of strengthened regional integration in ASEAN for a number of reasons. To start with, regarding the aforementioned exclusivity of ASEAN as an institution, there are two levels at which a strong elitist nationalistic stance could exist. At one level, there are the policymakers whose eagerness to pursue the formation of stronger regionalism will vary depending upon their perception of the costs and benefits incurred by such arrangements. In Indonesia's case, policymakers' decisions have been strongly associated with the personal economic benefits that can be gained or lost through further ASEAN regional integration. The decrease in economic gains resulting from such arrangements would normally provoke a stronger nationalistic stance among those policymakers. In this context, nationalism often equates to the economic or capital gains that can be acquired or lost by policymakers or other interest groups. At another level, the very fact that the country's foreign policy decisions represent largely the individual interests of members of government has been a catalyst in promoting the nationalistic stance held by many Indonesian citizens. Consequently, the exclusive nature of a regional institution can widen the gaps between the governments and the governed. Secondly, in both the economic and the security field, ASEAN countries are still very dependent on the United States (U.S.), Japan, and the European Union (EU). Therefore, any attempts to promote further regionalism in Southeast Asia cannot afford to violate various established agreements that have been made individually between ASEAN member and non-member countries. Finally, without continuous and comprehensive initiatives to eradicate the ethnonationalist movement within the country, the Indonesian state will most probably not favor any Southeast Asian regionalism since both regionalism and ethnonationalism still pose challenges to the established nation-state system.

Contribution of the Book

This book aims to contribute toward better understanding of the relationship between nationalism and regionalism. More specifically, this book is linked strongly to recent debates on NRA. Despite its flexibility and fluidity in characterizing recent patterns of regionalism, NRA still lacks the necessary comprehensive conceptual development to explain the nature of the relationship between nationalism and regionalism. In the past, most theoretical frameworks within the study of regionalism have focused upon the issue and process of the institutionalization of a regional grouping. This book, however, will specifically address the issue of the gap between a regional institution and the citizens of its member states, which has often been ignored in most analyzes on the political economy of regionalism.[12] It is only logical to address this particular issue since nationalism has long been seen as a contending variable within international fora or arrangements. While realizing this, however, most scholars have failed to elaborate further on the dynamic relationship between nationalism and regionalism.[13]

Moreover, this book will provide some new dimensions to the study of contemporary Indonesian foreign policy, and foreign economic policy (FEP) in particular, in ASEAN. This is in contrast to past Indonesian foreign policy studies that have taken for granted that Indonesian nationalism will be a contending variable in the future of ASEAN regionalism. The central conclusion of this book, however, offers a contrasting view. Past studies on this issue, such as those conducted by Weistein (1976) and Anwar (1994) have nevertheless provided an essential starting point from which to study the subject as well as a valid analysis of the logic behind such nationalistic stances. It must be taken into account, however, that the study of international political economy is not static, and thus has to be re-assessed within specified time periods and the international situations that exist at these particular times. The periods of Indonesian foreign policy in which Weinstein and Anwar carried out their respective research, for example, were set against a relatively stable international political economic context. Consequently, this book should offer new and important contributions to the analysis of Indonesia's foreign policy within the *reformasi*[14] period. Finally, the analysis in this book that focus upon the relationship between Indonesian nationalism and ASEAN regionalism should be useful for future comparative regionalism research.

Research Methodology

In the making of this book, I carried out field research in Indonesia between September 2000 and September 2001. Fifty-two individuals representing forty-two institutions were interviewed to analyze the perceptions of selected Indonesian domestic state and non-state actors about their country's involvement in ASEAN. Aside from that, I also conducted interviews with several individuals from selected foreign embassies in Jakarta to gather their perceptions about the progress of ASEAN regionalism in light of Indonesian nationalism.[15] Most of the research interviews were conducted in Jakarta, while a handful of respondents from Surabaya[16] also expressed their interest in being interviewed. Attempts were also made to conduct interviews with employees of government institutions in several district towns surrounding Jakarta, particularly in the industrial area of Tangerang.[17] However, due to the respondents' personal or formal constraints, the interviews were not given. However, there were several governmental or non-governmental institutions decline to participate in research interviews, most of which due to either individual respondents' personal or formal constraints. The remaining respondents were chosen because of their familiarity with the subject, their roles in the policy making process, the degree of their representativeness in the institutions they work for (i.e., decision-makers or those directly involved in the policy-making process), as well as their availability to participate in a research interview.

During the research interview, each respondent was asked a set of open-ended questions to find out the following:
1. the respondents' general perceptions of the regionalism process in Southeast Asia;
2. the extent to which, according to the respondents, nationalism is detrimental to the regionalism process in Southeast Asia;
3. the respondents' perspectives on the development of AFTA and Indonesia's readiness to enter the scheme;
4. the respondents' perceptions of the process of information dissemination about ASEAN and its AFTA scheme;
5. the extent to which, according to the respondents, various recently issued national regulations, such as the Regional Autonomy Law (OtDa—*Otonomi Daerah*), would have an impact on the ASEAN regionalism process;
6. the respondents' views on other domestic and international trade issues including leadership changes, the country's involvement in the World Trade Organization (WTO), and so on.

Table 1.1.
Characteristics of Respondents

Maximalist	Convergence	Minimalist
Regionalist/Internationalist	New nationalism (i.e., logical nationalism over romantic nationalism)	Nationalist
Support ASEAN and believe that ASEAN is important for Indonesia	Support ASEAN as long as it improves Indonesia's national interest	Oppose ASEAN because Indonesia is still a relatively poor country
Support AFTA	Positive, but remain cautious about AFTA	Oppose AFTA
Indonesian nationalism is strengthened through increased commitment in ASEAN and its AFTA scheme	ASEAN and its AFTA scheme serve Indonesia's national interests	Indonesian nationalism is weakened as a result of an increased regionalization process
ASEAN increases Indonesia's international autonomy, bargaining power, and its ability to contain the negative forces of globalization	ASEAN's ability to promote member countries' international autonomy, bargaining power, and to contain the negative forces of globalization has only been significant since the economic crisis of 1997	ASEAN's contribution toward Indonesia's international autonomy and bargaining power has been minimal, as has its ability to contain the negative forces of globalization
There is limited information about ASEAN/AFTA disseminated to the public	Information is available to the public, but the dissemination process should be expanded	There is sufficient information about ASEAN/AFTA, and no improvement is needed in the dissemination process
OtDa has a negative impact on AFTA	**Potential negative effect of OtDa on AFTA**	**OtDa does not affect AFTA because AFTA is not significant**

Subsequently, the chosen respondents were grouped into three different categories in accordance with their answers. The three categories include *maximalist, minimalist,* and *convergence* (refer to table 1.1.). The respondents whose views fell somewhere in between the minimalist and maximalist groups will hereafter be referred to as the convergence group. Those respondents categorized in the maximalist group were either regionalists or internationalists who supported greater regionalism in Southeast Asia or held a commitment toward complete liberalization at the global level. More specifically, maximalists supported the Indonesian government policy of using ASEAN as the main pillar of the country's foreign policy. In addition, maximalists argued that Indonesian nationalism has hindered the progress of regionalism in Southeast Asia. Despite the slow progress of ASEAN regionalism, maximalists also maintained that Indonesia is still better off with than without ASEAN. Those categorized within the maximalist group also supported the existence of AFTA and believed that this framework of economic cooperation would improve Indonesia's bargaining power in international fora and will increase the country's competitiveness in the global economic system. Through better standards of welfare, they believed that Indonesia would be able to solve its domestic problems, including the threats posed to national unity by ethnonationalism, and would be better placed to promote its national culture abroad.

Despite their support of Indonesia's foreign policy in ASEAN, maximalists also felt that the attempts made to disseminate information on this subject have been inadequate. Maximalists also argued that if no attempts were made to address this problem, the future of regionalism in Southeast Asia would be uncertain. Moreover, maximalists believed that the implementation of the provincial autonomy would have a significant negative impact on the implementation of AFTA. As a result, respondents in the maximalist category felt that the government should concentrate on the effect of provincial autonomy toward AFTA, and *vice versa*, so that the implementation of AFTA would not be interrupted. This group of respondents also believed that the new the recent transformation of Indonesian leadership (i.e., from Suharto, Wahid, Habibie, to Megawati) has brought changes to Indonesian foreign (economic) policy. More specifically, maximalist respondents argued that the Indonesian government has shifted significantly its foreign policy to an international, rather than regional, outlook. Finally, some maximalists also supported the idea of improved economic cooperation beyond ASEAN (i.e., ASEAN plus Three [APT] or Asia Pacific Economic Cooperation [APEC]) and suggested that Indonesia should remain committed to multilateral arrangements under the auspices of the WTO.

Meanwhile, those respondents categorized as minimalists can be considered extreme nationalists. Generally, these respondents showed great reservation about regionalism and multilateralism. Minimalist respondents opposed the process of regionalism in Southeast Asia because they felt that Indonesia was still poor, both economically and politically (i.e., minimal experience in practicing full democracy). The minimalist respondents were thus against any governmental policies to improve regionalism in Southeast Asia. More importantly, minimalists did not believe that the underlying purposes of RIS have been realized through ASEAN. Although they agreed with maximalists that ASEAN has been successful in maintaining peace and stability in the region, they still felt that the Association had failed to produce other forms of cooperation. They felt, for example, that Indonesia's bargaining position in the international fora was still weak, and that the country's national interests were often sacrificed to the interests of a foreign state or international institutions. In addition, minimalists did not believe that ASEAN promotes economic growth in the region. They felt that the economic growth experienced during the pre-economic crisis period was primarily a result of economic assistance from countries outside ASEAN and the heavy pursuance of economic nationalism. Despite being more nationalistic than other respondents, minimalists believed that nationalism no longer exists. They argued that Indonesia has been contaminated by foreign culture through the recent processes of economic liberalization. Therefore, they would ask that the government do more to promote and to preserve Indonesian nationalism.

Respondents in the minimalist category were also opposed to the AFTA scheme. They argued that the implementation of this particular scheme is likely to have detrimental effects on the overall domestic economy. As a result, they supported any possible moves to postpone the implementation of AFTA until, at least, Indonesia achieved a state of autarky. Minimalists saw the dissemination of information regarding ASEAN and AFTA as irrelevant as the subject, in their view, was of little significance to the majority of Indonesians today. Indonesians were more concerned about the many domestic problems that have resulted from the economic crisis. They believed that sufficient information regarding ASEAN and AFTA had been disseminated, and no improvement was needed. Respondents within the minimalist category also believed that Indonesian foreign (economic) policy had remained unchanged despite the leadership changes in recent years. Finally, minimalists did not agree that the implementation of provincial autonomy would have any impacts on AFTA. After all, they felt AFTA was of no significance for the country and that the scheme merited little attention. On the whole, therefore, in the perception of minimalist respondents, Indonesia would be better off focusing on its immediate concerns, particularly measures to alleviate the economic crisis.

Finally, those respondents categorized within the convergence group were those whose views fell somewhere in between those of the nationalists and regionalists and/or internationalists. In general, respondents in the convergence category expressed a view that can be described as a new form of nationalism, or *new nationalism*. Convergence respondents, or new nationalists, held rather pragmatic views as regards Indonesian foreign policy in Southeast Asia. Generally, they perceived the emergence of regionalism in Southeast Asia as positive. As such, they regarded regionalism as a way to improve Indonesia's national interests. The majority of respondents categorized within the convergence group also emphasized *logical nationalism* over *romantic nationalism*. In this context, Indonesian nationalism should be used, for example, to promote the economic competitiveness of the country rather than as a tool to oppose foreign entities or individuals. However, although in theory respondents within the convergence group regarded regionalism as positive, they also felt that the process of regionalization in Southeast Asia had been limited, largely as a result of ASEAN member countries' excessive preoccupation with their respective national priorities. Respondents in this category also believed that AFTA could help to promote economic growth in the country. At the same time, however, they felt that this form of economic cooperation should be approached cautiously since full trade liberalization might have detrimental effects on the Indonesian economy overall. Moreover, although the ASEAN Secretariat and the Indonesian government have provided substantial information to the public regarding AFTA, respondents in the convergence category also believed that the wider public audience, particularly local CSOs and NGOs, should be included as well. Finally, respondents within the convergence category were concerned about the potential effects of the provincial autonomy on the implementation of AFTA. The majority of respondents in this category believed that it would be hard to implement AFTA if the issues surrounding the implementation of provincial autonomy were not addressed properly.

The questions outlined above were intended to gain an insight into the contemporary perspectives of Indonesian state and non-state actors toward ASEAN and AFTA. With regard to the first question, the author tried to find out the respondents' general perceptions of ASEAN and its AFTA scheme. While maximalist respondents viewed positively the existence of regionalism in Southeast Asia to date, minimalist respondents expressed their opposition toward the concept of regionalism in general. Meanwhile, those respondents categorized within the convergence group held more moderate and mixed views on the existence of regionalism in Southeast Asia. Not only did Indonesian state and non-state actors place a high value on the existence of ASEAN, a similar view was also held by the majority of foreign representatives interviewed.[18] The second question deals with the respondents' views on the relationship between nationalism and regionalism. In the view of those placed within the maximalist camp, Indonesian nationalism can be strengthened through the country's commitment in ASEAN and its AFTA scheme, while those in the minimalist camp argued Indonesian nationalism was weakened as a result of increased regionalization and/or globalization processes. Generally, however, the majority of the respondents expressed a convergence point of view, arguing that Indonesia's involvement in ASEAN is in the country's overall national interests.

All the respondents were also asked about their perceptions of the development of AFTA and their country's involvement in the scheme. To start with, it is necessary to differentiate between ASEAN and AFTA, as each represents a different concept and sets of impacts on Indonesia. While ASEAN is generally regarded as a regional institution, AFTA is understood to be one mechanism used by the Association to enhance the process of regionalism. The majority of respondents thought that Indonesia's participation in AFTA to be a delicate matter. In fact, most non-state actors indicated that the country was not ready for AFTA and should pull back from the arrangement. Most government officials held a maximalist view, and fully supported AFTA. However, it is important to note that the *personal* views of these state actors differed from their *official* views. The majority of governmental officials expressed their full support of AFTA out of a sense of professional duty, which commits them to support any governmental policies made at the ASEAN level. Another major issue examined during the research interviews was the extent to which the ASEAN Secretariat and the relevant Indonesian government institutions have disseminated information regarding ASEAN and AFTA to the general public. The public's lack of support of ASEAN and its activities in the past can perhaps be blamed on the failure of these attempts at information dissemination. While the majority of governmental officials believed that they, along with the ASEAN Secretariat, had provided adequate information to the public regarding AFTA, the majority of non-state actors were not satisfied. Although there is a wide range of information available regarding ASEAN and AFTA, the majority of non-state actors believed that the available information is still highly technical and too expensive.

Finally, the last two questions dealt with current issues within the domestic, regional, and international spheres. Within the domestic sphere, the economic crisis has triggered various economical, political and social problems throughout the country. These problems, and the way in which the Indonesian government has handled them, are thought to have complicated the ASEAN regionalization process. One major concern expressed by the majority of respondents was the threat of national disintegration in Indonesia. Accordingly, the Indonesian government introduced the provincial autonomy to minimize the possible threat of national disintegration. Prior to carrying out the fieldwork, the author had hypothesized that the provincial autonomy would have a substantial negative impact on the implementation of AFTA, at least in the short-term. The fieldwork confirmed this hypothesis by revealing that the majority of Indonesian state and non-state actors both agreed that AFTA would be difficult to implement, unless further measures to address domestic problems were taken. Issues such as the changes in Indonesia's national leadership and its involvement in other multilateral organizations were also introduced to the respondents. The first issue is important in detecting a possible shift in the conduct of Indonesian foreign (economic) policy as a result of the new leadership. The majority of Indonesian state and non-state actors saw few changes in Indonesian foreign (economic) policy, which emphasizes the importance of regional cooperation, although the government's focus has now been expanded to secure aid from various international organizations and other countries beyond the Southeast Asian region.

Structure of the Book

There are three major questions that underlie this book. The first question is concerned with the reasons why regionalism has been one of the most important features of the global political economy in the last few decades. The second question focuses on why nation-states, particularly developing countries, employ a regional integration strategy (RIS) in international relations. The third question concerns domestic state and non-state actors' reactions and perspectives toward regional integration vis-à-vis globalization. Two main perspectives have emerged in recent writings on regional integration. On the one hand, there are scholars who see the development of regional integration as a stepping-stone or building block toward greater multilateralism in the world trading system (e.g. Lawrence 1995; Summers 1991; Anderson and Blackhurst 1993). For Bhagwati (1995a), on the other hand, regionalism can be seen as a stumbling block toward greater multilateralism in the world trading system. Accordingly, he insists on the persistence of multilateralism and global governance. From the mid-1990s, the issue has become increasingly controversial owing to the substantial rise in the number of domestic non-state actors that simply reject the idea of regional integration and globalization. Meanwhile, those who oppose regional integration, such as labor and environmental activists, tend to view regionalism as a similar phenomenon to that of globalization, although on a smaller scale. Ideas about the surrender of sovereignty and the spread of the negative forces of capitalism can lead to skepticism about regionalism among the general public. Therefore, deeper exploration of each of these questions is required for us to understand the logic behind the creation of various regional grouping in the world as well as the logic behind regional actors' decisions in pursuing an RIS. To deal with all these questions, this book is divided into seven chapters which deal with specific issues concerning the theoretical background of regionalism and nationalism, as well as an analysis of the case study that focuses on the dynamic relationship between Indonesian nationalism and ASEAN regionalism.

In Chapter 2 I attempt to analyze the theoretical background within the study of regionalism and nationalism. The chapter will start with an analysis of the logic behind regionalism as a contemporary phenomenon. The second part of this chapter will focus on recent trends in regionalism in the world today and the theoretical background to regionalism. There are two main disciplinary perspectives in the study of regionalism, that have emerged from international relations (IR) and economics. While IR perspectives on regionalism have experienced a major shift since their first appearance following the Second World War (i.e., neo-realism to social constructivism), much economic analysis of regionalism is still focused upon the traditional Vinerian approach. In recent years, however, NRA has added a new dimension in the study of regionalism. This new theoretical approach attempts to bridge the gap that exists between IR and economic perspectives on regionalism. Following the analysis of the theoretical background of regionalism, the third part of this chapter will focus on nationalism. More specifically, this part of the chapter will analyze the concept of nationalism and its application to international affairs.

Chapter 3 is concerned with the key conceptual framework of this book. The main focus in Chapter 3 is on the analysis of NRA. This chapter begins with an analysis of the relationship between NRA, as a new regionalism approach, and nationalism. This analysis aims to explore the dynamic relationship between nationalism and regionalism. Furthermore, this section is designed to fill the gap between established perspectives on regionalism and NRA, since most regionalism theorists have to date only mentioned the importance of the national domain but yet to provide any conceptualization of this issue. In addition, specific attention within this chapter will also be given to an analysis of contemporary nationalists' interest in pursuing a regional integration strategy. Finally, Chapter 3 will include a brief analysis of the relationship between NRA, Indonesian nationalism and ASEAN regional integration.

Detailed analyzes of Indonesian nationalism and ASEAN regional integration will be provided in both Chapter 4 and Chapter 5 respectively. Through a detailed examination of both the historical and contemporary perspectives on Indonesian nationalism and foreign economic policy, this book seeks to establish the logic behind Indonesia's pursuit of RIS, despite its strong nationalist historical background. The primary focus of Chapter 5, however, is on ASEAN regional economic integration attempts, both past and present. Since this book is primarily concerned with AFTA, early ASEAN regional economic integration attempts, such as the ASEAN Preferential Trading Arrangement (PTA), ASEAN Industrial Projects (AIPs), ASEAN Industrial Complementation (AIC) and ASEAN Industrial Joint Venture (AIJV), will only be analyzed briefly. The analysis of AFTA will include a historical account of the trade agreement and its prospects and challenges within and beyond Southeast Asia.

Chapter 6 provides a detailed analysis of Indonesian perspectives toward the country's involvement in ASEAN, with particular reference to AFTA. This investigation has been made possible through field research carried out during 2000–2001, which involved research interviews conducted with representatives from various government agencies and domestic interest groups in Indonesia. Moreover, this section also analyzes several contextual factors which have influenced public perceptions toward ASEAN at the present time. These include the regional crisis of 1997, contemporary Indonesian nationalism and ethnonationalism, and the organizational structure of ASEAN. The subsequent sections in this chapter are divided according to the questions set during the field research. Finally, Chapter 8 concentrates mainly on the findings of the study, which analyzes the dynamic of the relationship between Indonesian nationalism and ASEAN regional integration

Conclusion

The relationship between nationalism and regional integration has traditionally been viewed as conflictual, particularly since the latter can undermine the integrity of the former. This book offers a new approach to the study of regionalism and nationalism. The examination of Indonesia's relationship with ASEAN as a case study serves as a focal point in which the nature of the contending forces between nationalism and regionalism can be better comprehended. Indonesia is known traditionally as one of the most nationalistic country in the Southeast Asian region, which is not only due to her pride in the sheer size and richness of her natural resources, but also due to her long historical struggle against imperialism. Such attributes and historical background give Indonesia a sense of confidence in herself and, thus, over time, may be see to have produced excessive nationalism. Although ASEAN has existed for over three decades, it has as yet been unable to make any progress in further promoting Southeast Asian regionalism. Excessive emphasis on the national interests of member countries has further obscured the regionalization process in the Southeast Asian region.

In 1992, ASEAN member countries agreed to form AFTA, which has the objective to increase the international competitiveness of ASEAN industries and to make the Southeast Asian region an attractive investment location. During the signing of this trade agreement, there were little opposition expressed among Indonesian domestic actors because Indonesian politics at the time treated the conduct of the Indonesian foreign economic policy as exclusive affairs of the President, the Ministry of Foreign Affairs, the military, and a handful of members of the academic community. Recent developments within the region, however, depict a different picture where many Indonesian state and non-state actors have finally become more conscious about regional issues and problems. The conclusion of this book argues that although the majority of the Indonesian political elite remain supportive to AFTA, some Indonesian pressure groups, particularly NGOs and CSOs, are still concerned about this regional trade liberalization scheme. Despite this, skepticism toward AFTA was not borne out as a result of the emergence of nationalist sentiment in Indonesia, but because of the distance exhibited between ASEAN and the citizens of Southeast Asia, as well as the lack of proper information disseminated to pressure groups. For the majority of Indonesian state and non-state actors, ASEAN and its AFTA scheme remain part of Indonesia's national interest because they help to promote sustained economic development, the preservation nationalism and sovereignty, the enhancement of autonomy and bargaining in international arena, and the ability to resist the negative forces of globalization.

Notes

1. The rise of NGOs and CSOs is not actually a new phenomenon. International organizations (IOs), such as the UN, have been promoting such organizations for the past fifty years. One of the main factors that drives IOs to support these non-governmental agencies is the fact that their actions can be felt directly or indirectly by both their endorsers and recipients (Gordenker and Weiss 1996: 17). Moreover, Makito (1999: 177) also argues that one of the main factors that drive states to allow non-state actors to promote regionalism is the fact that many domestic non-state actors, particularly NGOs and CSOs, are "naturally issue oriented or even issue specific." By being issue oriented or issue specific, NGOs and CSOs are in a position to act as major advisory groups for the state.

2. Refer to appendix 1 for a detailed list of current ASEAN-affiliated NGOs.

3. APA is mainly "a general meeting of civil society organizations, non-government organizations, and civic organizations from the ten member-states of ASEAN. . . . [It] aims to serve as a vessel for articulating and conveying the people's view and interests outside of the formal political channels" (Hernandez 2003: 1). The first APA was initiated by the ASEAN Institute of Strategic and International Studies (ASEAN-ISIS). The Institute currently has eight members, including the Brunei Minister of Foreign Affairs, the Cambodian Institute for Cooperation and Peace (CICP), the Indonesian Centre for Strategic and International Studies (CSIS), the Laos Institute for Foreign Affairs, the Malaysian Institute for Strategic and International Studies (ISIS), the Philippines' Institute for Strategic and Development Studies (ISDS), the Singapore Institute of International Affairs (SIIA), Thailand's Institute for Security and International Studies (ISIS), and Vietnam's Institute for International Relations (IIR). The APA was based on the

rationale that community building in Southeast Asia must include all sectors of society. It was deemed imperative that ASEAN, as a regional institution, must be made relevant to the ordinary citizens of each of the member states (ASEAN-ISIS 2000).

4. Unlike APA, which is recognized as a formal ASEAN civil society forum in many ASEAN documents, ACSC is an alternative forum that is used by Southeast Asian civil society groups to engage with ASEAN and directly provide inputs to this regional organization. ACSC was established as a result of dissatisfaction among civil society groups that were dissatisfied with the limited role of APA in influencing ASEAN policymakers. ACSC was actually initiated by the Malaysian government, which commissioned the ASEAN Study Center, Universiti Teknologi MARA (UiTM), to hold the event parallel to the eleventh ASEAN Summit in Kuala Lumpur, Malaysia, in December 2005. The event was also supported by the ASEAN Secretariat, as well as another Malaysian NGO, the Third World Network (TWN). Although UiTM, an academic organization, took the coordinating role, the difference between ACSC and APA was that NGOs also played a role in the formation of ACSC. The First ACSC, which was attended by more than 120 participants from CSOs throughout Southeast Asia, produced a statement to be presented to the ASEAN heads of states. This was, of course, the first time that ASEAN leaders had been invited to hear representatives from civil society groups in the region air their views on the process of ASEAN Community-building. Initially, ACSC was meant to be a one-off event, with no follow-up events planned for the subsequent ASEAN Summit. However, during meetings between ASEAN leaders and representatives of civil society groups at the eleventh ASEAN Summit in Kuala Lumpur in December 2005, ASEAN leaders recognized the ACSC, and supported its annual convening. Since then, the Solidarity for Asian People's Advocacy (SAPA) Working Group (WG) on ASEAN takes the coordinating role of ACSC. For further information on ACSC and SAPA see Chandra (2006) or visit the official website of SAPA (accessed 2007) at http://www.asiasapa.org.

5. Refer to appendix 2 for data on the level of tariff barriers since the collapse of bipolarity in the late 1980s.

6. ASEM is comprised of ten Asian nations, fifteen European nations, and the European Commission. The prime motive for this meeting grew from the recognition of the need to strengthen the linkage between Europe and Asia. The first meeting was held on 1–2 March 1996, in Bangkok, and was followed up in London, on 3–4 April 1998. Prior to the creation of ASEM, however, both Southeast Asia and countries of the then European Community (EC) had a long-standing partnership, and such a relationship has been regarded as a model for a group-to-group inter-regionalism (Lukas 1989; Mols 1990). Although ASEM has different, even conflicting, agendas to other regional groupings that ASEAN countries are involved in, such as APEC, both forums allow the East Asian policymakers to consolidate political and economic communication with North America via APEC and the EU via ASEM (Higgot 1999: 194). Further information on the background to ASEM's creation can also be found at the ASEM official website (accessed 2003) at http://asem.inter.net.th/asem-info/background.html.

7. In Charrier's (2001: 315) analysis, the evolution from countries to a region also implies "the recurrence of the concept of the region over time in a cultural context, both within the region and beyond it. . . . Thus regional spaces develop an increasingly durable identity over time by the very fact of being repeatedly recognized as such in contemporary culture [*sic*]."

8. Non-state actors will henceforth be referred to as domestic actors and will include the business and academic communities, and pressure groups, such as civil society organizations (CSOs) and non-governmental organizations (NGOs). It is also important to

make a distinction between CSOs and NGOs. According to the World Bank's (2000) Operational Directive 14.70, NGOs may be defined as a "myriad of different types of organizations. At its broadest, it includes all groupings of individuals that fall outside the public and for-profit sectors, whether legally constituted or informal, established or transient." NGOs, therefore, are a diverse group, yet the term NGO is often used interchangeably with that of CSO, which normally "includes all associations and networks between the family and the state except firms [that] NGOs cannot represent" (Edwards 2000: 7–8). More specifically, CSOs are "the wide array of non-governmental and not-for-profit organizations that have a presence in public life, expressing the interests and values of their members or others, based on ethical, cultural, political, scientific, religious or philanthropic considerations" (World Bank website, accessed 2003). While organizations such as Friends of the Earth and Amnesty International are examples of NGOs, trade unions and religious or cultural groups are some examples of CSOs.

9. ABMI was initially endorsed at the ASEAN plus Three Deputies Meeting in Chiang Mai, Thailand, on 17 December 2002. The main objective of ABMI is to develop efficient bond markets in Asia that would enable the private and public sectors to raise and invest long-term capital without currency and maturity risks. A review of ABMI 2003 can be obtained from the Asia Recovery Information Center website at http://aric.adb.org/docs/asiabondmarket/asean.asp.

10. See also Dajin Peng's (2002: 425) analysis of the contribution of Japanese and ethnic Chinese economic networking to informal integration in East Asia. In this context, Dajin Peng defines informal integration as "integration through economic factors, facilitated by "natural" channels such as geographic proximity, ethnic ties, and industrial divisions of labor."

11. The principle of non-interference prohibits ASEAN member countries from interfering in any issues which can be regarded as the domestic affairs of other members. This principle is also regarded as one of the key elements, along with the principle of quiet diplomacy, the non-use of force, and decision making through consensus, of Asian value or the ASEAN way. For detailed analysis of the non-interference principle see Robison (1996), Ramcharan (2000), and Katsumata (2003).

12. The problem of the gap between citizens and regional institutions is best illustrated in the context of the European Union (EU). In recent years, the strengthening of the EU has led to an emerging "democratic deficit," a concept based on the notion that the EU lacks democracy due to its complex operational method. The EU is becoming increasingly remote from its citizens because Europeans put too much emphasis on the European Parliament, which is the only branch of the EU that is directly elected by the citizens (Moravcsik 2002). The debate over the EU's democratic deficit seems to raise further questions about the Union's social legitimacy (Smith 2003).

13. Although a closer attempt at analyzing domestic attitudes toward regionalism has been made by Haggard (1997), this study lacks any specific analysis of the dynamic relationship between nationalism and regionalism. Most publications on NRA, such as those produced by Hettne (1999) and Schulz et al. (2001a), also do not provide any specific explanation on the dynamic relationship between the two variables.

14. This period is marked by the regional crisis and followed with the resignation of Suharto as the President of the Republic of Indonesia on 21 May 1998.

15. Refer to appendix 4 for a complete list of all respondents interviewed in this research.

16. Surabaya is the second largest city in Indonesia, situated on the east coast of Java.

17. Tangerang is a regency area in the newly established province of Banten. Banten has recently obtained provincial status following the introduction of the Regional Autonomy Laws in 1999.

18. Foreign representatives (i.e., officials from the ASEAN Secretariat and foreign embassies) were interviewed due to their ability to provide an outsider view toward the relationship between nationalism and regionalism in Southeast Asia. More importantly, interviews with foreign representatives were useful to gather information concerning the experiences of their countries in dealing with nationalism and regionalism.

Chapter 2

Regional Integration and Nationalism in Theoretical Perspectives

The relationship between nationalism and regionalism is one major issue that has been neglected by political science (Shulman 2000: 365). Generally, however, the relationship between nationalism and regionalism has been characterized as contentious. For example, Breuilly (1985: 10) has mentioned that scholars often regard the term nationalism as referring to "offensive and aggressive policies" in world politics. The main objective of this chapter is to revisit some of the theoretical backgrounds in the study of nationalism and regionalism, as well as to identify some of the gaps in the existing literature on each respective subject. The next section analyzes different theoretical perspectives of regionalism. The theoretical analysis in this section is divided into two periods of regionalism; namely the *old regionalism* period and the *new regionalism* period.[1] The subsequent focus of this chapter is to analyze different theoretical perspectives within the study of nationalism. Here, the principal focus will be given to the concept of nationalism and the development of nationalism in the international context. Moreover, this section also attempts to identify the gaps within the existing literature on both nationalism and regionalism. Finally, the chapter will conclude with a general analysis of main findings within the literature of regionalism and nationalism.

Theoretical Perspectives on Regionalism

In recent years, interest in regionalism has been resurrected among scholars and policymakers as a result of emerging patterns of this phenomenon in world politics. Analysis in this section will be devoted to different theoretical perspectives on regionalism, particularly those relevant to a study of regionalism in the Southeast Asian region. The analysis in this section will be divided into two frameworks; namely "old regionalism" and "new regionalism." Within the old regionalism (first wave of regionalism), four international relations theories are relevant to our analysis of regionalism in Southeast Asia. These are (neo-)realism, neo-liberal institutionalism, social constructivism, and structuralism. Another mainstream theory during the first wave of regionalism is based on an economic perspective.[2] However, the old regionalism period faded out in the

27

late 1970s. In the wake of the re-emergence of RIAs throughout the world during the early 1990s, or during the second wave of regionalism, a new line of theory has been introduced. Scholars commonly term this new theory the New Regionalism Approach (NRA).[3] This approach attempts to bridge the gaps between both the international relations and economic perspectives upon regionalism. However, there are some existing limitations in the analysis of NRA, which are particularly evident in a vague and limited analysis of the relationship between nationalism and regionalism. This issue will be further explored and analyzed in this chapter.

Definitions and Associative Concepts of Regional Integration

In general, regional integration arrangements (RIAs) can be described as agreements between nation-states, within a specified geographical area, to minimize barriers.[4] Such an agreement is normally created with the aim of achieving gradual moves toward an elimination of political boundaries between the participating states. In addition to the term of RIA, this thesis also uses the concept of a regional integration strategy (RIS). The two terms differ in the sense that an RIS specifically refers to a *strategy* of regional integration used by domestic state and non-state actors to enhance their interests either at the domestic, regional, or international levels. Certain domestic actors (i.e., nationalists) may use an RIS for the purpose of, *inter alia*, enhancing their country's bargaining power vis-à-vis world economic powers. While this thesis primarily uses the terms RIA and RIS, other scholars have also used other terms, such as international economic integration (IEI)[5] and regional economic integration (REI).[6] Although these three terms have been used interchangeably by most scholars from time to time, each term is significantly different from the others. To start with, it is important to note that when one speaks of regionalism, one must bear in mind that "regionalism is regional" (Ethier 2001: 3), in that it specifies certain geographical limitations. Thus, there are differences between REI, IEI, and RIA.

The term REI is mostly limited to discussions of regional integration in the context of economics. In this sense, REI is normally defined as "the process of reducing the economic significance of national political boundaries within a geographic area" (Anderson and Blackhurst 1993: 1). Alternatively, it may also be "loosely defined as any policy designed to reduce trade barriers between a subset of countries" (Winters 1999: 8), and as such reflects the notion within trade theory that a partial move toward freer trade will improve welfare among member states. REI is similar to IEI, which can be broadly defined as "a state of affairs or a process [that] involves the amalgamation of separate economies into larger regions. [It is] more concerned with the discriminatory removal of all trade impediments between the participating nations and with the establishment of certain elements of cooperation and co-ordination between them" (El-Agraa 1988: 1). Although this definition of IEI mentions the word *region*, it is actually referring to international or global integration, which implies a larger geographical context than that of *region*. Finally, the concept of RIA carries a rather loose notion of regionalism. It is limited to the context of *region*, rather than *global* or *international*, and it does not denote a specific form or nature of regionalism, such as economic integration. Therefore, for the remainder of this thesis, the term RIA is used since much of the analysis will not focus solely on economic integration, but also on the framework of the political and social integration of a *region*. After all, regionalism is not, and should not be, purely centered around the issue of economics alone, in spite of much discussions and empirical evidence that prove the notion that trade fosters the growth of regionalism and *vice-versa*.

A distinction must also be made between regionalism and regionalization when analyzing RIA. Regionalism is primarily an "ideology that we ought to live in geopolitical domains greater than states, though not worldwide. Regionalization, [on the other hand], is the description of an empirical trend that ostensibly inspires or bears out this basic belief" (Pettman 1999: 181). In practical terms, regionalism consists of policies initiated by regional state actors to promote greater integration in a region (e.g., a state-led project, such as the formation of a growth triangle initiative). Meanwhile, regionalization normally refers to regional activities that are initiated by regional non-state actors (e.g., market or business-led projects). Moreover, despite being specifically *regional*, RIA is often associated with the concept of globalism or globalization. In line with his earlier definition of regionalism and regionalization, Pettman (1999: 181) also proposes that globalism is an intention "to live in ways that unite people worldwide, [while] globalization is the description of an empirical trend that ostensibly inspires or bears out this basic belief." Whereas the former is associated with a vision of a borderless world, the latter is often interpreted as being the process through which globalism could be achieved. Meanwhile, most economists associate globalism with "the principle of non-discriminatory and multilateral free trade in promoting non-restrictive movements of various commodities, including those of goods and services" (Okita 1994: 72), while globalization, on the other hand, "involves more precisely a quantum leap in the transnationalization of production, distribution of goods and services, and financial flow" (Tussie 1998: 82). Both terms refer to a form of international trade and economic liberalization in which tariff barriers between countries are non-existent, which is also known as multilateralism, regardless of the region in which a country is located.

There are some other important terms related to the notion of RIA and globalization, many of which relate to economic perspectives on RIA. It is important to understand these definitions prior to analyzing some of the mainstream theoretical frameworks of regional integration, particularly those related to economic issues. These terms include the following: "outward vs. inward looking policies; trade creation vs. trade diversion; and market integration vs. discriminatory integration" (Okita 1994: 72–75), and also homogenous vs. heterogeneous economies. Economists often refer to two different effects of regionalism on globalization, seeing it either as a stepping-stone or a stumbling block (Bhagwati 1995a). Regionalism as a stepping-stone is normally equated with open regionalism (outward regionalism), while regionalism as a stumbling block is usually associated with that of a trading bloc (inward regionalism). Both terms are also related to traditional RIA theory or the Vinerian *trade creation* and *trade diversion* theory.[7] An outward regionalism normally implies an RIA that proposes an open economy, and holds to the principle of trade creation both within and beyond the region. Meanwhile, the principal characteristics of inward regionalism can be seen in RIAs formed among countries that pursue a closed economic policy with a high level of protectionism, which leads to trade creation within the region, but trade diversion beyond the region.

Debates on whether regionalism is a stepping-stone or a stumbling block have been lively among economists. On the one hand, there is an argument that regionalism should be seen as a stepping-stone toward global economic multilateralism since regional activities themselves are "heavily influenced by increasingly regionalized forms of capitalism" (Stubbs 2000a: 233). Moreover, it has also been suggested that the re-proliferation of regionalism in recent years has resulted from many countries' "frustration [toward] multilateral approach within the [General Agreement on Tariffs and Trade (GATT)] framework" (Srinivasan et al. 1993: 73). The WTO has largely focused upon an individual country's preference in phasing out a protectionist policy. Meanwhile, regionalism could be a stumbling block in the sense that the rise of production networks and a single currency might eventually lead to the creation of competing blocs in the world economy. Multilateral trade is argued to have grown faster in the absence of RIAs (Bhagwati 1995a). However, GATT rules specifically regulate the pursuance of RIA between countries. Article XXIV, Clause 4, in particular, includes some prerequisites in which an RIA can be formed. Member states of an RIA must recognizes that "the purpose of a custom union or a free trade area should be to facilitate trade between the constituent territories and not to raise barriers to trade of other contracting parties with such territories" (GATT 1947: 41). This particular regulation applies not only to those countries that wish to establish new RIAs, but also to all established RIAs that wish to strengthen their cooperation. Thus, GATT rules have made it clear that the formation of an RIA should not be made at the expense of multilateralism.

Another important distinction has to be made between market and discriminatory integration. Market-led integration is a regional integration scheme where governments play a limited role in determining the direction of the market while discriminatory integration involves heavy interference from the government in determining the shape and size of a regional grouping. In market integration, market actors, such as transnational corporations (TNCs), are the most crucial players in determining the future of regionalization in a defined region. Their actions are closely associated with the movement of capital, goods and services, as well as financial mobility. The nature of the economies of regional groupings can be characterized as either homogeneous or heterogeneous. While a homogenous regional grouping includes member states that possess identical economic structures, a heterogeneous regional grouping normally consists of member states whose economic structures differ from each other. Lastly, there are also some other terms, such as shallow integration and deep integration (Robson 1993; Haggard 1995), that should also be acknowledged. While shallow integration refers to regionalism in the form of trade in goods and services only (i.e., FTAs, such as the North American Free Trade Agreement (NAFTA) and the Baltic Free Trade Area (BAFTA)), deep integration involves integration in the level of production (i.e., custom unions, such as the Southern Cone Common Market (MERCOSUR) and the Caribbean Community, and Common Market (CARICOM)).

Mainstream Old (First Wave) Regionalism Theories

Any attempt made to transcend mainstream theorizing in regionalism requires a comprehensive understanding of previous theoretical analyzes of the subject. There were four mainstream theories that dominated the analysis of regionalism during the first wave of regionalism, including (neo-)realism, neo-liberal institutionalism, structuralism, and social constructivism. Each of these theories falls within the sphere of international relations (IR) analysis, and each demonstrates certain characteristics, in that they all reflect the international political economy in which they were developed. Neo-realism, for example, was developed through a belief in the importance of the nation-state system in international relations. Neo-liberal institutionalism, on the other hand, rejected this notion and challenged the (neo-)realists' view by recognizing new important forces in world affairs; namely non-state actors or agencies. The same approach is also applied to the other remaining two newer IR theories. Economists, such as Viner (1950), Tinbergen (1954), and Balassa (1961), have also given us an equally important analysis of the first wave of regionalism. REI theory is generally concerned with the deepening of regionalism through the free trade area (FTA), custom union, common market, and total integration. This book, however, pays particular attention to FTA. The aim of this section is to examine and to analyze each of these mainstream theories, as well as to highlight their relevance to our study on regionalism in Southeast Asia.

Initially, regionalism was perceived as "state-driven processes in response to the changing structural condition of the international economic system" (Dent 2001a: 733). This is the predominant view held by the majority of *realists* about the emerging pattern of regionalism in the 1950s and 1960s. For realists, regionalism is the pursuit of national interests by nation-states. Another predominant feature in realists' thinking is security. The international system is assumed to be anarchic and run by egoistic actors, so that each state is forced to prioritize its own needs and interests as the basic means for its survival.[8] It is, therefore, necessary for a state to exercise power within the international arena. Its capacity to fulfill this role is normally determined by its military capability. In this sense, a state has the "monopoly of legitimate violence" (Lähteenmäki and Käkönen 1999: 205), which can be used to contain both internal and external threats. This line of thinking, moreover, stresses the notion of the balance of power, whereby

a strong country will act as a hegemon in order to minimize conflicts, or to foster cooperations, among nation-states. The elements of hegemonic power normally comprise "control over materials, markets, and capital as well as competitive advantages in the production of highly valued goods involving the use of
complex or new technology" (Keohane 1984: 32–33). However, while acknowledging the anarchic international system, realists also believe that the relationship between nation-states is hierarchical since each nation-state possesses a
different level of resources, wealth, and power. In the context of regionalism,
therefore, the realist perception tends to stress "the outcome of a situation where
the major power acts as either an imperialist, the player whose presence is to
maintain the balance of power, or as a hegemon" (Hveem 1999: 91–92).

As with realism, neo-realism considers the state as the main determinant in
neo-realist analysis while, at the same time, the "internal characteristics of nation-states [are considered] as irrelevant" (Dent 2001a: 732). Another major
characteristic of this theoretical perspective is that states act rationally in order
to acquire substantial power in the international arena. The main actors in this
theoretical approach are the nation-states who make their decisions based on
relative gains and losses, depending on the domestic concerns of their countries.
The main departure of neo-realism from realism concerns the structure in which
states function. Intense interaction among states enables a structure to develop
that makes up the order or the arrangement of the international system (Waltz
1979). Moreover, the international system is perceived as anarchic rather than
hierarchic, as realists would have suggested earlier. The international arena is,
therefore, unpredictable. With the collapse of the Cold War, Waltz (1993) added
the concept of *cyclical change* within the neo-realist paradigm. In his view, the
world observes the rise and the fall of the Great Powers. In this context, for example, he suggests that Germany or Western Europe, Japan and China will rise
to rank as great powers alongside the United States (Waltz 1993: 50). Therefore,
as a result of an anarchic international system, nation-states are more concerned
with relative rather than absolute gains.[9]

The theoretical perspectives provided by realists and neo-realists are particularly important in explaining the rise of regionalism in Southeast Asia. The
Association of Southeast Asian Nations' (ASEAN) member states, for example,
opted for a regional strategy to cope with the changing international economic
condition. ASEAN has often changed course to suit the unpredictable international political economic conditions. AFTA, for example, was introduced partly
as a response to strengthening regionalism in Western Europe and North America in the early 1990s. There are, however, some main fallacies prevalent in both
realist and neo-realist perspectives on regionalism. One main deficiency lies in
the tendency of both theories to see the aggressive behavior of nation-states, in
the form of military actions, as a way to maintain peace. Thus, realism and neo-
realism assume that regionalism is often shaped by political polarization in the
international system. Such political polarization is best illustrated through ob-
serving the Southeast Asian region where, during the Cold War period, two
main political ideologies, capitalism and communism, divided the region into

two camps. On the one hand, some countries, Singapore, Thailand, Indonesia, Malaysia, and the Philippines, joined ASEAN as the supporters of liberal capitalism, while, on the other hand, the socialist countries, such as Vietnam, proponents of communist based regionalism, joined the CMEA. Another major criticism of both theories is their emphasis on the importance of the nation-state in determining the international system (Underhill 1994: 26; Miller 1998: 77). Throughout the late twentieth century there were other actors, apart from the state, that played important roles in shaping and determining the international system. The significant rise of both civil society organizations (CSOs) and non-governmental organizations (NGOs), for example, has been influential in determining the state's behavior in the international arena today.

Another relevant theoretical framework for an analysis of Southeast Asian regionalism during the first wave regionalism period is neo-liberal institutionalism.[10] Neo-liberal institutionalism perceives the emergence of regionalism differently to (neo-)realists. Regionalism, according to this line of thinking, can be fostered through the formation of regional institutions or regimes (Keohane 1984; Grugel and Hout 1999). As with realism, however, neo-liberal institutionalism stresses the notion of individual self-determination and rationality. The expression of this notion has been best illustrated in the *laissez faire* principle of free trade and comparative advantage (Dent 2001a: 734). For neo-liberal institutionalists, "the idea of politics is equated with the need to develop social institutions (such as the state and market) that conform more closely to a possessively individualist model of motivation and the propensity of ostensibly free individuals to pursue their material self-interest" (Gill 2000: 50). However, unlike (neo-)realists who emphasize the importance of state actors, neo-liberal institutionalists are more concerned with non-state entities or actors, such as TNCs, NGOs and other international agencies. These entities have not only become major forces in international political-economics, they have also become the main determining factors for governance in the international arena (Risse-Kappen 1995).[11]

Apart from an emphasis on non-state entities, there are several other main characteristics that embody neo-liberal institutionalism theory. The first is the theory's preoccupation with the notion of interdependency (Keohane and Nye 1977). Interdependency is generated through intense interactions among non-state entities or actors. Neo-liberal institutionalism treats interdependency among states as the main feature of an *international regime* in regulating specific policy issues (Rittberger 1993). Subsequently, an increased level of interdependency will generate greater demand for the formation of international (or regional) cooperations. The second major characteristic is the use of a bargaining system between states as well as functional incentives for institutionalization to provide the outcome of inter-state bargains (Moravcsik 1993: 517). The third characteristic prevalent in most neo-liberal institutionalist literature is the stress on the institutionalization of such cooperation.[12] These international (regional) institutions are important because of their capacity to disseminate relevant information to the actors concerned, the promotion of transparency and monitoring, and to mediate divergent interests among different actors (Schulz et al. 2001a: 9).

There are some major deficiencies in the analysis provided by neo-liberal institutionalists. According to (neo-)realists, for example, neo-liberal institutionalism fails to take account of two major barriers in international cooperation, which include cheating and relative gains (Grieco 1988: 487). Neo-liberal institutionalism, however, argues that the problem of cheating in international affairs can be overcome through conditional cooperation. Despite this, neo-liberal institutionalism still fails to deal with the second problem of relative gains, which, according to the neo-realist school of thought, is a major characteristic in relations between states. Another main deficiency in this theory is its excessive reliance on the market and the principle of trade liberalization. The results of the implementation of this approach can be seen across the world. There is a great deal of skepticism among the political elites of developing countries about the advantages of the unregulated nature of global capitalism (Bowles 2000; Phillips 2002). This has been particularly evident since the economic crises in the late 1990s.[13] Despite these criticisms, the neo-liberal institutionalist explanations of the rise of regionalism have provided insights. In the Asia-Pacific region, for example, the formation of the Asia-Pacific Economic Cooperation (APEC) has been driven by increased interdependency not only among countries in the region, but also among non-state entities and actors. The forum itself has become the only major institutionalized mechanism to facilitate economic growth, increasing cooperation, trade, and investment in the Asia-Pacific region. The same also applies to the relationship between Europe and Asia under the framework of the Asia-Europe Meeting (ASEM). This forum was also formed as a response to "growing complex interdependency between the two regions" (Dent 2001a: 734).

Another important theoretical perspective on regionalism during the first wave period was structuralism. This theory's perspective on regionalism is based on the importance of economic, political, and social structures (Wallerstein 1979; Chase-Dunn 1989; Halliday 1994). In its broadest sense, structuralism analyzes a large scale system through a thorough examination of the functions and relations of the small constituents that make up that system (Underhill 2000: 17). Primary analysis within structuralist perspectives is drawn from Marx and Lenin. In Marx's view, for example, economic structure is the strongest single influence on society.[14] Based on his observations of the production structure inherent in capitalism and the dynamics that produce classes, Marx contended that such conditions would lead to class struggle, and, subsequently, revolution and the next stage of history. Marx's idea was further expanded by Lenin (1966), who regarded imperialism as the highest stage of capitalism.[15] According to Lenin, imperialism is a transitional stage that the world must pass through to reach communism.[16] This theory advocates the reform of the structure of global capitalism, particularly for the sake of developing countries (Isaak 1991: 3). The tendency for capital flow to come from developing countries to developed countries, for example, is a result of trade terms that are structured against the poor (Prebisch 1964). Moreover, structuralists also find an asymmetry between *the center* and *the periphery* areas (Singer 1950; Prebisch 1951). The asymmetry between the two areas emerges as a result of imbalances between the excessive demand made by the center, or developed countries, for manufactured and industrial goods and the demand made by the periphery, or developing countries, which specialize in agriculture and other basic natural resource production. This structural imbalance will result a trade gap between the two respective areas.[17]

Two major contemporary variants of structuralist perspectives have been *dependency theory*[18] and the *modern world-system theory* or *global social theory*. Dependency theory began to emerge during the 1970s and attempted to expand previous structuralist thinking on the divide between developed and developing countries. This theory holds that "the economy of certain countries is highly conditioned by the development and expansion of another economy to which the former is subjected" (Dos Santos 1970: 231). According to dependency theory, the gap that exists between the center and peripheral areas is normally sustained due to the dependency of developing countries on developed countries to supply capital, technology, trade, and so on. In a similar line of argument, modern world-system theory contends that "world politics occurs within a world-system dominated by the logic of global capitalism" (Hobden and Jones 1999: 126). One such prominent thinker is Wallerstein (1974), who argues that the world economy acts as a determining factor in the international system. Some of the main characteristics within the modern world system, according to this line of theory, are: first, a single division of labor that makes nation-states mutually dependent upon each other for economic exchange; second, the accumulation of profit through the sale of goods; and third, the functional areas or socioeconomic units within the world system.[19] Unlike dependency theorists, however, the modern world-system theory emphasizes the concept of the *core* to represent a geographical region made up of nation-states, all of which play an important role in the modern world system. Due to the varying degrees of bourgeois interests in each of these countries, all nations have different elements of core, periphery, and semi-periphery. Consequently, it is the core states that have the capacity to dominate the peripheral states through the unequal exchange between them.[20]

More recent analyzes of structuralism have also been developed through an analysis of two kinds of power in the international political economy, namely structural power and relational power (Strange 1994: 24). Within this context, structural power refers to the power that shapes and determines the systematic structures within which other actors must operate. Relational power, on the other hand, is the direct exertion of the power of international actors on the behavior of other actors. Within a global political economy where competition is evident between state and international capitalist forces (i.e., TNCs), structural power counts more than relational power. Structural power in an international economic structure, as Strange (Strange 1994: 29–30) further postulates, emerges from four sources, including security, production, finance, and trade. Those who possess such power will be able to change the range of options available to others. In this context, not only are international capitalist forces able to influence the policies pursued by international organizations, but they are also able to influence the environment in which economic activities take place (Dent 2001a: 736). Structuralism is useful to explain the failure of regional economic integration in Southeast Asia. The economies of ASEAN member countries, for example, have been greatly dependent upon the economies of non-member countries, particularly the United States, Japan, and the EU. Moreover, structuralism would view that the formation of AFTA, with its open economic policy, would further consolidate ASEAN member economies with those of North American, European, and Northeast Asian economies. This condition, in turn, will further marginalize other global peripheral regions, such as African countries.

In recent years, regionalism has also been explained through the adoption of a social constructivist point of view. Social constructivism was developed during the early 1990s[21] and has become the backbone for the development of NRA. Social constructivism is mainly concerned with the notion of culture and identity, both of which have been undervalued in other mainstream regionalism theories (Lapid and Kratochwil 1996).[22] The core analysis of social constructivism, however, is similar to (neo-)realism and neo-liberal institutionalism in that they all emphasize the notion of rationalism (Smith 1997: 183). Additional similarities also exist between social constructivism and neo-liberal institutionalism in the sense that both theories are concerned with the norms and beliefs that shape the behavior of international (regional) actors (Hette and Söderbaum 2000: 460). Moreover, social constructivism can also been seen as structuralism in the sense that it stresses "the interests of individual states are in an important sense constructed by the structure of the international system" (Baylis 1997: 204).[23] The underlying difference between social constructivism and other IR theories is that the former argues that norms and beliefs are socially constructed and not exogenously given.

In general, social constructivism offers a comprehensive understanding of "material incentives, inter-subjective structures, and the identity and interests of the actors" (Hurrell 1995: 72). In its broadest sense, social constructivism "places emphasis both on material forces and on its standings, including norms, that emerge from social interaction" (Adler and Barnett 1998: 10). For social constructivists, the meaning of material resources for human actions can only be acquired through the structure of shared knowledge in which they are embedded (Wendt 1995: 73).[24] In the social constructivist view, norms, culture, and ideas are ideational factors that should operate above any functional utility they may have, which would include the way in which they shape the identity and interests of the actors (Wendt 1994; Katzenstein 1996). In the framework of international affairs, social constructivism holds that "the system of states is embedded in a society of states, which includes sets of values, rules, and institutions that are commonly accepted by states" (Ruggie 1998: 11). This condition, in turns, enables the system of states to function properly. In Wendt's (1992) analysis, for example, international anarchy is not fixed since it does not reflect self-interested state behavior. Social constructivists, therefore, view anarchy as the reflection of selfish identities and interests and the product of interactions among states.

In reference to regionalism, social constructivism argues that a region is socially constructed and, as such deals specifically with the concept of a *region* (Schulz 2001a: 15). The term is most often used in the geographical sense to denote a certain geographical area. However, as Nye (1968: vi) points out, "region is an ambiguous term . . . . There are [no] absolute [or] nationally defined regions. Relevant geographical boundaries vary with different purposes . . . . [A] relevant region for security may not be one for economic integration." Indeed, as a concept, a region is relative matter. As Schulz et al. (2001a: 14) have added, the socially constructed character of a region also implies that "regionalization can be deconstructed," as it can be constructed. It is also important to note that some regions are too loosely defined. Again, by taking an example from the Asia-Pacific geographical area, Palmer (1991) insists on certain geographical limitations of this particular region. Due to the region's vast geographical size and its cultural and racial heterogeneity, it is almost irrelevant to regard the Asia-Pacific area as a *region*. It should instead be regarded as a "series of regions" (Palmer 1991: 21). Moreover, when one analyzes the concept of a region, it is also imperative to note some of the characteristics that make up a region, which include geographical proximity, social and cultural homogeneity, shared political attitudes and behavior, and economic interdependence. These are the elements that make up a sense of regional identity. These elements may seem vague and abstract, yet they provide clearer guidelines than those of modern frontiers. In addition, social constructivists also argue that the institutionalization process within regionalism is very much related to intense interactions conducted among actors (Smith 1997: 185). In this context, regionalization is considered a *process*. Through an understanding of various inter-subjective structures, it is possible that the interests and identities of international (regional) actors could change overtime.

Economic Perspectives upon Free Trade Areas

Neoclassical economic analyzes of regionalism are generally based on the orthodox theory of REI (Schulz et al. 2001a: 10). The underlying concept within the study of REI has been the theory of the customs union, which refers to the creation of the advanced stages of REI in linear succession. These stages normally include the formation of a preferential trading agreement (PTA), FTA, customs union, common market, and, finally, economic and political union (Ballasa 1961; Robson 1987; El-Agraa 1997; Jovanovich 1998). As with most other regional groupings in the world, with the exception of the EU, REI in Southeast Asia has only advanced at the FTA level. In the past ASEAN has also practiced economic cooperation under the framework of the ASEAN Preferential Trading Agreement (ASEAN-PTA) in 1977. In the early 1990s, however, ASEAN countries agreed to form a more advanced level of economic cooperation in the form of AFTA. This framework of economic cooperation was only implemented in January 2002. It is for this reason that the main focus of this section is given to an economic analysis of FTAs.[25]

While mainstream IR theories place much emphasis on institutional factors, economic analysis of regionalism define regionalism in terms of the movement of capital, goods, services, and labor. International trade theories have evolved from the seventeenth- and eighteenth-century mercantilist approach, such as absolute advantage[26] and comparative advantage,[27] and the early twentieth-century factor endowment theory.[28] These traditional international economic theories, however, are deficient in some respects, particularly in their emphasis upon individual actions in initiating trade and the assumption that perfect information disseminates among economic actors. In addition, these traditional theories do not explain the issue of the transfer of goods or FDI, technology, management, and marketing (Bende-Nabende 2002: 26). In spite of these shortcomings, these theories have proved useful in providing initial analyzes for the development of contemporary REI theory. This is evident in the development of the comparative advantage and factor endowment theories. While the comparative advantage theory perfected the absolute advantage theory by introducing the term *specialization*, the factor endowment theory corrected other previous theories by focusing upon land, labor, capital, technological, and management. The theory of comparative advantage has underpinned the development of recent REI theories by insisting on global free trade as the *first best* policy of realizing free trade. Under a global free trade condition (i.e., tariff free global trade), trade-creation is encouraged through tariff level cuts between all countries. In this context, each country is assumed to produce only the goods that it can produce more efficiently than other countries. This leads to optimum efficient production on a global scale if the neo-classical assumptions of comparative advantage theory hold true, namely a constant return of scale, no transport costs, perfect competition market conditions, etc. This theory is essential within the study of REI. A grouping that decides to co-operate economically aims to achieve welfare enhancement.

As mentioned earlier, prior to achieving a condition of total economic integration, countries in a region normally conduct an FTA, or in a simpler form, a PTA. A PTA normally exists when member countries charge each other lower tariffs than those they charge non-members (Schulz et al. 2001a: 10; Bond 2001: 16). However, it is important to note that PTAs normally involve one or more types of economic integration, including FTA, customs union, etc. Generally, economists differentiate between two types of PTAs: Partial Preferential Trading Agreements (PPTAs) and Full Preferential Trading Agreements (FPTAs) (Grether and Olarreaga 1998: 9). PPTAs generally refer to trade preferences that are granted to either specified products or unilaterally to a set of member countries by more developed member countries. At this stage, member countries are more concerned with their tariff barrier levels than with the free movement of goods. FPTAs, on the other hand, refer to trade preferences that include full product coverage and where all members grant preferential access to other members.

PPTAs normally involve a significant decrease of tariffs between member countries through a *product by product* base and/or sectoral based mechanisms. Some examples of PPTAs that involve product by product based mechanism can be found in the 1977 ASEAN PTA and the more recent South African PTA. Examples of sectoral based PPTAs, on the other hand, can be found in the European Coal and Steel Community (ECSC) of 1951 and the U.S.-Canada Auto Pact of 1965.[29] FTAs normally fall within the category of PPTAs. In other circumstances, FTAs may also be formed as an addition to previously established PPTAs. In this context, FTAs normally involve the initial equalization of various trade barriers between different states, normally at much lower rates than those imposed during the PTA level. The transformation of the ASEAN PTA into AFTA is a case in point whereby AFTA can be seen as an extension of the former. Unlike the more advanced stages of REI, however, both PTAs and FTAs do not require member states to harmonize trade policies among themselves.

An FTA has two basic features, which include, first, the ability of each member country to fix its own tariff rates against non-member countries; and, second, the use of a *country of origin* mechanism as a determination of intra-trade. The country of origin mechanism is useful "to limit trade deflection, [which] is a redirection of imports through the country with the lowest tariff for the purpose of exploiting the tariff differential" (Robson 1987: 23). At the FTA level of regional integration, it is true that trade deflection is likely to emerge (Dent 1997: 27), which is primarily due to the divergent rates imposed on the third countries. Thus, trade deflection occurs when member countries with more protectionist external policies are circumvented. The rule of the country of origin is particularly useful in determining the country origin of the traded goods. Therefore, "free trade performs the same function for international trade as competition laws in domestic economies" (Oxley 1990: 194).

Another major constraint in employing an FTA is that it generates unequal prices for the products being offered to consumers. This is mostly due to the price differences between products produced within an FTA region and products imported from non-member countries. As both Panagariya and Duttagupta (2001: 41) maintain, the "free mobility of goods produced within the union ensures there is a single union wide price for them. However, goods imported from outside [an FTA] pay different duty." Therefore, at this stage, while tariff levels between member countries equalize, tariff levels posed to non-member countries are not yet uniform. This condition normally enables producers to enjoy cheap prices for products coming from other FTA member states. However, this depends on the external tariffs set by member countries toward non-member countries. As a result of the different tariff levels posed to non-member countries, prices of products coming from these countries will vary greatly. Therefore, producers in a member country could only enjoy cheaper prices for goods coming from other member countries if the former set high external rates on imports from non-member countries.

In the global context, there are also some costs and benefits incurred through the creation of PTAs and/or FTAs (Edmond and Verbiest 2002: 2–3). In terms of benefits, firstly, the creation of either a PTA or an FTA enables a group of countries to deal with more complex issues of trade and regional cooperation (Freund 2000). Secondly, the creation of PTAs and FTAs also increases domestic competition, which can lead to greater productive efficiency among domestic producers. As a consequence, thirdly, the quantity and quality of goods available in the economy improves. Fourthly, these trade agreements may also foster greater economic regionalism among member countries. Fifthly, such agreements offer countries the opportunity to liberalize their economies in a limited and smaller scale than those agreements made at the multilateral level.[30] In terms of its costs, firstly, PTAs and FTAs can be interpreted as an easy way out for policymakers who are reluctant to actually commit to trade liberalization measures, but face an increasing domestic pressure for trade liberalization. Secondly, there is the fear of what Bhagwati (1995a) calls the *spaghetti-bowl* phenomenon. This phenomenon refers to the situation whereby products in a particular country enjoy access on varying terms based on their country of origins. If this occurs, then the fear is that such PTAs and/or FTAs can lead to an inward-looking regionalism.[31]

New Regionalism Approach (Second Wave)

The global tendency toward regionalism started to fade away during the late 1970s, and only re-emerged during the early 1990s. The resurrection of interest in regionalism in this latter period did not only prevail among policymakers and academia, but also among a wider spectrum of non-state actors, particularly business executives. In light of increasing interest in regionalism, political-scientists began to search for possible explanations for the proliferation of regionalism at the time. Aside from social constructivism, which had largely developed since the dismantling of the Cold War, a new theory was created to explain "the second wave of regional cooperation and integration" (Hettne 1999: 8). This approach was later called the New Regionalism Approach (NRA).[32] NRA's principal difference from other mainstream theories lies in its conceptual approach in defining an RIA. It is particularly concerned with the issue of regionalization, or the degree of *regionness*, where the "ultimate outcome [is the creation of] a *region-state*" (Hettne 1999: 11). It describes a *voluntary evolution* process in which nation-states are transformed into a supranational community. Although NRA is quite similar to other mainstream theories in respect of the voluntary transformation process, NRA is largely connected with the broader theoretical debate within IR and international political economy (IPE) (Schulz et al. 2001a: 12–13). In addition, NRA also emphasizes that the roles of non-state actors in regionalism is central to its analysis. Accordingly, NRA theorists, such as Hettne and Inotai (1994), argue that regionalism is not merely the institutionalization of a regional project or regional organization, nor is it merely a state mechanism. Rather, it has to be seen as a process, or as a regionalization process. This process will enable the states involved to gradually transform their relative heterogeneity and lack of cooperation into an increased demand for cooperation, integration, convergence, coherence and shared identity (Schulz et al. 2001a: 5). The new regionalism, then, is heterogeneous in character, encompassing a wide range of issues, actors, and institutions involved in the process of regionalization.

Departing from two most influential theoretical analyzes of global social theory (the modern world-system theory) and social constructivism, NRA has been developed to inform a more "comprehensive, interdisciplinary, and [to provide a] historically based social science" (Hettne and Söderbaum 2000: 460). The modern world-system theory has been particularly important to the development of NRA since this theory attempts to bridge the gap that exists between development theory and IPE approach (Hettne and Söderbaum 2000: 459). The political economy dimension of modern world-system theory enables an analysis of historical power structures and their contradictions, as well as an analysis of the changes and transformations expressed in normative terms to take place (Murphy and Tooze 1991; Hettne 1995; Cox with Sinclair 1996).[33] In addition, while the modern world-system theory highlights the dichotomy between *micro* and *macro* regionalism, NRA attempts to bridge such a gap.[34] More importantly, however, global social theory has been useful to NRA analysis because it abandons the idea of the state centrist determinant. Social constructivism, on the other hand, has influenced the development of NRA because of its emphasis upon the relative nature of a region. Moreover, by departing from social constructivism, NRA also attempts to transcend hard structuralism (Hettne and Söderbaum 2000: 459), as an emphasis is placed on the *process* (Wendt 1992) of regionalization. In this context, therefore, the focus of regionalism studies is placed on the agency and actors responsible for the formal institutionalization of a regional grouping or a regional project.

Moreover, the analysis of NRA has been developed through the detailed examination of the difference between the first wave and the second wave of regionalism or integration (Palmer 1991; Hettne 1994; 1999; Bhalla and Bhalla 1997; Hettne and Söderbaum 2000). The first wave of regionalism, according to this line of thinking, was primarily characterized by international bipolarity, an institutional drive to regionalism, inward-looking economies, economic discrimination against the rest of the world, emphasis on intra-regional trade, and membership of only one regional grouping. The first wave of regionalism was much influenced by two political ideologies, capitalism and socialism. The bipolar global political system that existed during the first wave of regionalism, between mid-1950s until late 1980s, was mainly associated with the notion of hegemony, which although it may "contain social conflict, [and] it does not eliminate it altogether. [Alternatively, it can be said that] hegemony is not a stable condition; it is always being created and undermined" (Mittelman 1996a; 1999: 47).[35] Hegemonic Stability Theory grew during the 1970s as a result of heated debates over a possible United States decline as a hegemon, which, in turn, would pose a problem of how to preserve the trade system from protectionist state policies (Bajo 2001: 23). Secondly, many RIAs during the first wave of regionalism were primarily set up under government initiatives to create a system of regional peace and harmony. The logic behind the formation of RIAs at the time was mainly concerned with creating political cohesion among member countries in a region. ASEAN, for example, was primarily founded for strategic and security reasons to end conflicts in the Southeast Asian region (Wanandi 2000: 25). Concern for other crucial aspects of integration, such as social and cultural aspects, was limited. Aside from the fact that an RIA was primarily triggered by the patterns of trade within a defined region, a state generally discouraged the involvement of non-state actors in determining their regional policies.

Thirdly, many states' strongly nationalist economic policies prevailed during the first wave of regionalism. Within this type of policy, the direction of the market was largely determined by the state and its policies. In a country where strongly nationalist economic policy prevails, such as those in Latin America and Asia, import substitution industrialization (ISI)[36] is normally seen as the predominant economic mechanism for the protection of national industries. ISI itself, as Dicken (1992: 177) posits, was normally aimed "to protect a nation's infant industries so that the overall industrial structure could be developed and diversified and dependence on foreign technology and capital reduced." In this type of trade strategy, the state normally imposes high tariff barriers on certain industrial sectors through various means, including quotas, licenses, multiple exchange rates, and so on. This particular trade strategy eventually drew many critics. In Dicken's (1992: 178) view, for example, ISI can be described as "a *halfway* industrialization or as *getting stuck* at the consumer goods stage." This is particularly common in a small domestic market where local production of consumer goods cannot attain an appropriate economy of scale, which leads to high domestic prices. Others, such as Genberg and De Simone (1993: 178–79), are more concerned about the delayed adjustment that ISI produces in the light of an external shock. Nevertheless, the majority of small countries throughout the world employed such a strategy (Hewitt et al. 1997: 19). As this economic nationalism spread, it became subsumed within a wider regional context, leading to the creation of regional trade bloc (Hewitt et al. 1997: 21). Within such a context, third countries are normally neglected by members of a regional grouping in the process of trade liberalization.

Another important characteristic of first wave regionalism is that many regional groupings at the time were mainly composed of countries that were economically competitive (homogenous) in nature. At the same time, intra-trade intensity was also used as a benchmark in many scholarly analyzes on the development of these regional groupings. Economists, such as Kemp and Wan (1976), examined the type of countries that can be the most desirable partners to form an RIA with. The appropriate level of intra-trade suitable for the promotion of further integration is normally supported with conditions of high economic diversity among member countries. While one country might have, for example, a comparative advantage in the production of manufacturing goods, another country's comparative advantage may rest in the richness of its natural resources. These complementary economic conditions among member countries will lead to efficiency and eventually to higher intra-trade level. In stark contrast with these conditions, however, many RIAs during the first wave of integration were homogenous in nature, which therefore led to slow progress toward deeper integration, such as in the case of ASEAN, or led to their demise, such as that in the case of CMEA.

Finally, a variety of policies were pursued by most states when determining the appropriate regional grouping they wished to join. While some countries preferred to join only one RIA, others pursued a strategy of overlapping membership. This can be seen in the case of RIA attempts in Latin America. During the late 1960s, while all Latin American countries were members of LAFTA, some had also formed an alternative RIA such as the Andean Pact. Among other things, this situation existed mainly as a result of the frustration held by some member countries over slow regionalism in LAFTA (Finch 1988). Moreover, geographical position did not necessarily hinder the pursuance of RIA among countries in different regions of the world. Initially, when international trade was not yet as fully intensified as it became during the 1980s onward, states tended to form RIAs with their closest neighbors. Some exceptions in this pattern, however, can be found in the case of CMEA, where membership include those non-Eastern European countries, such as Cuba, Mongolia, and Vietnam (Hewitt et al. 1997: 18).

In the view of many NRA theorists, however, recent regionalism differs to the first wave of regionalism in that it takes place in a multipolar world order spontaneous process; is open and outward oriented; and is a multidimensional process with the involvement of non-state actors (Hettne 1999: 7–8; Bhalla and Bhalla 1997: 21). Firstly, the collapse of communism transformed the world order system from a bipolar into a multipolar system in which regional groupings play important roles. This international political condition has led to the re-emergence of regionalism, particularly with the strengthening of European integration, which signifies the importance of regional rather than global interdependencies. Secondly, recent regionalism has been described by NRA theorists, such as Hettne (1994; 1999) and Schulz et al. (2001a), as a *spontaneous process* in the sense that it is not merely process instigated by institutions, but involves a number of other actors all contributing to the process of regional integration. A third and equally major transformation is the recent intensification of global economic activities. This has prompted nation-states to form regional groupings in order to contain the forces of globalization, but also to remain open according to their commitment toward multilateralism (overlapping commitment). Lastly, the involvement of non-state actors has been crucial in the promotion of regionalism. According to Hettne (1999: 7), because the new regionalism is a more spontaneous process from within and from below, non-state actors (i.e., TNCs and non-governmental organizations (NGOs)), are increasingly becoming the main proponents for regional integration.

The relevance of NRA analysis toward the regionalization process in Southeast Asia has been significant. The region itself has been recognized as a testing ground for both old and new waves of regionalism in the so-called Third World (Palmer 1991: 59). Although the formation of ASEAN in 1967 has done little to promote deeper integration among Southeast Asian countries (Wong 1989: 121), this regional grouping has been able to achieve substantial success in some areas of cooperation, particularly in the security field. The Southeast Asian region, with its diverse political and sociocultural backgrounds, as well as its heterogeneous economies, presents many obstacles to the emergence of formal regionalism among ASEAN member countries. However, as Palmer (1991: 12) convincingly reminds us, "regionalism may be well advanced even if it has not led to the establishment of major organizational form." This has been the case with the regionalization process in Southeast Asian region. With its limited capacity to foster deeper integration among Southeast Asian countries, ASEAN has to rely on the concept of *regionalization from within* the region. Demand for deeper regional cooperation has not only existed among state actors, but also among non-state actors. In the global economic context, the region is both committed to maintaining an open economic regime while at the same time, exercising overlapping memberships with other regional groupings. One recent study conducted by Lloyd (2002), for example, has indicated that there has been an increase in the demand for formal regionalism in the Asia Pacific, involving one or more countries from the Southeast Asian region. All these factors suggest that the Southeast Asian region has become one of the major players in the promotion of new regionalism across the world.

Theoretical Perspectives on Nationalism

Contemporary analyzes of nationalism have paid little attention to the relationship between nationalism and regionalism and/or globalism (e.g., Halliday 1997: 360; Shulman 2000: 365). Traditionally, nationalism is generally regarded as detrimental to both regionalism and globalism. For many IR scholars, such as Cobban (1969) and Roessingh (1996), nationalism can be considered as a territorial ideology, which is internally unifying and externally divisive. States that are not homogenous in culture and language are undermined from within and assaulted from without. It is, however, important to point out that nationalists today confront a complex set of considerations when dealing with various international forces. It is, therefore, incorrect to assume that all nationalists are uniformly hostile to regionalism or globalism (Shulman 2000: 365). Nationalism today does not necessarily pose a threat to regionalism, and can, in certain circumstances, be seen as a stepping-stone toward both regionalism and globalism. Whatever the case, nationalism is still an important element within the international system and a major constituent in determining the future of regionalism and further global integration. The primary focus of this section is to analyze the existing literature on the relationship between nationalism and regionalism.

The Concept of Nationalism

Unlike the concept of RIA, which grew only during the post Second World War period, nationalism is much longer. In fact, it evolved even before the conception of the Westphalian State system in 1648.[37] Nationalism, for some, has been regarded as "the most successful ideology in human history" (Birch, 1989: 3). The word nationalism derives from the Latin word of "*natio* [that] was used by the ancient Romans to refer to foreigners. Later it was used to refer to the assembly of nobles and clergy drawn from particular people" (Zernatto, 1944),[38] which differs from our use of the word *nationalism* today.[39] In its original classical sense, nationalism was also associated with "the word *nasci*, [which] means a tribal-ethnic group, a people born in the same place and territory" (Oomen 1997: 28).[40] It was only in the late eighteenth and nineteenth centuries that the debate on nationalism started, particularly among political philosophers who attempted to investigate the concept as it manifested during that period.[41]

Different scholars have interpreted nationalism in different ways, which has led to a continuous debate about nationalism in both theory and practice. In general, however, distinctions should be made between some of the associative terms related to nationalism. These terms include a nation, a nation-state or a country, people, national, and, finally, nationality.[42] A *nation* is generally understood to be "a social group that shares a common identity, history, language, set of values and beliefs, institutions, and a sense of territory. Nations do not have to have a homogenous ethnic culture but [it] usually exhibits a sense of homogeneity" (Balaam and Veseth 1996: 456). Subsequently, as Balaam and Veseth (1996: 456) further point out, a *nation-state* or a *country* generally refers to "a legal concept describing a social group that occupies a territory and is organized under a common political institutions and an effective government [*sic*]." The *people*, furthermore, refer to the members of the nation-state, and they often denote a specific political unit, which is the state, and an ethnological unit, the *race*. Moreover, the word *national* characterizes the whole body of citizens as distinct from any section or locality within the given area. It is normally used to describe certain issues that cover the entire nation-state, i.e., national policy, national ideology, etc. National, then, becomes *nationality* by virtue of the people's membership to a nation. Finally, *nationalists* are those who support nationalism in the sense described above. A nationalist, alternatively, may also refer to someone who tends to exalt devotion to his or her nation at the expense of all other considerations.

In the field of international political-economy, the term *economic nationalism* is often used as an as an associative term to that of nationalism. Generally, economic nationalism is a mercantilist ideology that emphasizes the partnership between the state and market (Balaam and Veseth 1996: 452). The term itself was widely used during the interwar years of the twentieth century (Heilperin 1960: 17).[43] Since then the concept of economic nationalism has been interpreted through various theoretical discourses (i.e., realist, liberal, and Marxist), most of which focus on the way in which production, exchange, consumption, and investment are governed by the state's interests (Crane 1998: 56–57). According to realists, for example, economic nationalism is logical because the state must turn all national economic activities to its national advantage in order to minimize its relative material losses in the international arena (Gilpin 1987: 31). For neo-liberalists, on the other hand, economic nationalism is viewed as something that does not fit with liberal ideals of economy and development (Koffman 1990).[44] Finally, from a Marxist standpoint, economic nationalism is simply the expression of capitalism that is conditioned by historical forces (Cox 1987).[45] Regardless of these different interpretations of the concept of economic nationalism, the term more generally refers to the "proclivity of the state, firms and individuals for economic decisions, actions and alliance formation that seeks to advance the nation's domestic or international position at the potential commercial expense of foreign national or international interests" (Dent 2002a: 25).

Current debates around nationalism have given rise to other contemporary terms associated with the concept of nationalism, which include *forced nationalism* and *ethnonationalism*. While forced nationalism refers mainly to the "extension, or a merger, of boundaries of states, [and is] related to homogeneous cultures between the states involved" (Hechter 2000: 15–17), ethnonationalism refers to the promotion of "the principle of self-determination and the politics of opposition of an ethno-nation or a people, and challenges the state to change its discriminatory policies and oppressive behavior" (Jalata 2001: 285–86). Forced nationalism is also often associated with the notion of *irredentism*,[46] which can be identified as the "desire to reconstitute or redeem the unity and integrity of a particular ethnic group, historic entity or community" (Christie 1996: 131). A forced nationalism or irredentism, then, might manifest as the annexation of a nation to become part of another, more powerful, nation (i.e., Indonesia's annexation of East Timor in 1975). Thus, geographical boundaries can be changed over time depending on the political relationship between a country and its neighbors, signifying the relativity of the nation-state concept. Ethnonationalism, on the other hand, is associated with the concept of secessionism from a large political unit under the nation-state due to differences in political ideology, language, unequal distribution of incomes, race, and cultural or historical backgrounds from the rest of the country. A major example of ethnonationalism can be seen in the experience of Canada in dealing with its province of Quebec. Because of their cultural differences Quebecois insist on being separate from the rest of Canada. This sense of *provincial* or *smaller* scale nationalism is called ethnonationalism.

Nationalism in International Political Economy

Early studies of nationalism in the international politics have been linked closely with the rise of nation-state systems (Carr 1945; Cobban 1969), wars and tensions between nation-states (Howard 1991), and secessionist movements that are often characterized by ethnic and religious conflicts within a nation-state (Horrowitz 1985; Mayall 1990). From the 1970s onward, however, the focus of international politics shifted from military to economic issues (Katzenstein 1978a). The increasing internationalization of economic activities over recent years, particularly through regionalism and globalization, has undermined the coherence of nation-states' nationalist ideology. In the late twentieth century, for instance, there have been claims that "nationalism has become an anachronism" (Heywood, 2000: 256). Indeed, any interpretation of the relationship between nationalism and RIA or globalization will often be contentious since RIA and globalization normally act as a destabilizing factor to nationalism. Not only do the processes of both RIA and globalization require a nation-state to lower its barriers and allow outside influences within its sovereign borders, but they may also produce clashes between and within nation-states. It is, therefore, hardly surprising when nationalists pursue a strategy that undermines regional or global projects.

Traditionally, one key variable in analyzing the dynamic of nationalism in international politics and economics is the concept of *national interest* (Krasner 1979).[47] Despite its wide use in foreign economic policy (FEP) analysis, the meaning of the term national (economic) interest remains vague (Frankel 1970: 15). Nevertheless, as Frankel (1970: 31–33) describes, national interest can be classified into aspirational, operational, and explanatory and polemical. At the aspirational level, national interest is seen as an ideal set of goals which, if possible, the state wishes to achieve. At the operational level, the national interest can be understood as the total sum of interests and policies actually pursued by the state. Finally, the explanatory and polemical level of national interest refers to the interrelationship between the aspirational and operational level. It is at this final level that the concept of national interest proves most significant since the distance between the two levels determines political dynamism. For Rosenau (1968: 34), however, the concept of national interest can be defined as both an analytical tool or as an instrument of political action. As an analytical tool, the national interest is the benchmark which the adequacy of a country's foreign policy is analyzed. As a political action, on the other hand, the national interest can be described as the way in which such a policy is justified. At both levels, the concept simply means what is best for the society of a nation. As a whole, however, it is right to suggest that national interest is "of great significance to the survival of the state" (Fifield 1979: 20).

It is, however, very difficult to determine a nation-state's national interests. Such difficulty primarily stems from the miscalculation or misinterpretation of the "perception, priority, and permanence" (Fifield 1979: 19) of various domestic interest groups in the country. The perceptions of domestic interest groups are shaped by various factors, including geopolitics, history, and social and economic factors. Furthermore, the national interest only specifies the state's FEP *objectives*, not the way in which the state implements such aspirations (Katzenstein 1978b). It is for this reason that, as Katzenstein (1978b: 297–306) further postulates, it is necessary to distinguish between policy objectives and policy instruments when analyzing a state's FEP. Here, policy objectives imply certain values that are ascribed to a state and the society in a country. Thus, great variations in policy objectives are only to be expected between different nation-states. Policy instruments, on the other hand, determine the success of such objectives in the process of policy implementation. There are vast array of policy instruments that a state can utilize, including licenses, tariffs, quotas, fiscal policies, tax credits, etc.

Apart from its emphasis on the concept of national interest, traditional analysis of FEP has also focused on the international factors that influence the way in which FEP is formulated, while ignoring the importance of domestic structures (Katzenstein 1978a). Here, it is useful to utilize the three approaches to FEP formulation proposed by Ikenberry et al. (1988: 1–2). The first approach is a system-centered, and explains a nation-state's FEP as a function of the attributes or capabilities of that nation-state relative to other nation-states. In this context, government officials respond to a set of opportunities or constraints that their country confronts at a specific point in time and, thus, international systems condition the state's FEP. The second approach is a society-centered, and views the formulation of a nation-state's FEP as either reflecting the preferences of the dominant group or class in society, or as resulting from the struggle of influence among various interest groups or political parties. This approach is most applicable to a democratic society. Here, FEP is a reflection of the ideal of the majority of the population, which is then transformed into policy by the policymakers. Finally, the third, or state-centered, approach shows the state to be the most important independent variable in the FEP formulation process, where FEP is mainly employed by the state under an autocratic political system. In this context, the objective of FEP formulation is associated with the justification of policymakers' will to pursue a certain course of action. Such action is assumed to represent the best interests of the majority of the population.

Another important analytical framework that focuses on the relationship between national domestic constituencies and international policy-making processes has been put forward by Putnam (1988) in his two-level game analysis. In his theoretical framework, Putnam (Putnam 1988: 434) asserts that "at the national level (level II), domestic groups pursue interests by pressuring the government to adopt favorable policies, and politicians seek power by constructing coalitions among those groups. At the international level (level I), national governments seek to maximize their own ability to satisfy domestic pressures, while minimizing the adverse consequences of foreign development."[48] Putnam's argument stresses the sovereign nature of the state, while pointing out that nation-states have to realize the increasing interdependencies between one another themselves. Neither level of the game should be ignored for to do so would result in conflicts between the constituents in either the domestic or international arena. A variation to Putnam's two-level game theory was offered by Guerreri and Padoan (1989: 21–29), who hold that a win-set situation is characterized by "popularity and reputation." While popularity depends on the ruling regime and ideological preferences, the reputation of a country depends on the country's ability to resist external or international pressures. With regard to the way in which international (or regional) economic integration policy might be pursued, Guerreri and Padoan (1989 24–25) propose that "this can be done in two, not mutually exclusive, ways." One is to conduct an outward looking strategy, which requires a government to be strong internationally, while the other is to conduct an inward looking strategy, which requires strong domestic conditions. National economic policy choices with regard to a country's involvement in an RIA or any other multilateral arrangement would depend on the definition of that country's long-term goals and strategies and the relationship between the state and its constituencies. Such national choices are characterized in terms of the supply and demand of the policies. While it is the state that supplies the policy in exchange for popularity, interest groups are those who determine the demand.

In recent years, scholarly analysis of FEP has attempted to explore further the importance of domestic structure in the FEP formulation process. Among others, Dent's (2002a) analysis of contesting actor-based influence is particularly useful. From a domestic perspective, Dent (2002a: 24–25) asserts that the process of FEP formulation is contingent upon: first, state bureaucratic power, culture, and dynamics; second, level of democratization; third, internationalization of civil society; and, fourth, economic nationalism. Firstly, state bureaucratic power, culture and dynamics determine FEP since policymakers have the ability to develop their own predilection toward the setting of specific policy objectives. A strong emphasis on state bureaucratic power, culture and dynamics generally occurs in a state-centric society where constituents hold limited influence over FEP formulation. Secondly, the formation of the state's FEP is also dependent upon the level of democratization in the society. Countries with a higher level of democratization are more likely to be influenced by constituents in the FEP formulation process. Thirdly, the level of a civil society's influence over FEP is also dependent upon their knowledge regarding international political and economic conditions. More outward-looking societies are more likely to assert a greater stake in the FEP formulation process, and *vice versa*. Fourthly, the level of economic nationalism also plays an important role in determining the FEP of a state. Nationalist economic measures are invariably implemented through strong industrial policies or the implementation of high import barriers (i.e., protection), much of which are applied to infant strategic industries within a country. There are also some cases where the huge assets of foreign firms may be confiscated after their operation inside a country for some time. At other times, foreign firms may not be allowed to enter a country to invest in large industries since these industries are seen to serve only the interests of local economic or political constituents.

It is, therefore, clear that an analysis of contemporary FEP is incomplete when a focus upon domestic structure is neglected (Katzenstein 1976: 2). A country's FEP can either be economically nationalist or liberal in nature, or somewhere in between, depending upon the immediate interests of domestic constituents. However, the recent nationalist interest in RIA and globalization have varied, at least since the post Cold War period, depending upon the degree to which such schemes are seen to serve the interests of a nation. It is important to note that there are times when nationalists may also express strong support for their country's involvement in a regional cooperation scheme, or even in a multinational arrangement. While the issue of sovereignty marks the foundation of much of the criticism attached to RIA, it is also important to stress that "when two or more countries sign a treaty, they agree to do and/or not to do specified things. Therefore, it is not a valid criticism of any international treaty to say that it entails a loss of national sovereignty" (Jovanovich 1992: 10). Furthermore, there are also times when nationalists may express great interest in regionalism, especially as a means to promote their nation autonomy, identity, and unity (Shulman 2000). Nevertheless, nationalist support for regionalism and globalization only exists when it is seen to serve their national interests.

The Gap within the Existing Literature Concerning the Relationship between Regionalism and Nationalism

Limited attention has been given to the dynamic nature of the relationship between nationalism and regionalism. Nationalists' reactions toward regionalism are often hostile while most proponents of regionalism insist that nationalism should be weakened or overcome (Shulman 2000: 365). This hostile attitude has been prevalent among nationalists since "the increase in the volume of trade, migration and cross-border financial transactions, the emergence of regional trading blocs, and the global reach of TNCs signal the erosion of national borders" (Goff 2000: 533). This book, however, argues that there are ways in which a *symbiotic* characteristic can be established in the relationship between nationalism and regionalism. Moreover, previous studies on nationalism and regionalism tend to treat the two as mutually exclusive. As a result, most previous studies fail to explain why convergence can emerge from the seemingly divergent national interests of the states involved in a regional grouping (Schirm 2002: 8).

Regionalism theories themselves are fragmented in their view toward nationalism; all placing different weight upon the concept of nationalism. Although (neo-)realists regard states as the most important players in the international arena, they fail to pay attention to other major domestic constituents (i.e., nationalists or liberals) that also have the potential to change the course of the state's FEP. Meanwhile, both the neo-liberal institutionalists and the structuralists have been too preoccupied with the issue of global capitalism. Moreover, both social constructivists and NRA theorists are correct to propose that regionalism is a process. However, both theories have been vague in their explanation of the way in which the institutionalization of regional projects or activities must take place in order to create a specific market or economy (Bajo 2001: 42). In addition, although NRA theorists have constantly maintained that the relationship between nationalism and regionalism is symbiotic (Hettne 1999; Schulz et al. 2001a), their explanations are still flawed and lack significant depth on this particular issue. Finally, REI analysis of free trade areas has been too preoccupied with intra regional trade as the benchmark of regionalism. REI theory has an implication, particularly on the results of implementation (Lawrence 1995: 7). If, for example, tariffs have been removed, problems can emerge where the countries involved have different regulatory policies. Thus, changing a regulatory policy within a country can affect the social policy of other member countries.

Gaps also exist in previous analyzes of nationalism, mainly because scholars, such as Geertz (1963) and Connor (1978) of nationalism have been too preoccupied with the notion of commonality among people within a specific geographical area. Such commonality is seen to derive from common language, race, tradition, historical background, and even religion.[49] Although this analysis is important in explaining why nationalism persists even in modern times (Birch 1989: 3), it fails to explain the supportive role that nationalism can play within the growing pattern of regionalism. Moreover, nationalism has been dubbed as an agency of destruction (Cobban 1969: 249) that often acts as a catalyst in propagating wars between nation-states. In the view of Fukuyama (1989), for example, nationalism has emerged as one of the most potentially powerful ideological rivals to economic liberalism. It is, however, possible to find some common ground between nationalists and regionalists. As will be argued throughout this book, nationalists do not necessarily feel hostile toward regionalism.

The final gap that will be addressed in this book is the fact that most existing FEP literature focuses on the context of developed countries. Much of the FEP analysis, from Katzenstein (1976; 1978a; 1978b), Hawley (1983), Ikenberry et al. (1988), Hocking and Smith (1997), to more recent analyzes, such as Dent (2002a), have focused primarily upon the formulation of FEP in developed countries and newly industrialized economies (NIEs).[50] An attempt to bridge this gap has been provided by Shulman (2000) who tries to analyze the FEP of nationalists in both India and Ukraine. However, analyzes of this subject in the context of Southeast Asian developing countries have been limited. Many analyzes, particularly with reference to Indonesia, have been subsumed into the context of foreign policy in general.[51] It is, therefore, necessary to provide a new focus upon the formulation of FEP in developing countries in order to examine and understand current debates on the new pattern of regionalism.

Conclusion

This chapter has provided a detailed theoretical analysis of the relationship between regionalism and nationalism. The analysis has demonstrated that the relationship between nationalism and regionalism is dynamic. This chapter began with an analysis of the various different perspectives that prevail within the theoretical study of regionalism. Regional integration theory has gradually transformed since its first wave into a second wave of integration. Many regional integration theories during the first wave were dominated by (neo-)realist, neo-liberal institutionalist, and structuralist points of view. Each perspective provides a different focus on regionalism. Realists and neo-realists, for example, focus upon the state's aggressive behavior, and argue that regionalism emerges as a result of political polarization in world politics. Meanwhile, the neo-liberal institutionalist analysis rests on the principle of market and trade liberalization, and offers the theory that regionalism emerges as a result of an increasing economic interdependency among countries in a specific region. Structuralists, on the other hand, challenge the neo-liberal institutionalist idea, and hold that an increasing pattern of regionalism will only further marginalize a peripheral region. Another analysis of the emerging pattern of regionalism looks instead through the lens of economics, and this approach has become a common focus for the study of the various regional groupings forming throughout the world. Despite some fallacies within these approaches, such theories provide useful stepping-stones for further studies of RIA.

New political science analyzes have emerged since the end of the Cold War. Both social constructivism and NRA attempt to provide a mediating status for regionalism, particularly in reference to the much-debated conflict between nationalism and globalization. The recent proliferation of regionalism is a response to the new challenges that states have met in the international arena. From such a viewpoint, regionalism is functional and fully compatible with the concept of national interest (Schirm 2002: 10). The emergence of regionalism does not mean the full erosion of the nation-state system. Such an analysis would propose that the emergence of regionalism is logical in that it can provide strategies for nation-states when dealing with globalization issues and effects. The role of regionalism within the world order, as Falk (1999: 80) asserts, "is to help create a new equilibrium in politics that balances the protection of the vulnerable and the interest of humanity as a whole against integrative, technological dynamic associated with globalism." Therefore, regionalism can be seen as a middle ground that is able to accommodate the notions of both nationalism and globalization.

The analysis of nationalism presented in this chapter has focused upon the literature provided by the discipline of international political economy. Largely speaking, the traditional literature interprets nationalism in terms of feelings about the country in which one is born and resides. Such feelings stem from the establishment of a commonality among the people that live within a particular area or region. An analysis of nationalism at the level of international politics and economy, however, suggests that contemporary nationalism constitutes a much more complex issue. This is particularly true when nationalism is examined vis-à-vis regionalism and/or globalization. While the traditional approach to nationalism focuses upon the concept of nation building and the modern nation-state, contemporary literature on nationalism places greater emphasis on inter-state relations. The dynamic relationship between nationalism and regionalism is significant in the case study that will be presented in this book. Indonesia's position in ASEAN is seen as *problematic*, because while the country is seen to have the potential to be the region's leader, domestic economic, social and political problems render it incapable. Despite this, the Association continues to exist and has conducted an initial form of economic integration through the implementation of AFTA in 2002.

Notes

1. The old regionalism is also known as the "first wave" of regionalism while the new regionalism can be referred to the "second wave" of regionalism (Hettne 1999; Schulz et al. 2001).

2. Generally, economists' analyzes of regionalism are based on four different economic structures, namely Free Trade Areas (FTA), Custom Union, Common Market, and total integration or Optimum Currency Areas. However, since the main focus of this thesis is on the ASEAN Free Trade Area (AFTA), specific concentration in this section will be given to FTA.

3. Some scholars, such as Schulz et al. (2001), also term this new theory the New Regionalism Approach (NRA). However, for the rest of the thesis, the term NRA will be used.

4. The term RIA was primarily derived from the concept of *regional integration*. Although there are no clear historical accounts which indicate the exact time that the concept of *regional integration* was first initiated, Machlup (1977: 63) suggests that the "concept made its first appearance in 1939 and 1942." Thus, it is a relatively new term, dating back to the World War II period. In addition, Machlup (1977: 61) also points out that the word *integration* itself was "taken from the Latin word *integratio*, which [was] mainly used in the sense of renovation." During its conception, the word *integration* was normally associated with industrial organization, and referred to the act of combining business firms through agreements, cartels, and so on. By 1950, however, the term regionalism had been given a specific definition by most economists as "a process and as a state affair" (Balassa 1961: 1). Regionalism is regarded as a process because it encompasses *measures* designed to abolish economic discrimination between participating countries. At the same time, it is also viewed as a state affair due to the absence of various forms of discrimination between national economies.

5. The term used by some scholars, such as Tinbergen (1954), El-Agraa (1988), and Robson (1987).

6. Multilateral trade bodies, such as WTO use the term regional trade arrangements (RTAs). This term specifically refers to free trade agreements made between two or more participating countries. The WTO, however, regards RTAs as not specifically constrained

by region *per se*. This is mainly due to the fact that many RTAs today do not necessarily involve countries within the same region. Further details on RTAs can be found at the WTO web site (accessed 2003) at http://www.wto.org.

7. The concept of trade creation and trade diversion are primarily used in the advanced level of REI, particularly at the custom union level. In his analysis of the static measure of a custom union, Viner (1950) argues that, as a result of the introduction of a common external tariff (CET), trade with non-member countries will result in either trade creation effect or trade diversion effect. A trade creation effect occurs when the imposition of a CET does not distort trade with non-member countries. In this context, a lack of inefficient products within an RIA will be replaced with cheaper imports from non-member countries, which eventually lead to producer and consumer gains. A trade diversion effect, on the other hand, occurs when "cheaper external imports being replaced by more expensive partner equivalent as a consequence of CET's imposition" (Dent 1997: 30) on non-member countries. A trade diversion effect, therefore, refers to higher levels of trades generated within an RIA rather than outside it.

8. The work of Thomas Hobbes (1968) was one of the main inspirations for the development of (neo-)realist thinking. For Hobbes, human nature is selfish: life is a struggle of individual wills in a battle for survival. Accordingly, in an international system where forces capable of producing order are absent, it is inevitable that wars occur as a result of human fear, greed, and competition.

9. In this context, for example, Waltz (1979: 67) suggested that, in the near future, it is likely that both Japan and Germany could become nuclear powers.

10. See in particular Moravcsik (1993), one of the main proponents of neo-liberal institutionalism.

11. Despite this, neo-liberal institutionalists also concur with (neo-)realism analyzes, particularly with regard to the state's role in world affairs. Here, neo-liberal institutionalists also maintain that states play a determining factor in world affairs, and that they act with a unitary and rational manner. Moreover, neo-liberal institutionalism also agrees with the (neo-)realists argument that anarchy is the major force that shapes the motives and actions of the states. For a further review on the differences between (neo-)realism and neo-liberal institutionalism, see Grieco (1988).

12. See also Moravcsik (1998) for his ambitious work on developing a theory of economic and political integration on the basis of intergovernmentalism. His work concentrates on national governments' pivotal responses to the increase of interdependence among national economies. Other attention is also given to the importance of international (regional) institutions in solving problems generated by economic interdependence.

13. Breslin et al. (2002) also add that, with regard to the Asian regional economic crisis of 1997, the underlying task is not to find a regional solution to the economic crisis, but also to question the advantages that can be accrued by pursuing neo-liberalism *per se*.

14. See, for example, Marx and Engels (1955: 5).

15. Lenin's analysis, *Imperialism: The Highest Stage of Capitalism*, was first published in 1917. It is important to note that an earlier comprehensive analysis on the role of economics in imperialism was first developed by John Hobson (1965). In Hobson's view, imperial expansion was primarily driven by the desire to search for new markets and resources, as well as to seek the opportunity for investment overseas.

16. This theoretical doctrine has been adopted by a number of socialist countries. Russia under Joseph Stalin and China under Mao Zedong, for example, adopted a centralized system to achieve the transformation from capitalism and imperialism to communism.

17. Structural or trade imbalance normally refers to the incapacity of peripheral areas, or developing countries, to earn enough from exports to cover the cost of imports. Developing countries normally require imports for the purpose of development. For a further review on structural or trade imbalance see Tussie (1987: 22–37).

18. Dependency theory was developed largely by analysts within the Economic Commission on Latin America (ECLA). This theory was later developed by other scholars, particularly those associated with the United Nations Conference on Trade and Development (UNCTAD), who were dissatisfied with the assumption that the failure of development in many developing countries was a result of religion, culture and tradition, which acted as a bulwark against modernization. Further analysis of dependency theory can be found in Dougherty and Pfaltzgraff (1990: 249–52) and Ghosh (2001).

19. Moreover, Wallerstein (1991) also argues that a world system analysis is the appropriate mode of analysis to explain all social phenomena over time.

20. Throughout the late 1980s, however, Wallerstein's work received stiff criticism by a number of scholars. For example, Chase-Dunn (1989) believes that the inter-state system is equally important in determining the international system. In his view, the capitalist mode of production has a single objective in which both politico-military and exploitative economic relations play key roles. Another criticism of Wallerstein's view is also present in Abu-Lughod's (1989) work, particularly with regard to the framework of the world system during the sixteenth-century. In her view, during the medieval period Europe was peripheral while the core region was the Middle East.

21. Prior to 1989, the term social constructivism was hardly used. Most scholars used the term *structuration theory* to relate to a constructivist approach in IR theory. This is particularly apparent in the works of Giddens (1979), Ruggie (1983), Wendt (1987), and Dessler (1989).

22. In recent years, however, the notion of culture and identity has also been predominantly used by neo-liberal institutionalists. For further analysis of the importance of culture and identity in neo-liberal institutionalists' perspectives see, *inter alia*, Caporaso (1992) and Zacher and Matthew (1995).

23. One major difference between structuralism and social constructivism is the latter's argument that structure has no existence or causal power apart from when it acts as a process. As a result, structure does not explain the outcomes. For further analysis on the differences between the two theories see, *inter alia*, Wendt (1992).

24. For Ruggie (1998: 4), social constructivism allows for the formation of various international (regional) agencies not only as the enactment of pre-programmed script, but as a reflection of social creation, within structured constraints.

25. It is still highly speculative to assume that REI in Southeast Asia will advance to any level beyond the FTA. Among other things, this problem is a result of the lack of will among ASEAN member governments to surrender part of their sovereignty. At an advanced level of REI, a regional grouping must suppress any discrimination in commodity movements as well as impose an equalization of tariffs toward non-member countries (custom union), abolish restrictions on factor movements (common market), harmonize national economic policies among member countries (economic union), and, finally, unify monetary, fiscal, social, and countercyclical policies (total economic integration). Many of these requirements are still too difficult to achieve in ASEAN. For further analysis on each of these stages see, *inter alia*, Balassa (1961).

26. The concept of absolute advantage was based on Adam Smith's most influential work, *The Wealth of Nations* (1776). Smith analyzed the consequence of economic freedom, covering issues such as self-interest, the division of labors, the function of market,

and the implication of the *laissez faire* economy. For a detailed analysis of Adam Smith's works see also Smith et al. (1986).

27. The theory of comparative advantage was developed by a British MP and economist, David Ricardo, in the early nineteenth century. For a detailed analysis of Ricardo's work see Sraffa and Dobb (1951).

28. Factor endowment theory was developed by Bertil Ohlin (1933), in his work *Interregional and International Trade*. In this work, he developed an earlier theory introduced by his mentor, Eli Heckscher, and his own earlier doctoral thesis. The factor endowment theory is now known as the Heckscher-Ohlin theory and has become the basis for many contemporary economic theories, such as the regional economic integration theory developed by Viner (1950) and Balassa (1961).

29. The U.S.-Canada Auto Pact of 1965 provided free trade for trucks, cars, and auto-parts between the two countries. Apart from that, this Pact was also formed to facilitate free trade on cars for the U.S. Big Four auto manufacturers, General Motors, Ford, Chrysler, and American Motors (Marxist Leninist Daily 2001). By 1999, two-way trade between the two countries rose to US$104.1 billion from an initial US$715 million in 1964. Nowadays, the Auto Pact has been incorporated into NAFTA.

30. An illustration of the benefits accrued from the implementation of PTAs or FTAs can be observed from the experience of the United States and Mexico through their involvement in NAFTA. During the first year of NAFTA's implementation, in 1994, bilateral trade between the United States and Mexico grew from US$84.7 billion (in 1993) to US$102.6 billion. Subsequently, in 1995, the bilateral trade between the two countries rose to US$112 billion while Mexico's exports to the United States amounted to US$66.7 billion. Meanwhile, the influx of direct investment to Mexico rose to US$10.9 billion in 1994 from an annual average of US$2.6 billion between 1985 until 1990. Therefore, since the formation of NAFTA, North American countries have become competition-oriented and have become an attractive investment location. For further assessment of the benefits accrued by Mexico and the United States from NAFTA see Schirm (2002: 140–41).

31. For further analysis on the way country of origin mechanisms enhance protectionism, see Krueger (1993).

32. One major early work on NRA was developed by Hettne and Inotai (1994), a research project sponsored by the United Nations University (UNU) and the World Institute for Development and Economic Research, and was summed up in their work entitled *New Regionalism: Implications for Global Development and International Security*. Subsequently, Hettne, Inotai and Sunkel elaborated further the concept of NRA by editing five publications, entitled: (1) *Globalism and the New Regionalism* (1999); (2) *National Perspectives on the New Regionalism in the North* (2000a); (3) *National Perspectives on the New Regionalism in the South* (2000b); (4) *The New Regionalism and the Future of Security and Development* (2000c); (5) *Comparing Regionalism: Implications for Global Development* (2001). Another important study focusing on the new regionalism phenomenon has also been conducted by Palmer (1991), with specific reference to the Asia-Pacific region.

33. As cited in Hettne and Söderbaum (2000: 459).

34. The modern world-system theory has also been useful in the development of NRA because it concentrates upon the big process of macro-regionalism, or regionalism between the three core regions, which include Europe, North America, and the Asia Pacific (triad regionalism). Examples of both macro and micro regionalism are best illustrated by Öjendal (2000: 1), who postulates the "maximalist and minimalist versions of regionalization." The maximalist form of regionalism is associated with the concept of

macro-regionalism, such as in the case of the Asia-Pacific, European, and the American regionalisms. The minimalist form of regionalism, on the other hand, is associated with the concept of micro-regionalism, such as in the context of ASEAN, or, alternatively, it can also be viewed in the context of the growth triangles whereby close trade cooperations among provincial or district areas of member countries in an RIA occur.

35. Hegemonic Stability Theory primarily derives from the (neo-)realists' analysis (Dent 2001a: 733) and is considered one of the variations within the liberal IPE perspective (Balaam and Veseth 1996: 51). Within the realm of (neo-)realists' analysis, Hegemonic Stability Theory contends that there is a tendency for a hegemonic state to play a stabilizing role within the international economic system. A hegemon tends to exploit its techno-industrial superiority through exports to foreign markets. Within the sphere of liberal IPE perspective, Hegemonic Stability Theory looks at the state and market in the global economy and holds that international markets work best when certain international public goods (i.e., free trade, peace and security, a balance of power, and sound international payment system) are present. Thus, a hegemon is likely to support an open and free trading system. For detailed analyzes on Hegemonic Stability Theory see, *inter alia*, Kindleberger (1973), Gilpin (1975), and Krasner (1983).

36. ISI strategy was initially developed by an Argentine economist, Raul Prebisch (Miller 1998: 151–52). This strategy forms an integral part of the implementation process of the dependency theory. For an analysis of Prebisch's contribution to the development of dependency theory, see also di Marco (1972).

37. For Koht (1947: 265–66), however, the concept of a nation was established far before the conception of the Westphalian State system, or after the dissolution of the Roman Empire.

38. Quoted from Oomen (1997: 4).

39. However, Sturzo (1946: 5) also stresses the errors and fallacies in the term nationalism and showed the error in connecting patriotism with nationalism. The word nationalism was first used during the nineteenth century, soon after the birth of the three "isms": liberalism, socialism, and communism. All four words have highly respectable origins. The words national, social, liberal, and communal were originally adjectives. "Ism" was added to these adjectives, thereby transforming them into nouns, so liberal became liberalism, social-socialism, common-communism, and national became nationalism.

40. The Latin word *nasci* literally means *to be born*. For a general analysis on the historical meaning of the word nation and nationalism see, for example, Haywood (2000: 251–56).

41. See, for example, Renan (1882) with his published work of *Qu'est-ce Qu'une Nation?* (What Is a Nation?).

42. Early distinctions between these different terms were made by the Royal Institute of International Affairs (RIIA) in its published work *Nationalism: A Report* (1939).

43. The study of economic nationalism, however, began in the nineteenth century. One of the most prominent scholars during that period was Friedrich List (1789–1846), who wrote *The National System of Political Economy* (1904). Since then, many scholarly analyzes of economic nationalism have drawn upon List's work. For a comprehensive analysis of List's concept of economic nationalism see, for example, Levy-Faur (1997a; 1997b).

44. For other liberals' view on economic nationalism see also Johnson (1967). Although Johnson contends that economic nationalism does promote national identity, he also maintains that the pursuance of this policy does not produce real economic advancement.

45. For other Marxist inspired works on economic nationalism see also Arrighi (1994).

46. The doctrine of irredentism, according to Mayall (1990), derives from the Italian *irridenta*. This word was associated with those territories, *Trente, Dalmatia, Trieste, Fiume,* all of which were culturally Italian, but remained under Swiss or Austrian rule and were *unredeemed* after the unification of Italy in 1861.

47. As mentioned earlier, the concept of national interest is also central in neo-realists' analysis. In Morgenthau's (1952: 961) view, for example, international politics can be seen as a process in which national interests are adjusted. Accordingly, policy-makers "think and act in terms of interest defined as power" (Morgenthau 1978: 5). See also Thompson and Myers (1984) for the assessment of Morgenthau's political philosophy on national interest.

48. For a detailed explanation of the two-level game theory analysis see also Evans et al. (1993).

49. For an analysis of the main narratives on nationalism see, for example, A. D. Smith (2000: 2). Here, Smith observes that the narratives of nationalism can be summarized into four paradigms, including primordialism, perrenialism, modernism, and ethno-symbolism. While the former two are mainly concerned with the question of which element, nationalism or a nation, comes first, the latter two are concerned with the contemporary development and the fragmentation of nationalism.

50. Although Dent (2002a) attempts to make a universal application in his analysis of FEP, his case study focuses on the newly industrializing countries of Northeast Asia and Southeast Asia, such as Singapore, Taiwan, and South Korea.

51. See in particular, Leifer (1983) and Anwar (1994; 2000; 2001a).

Chapter 3

Nationalists and Regional Integration Strategy

The global political economy is continuously changing and in today's world, globalism and regionalism exist alongside growing nationalism and ethnonationalism, in spite of their apparent contradiction of each other (Bereciartu 1994; Halliday 1997; Lähteenmäki and Käkönen 1999). Indeed, one main aspect that has to be addressed in analyzing the local-regional nexus is the concept of nationalism, which is one of the most potent ideologies in modern history, and as such is capable of undermining the process of regionalism. Traditionally, nationalists' major concern about their country's involvement in a regional grouping is the loss of sovereignty that may ensue. The prevalent assumption among nationalists in the past was that regionalism involves a series of compromises made among different states and, thus, does not *fully* represent the national interests of the country. Given today's increasing international economic integration, nationalists, like other domestic actors, are being forced to change or adjust their ideas and strategies. Nationalists are "by no means uniformly hostile to free trade and close economic ties with other states or nations" (Shulman 2000: 364). This chapter provides a detailed analysis of the factors that motivate nationalists to support or to pursue a regional integration strategy (RIS). More specifically, it offers a detailed theoretical framework to analyze the symbiotic nature of the relationship between nationalism and regionalism. This symbiotic relationship refers to the notion that the existence of both nationalism and regionalism can be mutually beneficial, although in some cases one variable benefits at the other's expense, or, in other cases, neither variable benefits at all.

In order to facilitate this argument, the New Regionalism Approach/Theory (NRA/NRT) is used as an analytical tool to examine the symbiotic nature of the relationship between the two variables. This is because NRA persists in stressing the flexible and fluid nature of recent patterns of regionalism. Consequently, the analysis in this chapter is divided into three sections. The first section focuses upon a broad explanation of the position of nationalism as a new focus within NRA analysis. The second section analyzes the ways in which nationalists pursue an RIS. The examples in this section reflect the experiences of Indonesian nationalists in dealing with an RIS. Finally, the relationship between Indonesian nationalism and ASEAN's efforts to build up regionalism is presented and analyzed as empirical evidence to explain the symbiotic nature of the relationship between nationalism and regionalism.

Nationalists' Interests toward Regional Integration Strategy

Although the concept of nationalism has been discussed at great length in many NRA analyzes, not much attention has been paid to the analysis of the relationship between nationalism and regionalism in NRA.[1] The contemporary wave of regionalism is only perceived as an extended form of nationalism (Seers 1983; Hettne 1999), or as an instrument that supplements and enhances the role of the state. This section of the chapter will provide expansion on the current analysis of NRA by arguing that the nature of the relationship between regionalism and nationalism is symbiotic. To begin with, it is important to start with an analysis of the importance of trade in diplomacy. As with bilateralism and multilateralism, RIA is essentially a form of diplomacy (Schiff and Winters 1998). Consequently, it is important to ask why trade might be used as a diplomatic measure (Winters 2001). One premise is that trade tends to increase understanding and harmony between partners, and the implementation of an FTA could be particularly beneficial if domestic actors hold such values in high regard (Schiff and Winters 1998). The second premise is that trade diplomacy in the regional context would encourage a higher degree of trust among the participating states (Bastian 1996). The third possible premise is that, in the politico-military context, an increase in trade among countries in the same alliance will allow member states to raise defense expenditures (Mansfield 1993).[2] In a specific reference to RIAs, Fawcett and Hurrell (1995) also hold that the promotion of an RIA among different states is logical since this strategy allows the states involved to pool their sovereignties, enabling member states to acquire greater leverage to manage global pressures.

Any analysis of the symbiotic nature of the relationship between nationalism and regionalism should draw upon the wide range of literature that specifically analyzes the domestic rationale behind regionalism, "much of which highlights interest group politics and societal pressures" (Mansfield and Milner 1997: 12). Some of this literature has focused on the distributive consequences accrued by domestic politics in pursuing certain (foreign) economic policies (Caves 1976; Pincus 1977; Baldwin 1985). This line of study analyzes the degree of support or opposition toward certain (foreign) economic policies, which is largely dependent upon the costs and benefits to be gained by the domestic politics. Certain foreign economic policies are pursued if the benefits accrued by domestic groups exceed those of the costs, and *vice versa* (Mansfield and Milner 1997: 12). Other literature analyzes the interactions between social and state actors. Here, Krasner (1979), in particular, contends that the formulation of an (foreign) economic policy is intended to advance the nation-state's national interests. On the other hand, however, Magee et al. (1989) and Grossman and Helpman (1994) maintain that the formulation of (foreign) economic policy is strictly intended to advance the personal interests of the policymakers (i.e., to maintain political power or to secure economic resources for personal use).

There are a few hypotheses that have been developed to analyze the reactions of politico-economic actors to regionalism. One hypothesis, for example, focuses upon the type of domestic pressure groups capable of pushing for protectionist measures in a regional trade liberalization process (Hoekman and Leidy 1993). In this context, Hoekman and Leidy divide domestic industrial sectors into two types, namely holes and loopholes. While some domestic actors support the protectionist measures attached to all domestic industries (also called *holes*), others are satisfied with the provisions that allow for only temporary protection such as import restrictions, import subsidies, etc. (also called *loopholes*). Other scholars, such as De Melo et al (1993), argue that the "preference dilution effect" and the "preference-asymmetry effect" may limit the power and the rent-seeking behavior of domestic pressure groups. The preference dilution effect implies that the larger the political community, the less influence can be exerted by domestic pressure groups on the policy-making process. The preference asymmetry effect, on the other hand, allows for compromises on a specific issue to take place among different state actors and domestic pressure groups across a region.

Another argument focuses on the formation of an RIA as a response of policymakers to domestic pressures. In Milner's (1997: 76–77) view, the formation of regional trade agreements can be seen as a government's attempt to balance consumer interests with the pressures that emerge from private economic agents, such as firms. For Cohen (1997: 65–67), it is the conflict between the state and social actors that has to be considered. He maintains that the formation of a currency region tends to reduce a government's ability to finance public spending via inflation. In this case, it is likely that private economic actors would want to switch their investments from a local currency to investments in a foreign currency. However, Cohen also reminds us that certain segments of society would find it easier to make such an adjustment than others (Cohen 1997: 73).[3] Another attempt to link patterns of regionalism with domestic economic conditions is provided by Haggard (1997), who argues that deeper integration in Latin America, in comparison to the Asia-Pacific region, has been facilitated by Latin America's numerous domestic economic crises. These crises have fostered a greater demand for formal institutionalization to take place in Latin America than in the Asia-Pacific region. Nonetheless, most of the aforementioned literature fails to provide any distinct focus on the attitudes of nationalists toward the formulation of a state's foreign economic policy (FEP) in an RIA.

In order to establish a more constructive analysis on the interests of nationalists toward an RIS, it is necessary to first of all identify the different types of nationalism (refer to figure 3.1). At the broader level, there is a so-called *generic nationalism*, which is associated with the concept of nationalism as a political, cultural, and ethnic ideology (Heywood 2000: 254). This type of nationalism involves using the nation's ideal to further specifically political ends (political nationalism), defending or promoting a national language, religion, or a way of life (cultural nationalism), and practicing distinctiveness and exclusivity (ethnic nationalism). Within the context of this book, generic nationalism will be regarded as a popular expression of nationalist sentiment among the general public within a country. Subsequently, there are three sub-types of nationalism that make up the generic nationalism, which include bureaucratic nationalism, economic nationalism, and bureaucratic nationalism. To start with, bureaucratic nationalism refers to the nationalist expression that is prevalent among the political elite and decision makers within a country. Central to an analysis of bureaucratic nationalism is the materialist and instrumentalist explanation or approach[4] to the dynamism of romantic nationalism (Gellner 1964; Nairn 1977),[5] which primarily argues that the nation was invented by political elites (bureaucratic units) in order to legitimize their power (Hobsbawn 1983).[6] Secondly, echoing an earlier analysis in Chapter 2, economic nationalism can be described as an expression of nationalism among political and economic actors within a country with the purpose of reducing foreign economic control in their country (through the imposition of high tariff barriers, quotas, the nationalization of foreign firms, etc.). Thirdly, ethnonationalism refers to the "emotional identification of a [smaller] group [within a nation-state] which shares culture, values, language, and genealogical line to real or fictive ancestors" (Andaya 1997: 131).[7] Ethnonationalism is normally a weapon with which to challenge the established nation-state, particularly in response to discriminatory or oppressive policies directed toward the ethno-nations.[8]

Moreover, all forms of nationalism can either be expressed romantically or logically. *Romantic nationalism* here is defined as a form of nationalism that feels pride in the achievements and the conventional values of the nation. In the Indonesian context, romantic nationalism would involve excessive pride about the historic struggle against imperialism, the richness of natural resources in the country, and the geographical size and large population of the country. These normally generate an inward-looking attitude among Indonesian nationalists. In the international arena, this attitude is characterized by arrogance and hostility to other nations. For example, the hostility expressed by the Indonesian government toward Malaya[9] in the early 1963 was partly motivated by the long-standing expansionist sentiment held by many Indonesian nationalist leaders (Gordon 1966; Reinhardt 1971). The decision made by Sukarno, the Indonesian President at the time, to *crush Malaya* was viewed by some section of the Indonesian politics, particularly the army, as part of his nationalist cause (Smith 2000a: 11). *Logical nationalism*, on the other hand, is a more moderate form of nationalism. In the Indonesian context, logical nationalism would suggest a more outward approach toward international affairs and a more pragmatic approach in the use of Indonesian foreign policy. The expression of logical nationalism can be illustrated in the increase use of regional integration strategy (RIS) among Indonesian policymakers in the early 1990s as a response to the strengthening of regionalism in Western Europe and North America (Hill 2000: 85).

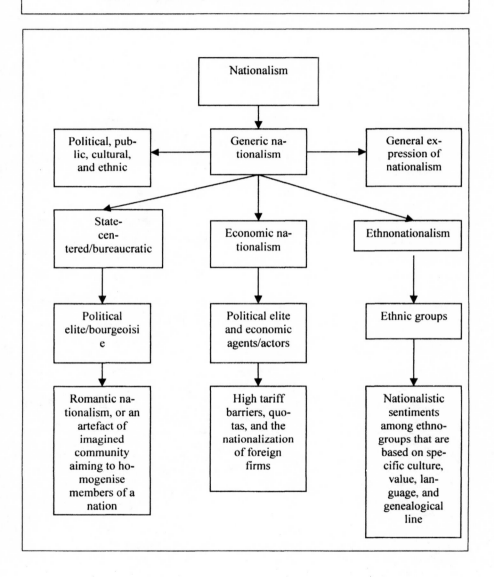

Figure 3.1.
Types, Composition, and Characteristics of Nationalism

Nationalism

Political, public, cultural, and ethnic ← Generic nationalism → General expression of nationalism

State-centered/bureaucratic

Economic nationalism

Ethnonationalism

Political elite/bourgeoisie

Political elite and economic agents/actors

Ethnic groups

Romantic nationalism, or an artefact of imagined community aiming to homogenise members of a nation

High tariff barriers, quotas, and the nationalization of foreign firms

Nationalistic sentiments among ethno-groups that are based on specific culture, value, language, and genealogical line

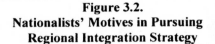

Figure 3.2.
Nationalists' Motives in Pursuing
Regional Integration Strategy

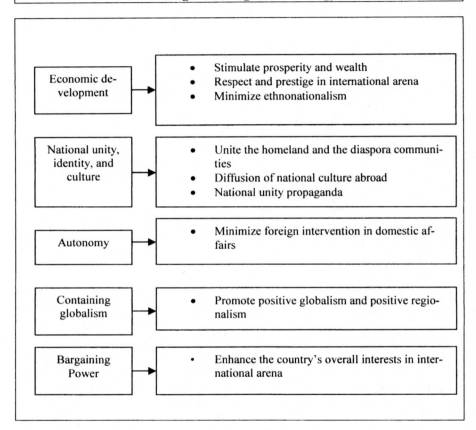

The relationship between nationalism and regionalism is symbiotic; the two variables can sometimes be mutually reinforcing, and sometimes mutually exclusive and conflicting. In order to understand this relationship further, it is necessary to analyze the attitudes and preferences of domestic actors. This analysis will be confined to contexts in which the state is attempting to conduct closer economic ties with foreign nations through the pursuance of an RIS, and on the support or opposition of domestic actors toward such an agreement. Particular attention here will be given to any nationalist reactions to such an agreement. Nationalists are one of many domestic groups that may adjust or change the state's FEP. Although previous international relations studies have tended to identify nationalists as opponents of FTAs, over recent years nationalists have not necessarily been hostile to free trade and closer economic ties with other states (Shulman 2000: 365). As with other domestic actors, nationalists today have to adjust to the ongoing and intense pressures of globalism and regionalism. Consequently, it is possible to identify general incentives that nationalists may benefit from by supporting an FTA.

Nationalist support toward the promotion of an RIA is dependent upon many factors, as outlined above. It is, however, important to identify some of the main benefits that nationalists may accrue by pursuing an RIS. Here, the works of Shulman (2000) and Falk (1999) are particularly useful to explain the nationalists' interests toward the pursuance of an RIS. However, these analyzes can be further explored and expanded. On the whole, nationalists pursue an RIS for the purpose of: first, the achievement of sustained economic development; second, the promotion of national unity, identity and culture; third, the promotion of the state's autonomy in international fora; fourth, the formation of regional collective action to contain the negative forces of globalism and to achieve regional governance through positive globalism and regionalism; and, fifth, the elevation of the nation-state's bargaining power at the international level (refer to figure 3.2). Some of these points can be interrelated.

The Achievement of Sustained Economic Development

The first major motive behind nationalist support for an RIS is the promise of sustained domestic economic development. Economic development has been one of the major objectives of various regional groupings throughout the world. From more advanced regional groupings, such as the EU, to less institutionalized ones, such as NAFTA, ASEAN, and MERCOSUR, these groupings all have economic development as part of their stated objectives. Although regionalism as a development policy has been tried in nearly all parts of the world, it has been a failure as far as development is concerned, much of which is due to excessive concerns with trade (Hettne 2001: 14).[10] Since the late 1990s, however, NRA has been trying to promote regionalism as a development policy by broadening the concept of development regionalism. In this context, development regionalism can be defined as "concerted efforts from a group of countries within a geographical region to increase the complementarity and capacity of the total regional economy as well as finding the right balance between function and territory" (Hettne 2001: 14). The new wave of regionalism, therefore, provides a new alternative for nationalists to achieve sustained domestic economic development. In this context, instead of focusing upon the promotion of regional autarky and the creation of trade blocs (or *inward-looking development*), more emphasis is placed on the co-ordination of production, improvement of domestic infrastructure, and making use of the available complementarities as a regional development strategy (or *development from within*) (Hettne 2001: 16).

One fundamental aspect of domestic economic development through RIS is the notion of economic openness (Pernia and Quising 2002: 4). Economic openness here is defined as a full engagement in international trade (Lipsey and

Chrystal 1999: 578), which allows the free movement of goods and capital and limits import protectionist quotas and foreign exchange controls. Nationalists today are, therefore, not solely associated with the promotion of protectionist policies but are keen to pursue trade liberalization measures. One main factor behind this transformation is that nationalists have had to change or adjust their strategies to bolster their countries' power, prestige, and prosperity in an increasingly economically interdependent world (Crane 1999; Shulman 2000; Helleiner 2002; Pickel 2003). The notion of economic openness is particularly important because it is held to promote, *inter alia*, domestic economic competitiveness and economic growth. A country is said to be competitive if it is willing to "meet the test of international markets while simultaneously maintaining and expanding the real incomes of its citizens" (OECD 1992: 242). Countries within a region normally pursue an RIS to push for greater efficiency in some of their domestic industries, thus enabling them to compete in the global markets. Subsequently, improved efficiency will allow these countries to experience economic growth.

Moreover, in a multicultural society, the achievement of economic development through RIS, particularly through trade liberalization mechanism, may not only stimulates prosperity and wealth throughout the country, but also reduces ethnonationalist sentiments. One of the reasons why certain areas within a country might demand greater autonomy is the failure of the central government to meet the demand of these ethno-nations' functional needs in terms of strategic planning, co-ordination of governmental and non-governmental activities, and large-scale public service delivery (Parks and Elcock 2002: 87).[11] Unequal economic distribution as conducted by the central government may trigger the demand for greater autonomy, or even independence, among the members of the ethno-nation. Therefore, an RIS or, specifically, trade liberalization mechanisms may appeal to nationalists because they can act as a stimulant to economic growth and as an appeasement of nationalist sentiments among the members of the ethno-nation. Likewise, the quest for autonomy or sovereignty will be less attractive to the population of the ethno-nation if their functional demands are met. However, it is also important to note that the strengthening of economic institutions and the financial sector in the ethno-nation can pose a challenge to the established nation-state (Martin 1997: 255). With improved domestic economic development, ethno-nations will be able to lessen their economic dependence upon the central government. Thus, areas within a country that possess strong cultures that are distinct from the rest of the country will be more inclined to demand greater autonomy, if not full independence (Shulman 2000).[12]

Although in the Southeast Asian context the pursuit of RIS has not been specifically aimed at promoting economic development *per se*,[13] the prevalence of support for ASEAN from the region's nationalists is largely due to the Association's capacity for fostering peace and stability in the region. Consequently, governments in the region are able to concentrate upon economic development in their countries.[14] Through the existence of ASEAN, for example, some major economies in Southeast Asia, such as Indonesia, Malaysia, Singapore, and

Thailand, have achieved tremendous economic growth since the 1970s onward, which has led to rapid modernization and an improvement in welfare in the region (World Bank 1993a). Economic growth in Southeast Asia, particularly prior to the economic crisis of 1997, was not only able to ease conflicts between states in the region, but also domestic conflicts. Indonesia is a prime example of the way in which Southeast Asian countries have used ASEAN as a means to promote national unity. Indonesians are comprised of nearly five hundred ethnic groups, practice nearly all the major religions, and speak nearly six hundred languages and dialects (Kooistra 2001: 5). The Indonesian political elite during Suharto's New Order regime perceived enhanced economic integration through ASEAN as an exploitation of the country's huge natural resources with very little to be gained in return (Smith 2000a: 24). In recent years, however, there has been growing support for greater economic integration in the region, particularly at the broader East Asian level from among the Indonesian political elite, owing to perceived benefits that Indonesia may accrue from such an arrangement (Hill 2000: 92). The Indonesian nationalists are concerned by the increasing threat of national disintegration in the country. Greater economic cooperation at the regional or broader East Asian level is hoped to bring about greater prosperity throughout the country. This, in turn, may bring about greater political and economic stability and minimize conflicts among Indonesian ethnonations.

The Promotion of National Unity, Identity, and Culture

The second major motive behind nationalist support of RIS is national unification and the promotion of national identity and culture. To start with, it is widely recognized that a principal nationalist objective is to unite all members of a nation both politically and emotionally (Shulman 2000: 371). This is because nationalist ideology reflects a sense of bonding or affiliation among a group of people as a result of political, cultural, and ethnic similarities (Heywood 2000: 254). For nationalists, an RIS may help to achieve this objective through its capacity to unite members of a nation that live in the *homeland community* and the *diaspora community* (Shulman 2000: 371).[15] People tend to move from one place to another in search of better living conditions. Today, the global pattern of migration is not only stimulated by increasing globalization, but also by the various violent conflicts, economic crises, and natural disasters that emerge throughout the world (National Intelligence Council 2001: 3). At the turn of the new millennium, for example, there were about 150 million migrants worldwide, which amounted to 30 million more than in the previous decade.[16] This trend, coupled with the historical vagaries of state boundary formation, has resulted in the fragmentation of members of nations (Shulman 2000: 371). For nationalists, an RIS may act to unite the fragmented members of each respective nation. Among other things, an increase in multinational linkage allows closer contact and communication between the dispersed members of a nation. One of the most widely cited cases where members of a nation linked together within a region is the Chinese community in Hong Kong, Taiwan, and Southeast Asian countries (Dobson 1998: 28–30; Yeung 1999; Peng 2002: 430–32). The ethnic business network in the East Asian region can be regarded as a form of informal economic integration, which facilitates economic transactions and the exchange of information between the fragmented members of a nation. Therefore, national unification among members of a nation who live in multiple states can be promoted through the pursuance of an RIS, and *vice versa*.

The objective of national unity is, therefore, a crucial element in understanding nationalist support for an RIS. Southeast Asian states, for example, have benefited greatly from RIS, such as ASEAN, in that an RIS can help maintain the national unity of the established states in the region. Indonesia, in particular, is one example. Although few studies exist that specifically analyze the direct contribution of ASEAN toward the maintenance of the national unity of its member countries, one motive behind Indonesia's support of ASEAN, as mentioned earlier, was the country's need to maintain domestic stability (Anwar 1994). The achievement of regional peace in the region has had a knock-on effect on economic development in each member state and, therefore, toward the promotion of national unity among countries in the region. One significant aspect is ASEAN's policy of non-interference, which primarily stems from "traditional notions in international relations of equality of the sovereignty of states . . . and the consequent right to exclusive sovereignty" (Ramcharan 2000: 60). The adoption of the Treaty of Amity and Cooperation (TAC), which highlights mutual respect for independence, sovereignty, equality, territorial integrity, and national identity of all nations,[17] is particularly central to the promotion of Indonesian national unity. The promotion of regional security in the Southeast Asian region has enabled Indonesia to focus on its economic development, and, in turn, reduce the social unrest that often jeopardizes domestic stability in the country.

Moreover, national unity and territorial integrity have become two main concerns of the Indonesian government since the economic crisis in 1997. Strong support from among Indonesia's immediate neighbors is crucial for the maintenance of national unity and territorial integrity in the country. During the Third ASEAN Informal Summit in 1999, for example, the Singaporean Prime Minister, Goh Chok Tong, highlighted how important it was for ASEAN leaders to support the integrity of Indonesia (Singapore Ministry of Foreign Affairs 1999). A Joint Statement was also signed among the APT Foreign Ministers in Bangkok on 24th–25th July 2000, which highlighted support for Indonesia's sovereignty, national unity, and territorial integrity.[18] Furthermore, ASEAN member countries were equally supportive when Indonesia attempted to crush the separatist movement in Aceh in 2003 (Baker 2003). The Thai Foreign Minister, Sihasak Phungketkeow, for example, stated that Thailand "would not allow any separatist movements to use Thai territory to cause trouble for ASEAN neighbors."[19] Initially, however, there were mixed feelings among ASEAN members when peace talks between the Indonesian government and Aceh broke down (Tan 2003). Singapore and Malaysia, in particular, expressed regret over the breaking down of the peace talks between the two sides and expressed hope that a peaceful resolution could be found to resolve the conflict in Aceh. On the whole, however, no country in the region would want to see the break up of Indonesia as such an event would bring about instability and the possibility of a refugee crisis in the region (Smith 2000a: 72). The existence of ASEAN is, therefore, crucial for the maintenance of Indonesia's national unity and territorial integrity.

Apart from the promotion and the maintenance of national unity, nationalists also pursue an RIS for the promotion and the expansion of their national identity and culture worldwide. Identity is an important term used by nationalists everywhere, along with unity and autonomy (Hutchinson and Smith 1994: 5). For most modern nation-states, a national identity can be interpreted as having a membership in a people, which is a fundamental characteristic of a nation (Greenfield 1992: 7–9).[20] The notion of identity in nationalism emphasizes "a complex set of themes about *us, our homeland, nations (ours and theirs), the world*, as well as the morality of national duty and honor" (Billig 1995: 4). It is, therefore, what members of a nation share which differentiates them from other nations. National culture, on the other hand, is the main feature of national identity, and plays an important role in shaping a nation. As a result, it is in the nationalist interests to preserve and to enhance their culture. While the pursuit of an RIS may impinge upon a nation's culture (Martin 1997), nationalists can benefit from such a strategy because it promotes their national identity regionally (Shulman 2000: 372). One process through which such an objective may be achieved, as Shulman further asserts, is cultural diffusion,[21] which enhances a nation's culture through a closer relationship with other nations, particularly those at close geographical proximity.[22]

One of the strategies that countries have used to promote their identity and culture today is tourism. In Southeast Asia, tourism has become an important "source of economic development, foreign exchange, and employment generation" (Hall 2001: 13). For Indonesian nationalists, RIS plays an important role in promoting their identities and cultures abroad. In order to achieve this, Indonesian nationalists may support the way in which ASEAN promotes regional tourism. It is clearer today that "cross border cooperation is of obvious importance for the mutual strengthening of the tourism industries of neighboring countries" (Grundy-Warr and Perry 2001: 64). As a result, during the Eighth ASEAN Summit in November 2002, ASEAN member countries signed a landmark Framework Agreement on ASEAN Cooperation in Tourism to boost the regional tourism industry, to facilitate domestic and intra-regional travel among member countries, and to harmonize visa procedures for international travelers.[23] Another attempt to promote tourism at the regional level has also been made through the ASEAN Tourism Forum (ATF), which is an annual meeting attended by individuals or entities involved in the ASEAN tourism industry with the objective of promoting the ASEAN region as a tourist destination.[24] In recent years, there has also been an attempt to incorporate tourism as an integral part of the Southeast Asian growth triangle initiatives (Chang and Raguraman 2001: 5 0–51). The cooperation of the Indonesian and the Singaporean governments in the Riau islands of Batam and Bintan has been a leading example of the incorporation of the tourism industry in the growth triangle initiative (Grundy-Warr and Perry 2001: 65).

For Indonesian nationalists, regional integration strategy in the context of the promotion of national identity and culture abroad contains some negative and some positive aspects. On the negative side, the promotion of an RIS can be perceived as a threat to national identity due to the increased penetration of foreign cultures among the population of the country (Martin 1997). This has been particularly evident among Indonesian youth who have been influenced by the heavy consumerism in foreign products and cultures. Many Indonesian youths today use foreign products to gain status and prestige; they drive a Jaguar and wear Armani shirts (Priyono 2003). Such fashions make traditional Indonesian culture appear less attractive to Indonesian youth. Another negative impact from the promotion of Indonesian identity and culture abroad through an RIS is the erosion of ethnic culture and economic and environmental degradation. This has been evident in the Tanah Toraja, in Sulawesi, where, without concerted efforts from both the government and local leaders, it would be impossible to preserve the Toraja's culture and identity (Hall and Page 2000: 16). Meanwhile, economic and environmental degradation as a result of the incorporation of tourism in an RIS is best illustrated in the case of the Singapore, Johor, Riau (SIJORI) growth triangle initiative. Large-scale resort development initiated by many Singaporean investors in both Riau and Johor, for example, has raised concerns over environmental and economic degradation in these two areas (Business Traveler Asia Pacific 1997). Singaporean tourists are perceived by locals in Riau and Johor as arrogant and major contributors to pollution and inflation (Lim 1999).[25]

On the positive side, however, there are two main objectives that the Indonesian nationalists wish to achieve through the promotion of national identity and culture abroad, namely political and economic objectives. The political objective includes the promotion of the Indonesian multi-ethnic character both at the national and the international level. At the national level, this can be used as propaganda to promote national unity among different ethno-nations in Indonesia. At the international level, the multiethnic character can be used as a symbol to attract international visitors (Wall 2001: 320). Therefore, the Indonesian government stands to gain substantially through the promotion of national identity and culture abroad. Meanwhile, the economic objective of the Indonesian government to promote national identity and culture lies in the increase of economic development, particularly in the peripheral areas of the country. Hence, it is not surprising that, as Hall (2001: 19) points out, "national tourism policies and plans are usually a deliberate tool of regional development strategies and/or broader trade policies." The achievement of even economic development throughout the country is seen to minimize possible conflicts between different ethno-nations in the country.[26] Therefore, although RIS may impinge upon Indonesian culture, the Indonesian nationalists benefits from this strategy through the promotion of national unity and economic development.

The Promotion of the State's Autonomy in the International Arena

The third motive behind nationalist support for an RIS is the promotion of their autonomy in the international arena.[27] One central analysis here rests upon the principle of collective self-determination, which is used by a nation as a whole to minimize foreign intervention in the domestic affairs of a nation (Shulman 2000: 369).[28] As with the aforementioned point on unity, the drive for national self-determination can also be stimulated by economic motive. Although isolationist economic policy, such as protectionism, may contribute to the self-determination, or independence, of a nation in the international arena (Shulman 2000: 369), economic nationalism does not necessarily lead to real economic improvements (Johnson 1967). However, what has become clear in recent years is that both regional economic integration and globalization are better means to promote wealth than economic autarky (Yergin and Stanislaw 1998). Since the end of the Second World War, countries around the world have gradually moved toward liberalization.[29] With regard to the Asian region, in 1999, the Asian Development Bank (ADB) issued a report that suggests the existence of a strong link between economic openness and growth. Such factors are behind the motives driving nationalists to conduct closer economic ties with other nations.

Indonesian nationalists perceive ASEAN as a "vehicle for a more autonomous regional order" (Anwar 1994: 212). This objective is particularly important because it coincides with the Indonesian free and active (*bebas aktif*) foreign policy. This policy does not imply that "Indonesia would necessarily adopt a neutralist stance but would establish a foreign policy course that was independent of great power concerns" (Smith 2000a: 9). Throughout the post-independence period, mistrust of the intentions of these great powers has been evident among Indonesian leaders. During the inception of ASEAN, many members of the Indonesian political elite perceived the creation of the Association as evidence of increasing regional independence (Anwar 1994: 54). Moreover, the objective of Indonesian nationalists of creating a more autonomous regional order also reflects the Indonesian government's concerns about the maintenance of Indonesian domestic security and territorial integrity from external threats (Anwar 1992: 13). It is quite fortunate that Indonesia's neighbors share similar concerns and, as such, are willing to adopt a similar approach to Indonesia in dealing with external powers. It is for this reason that Indonesia's policy of national and regional resilience is incorporated into ASEAN. While national resilience is built on the foundation of economic development, regional resilience subsequently emerges once national resilience has been achieved and countries in the region are able to co-operate fully with each other. It is at this point that "ASEAN countries will truly be able to become the master in their own house, no longer needing the political and military protection of foreign powers" (Anwar 1994: 213).

Collective Action to Contain the Negative Forces of Globalization and to Achieve Regional Governance

The fourth motive behind nationalist support of an RIS is the formation of collective actions with neighbors for the purposes of containing the negative forces derived from the process of globalization and for the purpose of achieving governance at the regional level. To start with, the concept of globalization is controversial (Rupert 2000: 43) and most debates have centered upon the issue of the threatened existence of the nation-state. The idea that globalization will lead to a borderless world and the end of the nation-state (Ohmae 1990; 1995) has been challenged by both academics and the mass media. Some scholars, such as Van Ruigrok and Van Tulder (1995), Hirst and Thompson (1996), Coleman and Underhill (1998), view the globalization thesis as exaggerated, believing that it is far too early to announce the emasculation, or even the disintegration, of the domestic institution as a significant focus in international economic, social, and political activities. Nevertheless, the process of globalization poses profound challenges to the nationalist objectives of national unity, international autonomy, and the preservation of their identity. After all, globalization has been perceived as the process that "subverts the [established] state's capacity to act in the interests of its citizens" (Stubbs 2000c: 197). Although the globalization process may have led to global cultural homogenization, it has also unleashed a cultural pluralism, particularly within nation-states themselves (Mittelman 1996b: 7–8). The explosion of cultural pluralism has given ethnonationalist movements a new start as a potent force to challenge the established nation-states. Since the end of the Cold War, for example, twenty-six new countries have been established, some of which were born out of ethnonationalist movements. One prominent example in the Southeast Asian region is East Timor,[30] which gained its independence from Indonesia on 30 August 2002.[31]

However, it should also be noted that the impacts of globalization can either be regarded as positive or negative depending upon the criteria being used to define each term. In an attempt to define the composition of positive globalism, Falk (1999: 69) asserts that the term mainly refers to "the democratizing of global institutions, creating accountability and responsiveness to more democratic social forces and establishing procedures for wider participation by representatives of diverse people." Consequently, negative globalism, as Falk further postulates, would point to "the conjuncture of largely non-accountable power and influence exerted by [transnational entities] and their collaborators with the ideology of consumerism and a development ethos weighted almost entirely toward return on capital mainly achieved by maximizing growth."

As with other domestic actors, nationalists today face intense pressure from the globalization process, particularly from its adverse effects.[32] It is for this reason that nationalists favor RIS to contain the negative forces of globalization. Although regionalism has not yet emerged as a potent source to contain negative globalization (Falk 1999: 72), it has achieved positive results in transcending the state's role to serve the interests of its citizens. Among other things, regionalism has been able to act as a forum to mitigate and to minimize conflicts, not only between states in a region, but also when internal conflicts emerge as a result of ethnonationalist movements. To date, there are a number of examples to illustrate the success of a regional grouping in mitigating conflicts at the national level. In Africa, for example, the Economic Community of West African States (ECOWAS) was successful in mitigating the fourteen year old civil war in one of its member countries, Liberia.[33] In Southeast Asia, however, little evidence exists to suggest that the regional grouping has had any success at mitigating conflicts at the national level. Nevertheless, ASEAN has been able to prevent conflict in the region through its adherence to the principle of non-interference, which makes it unlikely that an ethnonationalist movement in one country will be supported by other ASEAN member states (FfP 2002: 1). Southeast Asian countries, in fact, gave their support to the existence and the strengthening of the established nation-state system in the region. As a consequence, ASEAN states often involve non-members to mediate in domestic conflicts that arise between the central government and ethno-nations.[34]

Meanwhile, collective actions among states in a region may also act as a catalyst to achieve governance at the regional level. The term governance, in general, refers mainly to a social function that aims to produce collective choices in regard to matters that concern a specific group of people (Young 1995). Regional governance, therefore, is "the set of social functions concerned with making collective choices [among] people delineated by geographical proximity and other shared notions of sameness. . . . [It is also] also concerned with the regime that constitutes the set of fundamental rules for the intergovernmental institutions in the narrow sense" (Bøås 2002: 49). Regional governance is important nowadays as a result of the greater complexities that states have to confront. The increasing desire for regional governance among states is partly a result of the fact that governance is more difficult to achieve at the global level than at the regional level. If, for instance, globalization involves an extension of liberal values as the premise of policy making and an expansion of transnational elite networks working through a set of inter-linked international institutions, global governance, then, will create an explicit superstructure to facilitate these processes (Laux 2000: 268). The problem is that globalization and its *superstructure* will not necessarily accommodate every state's interests and concerns. In this context, globalization, as a historical epoch, will result in a new set of "winners and losers" (Reich 2001: 117). This is not to say that regionalism is not also problematic since, after all, regionalism also involves divergent national interests. However, convergence at the regional level is easier to achieve since most states are located within a similar geographic location, which suggests that their concerns and interests will be more uniform, although perhaps differing in context and scope. Regionalism, with its relatively smaller number of participants, is, therefore, preferable to multilateralism in two respects (Jovanovich 1998: 113). Firstly, member countries can enjoy cozier relationships, which makes monitoring easier to carry out. Secondly, friendly or positive cooperation within the group will offer a more conducive environment for the exchange of favors, mutual agreements, and dispute settlement to take place.

There are two possible ways in which regional governance can be achieved, which are the promotion of positive globalism and the promotion of positive regionalism (Falk 1999: 76–79). The promotion of positive globalism, which includes democratization, accountability, and responsiveness to democratic social forces, is a means to avoid centralism. Within this context, regionalism can be perceived as the "complementary and subordinate tools of global governance, shaped within the UN and contributing to either effectiveness or legitimacy or some combination of these" (Falk 1999: 77). It is imperative that the promotion of governance at the global level must also be forged at the regional level. Here, the promotion of positive regionalism, which contributes toward the goals of global governance at the regional level, is crucial. Yet finding any evidence of the promotion of positive globalism and positive regionalism in the ASEAN context is a difficult task. Throughout its existence, ASEAN has been far from transparent or accountable to the citizens of its member countries. However, given its willingness to change its organizational structure and its elitist tendencies, it is likely that regional groupings such as ASEAN will become more democratic and more responsive to the diverse needs of the citizens of its member countries.[35]

Nationalists may perceive regional governance as an important element to contain the negative forces of globalization. On the economic front, nationalists, in spite of their doctrine of economic nationalism, are not only concerned with trade protectionism and industrial policy (Crane 1998: 74). In the age of globalization, nationalists have come to see the logic of pursuing more liberal economic policies that will enhance the competitiveness of nationally based industries and increase the attractiveness of their country for the potential investments of TNCs (Helleiner 2002: 310). Moreover, most countries in the world today are pushed to pursue an open economic policy that will encourage higher incomes and economic growth (Meier 1984; Frankel and Romer 1999; Anoruo and Ahmad 1999).[36] However, this is not to suggest that nationalist economic policy is no longer valid for nationalists. As mentioned earlier, nationalists today have changed or adjusted their strategies to bolster their countries' power, prestige, and prosperity. Regionalism offers considerable opportunities for nationalists through its processes of collective action to tackle the various conflicts of interest that emerge between domestic industries and the forces of globalization. A regional institution, for example, will allow competitiveness to flourish as a result of the research funding made available for the development of local industries, a better organized industrial policy (Sally 1995), and the protection of local firms with long-term investments from the volatility of the international financial system (Hveem 2000: 77–78). Indonesia's position in AFTA is a case in point. Despite its poor economic performance as a result of the 1997 economic crisis, the country maintains its commitment to the agreement. After all, the elimination of tariff barriers among Southeast Asian countries allows member countries to enjoy greater production efficiency and long-term competitiveness (ASEAN Secretariat 2002a: 2), and thus generates economic incentive for Indonesian nationalists.

The Elevation of the Nation-State's Bargaining Position in the International Arena

Nationalists' fifth, or final, motive in supporting an RIS is to elevate their country's bargaining power at the international level. As with other domestic actors, nationalists may want to increase the bargaining power of their country vis-à-vis other countries, particularly in the framework of multilateralism. It has been asserted that "a nation's prospects in international negotiations depend principally on its bargaining power" (Hoekman and Leidy 1993: 258). Nevertheless, although concern over bargaining power is one reason why countries pursue an RIS, there has been little analysis of this issue in the regional integration literature. One exception is the regional economic integration (REI) analysis, which argues that countries, particularly small and developing ones, pursue a regional integration strategy to increase their bargaining power in economic relations (Robson 1987: 196). It is, however, necessary to analyze the two main objectives that underlie a country's desire to elevate their bargaining position in international relations. The first objective is that countries may desire to promote their national goals, such as an increase in domestic economic welfare, through international relations. Here, as mentioned earlier, an RIS may play an important role in promoting economic competitiveness and growth in its member countries. The second objective may be inspired by the state or other domestic actors' defensive reasoning that an increase in bargaining power in international relations will enhance their country's ability to counter the combined weight of regionalism pursued in other regions (Ravenhill 2001: 15–16).

However, one important aspect in the issue of bargaining power is the relative size of the regional grouping, instead of its absolute size, vis-à-vis its trading partners (Jovanovich 1998: 87–113). It is important to note that a regional arrangement implies "both a decision to include and a decision to exclude countries" (Padoan 1997: 130). In economic terms, for example, many countries pursue an RIS as an *insurance* that will protect them against possible trade bloc wars (Baldwin 1993; Perroni and Whalley 1994). Another analysis suggests that the external effects of integration may also trigger an enlargement process to take place (Mattli 1999: 59–64).[37] Here, a successful regional integration project creates a demand among non-member countries to join the established regional grouping (Dent 1997: 90).[38] Alternatively, negative external effects created by the establishment of a regional grouping, such as the diversion of trade, investment, and aid, may equally increase the demand among non-member countries to join the established regional grouping. Although the question of number optimality depends upon changes in the international environment, the increased size of an alliance normally increases the member countries' capacity to resist outside threats (Padoan 1997: 12 0–30). There can be no doubt that the size of a regional grouping is crucial. This applies not only to regional groupings composed mainly of developing countries, but also those composed of developed ones. The recent move by the EU to expand its membership eastward, for example, proves that the Union still wishes to strengthen its role in world affairs.[39]

For Indonesian nationalists, the issue of bargaining power is central to enhancing the country's interests in the international arena. It is for this reason that Indonesia strongly supported the enlargement process within ASEAN. It has been acknowledged that ASEAN's best achievement to date has been its efficacy as a united bargaining bloc in international diplomacy (Ravenhill 1995: 86 0–61; Anwar 2001b: 37). As a larger group, not only will ASEAN improve its position in Asia (i.e., vis-à-vis China), but it will also increase its bargaining power against some of the major powers, such as the United States and the EU. Throughout the 1990s, a number of initiatives have been taken by Indonesia to enhance its bargaining position in the international arena, particularly APEC. Indonesia was also indirectly involved in discussions over the proposed EAEC, which was a fearful reaction to the fortification of Europe following the adoption of the Single European Act of 1987 and the steady move toward Europe 1992 (Mattli 1999: 168). Unfortunately, the initiative was abandoned after the United States objected to APEC's East Asian member countries' proposals (Alvstam 2001). In recent years, it has become more likely that ASEAN will concentrate on strengthening APT cooperation to improve external relations (Abidin 2001: 271), and, as a result, policymakers in Indonesian hope to become involved in activities within the APT framework. Among other things, this hope has been fuelled by the slow progress of liberalization under the WTO, the enlargement process within the EU and the growing pan-American move to create the Free Trade Area of the Americas (FTAA), and, finally, the economic crisis of 1997 (Harvie and Lee 2002: 125).

The Relationship between ASEAN Regionalism and Indonesian Nationalism

For quite some time now ASEAN has been regarded as the most successful RIA formed among developing countries. The Southeast Asian region itself is dynamic as a result of its heterogeneous historical backgrounds, levels of economic development, and social patterns. More importantly, however, the dynamism of the Southeast Asian region is also due in part to an upsurge of nationalism, the growing interdependence of the global economy, and a new burst of regional cooperation, both outward-looking and inward-looking (Palmer 1991: 22).[40]

There is a definite correlation between ASEAN regionalism and Indonesian nationalism. For Indonesia, ASEAN has been a vehicle to promote its national interests at both regional and international levels. In order to illustrate further the relationship between the two ideologies, it is necessary to define ASEAN, AFTA, and Indonesian nationalism. To start with, ASEAN, in the simplest terms, can be defined as a regional grouping of Southeast Asian countries, which was established among the five Southeast Asian countries of Indonesia, Malaysia, the Philippines, Singapore, and Thailand, on 8 August 1967, in Bangkok, Thailand. The Bangkok Declaration of 1967[41] spells out the objectives of the regional grouping, which include, *inter alia*, (1) the acceleration of economic growth, social progress and cultural development in the region; (2) the promotion of regional peace and stability; (3) the promotion of active collaboration and mutual assistance in the area of economic, social, cultural, technical, scientific, and administrative fields.[42] Throughout the 1980s and 1990s, however, membership has been expanded to include Brunei Darussalam (1986), Vietnam (1995), Laos (1997), Myanmar (1997), and Cambodia (1999). Although the acceleration of economic growth was one of the prime motives behind the formation of ASEAN, another major focus was strategic and security cooperations (Wanandi 2000: 25).

Furthermore, AFTA is a reflection of the need for Southeast Asian countries to integrate the economies of the region into a single production base and to create a regional market for 500 million people (ASEAN Secretariat 2002a: 1). AFTA is, therefore, aimed at making the Southeast Asian region a free trade area. This trade scheme is an extension of previously established forms of economic cooperation which have been pursued since the mid-1970s. Starting with the ASEAN Preferential Trading Agreement (ASEAN-PTA), intra-ASEAN trade was "liberalized at the pace that was acceptable to all ASEAN members" (Wong 1989: 205–206). Following the creation of the ASEAN-PTA, the Southeast Asian region saw the emergence of various regional economic projects, such as the ASEAN Industrial Project (AIP), the ASEAN Industrial Cooperation (AIC), and the ASEAN Industrial Joint Venture (AIJV). Today, aside from AFTA, ASEAN economic cooperation is further extended through the promotion of the ASEAN Investment Area (AIA), and Growth Triangle (GT) schemes, such as BIMP-EAGA, IMS-GT, IMT-GT, the West-East Corridor (WEC) Mekong Basin River Growth Triangle, and SIJORI.[43] All these economic cooperation schemes currently being promoted are for the purpose of accelerating economic growth in the region.

Meanwhile, Indonesian nationalism is a form of nationalist expression among Indonesians that has been developing for nearly a century.[44] In the beginning, nationalism was used as an instrument to resist foreign colonial power in Indonesia. Indonesian nationalism, however, has dominated much of the country's post-colonial economic history. According to Robison (1997: 29–30), for example, four major agendas characterize the economic structures and policy frameworks in Indonesia, namely economic nationalism, economic populism, predatory bureaucratism, and economic liberalism. Firstly, economic nationalism in Indonesia stemmed from the desire to transform the economy from low value-added industrial production to a technologically advanced industrial economy. The Indonesian economy has been characterized by strong state intervention and trade protection. Secondly, economic populism is a form of economic nationalism that focuses on small business co-operatives and is heavily influenced by anti-Chinese xenophobia. Although economic populism was used as a tool to oppose the growing pattern of conglomeration, this ideology also played an important role in reinforcing political and social order in the political and military hierarchy. The third major agenda within the Indonesian economy was predatory bureaucratism, which can be defined as the appropriation of public authority by political and bureaucratic interests, or, sometimes, by powerful families. A high level of predatory bureaucratism prevents nationalism from producing significant results from economic industrialization, such as the economic success stories in South Korea or Japan. Fourthly, liberalism has been another key agenda in Indonesia's domestic economy, but it has received little support from among the domestic bourgeoisie due to the benefits that this group accrue from the state's heavy protection of their business activities.

Moreover, during the post-colonial period, Sukarno, Indonesia's first President, regarded colonialism and global capitalism as the twin evils of the colonial order. As a result, Sukarno pursued an economic ideology that was a hybrid of nationalism and socialism, which elevated trade barriers and discouraged foreign investments (Smith 2001a: 1). Following Sukarno's removal from office in 1967, Suharto, with his New Order regime, conducted one of the most successful stabilization programs anywhere in modern history (Booth 1998: 178). Indonesia began a trade liberalization program, which eased the restrictions on foreign trade and investment. Despite this, the switch from socialism to a capitalist or free market regime was never properly realized because of the widespread, deep-seated mistrust of market liberalism among the majority of policymakers in the country (Hill 2000: 95). In actual fact it was economic nationalism, economic populism, and predatory bureaucratism that triumphed over economic liberalism. On the whole, therefore, the Indonesian economy during the post-colonial era was characterized by the rhetoric of free trade on the one hand, and the apparent necessity of economic nationalism on the other. Indonesia's commitment to trade liberalization was at best half-hearted, and many in the policy-making circle remained unconvinced of the benefits that might accrue through closer integration at the global level (Booth 1998: 203).

The economic turmoil following the economic crisis of 1997 brought few changes to the way in which Indonesian state actors and domestic economic actors perceived the importance of economic nationalism. The Habibie administration's attempt to promote the *Ekonomi Kerakyatan* (People's Economy), for example, illustrated how important economic nationalism was to certain domestic actors in Indonesia (Smith 2001a: 7).[45] However, all the Indonesian governments during this period have remained fully committed to the trade liberalization program, at both regional and global levels. One important question to be answered is why Indonesia has been pursuing this strategy despite the country's strong tendency toward economic nationalism. The first outstanding factor that has driven Indonesia toward a rather liberal strategy is the economic crisis itself. Since the resignation of Suharto, Indonesia has had to comply with agreements made with the IMF and the World Bank, which include the promotion of an open market policy and privatization across various different sectors. The IMF, in March 2003, completed its eighth review of the Indonesian economy and has approved the disbursement of a further US$469 million.[46] The necessity to secure loans from these international agencies is clear to all Indonesia's post-crisis leaders. To that end, the pursuance of inward-looking economic measures would be highly unfavorable to the domestic economy, at least for the time being.

The second factor that drives Indonesia toward a liberalization strategy is the growing tendency toward greater regional economic integration in the Asian region, as well as trade liberalization measures brought about by the WTO. Throughout the 1990s, in particular, Indonesian policymakers began to take a serious interest in regional economic integration, especially with Japan and other Asian NIEs. Two main factors have contributed to the drive among Indonesian policymakers toward trade liberalization at the regional level. The first is the economic growth of the East Asian region. In trade related matters, Japan and other Asian NIEs have been the major benefactors of Indonesia's exports, accounting for 5 0–60 percent of the countries total exports, well in excess of the 25–40 percent destined for the EU-United States (Hill 2000: 85). The second is that these trade figures illustrate the growing complementarity between a low wage but resource rich Indonesia and high wage economies such as Japan and other Asian NIEs.

It is, therefore, clear that a profound relationship exists between ASEAN regionalism and Indonesian nationalism. To start with, it is important to reiterate the basic proposition of NRA theorists which has emphasized the symbiotic relationship between nationalism and regionalism. The proliferation of regionalism today should not be perceived as a distinct alternative to the promotion of national interests and nationalism, but rather as an element that enhances and protects the role of the state at both international (Palmer 1991; Axline 1994; Schulz et al. 2001) and domestic levels. In the case of Indonesia, although there is a strong tendency toward inward-looking, protectionist economic measures, Indonesian policymakers are beginning to comprehend the greater benefits that their country could gain by pursuing a much more liberal economic program. Although ASEAN countries play only a small part in Indonesian trade overall, ASEAN represents, nevertheless, the first and foremost circle of Indonesia's diplomatic relations. Regional economic integration with Japan and other Asian NIEs has, in fact, been propagated through ASEAN. This explains the recent expansion of ASEAN into APT, as well as the incorporation of the ASEAN membership into APEC.

Conclusion

This theoretical analysis has demonstrated the symbiotic relationship between nationalism and regionalism. In particular, this conceptual framework has shed light on the possible benefits that nationalists may accrue by conducting an RIS. Nationalists pursue an RIS for various reasons. Firstly, nationalists may find an RIS appealing because of its ability to stimulate economic development. Accordingly, a nation may acquire greater respect and prestige in the international arena as a result of sustained economic development. Moreover, sustained economic development may also enable a state to minimize the potential threat of national disintegration. Secondly, an RIS is also useful in helping nationalists unite the fragmented members of a nation. Among other things, increased regional linkage allows closer contact and communication between those who live in the homeland and those who live in the diaspora community. Thirdly, nationalists pursue an RIS in order to achieve international autonomy, thus, enabling them to minimize the potential threat of excessive foreign intervention in their domestic affairs. Fourthly, nationalists benefit from an RIS in that it can contain the negative forces of globalism through the promotion of positive regionalism and globalism, which includes democratization, accountability, and responsiveness to democratic social forces. Finally, nationalists pursue an RIS to elevate their bargaining power in international arena so that they could enhance their overall interests at the global level.

There is no doubt that both nations and nationalism will continue to survive in spite of global and regional transformations (Hoffman 1966; Strange 1995; Smith 1995). Therefore, the relationship between nationalism and regionalism is not necessarily always contentious. The case study of the relationship between Indonesian nationalism and ASEAN regionalism proves useful in illustrating the way in which nationalist policymakers use regionalism as a way to enhance their country's power, prosperity and prestige in the international arena. Although economic regionalism has been overshadowed by the quest for economic competitiveness in the region, ASEAN has managed to expand its economic interests to include Northeast Asian countries (as demonstrated by the APT). In recent years, inter-regionalism has also intensified through the increased promotion of the ASEM. All these factors suggest that the relationship between nationalism and regionalism is no longer contentious. Nationalist doctrine, instead, should be perceived as a symbiosis element in the emergence of regionalism.

Notes

1. The prevailing hypothesis in much NRA literature is that globalism and regionalism stand in a symbiotic relationship (see, for example, Hettne et al. 1999), particularly since the new regionalism is analyzed through the global structural transformation process (Schulz et al. 2001a).

2. This view, however, was challenged by Schiff and Winters (1997) for two reasons. The first is the fact that the very action of trade generates security benefits, regardless of the income effects that such actions may produce. The second is Mansfield's fallacy in assuming that the lowering of trade barriers would allow member states to generate income gains. For Schiff and Winters, however, trade preferences based on income should always be considered ambiguous (second best).

3. According to Cohen (1997: 73), the groups most capable of making such an adjustment are those that fall within the higher income group.

4. This explanation or approach is also known as the Marxist approach to the rise of nationalism.

5. For Gellner (1964), in particular, nationalism generally appeals to the educated, upper-middle classes. Nationalism, however, arises mostly in peripheral areas where the mobilization of the masses is more likely to take place. Such mobilizations would normally be able to reach the developmental goal of those local educated bourgeoisie.

6. Other scholars, particularly Anderson (1983) and Breuilly (1985), also employ a Marxist approach to bureaucratic nationalism. In Anderson's view, for example, the modern nation is an artifact of an imagined political community. He identifies print capitalism and new genres of newspapers and novels as tools used by the political elite to portray a nation as homogeneous. Similarly, Breuilly identifies the modern bureaucratic state as the genesis of nationalism. Breuilly also noted that during the seventeenth century nationalism seemed to offer the best solution to the conflicts prevalent between states and society.

7. In the Malay-Indonesian context, it could be described as *suku,* which literally means ethnic group.

8. By using a typology of ethnonationalism, or secessionism, based on levels of economic and educational progress or backwardness, Horrowitz (1985) demonstrates that ethnonationalism is most likely to occur among groups in poor regions rather than groups in more developed regions.

9. Malaya today is known as Malaysia.

10. Certain literature links regionalism and development, notably development integration theory, which has focused on two sets of distributive instruments that promote economic development, namely compensatory mechanisms (i.e., transfer tax system, budgetary transfer, etc.) and corrective mechanisms (i.e., planned industrial strategy, common investment code, etc.) (Schulz et al. 2001: 11). For further analysis regarding the development integration theory, see also Axline (1977), Robson (1987: 198–214), and Haarløv (1988: 23).

11. Another main reason behind a region's demand for greater autonomy, as Park and Elcock (2000: 87) assert, is the development of strong, distinctive cultures and identities, which lead these ethno-nations to demand a specific title as a national region or stateless nation.

12. Quebec is the most commonly cited case to illustrate an ethno-nations' support for trade liberalization for the purpose of lessening their economic dependence upon the central government's economy (Meadwell 1993; Martin 1997; Shulman 2000). Although Quebecois nationalists initially expressed resistance toward free trade in the 1970s (Meadwell 1993: 223), they have supported trade liberalization strategies since the 1980s. Since the introduction of NAFTA in 1994, for example, the United States has been perceived by Quebecois nationalists as a counter-balance toward the excessive English-Canadian dominance over Quebec. To date, greater integration among North American countries, under the auspices of NAFTA, has indeed lessened Quebec's dependence on English-Canada. For example, Quebec interprovincial trade increased to $69.41 billion

while international trade increased to $112.12 billion in 1996, from an initial $61.33 billion and $60.20 billion respectively in 1988 (Interprovincial Trade in Canada 1998: 7 0–74).

13. See, for example, ASEAN Secretariat (1993) or visit the ASEAN Secretariat official web site (accessed 2003), at http://www.aseansec.org/12374.htm.

14. Nevertheless, in recent years, as Parsonage (1997: 253) asserts, the focus on accelerating economic development has been considered the main source of solidarity in the region.

15. Homeland community here is defined as a community that is identified with a particular group of people or ethnic group. The members of a homeland community are born and reside in the same area, region, state, or territory throughout their lives. The diaspora community, on the other hand, is a community whose members have become dispersed from their original homeland community.

16. As reported by the *BBC News* (2000). For further information visit http://news.bbc.co.uk/1/hi/world/europe/1003324.stm.

17. See Chapter 1, Article 2 of the Treaty of Amity and Cooperation, which was signed on 24th February 1976, or visit the ASEAN Secretariat official web site (accessed 2003) at http://www.aseansec.org/1217.htm.

18. As reported in the ASEAN Secretariat (2000a) official web site at http://www.aseansec.org/597.htm.

19. As quoted in *The Nation* (2003), or visit *The Nation* official web site at http://www.nationmultimedia.com.

20. See also Tivey (1981) and Greenfield (1992) for a detailed analysis of a nation's self-confidence. Both scholars hold that prestige and success bring self-confidence. National identity is, therefore, a matter of dignity.

21. The use of the term diffusion was prominent as early as 1893 and was used to refer to the notion that most folklore was primarily borrowed from an Old World center of high culture, such as Egypt, Mesopotamia, India, and so on. Today, the term diffusion is used to describe *acculturation*, which means the transmission of culture from one community to another. For a detailed analysis of the concept of cultural diffusion see, for example, Wescott (1998).

22. This is, however, not always the case. In Shulman's view (2000: 372), for example, the process of cultural diffusion is most successful when a nation's culture is transferred to other nations that share a similar culture. Nevertheless, it is also argued in this book that, nowadays, the process of cultural diffusion does not necessarily require a close similarity between one culture and another, although close geographical proximity does allow the process of cultural diffusion to take place naturally. The recent increase in the use of information technology means that today members of a nation may access other culturally distinct cultures from their own without having to be *similar* or geographically close.

23. As reported by the ASEAN Secretariat (2002b), or visit the ASEAN Secretariat official web site at http://www.aseansec.org/13159.htm.

24. For details on the ATF main objectives, see the ATF (2003) official web site at http://www.atf2003.com/objective/index.html.

25. As quoted in Chang and Raguraman (2001: 61).

26. However, it has also been widely acknowledged that the "celebration of the manifestation of cultures living in peripheral locations may be viewed as encouraging [ethnonationalism]" (Wall 2001: 321). Through the promotion of regional tourism, for example, many Indonesian ethno-nations can hope for not only the promotion of their identities and cultures abroad, but also economic development. The incorporation of tour-

ism in the Brunei Darussalam, Indonesia, Malaysia, the Philippines East ASEAN Growth Area (BIMP-EAGA) and the Indonesia, Malaysia, Thailand Growth Triangle (IMT-GT), for example, has allowed some of the most restive Indonesian provinces, such as Maluku, Papua, and Aceh, to expect economic gains, particularly in terms of investment opportunities (PATA 1999). With sustained economic growth, Indonesian ethno-nations can lessen their economic dependence from the Indonesian government. As a result, the promotion of ethno-nation's identities and cultures through tourism may also be used as a leverage to increase resistance toward the Indonesian government.

27. The term autonomy, according to Heywood (2000: 118), literally means "self-rule or self-government." Autonomy implies a substantial degree of independence and states, institutions, or groups can be said to be autonomous if they enjoy a substantial degree of independence.

28. Other scholars, such as Hutchinson and Smith (1994: 4), have also observed that nationalists are always keen proponents of popular freedom and sovereignty. It is, therefore, imperative that the people or members of a nation should be liberated from any foreign interference, be able to determine their own destiny, be masters in their own house, be able to control their own resources, and obey only their own *inner* voice.

29. The WTO official web site indicates that the relationship between world trade and economic growth since the Second World War is evident through the cut in industrial products tariff rates (refer also to Appendix 2 for levels of tariff barriers since the end of the Cold War). By 1999, for example, tariffs on industrial products in developed countries had fallen sharply and averaged at less than 4 percent. For further WTO analysis on economic growth and open trade see the WTO official web site (accessed 2002) at http://www.wto.org/english/thewto_e/whatis_e/tif_e/fact3_e.htm.

30. East Timor today is known as Timor Leste.

31. Not all ethnic conflicts have resulted in the creation of a new nation-state. Some examples in Southeast Asia are the Acehnese resistance against the Indonesian government and the conflict between the Philippines government and the Moro Islamic movement. There is a similar tendency in Africa, where internal conflicts have been prevalent but new countries have not been born. One prime example is the conflict between the Oromos and the Ethiopian government (Jalata 2001).

32. However, this is not to suggest that nationalists themselves are not collaborators with these non-accountable international actors. As with other political groups, nationalists often need the financial and other support from these international entities to achieve their objectives.

33. ECOWAS sent its troops to Liberia to resolve the conflict between the Liberian government, led by Charles Taylor, and members of the Liberians United for Reconciliation and Democracy (LURD) and the Movement for Democracy in Liberia (MODEL). The peace deal was signed in Ghana, on 19 July 2003. For further details concerning the Liberian civil war and ECOWAS' involvement in the peaceful resolution to the conflict, visit the *BBC News* (2003a) official web site at http://news.bbc.co.uk.

34. The EU's involvement in the restoration or consolidation of democracies in Southeast Asian countries, such as Cambodia and East Timor, is a prime example of the use of inter-regional initiatives to resolve conflicts between the central government and ethno-nations. For further information concerning the EU's involvement in conflict resolution in the Southeast Asian region see the European Union Online web site at http://europa.eu.int/comm/external_relations/cambodia/intro/index.htm. (for Cambodia, accessed 2003), and http://europa.eu.int/comm/external_relations/east_timor/index.htm (for East Timor, accessed 2003).

In other cases, interregional initiatives to mitigate domestic conflicts have taken the form of formal pressure. One such example is the EU's arms embargo on Indonesia over East Timor. The EU was reported as taking a very pro-East Timorese stance vis-à-vis the Indonesian government. The embargo was imposed following the spread of violence in the former Indonesian province after the East Timorese general election on 30 August 1999. The embargo was later lifted on 17 January 2000 after the Indonesian government and the EU reached an agreement that the Indonesian government would seek peaceful solutions to other ethnonationalist movements in Indonesia (Reuters 1999).

35. See Chapter 7 for a further analysis of ASEAN's organizational structure and its elitist tendencies.

36. In recent years, substantial analyzes, such as those produced by Gundlach (1996), have been made on the impact of openness on the economic growth of developing countries. Most developing countries in the past supported the import substitution industry (ISI) mechanism that favored protectionism. Initially, the open economic policy was challenged by economic nationalists who favored protectionism. For the views of economic nationalists on the open economic policy see, for example, Myrdal (1957) and Prebisch (1962).

37. This external effect of integration can also be termed the multiplier effect (see, *inter alia*, Pederson 1994). This analysis argues that the lure to join an established regional grouping is greater when the critical mass of established regional groupings' members grows.

38. It is also possible that non-member countries' demands to join an established regional grouping may be rejected. As a result, as Mattli (1999: 43) further postulates, non-member countries may form their own regional grouping.

39. Apart from increasing the bargaining power of the Union in world affairs, the benefits of enlargement also include: (1) peace, stability, and prosperity throughout Europe; (2) the boosting of economic growth; (3) a better quality of life for the Union's citizens; (4) an increase in cultural diversity. For further information regarding the EU's enlargement, visit the European Union online official web site (accessed 2003) at http://europa.eu.int/comm/enlargement/arguments/index.htm.

40. In addition, Palmer also describes the region as the laboratory for the study of the new regionalism, as was the case with Western Europe's experience during the first wave of regionalism.

41. Also known as the ASEAN Declaration.

42. Quoted from the ASEAN Secretariat official web site (accessed 2002a) at http://www.aseansec.org/64.htm. Refer to Appendix 4 for details about the Bangkok (ASEAN) Declaration of 1967.

43. GT schemes were developed through the Growth Centre Theory (Lim 2001: 196–7), which attempts to narrow the wealth gap between central and peripheral regions or areas. This theory maintains that it is possible to achieve growth in both the central and the peripheral regions or areas. While it is the center that provides the peripheral with the capital injection needed for growth, the center also depends on the peripheral as suppliers of raw materials for industrial needs in the central regions or areas.

44. The October 28, 1928 *Sumpah Pemuda* (Youth Pledge) was a turning point in the promotion of Indonesian national identity. The delegates involved in this congress were representatives of many Indonesian political and ethnic groups. The congress resulted in the adoption of the Indonesian national language of *Bahasa Indonesia*, the Indonesian national anthem of *Indonesia Raya* (Great Indonesia), and the Indonesian flag of red and white.

45. The concept of the People's Economy was developed by the Minister of Co-operative, Small, and Medium Enterprises, Adi Sasono, during the Habibie administration. This concept will be analyzed in Chapter 5.

46. As reported in the IMF News Brief (2003), or visit the IMF official web site at http://www.imf.org/external/np/sec/pr/2003/pr0343.htm.

Chapter 4

Indonesian Nationalism and Foreign Economic Policy

Nationalism in Southeast Asia has been characterized as "reactive and creative as well as constructive and destructive" (Tarling 1998: 75). Nationalist movements in the region have varied throughout history. For Indonesia, nationalism has been a major feature of the country's foreign economic policy (FEP) during the post-independence period. During the first fifteen years after independence, for example, Indonesian economic policy moved in line with the inward-looking policies of the government (Paauw 1969; Myint 1971), which was evident, for example, in the process of nationalization that took place between 1957–1964 (Hill 2000: 109). The emergence of the New Order government in 1966 heralded in a major liberalizing reform of the Indonesian economy as well as a shift toward regional economic cooperation within the framework of ASEAN. Despite this, the Indonesian economy remained closed as inward-looking economic policies continued to prevail during this period (Hill 2000: 65). The present Indonesian economy is similar to that of the early independence period in that Indonesian economic policymakers are still "deeply concerned about potential foreign control of the economy" (Linnan 1999: 2).

The objective of this chapter is to provide an analysis of the dynamics of Indonesian nationalism and FEP, and, specific attention is given to both historical and contemporary aspects of Indonesian nationalism and FEP. The first section analyses the way in which nationalism played an important role in shaping the formation of Indonesian FEP in the past. Such analysis is crucial because it helps to explain the contemporary nature of Indonesian FEP. More specifically, this section analyses Indonesian nationalism and FEP in two periods. The first is the Old Order period, which was during the Sukarno administration. The Old Order government was in power from 1949, or the year in which the transfer of sovereignty from the Netherlands to the Republic of the United States of Indonesia (RUSI)[1] took place, to 1966 when Sukarno was removed from office. The New Order government, led by Suharto as the second Indonesian President, lasted for three decades, from 1967 until 1998. Here, attention is given to the New Order government's attempts to stabilize the domestic economy through the normalization of diplomatic relations with the West and Indonesia's immediate neighbors. Another major focus in this section is the government's attempts to enhance regional economic cooperation within the ASEAN framework. Meanwhile, the second section analyses the present state of Indonesian nationalism and FEP. This section analyses in particular the role that nationalism played during the Indonesian economic crisis in 1997 and the threat of national disintegration following the economic crisis.

The History of Indonesian Nationalism and Foreign Economic Policy

As with most other countries in Southeast Asia, Indonesia[2] experienced colonial domination.[3] The lengthy Dutch colonial presence in the East Indies[4] (some 350 years) led to a nationalist movement throughout the archipelago. During colonial times, Indonesia's FEP was subject to the interests of the colonial powers. When the Dutch gained substantial control of the country, it was the Dutch East India Company (VOC—*Vereenigde Oostandische Compagnie*) that mainly had control of economic policy in the East Indies. In international trade, the East Indies, as a colony, was transformed into an exporting economy (Glassburner 1971: 14). Coupled with the emergence of new export staples, the East Indies export trade grew dramatically in response to the growing markets in Europe and North America (Booth 1998: 203). Subsequently, during the Japanese occupation between 1942 and 1945, the Indonesian economy progressed in the same direction as that of the Dutch occupation. Japanese armed forces were able to secure supplies of strategic raw materials (Booth 1998: 47) to aid Japan economically in her further expansion throughout the Asia-Pacific.[5]

One of the most prominent features of the Indonesian economy during the post-independence period is the emergence of economic nationalism. Shortly after independence, for example, the Indonesian government introduced the so-called *Benteng* system in 1950, which was intended to promote native Indonesian businessmen (Mackie 1971: 47). Subsequently, following the introduction of Guided Democracy in 1957, the expropriation of foreign capital began to take place. During this period, many "Dutch trading and estate enterprises, the core of Dutch colonial capital, were expropriated together with Dutch shipping, banking and industrial enterprises" (Robison 1986: 79). The New Order government in 1966 made changes in the way economic nationalism was implemented. The New Order government's main priority in its economic stabilization program was to curb the rate of inflation that it had inherited from the previous government (Thomas and Panglaykim 1973: 145). As a result, Indonesia implemented an open-door economic policy, which "aimed at producing maximum economic growth and relying heavily upon investment by international corporate capital" (Robison 1986: 131). However, these economic policies lasted only until 1975, when there was a resurgence of economic nationalism (Robison 1986: 131). The New Order government began to take a more active role in foreign policy, particularly within the regional context, following the end of the Cold War in the late 1980s and the resurgence of regionalism in both Western Europe and North America. In any case, the New Order government pursued a rather pragmatic approach in its overall conduct of FEP

Nationalism and Foreign Economic Policy during the Old Order Period

As mentioned earlier, the Old Order period falls between the transfer of power from the Netherlands to the government of the RUSI in 1949 and the attempted *coup d'etat* in 1965. On the whole, the period between 1949 and 1965 can be seen as a time "in which the Dutch colonial economy was dismantled and new socio-economic and political forces gathered themselves within Indonesia" (Robison 1986: 36). Indonesia's economic policy during this period can be split into two phases. The first phase was from 1950 until 1957, during which time parliamentary democracy was implemented and the domestic economy was largely controlled by foreign and ethnic Chinese private business interests (Glassburner 1971: 4). The second phase was between 1957 and 1965, during which time the Guided Democracy policy was introduced and the concept of economic nationalism was strengthened. As a result, Indonesia's economic policy became inward-looking, as attempts to minimize foreign economic domination, particularly Dutch-owned capital, prevailed. Despite Indonesia's formal independence for nearly a decade, the Dutch were still largely in control of the relatively small but highly commercialized and industrial sectors, such as plantation agriculture, oil, and import trade (Thomas and Panglaykim 1973: 39). In the export and import sectors, for example, a mere five Dutch companies, including The Borneo-Sumatra Company (Borsumy), George Wehry and Co., *Internationale Credie en Handelsvereeniging* (Internatio), Lindeteves, and Jacobean van den Berg, controlled some 60 percent of operations (Allen and Donnithorne 1957: 60–63).

The pursuit of economic nationalism during the first phase of the Old Order period is best illustrated by the term *Indonesianization*, which refers to the process used to replace "Dutch officials and managers by Indonesian nationals in the government bureaucracy and private firms in Indonesia" (Lindblad 2002: 2). The Indonesian government at the time intended to bring indigenous Indonesians into the more complex sectors of the economy to lessen the domination of the Dutch and ethnic Chinese in the domestic economy. More specifically, Sutter (1959: 2) has outlined nine institutional changes that took place during this period. These were: (1) transfer of formerly colonial public enterprises to the Indonesian government; (2) establishment of state enterprises; (3) transfer of private alien enterprises to the Indonesian government; (4) increased government control over alien business; (5) transfer of private alien enterprises to Indonesian and their organizations; (6) establishment of new enterprises in sectors previously virtually closed to Indonesians; (7) increased Indonesian equity ownership in corporations established by aliens; (8) increased participation in the management of alien companies; and (9) return of landholdings by alien enterprises to the Indonesian community.[6] Shortly after the declaration of independ-

dence, various organizations were established to implement the Indonesianization policy, which included the National Trading Bank of Indonesia (BDNI—
Bank Dagang Negara Indonesia) and some twenty other newly established enterprises in the provisional capital of the Republic (Muhaimin 1990: 31). The
establishment of new organizations to foster an indigenous capitalist class continued until the early 1950s, which is evident in various business organizations
such as the Union of Indonesian Exporters (PEKSI—*Persatuan Eksportir Indonesia*), the Indonesian National Association of Importers (IKINI—*Ikatan Impor-
tir Nasional Indonesia*).

Two governmental plans were particularly important in realizing the Indonesianization process that took place during the Old Order period, namely the
Benteng program[7] and the Economic Urgency program. The Benteng program
was first implemented by the Natsir cabinet (1950–1951) and was enthusiastical-
ly prosecuted by the Ali Sastroamidjojo cabinet (1953–1954) (Robison 1986:
44). Through this economic program, the Indonesian government aimed "to protect the economically weak by reserving certain commodities and from specified
countries that could be imported by Indonesians only" (Thomas and Panglaykim
1973: 48). During its initial phase in 1950, Djuanda, the Indonesian Minister of
Prosperity at the time, announced that special protection would be given to national importers to help them compete with their foreign counterparts. Thereaf-
ter, the program altered the focus from national importers to indigenous Indonesians (*bangsa Indonesia asli*) and stipulated that 70 percent of the equity should
be owned by Indonesians, excluding the ethnic Chinese (Widihandojo 2000).
Meanwhile, the Economic Urgency program was launched in 1951 by Prof. Sumitro Djojohadikusumo who was Minister of Trade and Industry at the time.[8] In
essence, this program was introduced as a guide for government activities in the
agricultural and industrial sectors (Thomas and Panglaykim 1973: 49). Similar
to the Benteng program, the Economic Urgency program was a plan for industrial projects that involved extensive economic intervention in an attempt to establish indigenous industries (Djojohadikusumo 1954).

Both the Benteng and the Economic Urgency programs, however, failed to
produce any substantial results. In Chalmers' (1997: 10) analysis, for example,
both programs "serve to indicate the essential weakness of both private Indonesian capital and the state in the 1950s." Three main factors contributed to the
failure of both programs. The first was the ambivalent attitude of Indonesian
leaders toward foreign capital. On the one hand, the Indonesian government at
the time resented the fact that foreign capital still dominated the Indonesian
economy even after the granting of independence. The continued confrontation
with the Dutch over the West Irian issue also fuelled nationalistic sentiment
among Indonesian policymakers *vis-à-vis* foreigners. On the other hand, the
Sukarno administration publicly admitted that foreign capital and management
had an important role to play in strategies for the economic development of an
independent Indonesia (Linblad 2002: 17). The second factor contributing to the
failure of both programs was the overwhelming predominance of ethnic Chinese
capital in the domestic economy. Although joint ventures between Indonesian

and foreign nationals were encouraged, many companies that pursued such a strategy were owned and managed by ethnic Chinese (Booth 1998: 259). The third factor contributing to the failure of the Benteng and the Economic Urgency programs was the fact that there were favorable international economic conditions for the exporters of primary materials as a result of the Korean War (Chalmers 1997: 11). Indigenous Indonesians thus failed to recapture their lost territory within the domestic economy despite the Benteng and Economic Urgency programs.

The pursuit of economic nationalism was further strengthened through the introduction of *Guided Democracy* (the second phase of the Old Order period) in 1957.[9] Guided Democracy was uniquely Indonesian and largely associated with the concept of *musyawarah* and *mufakat*,[10] which is a process of decision-making traditionally practiced in Indonesian villages (Reindhardt 1971: 55). In principle, the Guided Democracy concept may also be referred to as *Socialisme à la Indonesia*, in that it rejects liberal thinking and places great emphasis on a collectivist organization of the economy, based on the family principle, or the *gotong-royong* (mutual assistance) method (Mackie 1971: 44–51). The most significant feature of this system is the overwhelming power invested in the political leadership because of the heavily paternalistic relationship between the leaders and the citizens. The decisions made by political leaders are seen as a reflection of the general interests of the public, thus allowing the supreme leader to take any necessary actions to solve any domestic crises. Sukarno had great influence during the introduction of this system after he had revoked the provisional constitution of 1950 and reinstated the older constitution that was established shortly after the declaration of independence. With reference to domestic politics, Sukarno believed that liberal democracy, which resulted in the emergence of numerous political parties and the conflicts that ensued between them, was not suitable for Indonesia. Following the introduction of the provisional constitution in 1950, the threat of disintegration as a result of the different views of political parties, particularly the Communists and religious groups, was looming. Sukarno finally introduced the new concept through the *gotong royong* cabinet and the National Council that represented all the major constituencies in the country.

The introduction of the Guided Democracy system produced substantial impacts on the development of Indonesian foreign policy. During this period, Sukarno was regarded as both the "draftsman for the blueprint of Indonesia's foreign policy and the driving force in its execution" (Agung 1973: 284). After launching the Asia-Africa Conference in 1955,[11] Sukarno believed that he had wide support from the leaders of other less developed countries (LDCs), and "launched himself as the champion of the New Emerging Forces (NEFOS) in Asia, Africa, and Latin America against the Old Established Forces (OLDEFOS) in the West" (Anwar 1994: 21). According to scholars, such as Bunnel (1966) and Legge (1972), Indonesian foreign policy during the Guided Democracy period was largely influenced by Sukarno's fervent nationalist idea that continuous anti-colonial struggle should be part of governmental strategy. Sukarno was convinced that colonialism and imperialism still prevailed in most parts of the world. It is for this reason that Indonesia had an active, yet militant foreign policy, particularly toward the West.

Nationalism was equally reflected in the general conduct of Indonesian FEP. One key aspect of Guided Democracy in the area of economy was the concept of the *Guided Economy*. As with Guided Democracy, Guided Economy gave substantial power to President Sukarno as the designated administrator of the national economy. Economic nationalism within the Guided Economy framework did not only include "the appropriation of the colonial economy, [but also] an attempt to build a national import substitution industrial section" (Robison 1990: 39), which meant that the state assumed a dominant role in the domestic economy. Although there is no authoritative definition of Guided Economy, its components can be seen in the Eight Year (Development) Plan of 1960 and the Economic Declaration of 1963, which include the strengthening of the role of the state in the national economy, the expropriation of foreign capital, and an attempt to create a more self-sufficient and more industrialized economy by replacing the colonial import/export economy with indigenous businesses (Robison 1986: 71).[12] Sukarno was able to draw support for his controversial foreign policy among Indonesian domestic constituents who were themselves frustrated by the continued Western domination of the Indonesian economy. As Weinstein (1976: 294) observes:

> In its trade and aid relations with the outside world, Indonesia looked almost entirely to the West; at home, Western capital still played a very important role in the country's economic life. [Meanwhile] the Dutch still occupied West Irian, a constant reminder that even the struggle for formal sovereignty remained incomplete.

Indonesian FEP at the time, as with its foreign policy in general, was dominated by "an apparent leftward drifts in domestic politics and a corresponding alignment internationally, especially in relations with the People's Republic of China" (Leifer 1983: 61) and the Soviet Union.[13]

On the whole, however, the Sukarno government paid little attention to the overall economic policy of the country (Chalmers 1997: 14). The Indonesian government was too engrossed with the West Irian issue and with Malaya's proposed plan to gain independence from the British. While the West Irian issue was settled through the Bunker Plan,[14] a confrontation with Malaysia became inevitable, particularly following Sukarno's announcement of the Crush Malaysia (*Ganyang Malaysia*) campaign in September 1963.[15] The Indonesian economy soon deteriorated along with Sukarno's plans to wage a war against Malaya. As Booth (1998: 65) observes, although GDP growth was positive from 1958–1965, it was still much lower than in the 1950–1957 period. More importantly, Pauker (1962: 617) notes that by 1961 Indonesia was experiencing high inflation due to high deficits in the rising national budget from Rp. 1.56 billion in 1956 to Rp. 16.65 billion in 1961, and with the figure expected to rise to Rp. 37 billion by the end of that year. The U.S. government, wishing to counteract Sukarno's military advances into West Irian and Malaya, pledged US$325 million in economic aid through the Humprey recovery plan to which would be added US$81 million from the IMF (Agung 1973: 446). Sukarno, however, preferred his militant foreign policy and discarded the West's help in economic rehabilitation.

Steps to end the conflict between Indonesia and Malaysia were taken when Macapagal, the President of the Philippines, proposed creating an organization comprising Malaysia, the Philippines, and Indonesia (Maphilindo) in 1963.[16] Later that year, serious talks began between the Foreign Ministers of the three countries. However, establishing Maphilindo was not an easy task. The Indonesian government, for example, received stern criticism from domestic political groups regarding the country's involvement in talks about the creation of Maphilindo. The Indonesian Communist Party (PKI—*Partai Komunis Indonesia*), in particular, announced their formal opposition to any regional initiatives that involved Malaysia, as well as the whole idea of Maphilindo. One of the reasons was that many in the PKI leadership, particularly Dr. Subandrio, had been influential in Sukarno's decision to implement the Crush Malaysia campaign. The talks soon ended after the Federation of Malaysia was formally established in September 1963. This event was marked by a mob attack on the Malaysian embassy in Jakarta, and Indonesia soon decided to break off its diplomatic relations with Malaysia.

In sum, Indonesian foreign policy during the Old Order period was mainly nationalistic in character, with a leftist orientation. In many ways it could be argued that Indonesian FEP was a reflection of the country's foreign policy in general. There were several reasons for this. The first was that Indonesia at the time had only just emerged from its colonial experience. This provided a fundamental basis for nationalist sentiments against anything foreign from among Indonesian policymakers, and explains the implementation of inward-looking economic policies. The *Benteng* and Economic Urgency programs exemplify the staunch nationalist attitude among Indonesian policymakers. Under these programs, the nationalization of foreign enterprises took place, particularly those owned by Dutch and ethnic Chinese private businessmen. Another reason was the leftward drift within the political spectrum in Indonesia. After successfully establishing himself as the supreme leader of the Republic, Sukarno was able to give vent to his rhetoric of anti neo-colonialism, colonialism, and imperialism (Nekolim).[17] which clearly indicated his suspicion of the West. Throughout the implementation of Guided Democracy, Indonesian foreign policy was radicalized and brought toward a closer relationship with the major Communist powers, particularly China (Anwar 1994: 21).

Nationalism and Foreign Economic Policy during the New Order Period

The failed coup d'état of 1965 marked the fall of Sukarno and the ascension of Suharto's New Order government.[18] If Sukarno played a major role in influencing Indonesian foreign policy during the Old Order period, Suharto was the main determinant of Indonesian foreign policy during the New Order period. General Suharto soon took charge of the government following the neutralization of President Sukarno in July 1966 and brought radical changes to Indonesian national policy. As the new leader, "Suharto [was] serious and dedicated, yet also somewhat distant and devious in pressing his policies. Delicacy and ritual [seemed] to mark his style of authority and he [was] committed to a compromising mode of operation" (Reinhardt 1971: 141). In order to carry out many of its objectives, the New Order government conducted "a notable reduction in the degree of pluralism within the system and not an assumption of power by new elements" (Leifer 1983: 111). One of the main determinants that ensured the long tenure of Suharto's Presidency was his emphasis on placing the military at the center of Indonesian politics and daily life, as demonstrated by the Indonesian military's adoption of the dual function (*dwi fungsi*) system.[19]

This system, as Kooistra (2001: 11) asserts, "allowed the [military] to place members of its socio-political wing' alongside government officials right down to the village level. The idea was to keep in touch with local communities, explain to people how great it was to be Indonesian." Suharto realized that the military had consistently played a significant role in Indonesian politics since the independence period. The military, and particularly the army, which had assumed command of the political heights of the Republic, had been of great political importance from the onset of the national revolution. Another important political element within the New Order period was the Functional Group (Golkar—*Golongan Karya*), which was a government-sponsored functional group that became the main Indonesian political party during the Indonesian New Order period.[20] Thus, the President, the armed forces, and Golkar became the main political players during the New Order period to determine Indonesian national and foreign policies.

With regard to foreign policy, "the New Order leadership had three key aspects: namely, strong anti-communism, a commitment to stability and economic development, and a pragmatic international outlook" (Anwar 1994: 35). Indonesian FEP had a similar direction. The first way in which the New Order government incorporated these aspects into Indonesian foreign policy was through appointing Adam Malik Foreign Minister (Leifer 1983: 113).[21] and by granting the Sultan of Yogyakarta[22] the position of Economic Minister. The major aim of Indonesian FEP at the time was to restore the country's credibility in international fora. It was only through the implementation of such policies that Indonesia would be able to acquire the necessary aid to restore the country's ailing economy. Upon resuming his position in the Ministry of Foreign Affair, Malik immediately declared Indonesia's intention to repair the country's relationship with Malaysia and to rejoin the UN, which were finally achieved in August and September 1966 respectively. Indonesia's credibility was gradually restored, particularly in the eyes of the United States and Japan who finally granted an emergency credit of US$59 million and US$30 million respectively (Palmer 1978: 27).[23] Indonesia's relationship with its major creditors was later formalized through the creation of the Inter-Governmental Group on Indonesia (IGGI) in February 1967. The Netherlands' led initiative aimed to co-ordinate the multilateral aid given to Indonesia.[24] The major creditors of Indonesia were convinced that the stability of Southeast Asia would be ensured if Indonesia could achieve political and economic stability.

Figure 4.1.
Indonesian Level of Inflation,
1966-1971 (%)

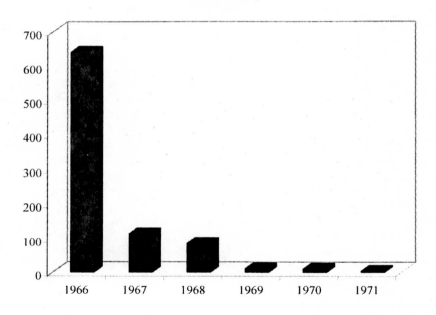

Source: National Development Information Service (1977: 34)

The major economic policies issued by the New Order government can be divided into three periods, all of which had substantial impacts on the Indonesian government's FEP. The first was from 1966–1973 when the New Order government concentrated on the issue of economic rehabilitation and recovery. The government priority in this period was to re-establish its relationship with its most major Western donors as well as to manage the inflation level. The second period was between 1974 and 1985, when Indonesia attained rapid economic growth. The sustained growth of the economy was particularly significant following the rise of the international oil price in the mid-1970s.[25] However, the Indonesian economy during this period was also highlighted by strong economic nationalism, economic populism, and a strong resurgence of predatory bureaucratism.[26] As a result, this period saw a substantial increase in indigenous-led enterprises as well as the rise of protectionist policies, particularly trade and investment policies. Subsequently, the fall in the international oil price in the mid-1980s forced the Indonesian government to cut back on its expenditures and to introduce a major economic reform, which concentrated on tax and banking policies. Finally, the third period runs from 1986 until the recent economic crisis. Within this period Indonesia conducted a rather active FEP, particularly through its commitment to various regional and international economic integration arrangements. There were, however, some substantial setbacks for the Indonesian economy, which included an increase in the practice of predatory bureaucratism among the New Order leadership as well as Suharto's continued reliance on certain technocrats.

During the first period, from 1966 until 1973, a major concern of the New Order government was to restore the deteriorating economy of Indonesia (Reindhardt 1971: 141–42; Leifer 1983: 112–13). As a result, Indonesian economic policy at the time was influenced by a *laissez-faire* approach, which aimed at increasing economic growth and attracting foreign investment (Robison 1986: 131). In 1967, for example, the Indonesian government issued the Foreign Investment Law No. 1/1967, which made the investment climate more attractive by providing substantial incentives, such as tax holidays, certain guarantees, etc, to foreign investors.[27] This was the New Order government's response toward the decline of the Indonesian economy.

When the New Order government took control, the inflation level was "accelerating, output was stagnating, poverty and hunger were widespread, and a tiny minority with access to import licenses were enriching themselves [while] incomes . . . were declining" (Booth 1998: 71). In 1965, the inflation level exceeded 500 percent (refer to figure 4.1), while the price of rice rose as much as 900 percent (Leifer 1983: 113). In the capital alone, the cost of living index rose from 166 in 1959 to 269,000 in 1965 (refer to table 4.1). Moreover, Indonesia's total debt reached "about [US]$2,300 million, of which about half was a Soviet and East European military debt. The immediate forecast, for 1966, was of foreign exchange earnings of $430 million (including oil) and minimum import requirements of $560 million; not to mention a debt servicing of $530 million" (Palmer 1978: 6–7).

Table 4.1.
Cost of Living Index in Jakarta,
1959–1966

End of the year	Index	Percentage of Increase
1959	166.0	19.4
1960	215.0	29.5
1961	380	76.7
1962	976.0	156.8
1963	2,226.0	128.1
1964	5,234.0	135.1
1965	36,347.0	594.4
1966	268,733.0	639.4

Note: Compared with the end of previous year
Source: National Development Information Service (1977: 18)

Between late 1958 and 1965, the Indonesian annual growth rate for net national products was 1.7 percent per annum, which was lower than for the 1950–1957 period. This percentage indicated a decline in the per capita income, as the population grew at around 2 percent per annum (Nugroho 1967: 539). In addition, the new Indonesian government also faced major problems concerning the balance of payments. In order to restore the Indonesian economy, the New Order government realized that it was necessary for Indonesia to acquire foreign aid and to reschedule its foreign debts. The government turned for help to some prominent Indonesian economists (Booth 1998: 74), who later become the main architects behind the Indonesian economic boom of the 1980s.[28] These economists soon approved the government's decision to acquire external funding. The Indonesian economy eventually made substantial progress through the implementation of various economic policies, such as an improved tax collection system and the government's focus on non-agricultural sectors (Sundrum 1986: 58), particularly the manufacturing and construction sectors.

Apart from the economic restoration of the country, there was also a major shift in Indonesian foreign policy during the first phase of the New Order period, particularly with regard to the government's perspective on regional order and stability. The shift was not only evident in the normalization of the relationship between Indonesia and Malaysia, but also in Indonesia's support of the creation of a regional forum in Southeast Asia. Following the signing of the final agreement to end the confrontation, the representatives of both Indonesia and Malaysia continuously conducted various discussions on the possibility of the formation of a regional grouping. Both sides decided to put the issue on the agenda during their formal talks at the end of May 1966 (Gordon 1969: 110). Many Indonesian politicians at the time were convinced that cooperation in the region would prevent future conflicts and promote regional prosperity. In his statement before the House of Representatives (MPR—*Majelis Permusyawaratan Rakyat*) on 16 August 1966, General Suharto (1966: 48) stated that:

If one day an integrated Southeast Asia can be established, this part of the
world then may stand strongly in facing outside influences and intervention
from whatever quarter it may come, be it of an economic nature, or a physical
military intervention [sic].[29]

Suharto's argument soon drew widespread public support. Most people believed that regional cooperation would act as a much needed bulwark against the
forces of neo-colonialism (Anwar 1994). Suharto was also greatly influenced by
other Indonesian army leaders, who also thought that a regional grouping in
Southeast Asia was necessary, largely for strategic purposes. More importantly,
however, Indonesia, as a member of ASEAN, was determined that its development would be oriented toward programs that strengthened its national resilience
and promoted stability in all fields (Panglaykim 1977: 38). Despite the fact that
Indonesia was known as the most nationalistic country in the region, it held, and
still holds, a vision of an integrated Southeast Asia. Despite this, little attention
was given to the development of ASEAN at the time. It was not until the second
phase of the New Order period that strengthened cooperation, particularly in the
field of economics, was fostered among Southeast Asian countries.

Throughout the period between 1974 and 1985 Indonesia saw an increase in
economic growth at an average of 7 percent per annum (Booth 1992: 1). At the
same time, however, Indonesia experienced another surge of economic nationalism within the second phase of the New Order economy. Such nationalistic sentiment was partly fuelled by the *Malari Riot* of 1974.[30] which gave added impetus to the momentum of public dissatisfaction with foreign capital (Chalmers
and Hadiz 1997: 71).[31] This resurgence of economic nationalism at the time can
be characterized as a "complex movement influenced less by a declining petty
bourgeoisie demanding state protection against the superior forces of foreign
capital than by emerging political and economic forces demanding the removal
of political and economic constraints upon their potential development" (Robison 1986: 147). Realizing that it was impossible to control nationalist discon-
tent, the Indonesian government introduced measures that would benefit indigenous Indonesian businessmen. Among other things, all new foreign investments
at the time were required to open as joint ventures with local businesses. More
specifically, all new foreign investors were required to offer Indonesian businessmen a share of as much as 20 percent of equity holding initially, and this
was to be expanded to 51 percent within ten years of operation.

The re-emergence of economic nationalism during the second phase of the
New Order government was caused by two factors. Firstly, Indonesia became
increasingly dependent on foreign aid, particularly from international financial
institutions, such as the IMF, World Bank, and other foreign advisers (Arndt
1984: 42). The Indonesian public resented the fact that Indonesia had to sell out
its natural resources to serve the interests of foreign capitalists. Aside from that,
indigenous Indonesians, mainly Muslims, were also unhappy with Indonesia's
open-door policy at the time, arguing that they could not compete with their

foreign counterparts. Secondly, the boom in oil prices in 1974–1975 also played a major role in shifting the orientation of New Order economic policymakers' toward more inward-looking policies. The Indonesian government, for example, was able to increase the corporate tax on oil from Rp. 344 billion in 1973–1974 to Rp. 8,627 billion in 1981–1982 (from 35.6 to 70.6 percent of total revenue) (Robison 1990: 144). The excess revenue accrued from the oil sector allowed the Indonesian government to implement more inward-looking economic policies.

Four institutions were particularly important in promoting economic nationalism (or statist-nationalist ideology) during the second phase of the New Order period, namely the Indonesian Gas and Oil Company (Pertamina—*Perusahaan Pertambangan Minyak dan Gas Bumi Negara*), the Ministry of Industry and Trade (Depperindag—*Departemen Industri dan Perdagangan*), the Investment Co-ordination Board (BKPM—*Badan Koordinasi Penanaman Modal*), and the Centre for Strategic and International Studies (CSIS) (Chalmers and Hadiz 1997: 72). Pertamina was actually a state corporation but, from when the New Order government took control until 1975, it was "a fiefdom controlled by a military officer directly responsible to the President in pursuit of a variety of nongovernmental interests" (Robison 1990: 15). Apart from its involvement in non-governmental activities, such as allocating drilling leases to foreign companies, Pertamina often used the "state's authority to force foreign capital to support Indonesia's own development" (Chalmers and Hadiz 1997: 72). On the other hand, the Depperindag promoted economic nationalism through the maintenance of tight regulations in Indonesian investment laws, and BKPM was established during the New Order period to study various investment applications from abroad.[32] Indonesia's trade and regulatory policy regimes had often been the *béte noire* of liberal economists (Hill 1990: 226), in that the investment process was often heavily bureaucratized. The last major institution that promoted the notion of economic nationalism was CSIS, which was a private research institution established with business funding. It had close links with Golkar, the State Intelligence Coordinating Agency (BAKIN—*Badan Koordinasi Intelijen Negara*), and a military organization called the Special Operation Service (OPSUS—*Operasi Khusus*).[33] The CSIS intellectuals were part of the nationalist bureaucrats who longed for state-led national capitalism, which would be integrated at the political level with authoritarian corporatism (Robison 1986: 134–35; 148). These four institutions were cornerstones for the formalization of economic nationalism in governmental economic policy.

The fall in the oil prices in the first half of the 1980s forced the Indonesian government to take structural adjustment measures. By 1985, the revenue collected from corporate oil taxes totaled a mere Rp. 6,338 billion (or about 57.1 percent of total revenues) (World Bank 1993b: 185), which represented a decline of about 13.5 percent from the 1981–1982 period. Coupled with rising debts and a sudden decline in economic growth, Indonesia ended its decade of oil-financed growth and abundance (Hill 2000: 16). Due to the worrying state of the Indonesian economy, "the World Bank began to press the Indonesian government to liberalize its economy and place less emphasis on [ISI]" (Chalmers and Hadiz 1997: 92). The World Bank, which had played a very important part in the policy-making networks during the first phase of the New Order period, was now growing uneasy about the state intervention mechanisms that had operated during the 1970s. The Indonesian government responded to the World Bank's concern by introducing a series of reform packages in the mid-1980s, which included the deregulation of the financial and trade sectors, the relaxation of foreign investment regulations, and the introduction of a privatization process (Robison 1997: 34). However, this reform package was not entirely successful for two reasons. The first reason was that the Indonesian government persisted "with a policy of import restrictions through more systematic and comprehensive licensing" (Booth 1998: 197). Although the Indonesian government took progressive steps in tariff reduction, foreign investments still had to include a minimum domestic equity, while foreign investors continued to be excluded in a range of sectors, particularly some of the still-lucrative import substitution areas (Robison 1990: 113). The second reason was the fact that many Indonesian domestic business groups had become increasingly comfortable with the nationalist economic policies introduced during the previous decade (Robison 1997: 35). Due to the bureaucratic capitalism that had emerged in the previous decade, it was only large conglomerates with close connections to governmental officials that were capable of making offers for corporations previously under the control of the government.

The second phase of the New Order period also saw major changes in the way the Indonesian government conducted its FEP, particularly as regards regional economic cooperation within the ASEAN framework. Starting with the ASEAN Preferential Trading Agreement (ASEAN-PTA) in 1977, the following decade saw increasing regional economic cooperation in Southeast Asia, which was evident in initiatives such as the ASEAN Industrial Joint Ventures (AIJVs), ASEAN Industrial Projects (AIPs), and ASEAN Industrial Complementation (AIC). The first discussion to initiate such cooperations began during the Fourth ASEAN Ministerial Meeting (AMM) in 1971, where General Carlos Romulo, the Foreign Minister of the Philippines at the time, pointed out how important it was for the Association to have a new sense of direction rather than being simply a tool to bridge the political divide between the major powers. As a result, a plan to create an ASEAN Common Market was submitted, and the 1970s was declared the *Decade of Development* for ASEAN. In response to General Romulo's idea, the Indonesian government agreed to get involved in an enhanced regional economic cooperation. At the same time, however, the Indonesian government remained convinced that "it would seem more realistic for the ASEAN states to proceed with a more selective approach to cooperation" (Kartadjoemena 1976: 206). With increasing public demand for a nationalist economic approach, the Indonesian government maintained that it "would like first to have a better grasp and control of the national economic life in order that the country's economic and social development could be directed toward the national objectives chosen" (Kartadjoemena 1977: 77). Given the strong influence that Indonesia had over the Association at the time, most of ASEAN's early attempts at economic cooperation failed to succeed.

Major economic liberalization began to take shape again in the third phase of the New Order period (1986–1997). The economic policies introduced during this period were more market oriented, and the private sector was given the role of achieving economic growth (Gray 2002: 3). A more significant development that occurred in Indonesian economic policy was the shift from ISI to a more export oriented approach. The Indonesian government devalued the *rupiah* in 1986 to support the national export sectors. In the following year, a reform package was introduced to further reduce import barriers, remove export licenses and other barriers, improve incentives for foreign investors, and to revive the moribund domestic share markets (Booth 1988). Although the national economy appeared rather bleak in both 1987 and 1988, the Indonesian government was able to provide a more optimistic forecast for the coming decade at the end of 1989 (Booth 1992: 23). The Indonesian government's forecast was correct. Investment values in 1994, for example, reached as much as US$39.9 billion from about US$23 billion between 1990 and 1993. On the whole, Indonesia experienced a major economic boom during this period, and this was to last until the economic crisis in 1997.

As a result of major economic reform in the mid-1980s, Indonesian pursued a more active FEP. The Indonesian government at the time was interested in enhanced economic cooperation in the Southeast Asian region, if not at the Asia-Pacific level. This indicated a major shift of interest among Indonesian FEP-makers from the traditional concentration on the Northern hemisphere to the Asian region, particularly Japan and the Asian Newly Industrializing Economies (NIEs). In Hill's (2000: 85) analysis, three rationales can explain such a shift. These were "the rapid growth of the Northeast Asian economies; the ever stronger economic complementarities between a low-wage but resource rich Indonesia alongside the resource poor, high-wage economies of Japan and the NIEs; and political-institutional changes which have gradually weakened old ties to Europe in particular." Another important factor that drove Indonesia to become more supportive of regional integration strategy (RIS) was the strengthening of regionalism in both Western Europe and North America. As a result, Australia's proposal to introduce regional trade liberalization at the Asia-Pacific level was welcomed warmly by Indonesian policymakers, and, subsequently, Indonesia became one of the APEC founders. In ASEAN, talks began on the possible development of established economic cooperation through AFTA, which was finally introduced in 1992.

To sum up, the New Order government made substantial changes to Indonesian FEP. Throughout its existence, the New Order government was committed to various forms of economic policy. From 1965 until 1974, economic liberalization measures were undertaken by the New Order government. Subsequently, from 1975 until 1985, economic nationalism became a response to the domestic business interests who had enjoyed hardly any benefits from economic liberalization. Following the stabilization period after the oil price shocks of 1981 and 1985, the New Order government once again introduced liberalization measures between 1986 and 1997. Economic growth reached its peak before the economic crisis of 1997. Since the economic crisis began the government has been blamed for the collapse of the Indonesian economy, but an open mind should be kept when analyzing the Indonesian New Order government. On the whole, since the New Order government took control, Indonesia was able to develop its economy through the implementation of a number of effective economic policies.[34] The real per capita GDP, for instance, trebled in just one generation, while poverty levels decreased (Hill 1994: 56–57). During the last phase of the Guided Democracy period, the average growth of real per capita GDP was only -0.4 percent. In contrast, the New Order government was able to increase average real GDP growth by 8.1 percent by 1995. The New Order government was also successful in reducing poverty (Hill 1994: 57). In Java alone, the poverty level was slashed from 61 percent in the mid-1960s to only 10 percent by the 1990s. In various provinces outside Java poverty was reduced from 52 percent in the mid-1960s to only 7 percent by the mid-1990s.

Contemporary Indonesian Nationalism and Foreign Economic Policy

The economic crisis in 1997 marked the fall of the New Order government. By October 1997, Indonesia was forced to seek assistance from the IMF to counteract the economic crisis.[35] However, questions regarding President Suharto's health and increasing opposition and protests from different groups within society demanding political change exacerbated further the economic deterioration of the country. Indonesia was suddenly transformed from a miracle economy, which had been heralded by many foreign economists as a development model for other developing countries, into a *melt-down* economy, dependent on various international financial institutions and donor countries for its survival (Thee Kian Wie 2001: 164). Subsequently, leadership changes saw the appointment of Bachruddin Jusuf Habibie, then Abdurrahman Wahid, Megawati Sukarnoputri, and, finally, Susilo Bambang Yudhoyono as Indonesian Presidents over a six-year period. This analysis of contemporary Indonesian nationalism and FEP is based upon these last four Presidential periods. There were two important problems that challenged the Indonesian leaders following the demise of the New Order government, namely economic recovery and the threat of national disintegration. Consequently, Indonesian FEP was directed both toward the alleviation of the economic crisis and toward protecting national unity.

Habibie Administration

Habibie was appointed the third Indonesian President following Suharto's resignation on 21 May 1998, which had been forced by the massive demonstrations that took place throughout the country. Habibie had been one of Suharto's most trusted followers throughout the existence of the New Order government. Initially, he had been appointed as the Minister for Research and Technology in 1978, a position that he held until his appointment as Vice President in March 1998. During his time as the Minister for Research and Technology, he was known as an eccentric, an arrogant *technolog* who was an advocate for notoriously expensive state-led projects that aimed to make Indonesia technologically self-sufficient. His views were criticized both within and outside Indonesia. When the news of his appointment as Vice President was broadcast in January 1998, the value of the rupiah fell drastically (Hill 2000: 280) to around Rp. 17,000 against the U.S. dollar. After assuming the Presidency, Habibie wanted to include foreign policy in his overall agenda, but could not do so owing to the short tenure of his office and the fact that the post of vice president was vacant. Regardless of such setbacks, Anwar (2000: 2), a political and foreign affairs adviser to the President, has described Habibie's three overall objectives. These were laying "the foundation for Indonesia's democratization," resolving "the East Timor issue once and for all," and securing "international assistance for Indonesian economic recovery." These three objectives were central to Indonesian foreign policy during Habibie's Presidency. In essence, these objectives were aimed at freeing Indonesia from the various foreign pressures that stood in the way of the government's attempt to achieve sustained economic recovery.

Habibie faced an immense challenge when he took the Presidency, particularly with regard to alleviating the economic crisis and trying to establish the foundations for democracy in Indonesia. By 1998, Indonesia's economic growth had contracted to an average of -15 percent, from an annual average of 7 percent per annum prior to the economic crisis. The value of the rupiah was also weakened against the US$, from Rp. 2,400 in July 1997 to an average of Rp. 16,000–Rp. 17,000, when Habibie took over (Abrash 1998: 1; Sunderlin et al. 2001: 767). The financial sector, in particular, was in a dire state with the total external debt of Indonesian private banks and businesses reaching as much as US$73 billion, while the Indonesian government owed a further US$66 billion. Moreover, unemployment, as a result of the contraction in the real sector of the economy, began to soar and inflation hit its highest level ever at about 80 percent (Abrash 1998: 1). The deepening economic crisis and the independence crisis in East Timor triggered nationalist sentiment in the country. Searching for possible scapegoats to take the blame for the economic crisis, the Indonesian authorities and media alike pointed their fingers at currency speculators (Henderson 1998: 155). The Indonesian Minister of Justice reportedly threatened that any currency speculators found conducting activities that might destabilize the country's economy would be guilty of subversion, while, at the same, a campaign of *defend the rupiah, defend the nation* was championed by the Indonesian media (Henderson 1998: 155). In economic terms, therefore, the Habibie administration faced the challenge not only of stabilizing the economy, but also regaining the confidence of foreign investors in light of heavy political instability and the possible re-emergence of economic nationalism.

The appointment of Adi Sasono, a former Islamic NGO activist, as the Minister of Co-operatives, Small, and Medium Enterprises also raised fears over the possible re-emergence of economic nationalism in Indonesia. In the past, he had developed the concept of the *Ekonomi Kerakyatan* (People's Economy), which can be defined as a participative economy, which allows fair and equal access to all members of society in the processes of production, distribution, and national consumption without sacrificing human resources and the environment to support the people (Sasono 1999).[36] In principle, the concept of the People's Economy involved activities conducted from the people, by the people, and for the prosperity of the people. Members of the business community saw People's Economy as a signal for another wave of the nationalization of foreign and ethnic Chinese capital. However, economic nationalization was not the main aim of Sasono with regard to the concept of the People's Economy. In an interview with *Asiaweek* (1998), he emphasized that the main intention of the Habibie administration was not to "nationalize [foreign-owned or ethnic-Chinese] assets, but . . . to limit the degree of ownership, which can create social tension." He further argued that 2 percent of Indonesians, most of whom were ethnic Chinese, controlled about 61 percent of the national GDP, which was not a healthy economic condition. True reform within the framework of the People's Economy, according to Sasono, would include the empowerment of the small and weak in order to create a strong middle class. Far from proposing a *racist* economic policy, Sasono's idea of the People's Economy, if implemented properly, would indeed foster not only economic stability, but also social equality for Indonesia.

During the Habibie administration, Indonesia's relations with one of its closest neighbors, Singapore, went sour despite the administration's commitment to improving relations with Indonesia's immediate neighbors (Anwar 2000: 2). The ethnic issue was once again the main theme behind the conflict between the two countries. Not only had this conflict undermined the special relationship that had been built over the years between the two countries, it also jeopardized the flow of future financial aid from Singapore to Indonesia. The conflict began with Habibie's irritation at the slow response of Singaporean leaders toward his appointment as the third Indonesian President. It seemed to indicate that the Singaporean leaders expected Habibie's tenure to be short owing to his close association with the former President Suharto. The relationship between the two countries worsened when a row between Habibie and the Singaporean leaders broke out over sensitive ethnic issues in Singapore, and in Indonesia itself.[37] In an interview with *Taiwanese China Times*, Habibie accused Singapore of discriminating against the ethnic Malays, particularly in the military (Suh 1999). The Singaporeans reacted furiously toward this accusation and were only calmed following a statement by the Indonesian Education Minister, J. Sudarsono, that President Habibie was misinformed about the level of Malay representation in the Singaporean military service. In actual fact, however, the conflict between the two countries was mainly a result of the frustration of the Indonesian elite about Singapore's overall contribution to help overcome the economic crisis in Indonesia.

Despite this major setback, Habibie's FEP was quite successful overall. Apart from his full commitment to the IMF's prescriptions,[38] the success of Habibie was also due to his ability to promote political democracy in Indonesia, which allowed the country to regain the necessary support from the international community to alleviate the economic crisis. The first move by the Habibie administration to achieve this objective was to release political prisoners taken by the New Order government and to guarantee freedom of speech for the press (Anwar 2001a: 8). The second major move of the Habibie administration to gain international support was to raise the issue of the future of East Timor. On 21 September 1999, President Habibie gave a speech before the People's Representatives Assembly (DPR—*Dewan Perwakilan Rakyat*), which revealed the President's policy on the question of East Timor (Mizuno 2003: 117–18). For Habibie, the question of East Timor, which had been a major embarrassment for Indonesia since its incorporation into the country, was particularly important to Indonesia. Habibie also believed that, by raising the question of East Timor, the international community would be more inclined to provide much needed aid and assistance to Indonesia during the economic crisis. Despite the resurgence of strong nationalistic sentiments, particularly among military officers and opposition leaders (Leifer 2000: 154), the Habibie administration continued to pursue this strategy. The third major move to secure economic support from foreign donors and international financial institutions was Habibie's intention to hold a fair and open election.[39] Finally, at the regional level, during his short tenure, Habibie managed to make close contact with Mahathir Mohammad, the Malaysian Prime Minister. As a result, the future of ASEAN regionalism, and the progress of AFTA in particular, was no longer in jeopardy despite the strained relationship between Indonesia and Singapore.

Wahid administration

Abdurrahman Wahid finally took over the presidency following the 1999 election despite the fact that his party, the National Awakening Party (PKB—*Partai Kebangkitan Bangsa*) ranked only fourth in the election poll.[40] As with Habibie, Wahid was considered eccentric, while at the same time different from Habibie in that he was considered a more moderate Islamic leader and a stronger supporter of democracy and pluralism. Shortly after his appointment as the head of state, President Wahid set out the main themes of his FEP, which included the promotion of foreign investment and free market reforms (Seymond 1999). This was President Wahid's nationalist appeal to build a stronger Indonesia in the face of the economic crisis. In addition, President Wahid also called for closer ties with Japan, China, and the member countries of ASEAN. The market reacted positively to the appointment of Wahid as the leader of Indonesia. The Jakarta Stock Exchange (JSE), for example, experienced a resurgence with a peak of US$63.7 billion after the news of Wahid's appointment as the new President was broadcast (Smith 2001b: 7). Moreover, the country achieved substantial growth of 0.1 percent by the end of 1999 from -13.2 percent in the previous year, while the rupiah was stabilized at between Rp. 7,800 to Rp. 8,000 to the dollar (refer to table 4.2).

Table 4.2.
Annual Economic Indicators, 1996–2000

	1996	1997	1998	1999	2000
GDP at market prices (Rp. bn)	532.6	625.5	1002.3	1119.4	1308.6
GDP (US$ bn)	0.2	0.2	0.1	0.1	0.2
Real GDP growth (%)	8.0	4.5	-13.2	0.1	4.8
Consumer price inflation (avg. %)	7.0	6.2	58.4	20.5	3.7
Population (m)	196.8	199.9	204.4	209.3	212.6
Exports of goods fob (US$ m)	50,188	56,298	50,371	51,424	65,507
Imports of goods fob (US$ m)	44,240	46,223	31,942	30,598	41,001
Current account balance (US$ m)	-7,663	-4,889	4,096	5,785	7,072
Foreign exchange reserves excl. gold (US$ m)	18,251	16,587	22,713	26,445	22,458
Total external debt (US$ m)	128.9	136.2	147.5	142.5	143.8
Debt service ration, paid (%)	36.8	30.0	33.2	32.6	25.3
Exchange rate (avg) Rp:US$	**2,342.3**	**2,909.4**	**10,013.6**	**7,855.2**	**8421.8**

Source: Economist Intelligence Unit (2001: 5)

Another major FEP theme in the Wahid administration was a commitment to fully support the IMF rescue loan package, which was linked with the IMF LoI. The disbursement from the IMF was important because it could be "taken as a measure of market confidence in the progress of economic reform. Therefore, . . . the credibility of Indonesian economic reforms [was] reflected in the successful and consistent implementation of the IMF program" (Feridhanusetyawan 2003: 238). The first LoI agreed between the Wahid administration and the IMF was signed on the 20 January 2000. This required the Indonesian government to achieve price stability in the market, to push for various restructuring measures including those related to corporate and banking policies, to rebuild key public institutions, to implement economic and social policies, and, finally, to manage natural resources.[41] However, the IMF did not enjoy a close relationship with the Wahid administration for long (Sadli 2003). The Indonesian government missed many deadlines and its commitment toward the agreed LoI was questioned (Feridhanusetyawan 2003: 238). The Wahid administration was also unable to maintain a close relationship with other international financial institutions and foreign donors (Sadli 2003: 190–93). The World Bank, the ADB, and the Japanese government, for example, have traditionally provided major development aid for the Indonesian government. However, during the Wahid administration, the World Bank scaled down Indonesia's rating from a "high case" to a "low (or base) case," which led to the incomplete disbursement of the much needed financial aid for economic recovery. These institutions claimed that they were dissatisfied over the progress of the Wahid administration while in power (Sadli 2003: 190–91). They were particularly unhappy with the Wahid administration's handling of the decentralization process (i.e., Regional Autonomy Law), regarding the amount of freedom given to local authorities regarding taxes and expenditure in their districts, which might damage central government balances. President Wahid is often cited as having criticized these international financial institutions for helping his political opposition by delaying the disbursement of the loans.[42] Therefore, throughout its short existence, the Wahid administration failed to create a suitable environment for the reform packages offered by these international financial institutions.

Despite unstable relationships with some foreign donors, the overall FEP of the Wahid administration did encourage foreign investments and private sector growth in the country, which was a direct reflection of the administration's commitment to alleviating the economic crisis. Although the Foreign Capital Investment Law of 1967, which gave substantial incentives to foreign investors (i.e., tax holidays, etc.), was still in effect as the basis for foreign investment in the country, the Wahid administration had amended the law to suit the overall objective of its FEP. Among other things, one major amendment was to remove unnecessary bureaucratic procedures that were considered problematic by foreign investors. In the past, for example, apart from dealing with the BKPM, foreign investors were also required to work closely with the relevant technical departments, such as the Ministry of Finance (MoF), the Directorate General of Custom and Excise, the Ministry of Justice (MoJ), and so on.[43] The new investment regulations, however, meant that foreign investors could deal directly with BKPM. In addition, the Wahid administration also speeded up the Initial Investment Approval (IIA), which had previously taken a few months, to a maximum period of fifteen working days. Nearly all industries were reopened, except for those industries stipulated in the Presidential Decree No. 96/2000, which were open to investment under certain conditions. The sectors that remained absolutely closed included mining and fishing, industry and trading, communications, and the energy sectors.[44]

In order to implement an FEP that was accommodating to foreign investment, President Wahid attempted to make significant changes to the overall conduct of Indonesian foreign policy. Internally, a radical change was made in the Ministry of Foreign Affairs (MFA) and Dr. Alwi Shihab.[45] an outsider to the MFA bureaucracy, was chosen as the Foreign Minister. Externally, inspired more by "Sukarno nationalism and high profile foreign policy than by Suharto's low profile" (Anwar 2003: 77), President Wahid shifted the overall Indonesian foreign policy by playing the *Asia Card*, in an attempt at lessening Indonesia's dependence on the West (Smith 2000b: 498). Apart from that, President Wahid also expressed his desire for a more international outlook or *ecumenical* foreign policy. This international outlook with regard to foreign policy was evident through his frequent travel abroad. The prime motive behind his policy was to provide the international community with comprehensive information regarding the real situation in Indonesia. Through this policy, the Wahid administration hoped that they would be able to regain the confidence of international investors. In a speech at a conference marking Indonesian National Press Day in Jakarta, Dr. Shihab (2000) reiterated President Wahid's foreign policy and maintained that Indonesian foreign policy would be geared to the economic situation, and to the realities of globalization and interdependence.

President Wahid's first foreign visit was made shortly after his appointment as Indonesian President. He visited Indonesia's neighboring countries, including Singapore, Cambodia, and Myanmar on 6, 7, and 8 November respectively. The visit to Singapore was made for two reasons. The first reason was to restore the old bilateral relations that had been strained during the Habibie Presidency. The second reason was to persuade Indonesian business people who had transferred their wealth to Singapore during the economic crisis to return to Indonesia. Within four months of his Presidency, President Wahid visited nearly twenty-six countries, which made him the Indonesian head of the state who had conducted the most foreign visits within such a short space of time (Smith 2000b: 505). Throughout this time, he gave voice to numerous controversial ideas that were often unrealistic or too difficult to implement. For example, following his visits to China and India in late 1999 and early 2000 respectively, Wahid proposed establishing a triangular relationship between Indonesia, China, and India, aimed at lessening their dependence upon the West. However, skeptics have commented that although such a proposal is interesting, it is also challenging as a result of the bilateral problems that still exist between India and China (Anwar 2000: 5). Aside from that, President Wahid also proposed a West Pacific Forum, which would include Indonesia, Australia, New Zealand, Papua New Guinea, and East Timor (Anwar 2003: 78). Not only were these proposals too ambitious, costly, and potentially ineffectual, such new fora would also have undermined ASEAN and its recent economic regionalism attempt, AFTA.

On the surface, President Wahid implemented quite controversial foreign policies. Some scholars, such as Smith (2000b) and Anwar (2000), however, are

skeptical, and suggest that Indonesian foreign policy during the Wahid administration was far more orthodox than others have indicated. Although the President
was able to gain enormous support from the international community for Indonesia's efforts at national integration, Indonesian foreign policy during the Wahid administration remained quite conventional and its main ideas were similar
to the foreign policy conducted by the New Order government (Smith 2000b:
523).[46] Although President Wahid's frequent travels were quite successful during the early stages of his administration, most of his later foreign visits were
ineffective (Anwar 2000: 4–5). Furthermore, Anwar indicates three main reasons for the failure of President Wahid's foreign policy. Firstly, with mounting
domestic problems, President Wahid's frequent travels abroad led to conditions
of lawlessness and lack of governance in the country. Secondly, it was illogical
for Indonesia to conduct an ecumenical foreign policy when the country needed
to focus on its immediate geo-strategic interests. Thirdly, President Wahid had
to face allegations that pointed to his involvement in numerous scandals, which
undermined the authority of his leadership in the government, MPR, and DPR.
Moreover, it should be added that President Wahid's insistence on the *Asia Card*
was overly ambitious. Economically, Indonesia was still dependent upon the
West for financial assistance and had been even before the economic crisis. As a
result, Indonesia would hardly benefit by conducting an FEP that was hostile
toward the West.

The Wahid administration finally came to an end because of the opposition
leaders' irritation over the inconsistency that the President had shown as leader
of the country. It was decided through a vote in the Parliament that the President
should step down,[47] and Megawati was sworn in to become the fifth Indonesian
President on 23 July 2001. As with her predecessors, the Megawati administration inherited the challenges of maintaining the country's integration, alleviating
the economic crisis, and ensuring long-term political stability in the country. Her
policy with regard to national integration was coherent and comprehensive. In
this context, she insisted that national unity should be placed as a priority in her
national agenda. As with her father, Sukarno, President Megawati has also
known as a staunch nationalist who was reluctant to jeopardize the current geographical existence of the country by allowing any separatist movements within
the country. The Megawati administration had been particularly relieved by the
fact that its policy of national integration was fully supported by the world's
major powers, particularly the United States. The United States, under the Clinton administration, had initially suspended its military aid to Indonesia due to
the human rights violations that took place under the New Order government.
Recently, however, both sides have tried for reconciliation and have resumed
their military relations. This reconciliation was demonstrated by President Megawati's visit to the United States shortly after the September 11th tragedy,
which made her the first head of the state to visit the United States after the
event. The Bush administration expressed its wish "to enlist Indonesia [as the]
host to the world's largest Muslim population in the fight against terrorism"

(Gershman 2001: 1).[48] However, as Gershman points out, U.S. support of an integrated Indonesia might undermine the democratization process in Indonesia because the Megawati administration is now capable of implementing stern, or even violent measures, to maintain the integration of the country.

Megawati Administration

Figure 4.2.
Three Concentric Circles of Indonesian Foreign Policy

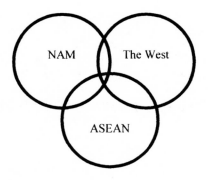

Source: Smith (2000a: 18)

In terms of improving economic conditions, Megawati appears to have put the appropriate FEP in place. One key feature of the Megawati administration's overall foreign policy has been a return to the traditional *concentric circle* formula (refer to figure 4.2), which was abandoned by the Wahid administration that favored instead the ecumenical approach to foreign policy (Anwar 2003: 78). This formula has identified ASEAN as the highest priority of Indonesian foreign policy.[49] Accordingly, President Megawati appointed Dr. Hasan Wirayuda as Foreign Minister, a senior career diplomat with vast experience of diplomacy who had served in the MFA since the mid-1970s. Soon after taking over from Dr. Shihab, the new Foreign Minister stated that the main Indonesian foreign policy was to restore relationships with neighboring countries, thus, once again, emphasizing the importance of ASEAN. Dr. Wirayuda's first step was to visit Singapore to conclude some major economic discussions for further bilateral cooperation (Manning 2001: 2). Afterwards, President Megawati visited all nine ASEAN countries to reassure regional leaders that she could handle Indonesia's problems as well as re-establish strong relationships with other ASEAN countries. Therefore, the overall foreign policy of the Megawati administration was, and is, moderate and very much in line with that of the New Order government.

Indonesia's return to the concentric circle foreign policy formula dismissed speculation that Indonesia would abandon AFTA and other ASEAN regional economic integration initiatives. During her speech at the inaugural meeting of the ASEAN Business Advisory Council (ABAC), in Jakarta on 10 April 2003, President Megawati pointed out that much could be gained from enhanced economic cooperation in the region. Specifically, she stressed that each ASEAN country should outline their own potential and realize these potentials by teaming up with other ASEAN countries.[50] In the same speech, President Megawati also called upon other ASEAN countries to expand their market to include the member countries of the Non-Aligned Movement (NAM). Later on in the year, the Indonesian MFA also announced some adjustments made to the concentric circle formula of Indonesian foreign policy. ASEAN and the Western countries remain within the first and the third circles of Indonesian foreign policy overall. Major adjustments, however, have been made to the second circle, which indicates that Indonesia will concentrate its foreign policy on the member countries of the Pacific Island Forums (PIFs), the Southwest Pacific Dialogue, and the Tripartite Consultation between Indonesia, Australia, and Timor Leste, and the three close economic partners of Indonesia, which include Japan, China, and South Korea.[51] The adjustments made to the concentric formula indicate Megawati's realization of the growing need to strengthen regional economic cooperation with the countries of the Southwest Pacific and Northeast Asia. In this way Indonesian FEP is decided according to the overall foreign policy of the country.

In order to fulfill her overall FEP objectives, President Megawati appointed a number of economic experts in her cabinet. The appointments of Prof. D. Kundjorojakti as the Coordinating Economic Minister and Dr. Boediono as the Minister of Finance were central to the process of economic recovery due to their impeccable credentials in the international arena. Their international reputations will be useful in helping to reactivate the suspended IMF/World Bank loans of US$400 million, which were suspended during the Wahid administration. Equally important for political stability in the country was the appointment of Dr. H. Haz as the Vice President and the well-respected S. B. Yudhoyono as the Coordinating Minister of Political and Security Affairs. The appointment of these two individuals will limit possible political maneuvering from both Islamic political groups and the military.[52] In sum, Megawati achieved a "balance between political representation and professional expertise [within] the new cabinet" (Manning 2001: 2). The economic and political team within Megawati's cabinet has been a positive sign for economic recovery. To date, although economic growth has been lower than in 2000 and 2001 (refer to table 4.2 and table 4.3), the economy is expected to grow at a moderate level in subsequent years.

Although the foreign press has often described Megawati's cabinet as the *dream team* (Sadli 2003: 185), the economy of Indonesia has remained unstable.

As was the case with President Wahid, the market reacted positively when the news of Megawati's Presidency was broadcast. At the time, the rupiah was impressively strengthened at around Rp. 8,500 to the U.S. dollar from around Rp. 11,500 during the last days of President Wahid's office. However, the rupiah weakened again by the end of 2002 at around Rp. 8,940 against the U.S. dollar, and only appreciated again by the beginning of 2003 to Rp. 8,210 (Economist Intelligence Unit 2003: 10). Meanwhile, Indonesia also experienced major problems with foreign investments. Although investments improved in the second and third quarters of 2002, they remained about 20 percent below the pre-crisis level (Waslin 2003: 10). In a press release issued in February 2003, the BKPM Chairman, T. Teomion, made a statement about the current investment performance of Indonesia, and added that the approved foreign and domestic investment levels for the year 2003 will be the lowest since the economic crisis began in 1997.[53]

Table 4.3.
Indonesian Economic Indicators during Megawati's Presidency

Item	2001	2002	2003*
GDP growth	3.3	3.0	3.6
Gross domestic investment/GDP	17.0	17.0	17.0
Gross domestic savings/GDP	25.5	23.0	21.0
Inflation rate (consumer price index)	11.5	13.1	7.7
Money supply (M2) growth	17.5	18	18
Fiscal balance GDP**	-2.3	-2.5	-0.5
Merchandise export growth	-9.8	10.5	8.0
Merchandise import growth	-12.2	10	10
Current account balance/GDP	**3.1**	**1.5**	**0.7**

Notes: *   Expected
           **   For 1999, the ratio of the fiscal balance relates to 1 April 31 March. For 2000, the ratio is estimated on an annual basis for 1 April-31 December. Thereafter, the ratio refers to calendar year data.
Source: Asian Development Bank (ADB) (2002).

The main obstacles to investment in Indonesia were international as much as domestic. At the international level, aggressive U.S. foreign policy toward Afghanistan and Iraq has had a damaging effect on the Indonesian economy. These two events stimulated threats and demonstrations against the United States and its allies in Indonesia (Anwar 2003: 75). At the domestic level, issues such as regional security, law enforcement, labor market problems, the overlapping responsibilities of central and provincial government, regulatory burdens, and distortions in the tax system remain major problems to be confronted by potential investors in Indonesia (Bappenas 2003).[54] In response to gloomy international economic conditions and domestic economic uncertainty, the Megawati administration declared the year 2003 as *Indonesian Investment Year*. During the launching of the program in early 2003, President Megawati promised that her administration would create a favorable climate for investment and would continue to introduce reforms in various sectors, particularly the fiscal and economic sectors (Sulistyowati 2003). This program was hoped to trigger more conducive conditions for the recovery of the national economy. Among other issues, improvements in the year 2003 and subsequent years will include a revision of the investment laws, tightened security, as well as an attempt to coordinate the regulations of the central and provincial governments.

Yudhoyono Administration

Dr. Susilo Bambang Yudhoyono (also referred to SBY), a retired army general, is the first Indonesian President that has been directly elected by the voters throughout the Indonesian history. He secured the majority of votes during two rounds of presidential elections, defeated his closest rival, Megawati Sukarnoputri. In the first round of presidential election, held on 5 July 2004, Yudhoyono gained 33 percent of votes, less than most had anticipated. Meanwhile, his closest rival, Megawati and (ret) General Wiranto, a former Chief of Armed Forces, only secured 26 percent and 22 percent of total votes respectively. Unlike his closest rivals, Yudhoyono did not belong to a well-established political party. Megawati's PDI-P and Wiranto's Golkar are two political parties that have significant influences in outlying provinces throughout Indonesia. Prior to the election process, Yudhoyono, who previously held the position of Coordinating Minister of Political and Security Affairs under the Megawati's administration, agreed to join a newly established party of Democratic Party. The second round of Presidential election was carried on 20 September 2004 and saw Yudhoyono secured an impressive 60.62 percent vote that made him the sixth Indonesian President. Yudhoyono was finally sworn in as the new President on 20 October 2004.

Several economic problems emerged during the early part of Yudhoyono administration. This first related to the tsunami that hit the war-torn province of Aceh and other parts of South Asia on 26 December 2004. This natural disaster left Aceh in ruin and thousands to die, which forced the Indonesian government to allocate more development assistance to rebuild this war-torn province. Fortunately, the tsunami became an international spotlight and the President was able to turn the situation around to his political advantage. Prior to the tsunami, there were signs of mounting public anxiety with the slow pace of reform. However, Yudhoyono's handling of the tsunami has largely met public's expectation (Economist Intelligence Unit 2005b: 1–2). Various economic problems and the natural disaster that hit Aceh forced the Indonesian government to focus their economic policy at improving investment climate and to develop the country's infrastructure. As a result, an Infrastructure Summit was held in January 2005, which led to the approval of 91 infrastructure projects worth an estimated of US$2.2 billion.

A more serious economic problem that hit the Yudhoyono administration was the international energy crisis during second half of 2005. The increasingly limited international oil supply, and the emergence of Hurricane Katrina that hit the Southern parts of the United States, have led the raise of oil prices all over the world from US$24/barrel to US$56.6/barrel. The Indonesian government was forced to revise its 2005 state's budget (APBN—*Anggaran Pendapatan Belanja Negara*), and no longer capable of subsidizing its oil sector. The increase in oil prices also meant that the government should allocate Rp. 113.7 trillion, or about one-fourth of its overall budget, for oil subsidy. The Indonesian government was, indeed, faced with a dilemma. On the one hand, if it was to proceed with its oil subsidy scheme, the Indonesian government would have to allow a Rp 46.3 trillion deficit in its state budget. On the other hand, the government was also risked of facing mounted demonstration from various elements within the society rejecting the government's policy of raising the oil prices. Despite this, the Indonesian government proceeded with its plan to raise the oil prices as much as 80 percent by 1st October 2005. At the time when this part of the book was written, it was still uncertain how well the Yudhoyono administration would cope with mounted public pressures.

Figure 4.3.
Yudhoyono Approval Ratings

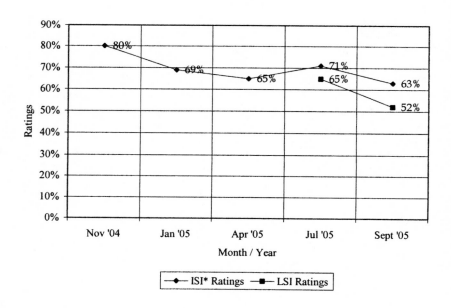

Note: * Indonesian Survey Institute (ISI)
Source: *Jakarta Post* (2005)

In terms of his leadership so far, Yudhoyono seems to have been providing a more concrete direction in comparison to other post-crisis leaders. Unlike Wahid that had experimented with a mix between liberal Islam and socialism, and Megawati who had shown ambivalence toward any political ideologies, Yudhoyono's strong commitment to neo-liberalism has made him a more decisive leader in comparison with his predecessors. A year after his appointment as the Indonesian leader, Yudhoyono still maintains his popular support. This is despite a number of mounted domestic problems that have previously been highlighted above. A survey carried out by the Indonesian Survey Circle (LSI—*Lingkaran Survey Indonesia*) among 1,000 respondents on October 2005, for example, showed that 52.4 percent of these respondents still expressed support for Yudhoyono's administration (refer to figure 4.3).[55] Although he lost about 9 percent of support since the presidential election run-off a year before, his ability to maintain popular support throughout 2005 was partly due to his ability to generate a sense of concrete direction in Indonesian political and economic lives.

Moreover, unlike his predecessors who were forced to fill in their cabinets with individuals from various different political backgrounds, Yudhoyono was able to appoint a number of influential individuals that share similar neo-liberal views to his. The appointment of Aburizal Bakrie, an industrialist tycoon and a former Head of the Indonesian Chambers of Commerce (KADIN—*Kamar Dagang dan Industri Indonesia*), as the Coordinating Minister of Economy highlights the increasing importance of business community for Yudhoyono's administration.[56] Moreover, Yudhoyono also appointed Dr. Mari E. Pangestu and Dr. Sri Mulyani Indrawati, both are well-known economists and strong neo-liberal advocates, as the Minister of Trade and Head of National Development Planning Agency (Bappenas—*Badan Perencanaan Pembangunan Nasional*) respectively. The appointment of Dr. Pangestu and Dr. Indrawati, in particular, has been crucial in determining the country's overall support toward open economy and trade liberalization.

Yudhoyono's conviction toward neo-liberalism has been consistent since he was first elected as the representative of the Democratic Party to take part in the presidential election. During his election campaign, for example, Yudhoyono ensured his supporters that the promotion of foreign investment would make a positive contribution toward job creation in the country (Economist Intelligence Unit 2005a: 1). Subsequently, in order to stress his strong commitment toward neo-liberalism, President Yudhoyono also stated during his inaugural speech that:

> My administration will stimulate the economy in order to achieve higher economic growth, which can absorb more employment and help alleviate poverty;

My administration will continue to adopt and implement open economic
policies, in order to integrate the economy with regional and international
economies. . . .

My administration will encourage more investors to build our infrastruc-
tures;

My administration will actively launch an anti-corruption program, which,
I, myself, will lead;

My administration will intensify constructive dialog with economic actors,
especially our business community, including investors, whom I really expect
to be the engine of our economy.[57]

All the points stated signify neo-liberal elements of Yudhoyono's leadership,
which he believes to have been crucial policy options for Indonesia in dealing
with mounting domestic problems.

One important element to support his neo-liberal policy was the strengthening Indonesia's relationship with the United States, a move which was welcomed by the Indonesian armed forces. Previously, as mentioned earlier, Indonesia's relationship with the United States went sour following the violent
incidence that took place in East Timor in 1999, as well as the murder of American teachers in Papua in 2002 (Economist Intelligence Unit 2005c: 14). The
United States had actually embargoed the selling of its weaponry to the Indonesian armed forces even after the East Timor in 1999. However, the 9/11 incident
also pushed the Bush administration to reconsider its stance toward the U.S.-
Indonesia relationship, particularly since Indonesia was capable of playing a key
role in the *War against Terrorism* in Southeast Asia. Elsewhere, Yudhoyono
(2005a) also stated that "there has been an incredibly deep emotional connection
between America and Indonesia since the tsunami" that stroke Aceh, and other
areas in South and Southeast Asia on December 2004.

Another important element of Yudhoyono's neo-liberal agenda was the active and aggressive participation of Indonesia in bilateralism, regionalism, and
multilateralism. To start with, although Indonesia was considered slow in concluding any bilateral free trade agreements (BFTA) in comparison to other key
Southeast Asian countries, the country had begun a number of BFTA negotiations with its major trading partners. The first BFTA to emerge was with China
owing to the initiation of the early phase of the ASEAN-China Free Trade
Agreement (ACFTA), with the implementation of the Early Harvest Program
(EHP), in January 2004. However, Yudhoyono's administration responsible for
the first Indonesia's *country-to-country* BFTA with the commencement of the
joint study groups (JSGs) and negotiations to conclude the Indonesia-Japan
Economic Partnership Agreement (IJEPA) since early 2005. Subsequently, on
April 2005, Indonesia's major trading partners, such as the United States, Australia, and even the European Free Trade Association (EFTA), had expressed
their interests to begin negotiations with the former. The Indonesian government
had finally agreed to sign a Trade and Investment Framework Agreement
(TIFA), an agreement for the commencement of the BFTA negotiation between
the two countries, with Australia on 29 September 2005.[58]

At the regional level, President Yudhoyono's arrival coincided with half-way regional efforts to strengthen the cooperation among Southeast Asian countries through the idea of the ASEAN Community (Bandoro 2005). As a keen supporter of democracy, President Yudhoyono reiterated the importance of ASEAN to be more open *vis-à-vis* the people of Southeast Asia, a call which has also been made by various civil society groups in Southeast Asia.[59] In his lecture at the ASEAN Secretariat in commemoration of the thirty-eighth anniversary of the Association, on 8 August 2005, Yudhoyono (2005b) stated that:

> The problem [with ASEAN] is not that [this Association] is not useful to the lives of the peoples of Southeast Asia—because it is. It has, in fact, made a great deal of difference in terms of the peace and the relative prosperity that they enjoy. The problem is that we still can do better in ensuring greater participation of the regional peoples in the decisions of ASEAN. (ASEAN Secretariat 2005b)

In essence, Yudhoyono convinced that democracy was an important element if ASEAN was to strengthen its integration process in the future.

Indeed, the Yudhoyono administration was generally supportive toward any forms of regionalism that Indonesia was involved in, at both macro (i.e., ASEAN) and meso (i.e., APEC) levels, as long as these regional groupings remained as open as possible to international trade (multilateralism). An open regionalism is a complementary to the ideological approach that was subscribed by the Indonesian leader. At the ASEAN level, Indonesia was anxious in undertaking aggressive liberalization measures to increase intra-ASEAN trade, a policy option that was not easily pursued by other previous Indonesian governments. At the thirty-seventh ASEAN Economic Ministerial Meeting (AEM), in Laos, on 28–29 September 2005, for example, Indonesia and other main ASEAN countries agreed to discuss ways to simplify the existing tariff classifications under the Common Effective Preferential Tariff (CEPT) mechanism of AFTA. At that meeting, Ong Keng Yong, the ASEAN Secretary General, stated that this development could lead to an increase in intra-ASEAN trade from US$180 billion, or around 23 percent, to US$300 billion, or about 35 percent within the next five years (Webb 2005).

Overall Contemporary Indonesian FEP

In sum, the collapse of the Indonesian economy in 1997 brought significant changes in the way that nationalism and FEP were integrated by the state. The conventional approach of implementing economic nationalism was no longer applicable. Faced with an ever-increasing dependency on various international financial institutions and other foreign donors, all the post-economic crisis Indonesian governments were forced to follow stringent measures to secure loans from these international institutions. The agreements made between these Indonesian governments and the IMF through the signing of LoI, in particular, have been particularly demanding. However, there have also been debates among the Indonesian political elite as to whether Indonesia should continue its relationship with the IMF, which officially expired of the end of 2003 (Economist Intelligence Unit 2003: 22). On the one hand, the Indonesian political elite is concerned that the Indonesian government will continue to lose its sovereignty by following IMF measures. On the other hand, the presence of the IMF has, indeed, improved the macroeconomic condition of Indonesia. Although the final outcomes have yet to be seen, the Indonesian public has shown growing dissatisfaction toward the IMF's stringent conditions. As regards Indonesian FEP in ASEAN, the shift of leadership from Wahid to Megawati allowed Indonesia to return to its more traditional focus on its immediate neighbors. As a result, Indonesia remains committed to the progress of ASEAN economic regionalism, particularly AFTA. After all, it has always been in the interests of Indonesia to put ASEAN at the cornerstone of its overall foreign policy.

Conclusion

This chapter has dealt with two fundamental issues, namely Indonesian nationalism and FEP. It is clear that, from crisis to crisis, and from government to government, nationalism has played and still plays a major role in shaping Indonesian FEP. The first section of the chapter provided a detailed analysis of Indonesian nationalism and FEP during the post-independence period. This historical analysis is crucial because it allows for greater understanding of policymakers' attitudes when making certain political decisions (Weinstein 1976: 362). During the Sukarno administration, in particular, nationalist doctrine was the major determinant of Indonesia's hostile FEP. The large-scale expropriation of Dutch and ethnic Chinese capital was conducted to promote indigenous capitalists. The demise of the Old Order government led to an economic deterioration that forced the country to seek assistance from various international financial institutions. The subsequent Indonesian government, led by Suharto, did not use economic nationalism until the increase in oil prices in 1974. Another economic adjustment was needed after the sudden collapse of the oil price in 1985. In response, the New Order government reacted wisely by allowing trade liberalization to take place, which helped to create an economic boom afterwards. In the early 1990s, Indonesia once again had a more active FEP. International relations were diversified and economic cooperation at the regional level was strengthened.

The sudden emergence of the economic crisis in 1997 brought significant changes to the Indonesian government's FEP. Indonesia was once again forced to seek assistance from both the IMF and the World Bank. Fear of reawakened economic nationalism grew. However, despite their nationalistic ideals, Indonesian policymakers were no longer able to impose protectionist measures due to the IMF's stiff conditions for economic recovery, which demanded the removal of trade and investment barriers (Feridhanustyawan 2003: 236). At the regional level, Indonesia's relations with its immediate neighbors were at a low point. The economic crisis stimulated debate on the future relevance of ASEAN (Tay and Estanislao 2000). During the Habibie administration, Indonesian policy-makers were frustrated by the lack of assistance provided by the Association during the crisis. As a result, friction emerged between Indonesia and its immediate neighbors, particularly Singapore. Indonesia's relations with its neighbors improved following the change of leadership from Habibie to Wahid. However, questions arose as to whether President Wahid's ecumenical foreign policy would undermine the existence of ASEAN and attempts for regional economic integration. It was only during the Megawati administration that Indonesia returned to its concentric circle formula, which redirected Indonesian FEP toward the member countries of ASEAN.

Notes

1. In November 1946, under the Linggarjati Agreement, Indonesian leaders and Dutch representatives agreed on the formation of RUSI with the Dutch crown as the head of state, following the Netherlands' recognition of the Republic of Indonesia's authority in Java, Sumatra, and Madura. Initially, however, Sukarno and Mohammad Hatta had proclaimed Indonesia's independence on 17 August 1945, but the Dutch were reluctant to recognise Indonesia as an independent state at the time. As a result, major conflicts between Indonesia and the Dutch broke out from the time Indonesian leaders proclaimed their country's independence until the signing of the Hague Agreement in November 1949. Soon after the signing of the Hague Agreement, Indonesia received *de jure* and *de facto* recognition from the following countries: Afghanistan, Burma, Egypt, Iraq, Lebanon, Saudi Arabia, Syria, Yemen (*de jure*), Australia, Britain, the Republic of China, India, the Netherlands, Pakistan, the Philippines, and the United States (*de facto*). On 17 August 1950 RUSI was transformed into a unitary state, and is presently known as the Republic of Indonesia.

2. As according to Smith (2001b: 80), the name Indonesia derives from the Greek word *Indos Nesos*, which simply means Indian islands, and gained popular usage among nationalists for its non-colonial etymology

3. Thailand, which was never colonised, is the exception.

4. Indonesia was previously known as the Dutch East Indies. The name Indonesia gained popularity in the early 1900s and became the official name of the country following the Youth Pledge of 1928, which promoted Indonesian national identity.

5. However, Glassburner (1971: 3) also notes that the Indonesian economy during the Japanese occupation was even more inward-looking and economic growth was further inhibited.

6. As quoted in Linblad (2002: 3).

7. The name *Benteng* literally means fortification.

8. The Economic Urgency program was later known as the *Sumitro Plan*.

9. Despite its widespread use in the late 1950s and early 1960s, the Guided Democracy concept had actually been developed by Sukarno in the early twentieth century when Indonesia was struggling to break free from colonial domination. The concept was referred to in a thesis that Sukarno wrote in 1926 concerning the possibility of cooperation between nationalism, Islam, and Marxism (Agung 1973: 283), which later became the basic principle of the Guided Democracy concept.

10. The term *musyawarah* is largely associated with the notion of consensus within a *mufakat*, or a meeting. As Hill (1994: 280) notes, the concept of *musyawarah* signifies "the recognition of consultation among all household heads before community decisions were made." These social forms continue to be used to this day.

11. The Asia-Africa Conference was held in Bandung in April 1955 and attracted delegates from twenty-four nations. Some prominent world leaders, such as Chou En-Lai, Nehru, and Nasser, also attended the Conference.

12. The formalization of the Guided Economy system was initiated through other nationalistic economic policies. One economic policy that stood out was the Nationalization Bill of 1958, which ended Dutch control over the modern sector of the Indonesian economy (Thomas and Panglaykim 1973: 56). The anti-Dutch boycott, however, had officially begun in October 1957, and resulted in the confiscation of some 246 Dutch private investments.

13. The socialist approach in the Guided Economy system, however, was not particularly a result of Indonesia's political drift toward the Left. Indonesia's fervent opposition to liberal capitalism was stipulated in the country's constitution of 1945, which stated that "the economy shall be organised as a common endeavour based on the principle of the family system."

14. The Bunker Plan was named after the U.S. diplomat Ellsworth Bunker, who proposed that the Netherlands give up West Irian to the UN administration, and a plebiscite held to decide the future of the territory. The transfer of West Irian from the Netherlands to the Indonesian government formally took place on 15 August 1962.

15. The Crush Malaysia campaign was a result of Sukarno's irritation over the continued existence of colonialism in the Southeast Asian region. Some scholars, such as Reinhardt (1971: 129) and Gordon (1966), argue that the confrontation with Malaysia was an implementation of the long-standing expansionist sentiment held by many Indonesian nationalist leaders. The validity of this argument was given weight by one of the Indonesian leaders, Yamin (1959: 131–32), who maintained that a greater Indonesia would include the Malayan peninsula within the projected nation. On the whole, however, Malayan independence was seen by most of the Indonesian elite as an "alien-inspired polity designed to perpetuate colonial economic and military interests in Southeast Asia which, by their nature, posed a threat to the viability and regional role of Indonesia" (Leifer 1983: 75).

16. Maphilindo, however, was not the first regional organization in the Southeast Asian region. In 1955 the United States initiated a military pact of eight nations, the Southeast Asian Treaty Organization (SEATO), to check the Communist expansion in the Asia and Pacific region. This grouping involved Great Britain, the Philippines, France, Thailand, Pakistan, Australia, New Zealand, and the United States. Subsequently, in 1961, another regional organization, the Association of Southeast Asia (ASA) was established between Malaysia, the Philippines, and Thailand. This organization, however, became defunct following the Sabah conflict that emerged between Malaysia and the Philippines.

17. Nekolim was a term first coined by General Achmad Yani.

18. The coup began on 30 September 1965 with the arrest and execution of six leading generals. The coup was blamed on the PKI, which led to the killing of 500,000 members of the PKI in the following next month (Smith 2001b: 77). Some scholars, such as Challis (2001: 82), argue that the coup was a subversive attempt sponsored by the Central Intelligence Agency (CIA), which has been very active in conducting its operation to remove President Sukarno since August 1965. To date, however, the circumstances surrounding the coup remain unclear.

19. *Dwi fungsi*, or dual function, is the Indonesian army's main doctrine that legitimises the military's involvement in political and social affairs. General Nasution was the first to introduce this doctrine through his "Middle Way" speech in November 1958. Although the dual function doctrine was implemented from the 1960s onward, it was not made law until 1982.

20. Golkar was first established in October 1964.

21. Adam Malik initially served as Indonesian Ambassador to Moscow during the Sukarno administration. He was a well-known politician from the small but influential Murba party. As Anwar (1994: 35) observes, the "appointment of Malik, who had close links with the Soviet Union was probably partly to convince the international community, especially the non-aligned countries, that despite the massacre of communists, Indonesia was not about to enter the American camp," thus confirming Indonesia's continued commitment to a free and active foreign policy.

22. Also known as *Sultan Hamengkubuwono IX*. The Sultan had previously held various important positions during the Sukarno administration and had continuously identified with the banned Indonesian Socialist Party (PSI—*Partai Sosialis Indonesia*). He was also largely responsible for the rescheduling of Indonesia's foreign debt following his appointment as Economic Minister.

23. West Germany later offered funds of US$7.5 million, the Netherlands US$18 million, and Singapore US$ 32.7 million in aid.

24. IGGI membership consisted of Australia, Belgium, Great Britain, Canada, France, Germany, Italy, Japan, the Netherlands, New Zealand, Switzerland, and the United States. IGGI was later transformed into the Consultative Group on Indonesia (CGI) in March 1992 as a result of Indonesia's rejection of continued Dutch leadership and membership of the group.

25. Indonesia is one of the world's major oil producers and a member of the Organization of Petroleum Exporting Countries (OPEC)

26. See Chapter 3 for definitions of these terms.

27. The law, however, did not apply to several crucial sectors, including the oil, gas, banking, insurance, and leasing sectors.

28. This group of economists included Prof. Sumitro and Sjafruddin, who were at the time teaching at the University of Indonesia. This group was later known as the *Berkeley Mafia* as most of them were trained at Berkeley University, U.S.A.

29. As quoted in Leifer (1983: 119).

30. The *Malari Riot* started on 15 January 1974, during the arrival of the Japanese Prime Minister, Kakuei Tanaka. A public demonstration of tens of thousands of people led to looting and violence. Today, this incident is also referred to as the anti-Japanese riot of 1974.

31. During the period leading up to the *Malari Riot*, Robison (1990: 145) points out that "associations and newspapers representing Muslim-oriented indigenous small capital had conducted a public and virulent anti-foreign, anti-Chinese campaign in an effort to halt their deteriorating position" in the domestic economy.

32. Initially, the Indonesian government created the Foreign Capital Investment Advisory Board (BPPMA—*Badan Pertimbangan Penanaman Modal Asing*) following the enactment of the Foreign Investment Law No. 1/1967. In the following year, 1968, the Indonesian government felt that it was necessary to improve the institutions involved in the investment process. To that end, the BPPMA was transformed into the Technical Committee on Investment (PTPM—*Panitia Teknis Penanaman Modal*). The task of the PTPM was not only to advise the President regarding the implementation of foreign investment, as was the case with the BPPMA, but this new institution was also responsible for the study and evaluation of investment applications. BPPMA was later changed into BKPM in 1973 as a result of the further need to improve the co-ordination of investment permits as well as the need to improve investment promotion. For a more detailed history of the BKPM, visit the BKPM official web site (accessed 2003) at http://www.bkpm.go.id.

33. OPSUS was shut down in 1985 following attempts to restructure the organization.

34. Suharto later proclaimed himself the *Bapak Pembangunan,* or father of development, in Indonesia.

35. The IMF-supported program was initiated by the first Letter of Intent (LoI), which was submitted to the IMF on the 31 October 1997 and was approved by the IMF on the 4 November 1997. The first LoI was built around three areas, which included: (1) economic reforms in the real sector, including improved transparency in governance; (2) a strategy for comprehensive financial restructuring that would include the closure of insolvent banks; (3) a strong macroeconomic policy for balance of payment stability. For a detailed analysis of the first LoI signed between the Indonesian government and IMF see, *inter alia,* Djiwandono (2003: 200).

36. As quoted in Thoha (2000).

37. These ethnicity issues have often been used as political propaganda in Southeast Asian politics, particularly in Indonesia, Singapore, and Malaysia. The racial diversity of these countries had apparently claimed the lives of many ethnic Chinese Indonesians, as evidenced by the May 1998 race riots in Indonesia. Since then the international community, particularly China and Singapore, had blamed the Indonesian government for failing to provide fair treatment for the Indonesian Chinese community. Although most national constitutions in Southeast Asian countries, with the exception of Malaysia with its New Economic Policy (NEP), do not specify special treatment for specific ethnic groups, racial issues continue to be used as propaganda by both the Singaporean and Indonesian governments.

38. As reported by the *BBC News* (1998), or visit the *BBC News* official web site at http://news.bbc.co.uk/1/hi/events/indonesia/latest_news/119700.stm.

39. On 13 November 1998, Habibie instructed his Minister of Home Affairs, Syarwan Hamid, to conduct a feasibility study on the implementation of a democratic election in the near future. Subsequently, the government appointed a group comprising mostly of academics, also known as the Group of Seven, to assist in the drafting of new election laws. Indonesia finally experienced one of the most fair and open elections to be held in a developing country and became the third largest democracy in the world.

40. The final result of the 1999 election was as follows: the nationalist Indonesian Democratic Party for Struggle (PDI-P—*Partai Demokrasi Indonesia untuk Perjuangan*) gained 153 seats; the incumbent Golkar took 120 seats; the Islamic United Development Party (PPP—*Partai Persatuan Pembangunan*) took fifty-eight seats; the Islamic PKB fifty-one seats; National Mandate Party (PAN—*Partai Amanat Nasional*) thirty-four seats; and lastly the Islamic Crescent Moon and Star Party (PBB—*Partai Bulan Bintang*)

gained thirteen seats. Although his party ranked only fourth during the election, Wahid gained enough popular support to become the fourth Indonesian President heading a coalition government formed between his own party, Golkar, PAN, PBB, and another Islamic party, the Justice Party (PK—*Partai Keadilan*). Wahid was appointed President while Megawati took the vice presidency post. They were sworn in on 20 and 21 October 1999 respectively.

41. For further details concerning the content of the 20 January 2000 LoI, visit the IMF official web site (accessed 2002) at http://www.imf.org.

42. As reported in the Down to Earth (2000–2001) official web site at http://dte.gn.apc.org/Au11.htm.

43. Quoted from the official web site of the U.S. Embassy in Jakarta (2000) http://www.usembassyjakarta.org.

44. The Presidential Decree No. 96 / 2000 can be read on the official BKPM web site (2000) at http://www.bkpm.go.id/bkpm/dni.php?mode=baca#ATTACHMENT%20I.

45. Dr. Shihab was previously a scholar of comparative religions at the University of Harvard's Divinity School. Despite his appointment as Indonesian Foreign Minister, Shihab never had any experience in conducting diplomatic relations.

46. The former Indonesian Foreign Minister, Alwi Shihab, further confirmed that ASEAN remained the cornerstone of Indonesian foreign policy and that Indonesian foreign policy was very much in line with the New Order's. For further details of Shihab's comments on Indonesia's foreign policy see *Time Asia* (1999), or visit the *Time Asia* official web site at: http://www.time.com.

47. The assembly voted 591 to 0 to remove President Wahid from office.

48. The Bush Administration has also provided further support for the Indonesian military following the terrorist bomb attack on Bali in October 2002.

49. The concentric circle, according to Smith (2000a: 17), places ASEAN as the first circle of the Indonesian foreign policy, while the member countries of the Non-Aligned Movement (NAM) and the West are placed as the second and the third circles of Indonesian foreign policy.

50. As reported by *the Business ASEAN Newsletter* (2003: 6), or visit its online version at http://www.aseansec.org/viewpdf.asp?file=/pdf/ba_jun03.pdf.

51. As reported by the official web site of the Indonesian Ministry of Foreign Affairs (2003) at http://www.deplu.go.id.

52. Dr. Hamzah Haz is from the PPP while Susilo B. Yudhoyono is from a military faction.

53. For further details regarding the BKPM Chairman's report on Indonesian investment performance visit the BKPM (2003) official web site at http://www.bkpm.go.id.

54. As quoted in Waslin (2003: 10).

55. As reported by *Jakarta Post* (2005). The article also mentions that over 61 percent of voters opted for Yudhoyono and his running-mate Yusuf Kalla in the run-off of presidential election a year before.

56. However, some observers also convince that the appointment of Aburizal Bakrie as the Co-ordinating Minister of Economy also highlights conflicts within Indonesia's ruling elite (Roberts: 2004). Initially, Dr. Sri Mulyani Indrawati, a former IMF Director for Southeast Asia, was the first choice of the President to take the post of the Coordinating Minister of Economy. Some Islamic parties, including PBB and PKS, were believed to have threatened to withdraw their support for Yudhoyono if he insisted to appoint a "pro-IMF" individual in such a ministerial post.

57. As quoted in Brotodiningrat (2005).

58. As reported in The Business Online (2005) official web site at http://www.thebusinessonline.com.

59. See Appendix 5 for details on the statement of recommendations/proposals from Southeast Asian civil society groups in building a just, democratic, transparent, and accountable ASEAN Community for the people of Southeast Asia. This statement was addressed by representatives of ASEAN civil society groups to the ASEAN policymakers during the Roundtable Discussion on "Building the ASEAN Community: Prospects and Challenges," in Jakarta, 4 August 2005.

Chapter 5

Indonesia in the ASEAN Free Trade Agreement (AFTA)

The ASEAN Free trade Area/Agreement (AFTA) is an agreement to liberalize trade among the member countries of ASEAN. This agreement was initiated in 1992 and was first implemented in January 2002. Specifically, AFTA has the objective "to increase the international competitiveness of ASEAN industries and [to make] the ASEAN region an investment location" (Tongzon 2002: 182). In the early 1990s, the Southeast Asian region saw significant changes as a result of global political and economic conditions. These new situations resulted in alterations in the way in which ASEAN conducted its economic cooperation. There were also calls to use the term *economic integration* in the region from economists from both within and outside the region during this period (Chirativat et al. 1999: 30). The major catalyst for such calls was the demise of the Cold War, which resulted in an increase in the formation of regional groupings throughout the world. Significant moves toward regional economic integration were strengthened not only within ASEAN, through the creation of AFTA, but also in terms of the Association's external relations, with the most significant move being the creation of the Asia-Pacific Economic Cooperation (APEC) and possible economic integration with the Northeast Asian countries of Japan, China, and South Korea through ASEAN Plus Three (APT).

The main objective of this chapter is to provide a detailed analysis of AFTA. The primary focus of the chapter is the evolutionary process and the current development of AFTA as well as Indonesians' initial perspectives toward the creation of this regional trade scheme. There will be four areas of discussion that will be raised in this chapter. The first is the analysis of the historical background of AFTA, which would explain the rationales that drove ASEAN leaders to promote enhanced economic integration in the region, as well as some basic mechanism that have been used in the implementation of AFTA. The second is the analysis of the prospects and challenges that confront the implementation of AFTA and other economic cooperation initiatives beyond this agreement. Issues such as the regional economic crisis, membership expansion, and the incorporation of the three Northeast Asian countries, Japan, China, and South Korea, into the ASEAN framework (i.e., APT) are some of the major challenges that ASEAN will face in the future. The third area of discussion is the analysis of the Indonesian political elite's perceptions of the creation of AFTA in the past. Finally, the fourth area of discussion presents a conclusion and highlights some of the main findings of this analysis of AFTA.

The History of AFTA

AFTA was first proposed at the Eighteenth ASEAN Economic Ministerial Meeting (AEM), which took place in the Philippines on the 28–30 August 1986. At that time, the Filipino delegation proposed a reduction in tariffs as well as the imposition of common external tariffs (CET), which were intended to drive ASEAN into forming a Custom Union. Indonesia and Singapore, however, rejected this idea for two contrasting reasons (Bowles 1997: 222). On the one hand, Indonesia was not very keen on either the idea of imposing a deadline to phase out tariffs, nor CET. Singapore, on the other hand, rejected the idea on the grounds that it did not wish to impose CET in its already tariff-free international trade. It was only at the Twenty-Second AEM in 1990, in Bali, Indonesia, that ASEAN Economic Ministers agreed upon the application of a Common Effective Preferential Tariff (CEPT) scheme on selected industrial items, such as fertilizer, pulp, and cement. By November 1990, the first Interim Technical Working Group (ITWG) meeting was held in Jakarta to further discuss the idea of AFTA. A year later, Thailand proposed the formation of AFTA during the ASEAN Senior Official Meeting (SEOM) in Kuala Lumpur.

There were two main motives that propelled ASEAN leaders to the pursuit of a trade liberalization strategy. These were: first, the changes in the international political economy during the late 1980s and the early 1990s and ASEAN's desire to maintain its position as an important organization in light of these changes; and second, the rise in the influence of economic actors' interests throughout the ASEAN region and their predisposition toward regional trade measures (Bowles and Maclean 1996: 327). To begin with, it was substantial change in the international arena that acted as the catalyst in making AFTA a reality in ASEAN. Some of the most important international political-economic changes that occurred during the 1980s were the appreciation of the Japanese Yen, the economic rise of China and the new emerging markets of the former Soviet bloc. The appreciation of the Japanese Yen began since the signing of the Plaza Accord in 1985, which led to substantial increases in Japanese investment in Southeast Asia. Japanese firms supported the idea of a free trade area in the Southeast Asian region due to possible cost minimizations in the production process and capital movement across the region (Webber 2001: 349). Meanwhile, the rise of the Chinese economy and the newly independent states of the former Soviet Union in the early 1990s also posed a threat to the overall competitiveness of the Southeast Asian states (Yew 2000: 382; Lim 2001: 191–92). It is for these reasons that ASEAN countries agreed to establish AFTA in 1992.

Other contributing factors that led to AFTA were the rise of new trading arrangements in North America and the strengthening of regional economic integration in Western European countries (Means 1995: 149–53). Southeast Asian countries were concerned about the possible trade-diversion effects that these regional groupings would pose toward the economies of Southeast Asia. A study conducted by Michigan State University, for example, estimated that the formation of the North American Free Trade Agreement (NAFTA) would produce a trade-diversion effect of about US$484 million, which would account for about 4 percent of ASEAN's total exports to North America. The trade-diversion effect would likely reach 8 to 12 percent of Southeast Asian exports in food, chemicals, textiles, metals, and electronics sectors.[1] To address this threat, ASEAN countries devised with three possible solutions. The first was that each individual country should support the GATT system and the completion of the Uruguay Round. The second was to enhance regional economic integration, while the third possible solution was to take initiatives to enhance economic cooperation with the North American and European integration mechanisms. Over time, it was clear that the third option was more feasible for ASEAN since member countries had longed for greater economic cooperation in the region, and had been unable to conduct such measures in the past for various political reasons.

Economic actors also played an important role in pushing the formation of AFTA. The role of the ASEAN Chambers of Commerce and Industry (ASEAN-CCI) was particularly crucial in influencing the governments of Southeast Asia to create AFTA (Bowles 1997: 221). Following the surge of trade liberalization in the mid-1980s, ASEAN economic actors began to realize the increasing diversification of the production structure and complementarity of ASEAN economies, which were a result of the growing activities of transnational corporations (TNCs) and the strengthening industrialization process within most ASEAN countries (Tongzon 2002: 182). More importantly, however, ASEAN economic actors were worried about the aforementioned threats that might jeopardize the competitiveness of the Southeast Asian economies. In Malaysia, for example, economic actors were concerned about China and its capacity to alter both the strategic balance and the economic growth patterns of Southeast Asia (Means 1995: 163). Economic actors in both Singapore and Indonesia, on the other hand, worried about the future trade-diversion effects from NAFTA and the EU. Indonesian economic actors, in particular, feared that the creation of NAFTA would bring about major changes to the general system of preferences (GSP), which would affect Indonesia's exports to North American markets (Means 1995: 168). It is for these reasons that ASEAN economic actors pushed the ASEAN member governments, through the ASEAN-CCI, to create AFTA.

In addition, AFTA was also created to replace or to complement the previous economic cooperation initiatives that were conducted by ASEAN, particularly the ASEAN Preferential Trading Arrangement (ASEAN-PTA), ASEAN Industrial Project (AIP), ASEAN Industrial Complementation (AIC), and the ASEAN Industrial Joint Ventures (AIJV) schemes.[2] Apart from a lack of economic complementarity, the failure of these schemes was due primarily to divergent national interests as well as the high levels of bureaucracy in ASEAN member countries. The ASEAN-PTA, for example, was a failure because it was effectively negated by a vast exclusion list (Lim 2001: 185). Although the number of items set in the inclusion list had expanded to 18,907 by 1986, the scheme was unable to significantly increase intra-regional trade. In fact, Chng's (1985: 33) examination proves that the trade flows of 1981 that covered some 9,000 preferences only accounted for about 10 percent of total ASEAN intra-trade.

The problem of divergent national interests was particularly clear in the case of both the AIP and AIC schemes (Suriyamongkol 1988: 118; Lim 2001: 189). The allocation of projects under the AIP initiative, for example, generated conflict amongmember countries. This was particularly evident in the allocation of the Diesel Engine Project in Singapore, which later drew criticism from Indonesia who was also trying to develop a similar line of production (Anwar 1994: 76).[3] On the whole, therefore, there was a lack of compatibility in production facilities in all ASEAN member countries (Rao 1996). Furthermore, the AIC scheme also encountered similar problems because "most ASEAN members have their own domestic automotive industries in collaboration with [various] multinational corporations" (Lim 2001: 189).[4] Meanwhile, the implementation of the AIJV was not supported by a strong enough bureaucratic process at both the national and regional levels (Narongchai 1992). The process of approval, for example, sometimes took up to one year or more, which made the scheme appear unattractive. In Indonesia alone, the business community was not particularly interested in ASEAN projects, although this can be explained by the fact that ASEAN governments themselves were reluctant to disseminate proper information to the business communities in the region (Pangestu et al. 1992: 335). To date, however, only the ASEAN-PTA and the AIJV schemes are complimented by the CEPT scheme. Those products covered under the ASEAN-PTA scheme may be transferred to the CEPT scheme,[5] while products covered by the latter may be allowed to slide in accordance to the benefits of the AIJV scheme (ASEAN Secretariat 1993).

In light of these new international challenges, the heads of ASEAN states finally agreed on the establishment of AFTA during the Fourth ASEAN Summit in Singapore in 1992, with the main objective of increasing "ASEAN's competitive edge as a production base geared for the world market" (ASEAN Secretariat 1993: 1). In order to implement AFTA, the ASEAN Economic Ministers also agreed on the CEPT as the main mechanism in which intra-regional tariffs and non-tariff barriers would be removed within a fifteen-year period. In 1993, member countries agreed upon the moderation of the CEPT scheme whereby all manufactured goods would reach tariffs of between 0–5 percent by 2008.[6] However, due to deepening economic challenges, ASEAN countries also agreed to reduce the target date for the realization of AFTA by five years, from 2008 to 2003, during the Twenty-Seventh AEM meeting in Chiang Mai.

Table 5.1.
Average AFTA/CEPT Tariff Rates

	1998	1999	2000	2001	2002	2003
Brunei	1.35	1.29	1.0	0.97	0.94	0.87
Indonesia	7.04	5.85	4.97	4.63	4.20	3.71
Laos	5.0	5.0	5.0	5.0	5.0	5.0
Malaysia	3.58	3.17	2.73	2.54	2.38	2.06
Myanmar	4.47	4.45	4.38	3.32	3.31	3.19
Philippines	7.96	7.0	5.59	5.07	4.80	3.75
Singapore	0.0	0.0	0.0	0.0	0.0	0.0
Thailand	10.56	9.75	7.40	7.36	6.07	4.64
Vietnam	6.06	3.78	3.30	2.90	2.89	2.02
ASEAN	5.37	4.77	3.87	3.65	3.25	2.68

Source: ASEAN Secretariat official web site (accessed 2003) at http:www.aseansec.org.

The CEPT scheme is composed of four main product categories, which include the *inclusion list, temporary exclusion list, sensitive list,* and *general exception list,* all of which fall within either the Fast Track Program or the Normal Track Program of tariffs reduction. Under the Fast Track Program it was agreed that all products with tariff rates above 20 percent would be reduced to 0–5 percent level within ten years (January 2003)[7] while those with tariff rates of 20 percent or below would be reduced within a period of seven years (January 2000) to 0–5 percent level. Under the Normal Track Program, on the other hand, items with tariff rates above 20 percent can be cut in two ways. Firstly, the tariff rates of these products can be reduced to 20 percent in five to eight years, and, secondly, the tariff rates are reduced to 0–5 percent in seven years. Finally, those goods with tariff levels of 20 percent or below are reduced to 0–5 percent within ten years. It is hoped that, eventually, the average tariff rates attached to inclusive products will reach 2.68 percent (refer to table 5.1).

The *inclusion list* category is largely composed of products that are undergoing immediate liberalization under the CEPT program, and should be included in the Fast Track Program tariff-reduction measure. Meanwhile, the *temporary exclusion* category is composed of products that were protected for a short-term period and then transferred into the *inclusion list* by January 1996 in order to reach the tariff level of 0–5 percent. The *sensitive list,* on the other hand, is made specifically to reduce tariff rates for agricultural products as well as other nontariff barriers. The sensitive list exists because ASEAN economies are composed mainly of agricultural producers and consumers. Therefore, some ASEAN countries, such as Indonesia and Thailand, may wish to postpone trade liberalization for their agricultural products. Lastly, the *general exception list* category involves all products that are excluded from the trade liberalization program for national security reasons. Unlike its predecessor, Margin of Preferences (MoP), that only covered about 19,000 items, before February 2000, the CEPT had covered about 53,026 items, or about 82.5 percent of total ASEAN trade. At present, the six major ASEAN countries have submitted 42,939 items on to the inclusion list out of a total of 43,636 items (refer to table 5.2 below).

Table 5.2.
CEPT Product List for the Year 2000, ASEAN 10

Country	Inclusion List	Temporary Exclusion List	General Ex-clusion List Sensitive List	Sensitive List	Total
Brunei	6,276	—	202	14	6,492
Indonesia	7,158	21	69	4	7,252
Malaysia	9,092	—	63	73	9,228
Philippines	5,571	35	27	62	5,695
Singapore	5,739	—	120	—	5,859
Thailand	9,103	0	0	7	9,110
Cambodia	3,114	3,523	134	50	6,821
Laos	1,247	2,126	90	88	3,551
Myanmar	2,356	2,987	108	21	5,472
Vietnam	3,573	984	219	51	4,827
ASEAN	**53,229**	**9,676**	**1,032**	**370**	**64,307**

Source: ASEAN Secretariat official web site (accessed 2003) at http://www.aseansec.org

Since the implementation of AFTA on 1 January 1993, there have been significant initiatives to improve the level of economic cooperation among ASEAN countries. One of these additional measures has been the introduction of the ASEAN Industrial Cooperation (AICO) scheme and ASEAN Investment Area (AIA), which was introduced during the Fifth ASEAN Summit in Bangkok on 15 December 1995. Both schemes were expected to complement the progress of AFTA. The establishment of AICO was primarily to replace the unsuccessful BBC and AIJV schemes, and the objective of the new scheme was to promote investment from technology-based industries (Lim 2001: 190). The AICO scheme is essentially open to all ASEAN companies with two main requirements. First, the cooperation should be incorporated and operated in ASEAN countries. Second, the ASEAN nationals involved in the cooperation should own at least 30 percent of the equity.[8] Third, resource sharing, such as technology and market sharing, has to take place between the involved parties. The scheme is based on the earlier established CEPT program, particularly with regard to the *rules of origin*, which requires a minimum of 40 percent ASEAN content. The AICO scheme became effective on 1 January 1996, while ASEAN's newest members, Laos and Myanmar, agreed to join the scheme in 1997. The Fifth ASEAN Summit also endorsed an important AIA document with the objective of enhancing greater investment in the region. Under the AIA agreement, ASEAN countries agreed to commit themselves to lower tariff barriers in line with the AFTA scheme, an improved liberalization of various strict regulations, and to making an effort to provide the necessary incentives for foreign investors coming into the region.

Prospects and Challenges for AFTA

Table 5.3.
ASEAN-6 Exports, 1999–2001*

	Intra-ASEAN Trade			Extra-ASEAN Trade		
	1999	2000	2001	1999	2000	2001
BD**	375	634	775	1,965	1,529	2,775
Ind	8,278	10,883	9,507	40,387	51,240	46,810
Mal	21,885	24,408	21,024	62,402	73,745	67,007
Phil	4,989	5,982	4,986	30,047	32,095	27,164
Sing	29,369	37,783	32,815	85,355	100,668	88,871
Thai	9,901	15,099	14,356	46,208	54,154	50,761

Notes: * Value in thousand US$
           ** Brunei Darussalam

Source: ASEAN Secretariat official web site (accessed 2002) at http://202.154.-
         12.3/trade/publicview.asp

There have been many scholarly analyses on the challenges and the future prospects of AFTA since its implementation in 1993. Proponents of AFTA primarily argue that the deepening of regional economic integration in the region will "help to attract foreign investment and . . . strengthen Southeast Asia's global trading position" (Petri 1997: 191). Such an analysis draws largely upon the insistence that AFTA is not an isolationist policy enforced by ASEAN member countries to create a trading bloc, as some have previously suggested. In addition, Chirathivat (1999: 31) maintains that AFTA will enable member countries to extend and to combine their natural resources, thereby limiting national barriers. Equally important is the fact that the formation of AFTA can help the Association prepare itself for further regional and global trade liberalization programs. This, in turn, will help member states to realize the necessity of having ASEAN, in that it helps them to address and solve various regional issues and problems. Moreover, AFTA was deemed crucial in increasing ASEAN's global competitiveness. In Soesastro's (2000: 24) analysis, for example, ASEAN represents more than AFTA and the objectives of free trade are not merely to increase intra-regional trade or to support regional import substitution schemes. AFTA is only a stepping-stone, which enables the Association to achieve a necessary competitive edge in the global economy. This is why ASEAN continues to expand its economic cooperation framework, which can be seen in the concept of *AFTA Plus*. The AFTA Plus concept involves mainly the expansion of agreements made within the AFTA framework. To date, such expansion includes the formation of various measures to reduce tariff and non-tariff barriers for products that are not covered by the original CEPT agreement, which can be seen in the aforementioned enhanced economic cooperation initiatives, such as in service, intellectual property, AICO, AIA, custom harmonization, etc. Therefore, according to such an analysis, AFTA is a necessary stepping-stone toward

greater economic cooperation in the region and to prepare ASEAN for further
global multilateralism.

There are also many critics of AFTA. Some of the important critics are Imada et al. (1991), who have pointed out the prevailing heterogeneous nature of
ASEAN economies. It is hypothesized that such an economic condition will
result in economic competitiveness rather than complementarity, which is an
inadequate measurement for any regional economic integration scheme. Although tariff levels in ASEAN countries are relatively low by comparison to
other developing countries, the region is only able to generate roughly a 20 percent intra-trade level, most of which is owing to its bilateral economic relationship with Singapore.[9] On the positive side, however, the competitive nature of
ASEAN economies also means that it is very unlikely that ASEAN will generate
a trade diversion effect to third countries. Table 5.3 demonstrates ASEAN exports within and beyond the region.[10] Other scholars, such as Denoon and Colbert (1998: 516), have also concentrated on the issue of the trade-creation and
trade-diversion effects of AFTA and the relative size of the ASEAN economies.
Owing to the small size of the ASEAN market, the level of trade-creation and
trade-diversion effects will also be small in this region. Therefore, ASEAN will
benefit more if the Association remains in a larger economic cooperation
scheme, such as APEC. Another critic of AFTA is Pangestu et al. (1992), who
are concerned with the scheme's ability to provide a larger market in the region
through intra-trade and investments. These scholars argue that AFTA will remain a matter of mere political rhetoric despite member countries' agreement on
the realization of AFTA by specified dates. The long process of negotiations on
the products included will remain the most significant problem during AFTA's
implementation phase. Another major problem is the excessive number of items
included in the exclusion category, which further undermines the effectiveness
of AFTA's progress.

After over a decade since AFTA was first initiated, ASEAN remains committed to its regional economic liberalization programs. Nevertheless, there have
been substantial challenges facing the Association during the phase of tariff liberalization, which include the issue of membership expansion, the regional economic crisis, and the expansion of ASEAN economic regionalism within the
framework of APT. The first important challenge was the entrance of new
members into the Association. There has been great concern over the entrance of
ASEAN's four new members, particularly with regard to politics and security
(Takeshi 1999). More specifically, there is fear about the impact of the inclusion
of new members into the ASEAN trade liberalization process under the AFTA
scheme. One problem is that the admittance of Vietnam, Laos, Myanmar and
Cambodia into ASEAN might sabotage the Association's earlier efforts to
achieve meaningful integration (Bello 1997). Enlargement might jeopardize the
already established development of AFTA since it is largely driven by political
factors. Another problem is that the process of enlargement means that the Association will have to adopt measures and schemes that are acceptable for the
new members (Akrasanee 2000). The new members are quite fortunate in that

the AFTA schedule remains flexible. However, their entrance into the Association could also be detrimental to ASEAN since AFTA will have to be modified to suit the interests of the new members. On the other hand, in his comparative study of the EU's and ASEAN's enlargement processes, Pomfret (1998: 8) concludes that the entrance of new members into the Association will be generally beneficial for the Association, apart from some minor discussion regarding the new member countries' lack of experience in dealing in the WTO type tariff reduction measures. At the same time, internal trade disputes between the old and the new members will be minimal since the issue of intra-trade remains an issue of only minor importance for ASEAN. One major benefit that the enlargement will bring is the enhancement of ASEAN's international bargaining position in international fora.

The second issue that challenges the progress of AFTA is the regional economic crisis of 1997. The economic crisis is particularly important especially where ASEAN's post-crisis role is concerned (Tay and Estanislao 2000). ASEAN's performance in alleviating the economic crisis has been limited, if not poor, and few measures to deal with the crisis have been implemented. In his analysis of the theoretical and empirical implications of the economic crisis on the Southeast Asian regionalization process, Ruland (2000: 428) argues that the "emerging symptoms of crisis were regarded as purely national problems." His analysis primarily stems from the fact that prior to the economic crisis much of ASEAN's policy mix was closer to a realist standpoint than to an institutionalist pole of a realism/institutionalism continuum. Since ASEAN's inception, efforts to conduct economic cooperation have been largely driven by political factors. This has been the primary reason behind the Association's poor performance in implementing the necessary measures to handle the economic crisis. The impact of the economic crisis on the progress of regionalism in Southeast Asia has been significant. In mainland Southeast Asia, for instance, Ruland (2000: 437) believes that the economic crisis will jeopardize various sub-regional mechanisms, such as BIMP-EAGA, IMS-GT, IMT-GT, SIJORI, etc., due to a lack of investment, aside from the fact that co-ordination of these projects has been largely absent. A similar argument has also been posed by Webber (2001: 365), whose analysis of ASEAN and APEC during the economic crisis, postulates that although "there will be no "funeral" for ASEAN or APEC, there is a high risk that the two organizations will remain to a greater or lesser extent incapacitated." With regard to ASEAN, Webber holds that the crisis has led to the loss of Indonesia as ASEAN's natural leader, while, at the same time, ASEAN's efforts at collective action to manage the crisis have been overshadowed by the relatively low economic development of ASEAN member countries.

ASEAN has indeed been rather slow in taking measures to alleviate the economic crisis, and it took more than six months for the Association to actually come out with any concrete measures to deal with the economic crisis. Two initial steps were the Hanoi Plan of Action (HPA) and the Statement on Bold Measures, which were finalized during the Sixth ASEAN Summit in Hanoi, on

15–16 December 1998.[11] During the Summit, ASEAN's Heads of States collectively agreed on various issues to enhance greater economic and financial cooperation in the region. Specific to the economic crisis, ASEAN leaders also agreed upon the introduction of the ASEAN Surveillance Process (ASP), as well as the enhancement of the process of ASEAN economic integration through the acceleration of AFTA's schedule. The ASP deals mainly with efforts to maintain regional macroeconomic and financial stability through the liberalization of the financial service sector, the intensification of cooperation in money, tax and insurance matters, as well as the plan to develop an ASEAN capital market. Although the ASP might be effective in alleviating the economic crisis, it is difficult to implement owing to the conflicting political and national interests of each member country. Since its conception, it has been suggested that the scheme's survival is largely dependent upon member countries' willingness to step aside from their national political considerations and interests (Monzano 2001: 96). As an institution, it is widely acknowledged that the "ASEAN Secretariat [is] nothing more than a glorified post office" (Anwar 2001b: 39), which lacks the necessary authority to implement any regional policies without prior consent from member governments. Moreover, staff members of the ASEAN Secretariat often complain about the member countries' inability to pass on the necessary and accurate information in a timely fashion. Therefore, it is unlikely that the Secretariat could issue any warning signs to prevent a possible future economic crisis in light of the heavy bureaucracy that exists at the national level.

Meanwhile, enhanced regional economic integration was envisioned in the Statement of Bold Measures, which called for the acceleration of the AFTA schedule. Under this initiative, the six original signatories of AFTA had to agree to advance the implementation of AFTA to 2002 from the originally agreed date of 1 January 2003. Moreover, member countries were required to reach a consensus on at least 90 percent of all products included in the CEPT scheme to meet the tariff requirement of 0–5 percent by 2000, which would account for nearly 90 percent of total ASEAN trade. The logic of such a policy lies in the realization that the region desperately needs to regain the confidence of both the business community and international investors. In line with the acceleration of AFTA's schedule, ASEAN also reiterated its earlier intention to implement the AIA to "attract greater FDI into the region from both ASEAN and non-ASEAN sources. [It is also hoped that] the goal of a liberal and transparent investment environment for ASEAN investors by 2010, and all investors by 2020" (Heinrich and Konan 2001: 143) can be achieved. Specifically, Article 4 of the Framework Agreement on the AIA sets out several guidelines for the improvement of the region's investment climate.[12] Firstly, ASEAN will co-ordinate its investment cooperation program to generate investments from both ASEAN and non-ASEAN investors. Secondly, all ASEAN investors will receive *national treatment* by 2010 while all other investors will receive this privilege by 2020. Thirdly, member countries must also commit themselves to opening all their industries to ASEAN investors by 2010 and other investors by 2020. Fourthly, ASEAN will also allow the private sector to play a greater role in various activities related to ASEAN investment issues and any other ASEAN activities. Finally, member countries also agree to promote various measures to allow the freer flow of capital, skilled workers, and technology amongASEAN members.

Table 5.4.
Foreign Direct Investment in ASEAN, 1990–2002
(in million US$)*

Country	1990–1995 (annual average)	1996	1997	1998	1999	2000	2001	2002
Brunei	102	654	702	573	748	549	526	1,035
Cambodia	80	586	168	243	230	149	148	54
Indonesia	2,135	6,194	4,678	-356	-2,745	-4550	-3,279	-1,523
Lao PDR	33	128	86	45	52	34	24	25
Malaysia	4,655	7,296	6,324	2,714	3,895	3,788	554	3,203
Myanmar	180	310	879	684	304	208	192	129
Philippines	1,028	1,520	1,261	1,718	1,725	1,345	982	1,111
Singapore	5,782	8,608	13,533	7,594	13,245	12,464	10,949	7,655
Thailand	1,990	2,271	3,882	7,491	6,091	3,350	3,813	1,068
Vietnam	947	1,803	2,587	1,700	1,484	1,289	1,300	1,200
ASEAN	16,932	29,370	30,369	18,504	19,691	11,056	13,241	13,957

Source: Chavez and Chandra (2008: 9)

Further attempts to improve the investment climate are also spelt out in the Statement of Bold Measures, which specifies several additional short-term measures in relation to the AIA scheme. These measures include: first, a minimum three year corporate income tax exemption or a minimum 30 percent corporate investment tax allowance; second, 100 percent foreign equity ownership; third, duty-free imports of capital goods; fourth, domestic market access; fifth, a minimum industrial land leasehold period of thirty years; sixth, employment of foreign personnel; and seventh, speedy custom clearance. At the institutional level, the AIA Council has been set up to monitor the progress of the AIA. However, it is important to note that each member country is expected to develop its own investment policy, which will nonetheless be subject to continuous review by the AIA Council every two years. As with the AFTA, member countries are expected to place their industries either on the TEL or the SL. All the original ASEAN-6 countries and Myanmar are expected to phase out their industries in the TEL category by 2003 while the remaining three members are expected to achieve this goal by 2010. Therefore, the implementation of AIA is hoped to improve the investment climate in the ASEAN region, which has deteriorated as a result of the crisis. Total ASEAN FDI has slumped from US$27 million prior to the economic crisis to a mere US$14.3 million in 1999 (refer to table 5.4). To date, the progress of AIA is expected to go in line with that of AFTA. It is for this reason that "most members' sensitive list will be fairly short, as the terms of AFTA provide for tariffs to be below 5 percent in most sectors by 2002" (Freeman 2001: 85).

Prospects and Challenges for Southeast Asian Regionalism Beyond AFTA

Southeast Asian RIA, while facing the challenge of the regional economic crisis, is also facing the new prospect and challenge of ASEAN's proposed expansion to include the three Northeast Asian countries, namely Japan, South Korea, and China, in the framework of APT. The idea was initiated by the Malaysian Prime Minister, Dr. Mahathir and was developed in the early 1990s. The idea proposes greater economic integration in the East Asian region through the formation of the East Asia Economic Caucus (EAEC), "whose memberships would exclude all the Western members of APEC including Australia, Canada, and the United States" (Acharya 2002: 28).[13] There have been many attempts to include the three Northeast Asian countries in ASEAN's regional integration discussions during meetings held under the auspices of the ASEAN-Europe Meeting (ASEM). It was expected that a strong impetus for the formation of a regional mechanism might come from the Northeast Asian countries through such an informal meeting (Soesastro 2000: 221), but this initiative failed to bring together the Southeast and Northeast Asian countries. Concrete moves toward the creation of APT began in 1997, when the three Northeast Asian countries were invited to the Second ASEAN Informal Summit in Kuala Lumpur. At that time the Foreign Ministers of the countries involved agreed to meet annually to strengthen the foundation of the APT. A year later, during the Sixth ASEAN Summit, President Kim Dae-Jung of South Korea proposed the creation of the East Asia Vision Group (EAVG), which would provide a long-term vision for East Asian regional cooperation. In addition, it was also suggested that an East Asia Study Group (EASG) should be established to conduct a feasibility study on EAVG. The Northeast Asian countries involved finally sent positive signals after their Economic and Finance Ministers met with their Southeast Asian counterparts to discuss the possibility of APT in April 1999. Initial efforts at cooperation began in 2000, following the Fourth ASEAN Finance Ministers' Meeting (AFMM), whereby ASEAN countries agreed with their Northeast Asian counterparts to conduct financial cooperation, otherwise known as the ASEAN Swap Arrangement (ASA). This mechanism sought to prevent or to minimize the possibility of future economic crises.

After a three-year feasibility study, the EAVG's report was finally approved by the EASG and became the fundamental vision for greater cooperation in the region. There were three main areas of cooperation highlighted in the report, which included economic, financial, and institutional cooperation. In the area of economic cooperation, it was suggested that the APT should establish the East Asia Free Trade Area (EAFTA) as well as calling for the establishment of an

East Asia Investment Area (EAIA) as an extension of the already established Southeast Asian AIA. Another important recommendation also included the formation of the East Asian Monetary Fund (EAMF), in line with Japan's prior suggestion to create an Asian Monetary Fund (AMF) at the onset of the regional economic crisis in 1997. For some observers within the region, the development of APT, especially during the recent economic crisis, is seen as a "fresh infusion of political stability and economic dynamism" (Alatas 2001: 1). Moreover, Alatas also holds that enhanced regional economic integration under the APT mechanism is logical for several reasons. First, it increases economic interdependence and complementarity in the region. Second, both regions have previously signified their intentions to implement such a cooperation. Thirdly, it is a response to the challenges that globalization poses to the East Asian region. Some examples of economic interdependence and complementarity in the region can be found in various analyses of the Japanese and Overseas Chinese network building throughout Asia (Sang-Ho 2001: 407–12). Both regions have indeed already indicated their intentions to implement greater cooperation and as far back as the 1960s, Japan proposed the idea of East Asian regional institutions, which would strengthen regional economic cooperation in the region. Throughout the 1960s there were several regional economic arrangements in the Asia-Pacific region, such as the Pacific Economic Cooperation (PEC), the Asian Development Bank (ADB), the Asian and Pacific Council (ASPAC), the UN initiative of the Economic Commission for Asia and the Far East (ECAFE), the Ministerial Conference on Economic Development in Southeast Asia (MCEDSEA), and so on. Some of these projects failed to succeed either due to internal conflicts amongthe countries involved or serious objections from the West.

There can be no doubt that the formation of APT provides a sound base for enhanced regional economic integration in the East Asian region. Aside from the highly complementary nature of the grouping, APT can also act as leverage for member countries in the international fora. However, internal conflicts amongcountries in each respective region remain a major problem for the future of APT. Some major constraints within the Northeast Asian region reflect those in the Southeast Asian region. As with the countries of Southeast Asia, the relationship among Northeast Asian countries has been blanketed by conflicts and the issue of excessive nationalistic interests. The deep mistrust between Northeast Asian countries, as a result of their shared histories, which is evident in the case of Sino-Japanese relations, has been a major setback to the process of regionalism (Cai 2001: 15). During much of the twentieth century, for example, Japan's colonization of Northeast Asia left an "indelible, brutal imprint on a generation" (Dent 2002b: 5). Another important factor worth noting is that, unlike their counterparts in Southeast Asia, regionalism has largely been absent in the history of Northeast Asian countries.[14] Furthermore, it is also important to question the extent to which APT would accommodate additional new members in East Asia, such as Taiwan and North Korea. To date, Taiwan has been partic-

ipating as an observer in the APT framework while discussions on the involvement of North Korea have been largely absent. The inclusion of these new
members would present a new challenge, and may threaten the continued existence of APT. The Sino-Taiwanese relationship, for example, has recently
soured by the sale of U.S. weapons to Taiwan. Meanwhile, despite South Korea's implementation of the *Sunshine Policy*[15] toward the neighboring North
Korea, it is still unclear if North Korea will guarantee reciprocity in security and
other areas to its southern neighbor (Sang-Ho 2001).

In addition to the APT framework of cooperation, Japan, South Korea, and
China have recently proposed a bilateral FTA with either ASEAN or each individual country within the Association. During the Eighth ASEAN Summit on 5
November 2002, in Phnom Penh, for instance, the ASEAN-China Framework
Agreement on Comprehensive Economic Cooperation was signed between China and its Southeast Asian partners. The agreement, which was implemented on
1 July 2003, aims to liberalize trade on goods and services, as well as create a
transparent and liberal investment regime between all parties. This ASEAN-
China FTA will open up a market for nearly 1.7 billion consumers, with a combined GDP of US$1.5 trillion and a two way trade level of US$1.2 trillion.[16]
Prior to the signing of this agreement, both Japan and South Korea also announced their interest in negotiating bilateral FTAs with some ASEAN countries. In early 2002, for example, Japan signed a bilateral FTA with Singapore,
which was implemented on 30 November 2002. The agreement is historical
since it is the first time that Japan has ever agreed to conduct an FTA with other
countries. The proposed scheme covers some 3,400 items and eradicates tariffs
on about 94 percent of Singapore's exports into Japan. Singapore, on the other
hand, has eliminated the remaining tariffs on imports from Japan, mainly on
alcoholic drinks.[17]

In response to China's effort to form an FTA with ASEAN, Japan also at-
tempted to push its Comprehensive Economic Partnership Program (CEPP) with
ASEAN, with elements of an FTA to be completed within ten years (ASEAN
Secretariat 2003). The agreement was made at the ASEAN-Japan Summit, following the Eighth ASEAN Summit in Cambodia. The decision to implement the
CEPP was based on the report of the ASEAN-Japan Closer Economic Partnership Experts Group, which was earlier commissioned by the AEM and Japan in
September 2001. It is expected that the agreement will increase economic interactions between ASEAN and Japan.[18] While ASEAN aims to boost its exports
to Japan by US$20 billion, Japan is expected to increase its exports to ASEAN
countries by US$20 billion (ASEAN Secretariat 2003: 3). Some areas of coop-
eration included in the agreement are financial services, information and communication technologies, sciences, the development of small and medium enterprises (SMEs), tourism, energy, human resources development, and
transportation. Leaders from both sides share the view that the program will
facilitate greater economic ties between the two parties. Along with the already
agreed Japan-Singapore's FTA, the Japanese government also intends to implement an FTA with the Philippines. To date, the free trade pact is still under ne-

gotiation between the two parties, and is expected to be concluded by 2004. In addition, on 11–12 December 2003, the Japanese government held the Japan-ASEAN Commemorative Summit in Tokyo, which made it the first ASEAN Summit ever to be held in a non-ASEAN country.

Meanwhile, as bilateral economic cooperation between ASEAN and China, and ASEAN and Japan increases, the South Korean government also announced its intention to conduct an FTA with ASEAN in September 2002. Earlier that year, the former South Korean Foreign Minister, Han Sung Joo, is reported to have claimed that the creation of an FTA pact between ASEAN and South Korea is more than likely as the agreement would boost additional foreign investments and competitiveness in the region (Fore 2002). The current South Korean Trade Minister, Hwang Doo-Yun, also added that his government was carrying out a feasibility study about implementing an FTA with all Southeast Asian countries (Maneerungsee 2002). Unlike its Northeast Asian neighbors, China and Japan, the South Korean government is rather cautious in taking major steps to conduct an FTA with ASEAN countries. However, the South Korean government is alarmed by the current development of other free trade pacts that have been implemented between ASEAN, Japan, and China. As a result, it is very likely that an FTA between ASEAN and South Korea will be implemented soon.

Moreover, ASEAN countries are increasingly interested in conducting FTAs with non-ASEAN member countries, which has been evident in a number of initiatives toward closer economic cooperation between ASEAN and the United States, India, and the Australia-New Zealand Closer Economic Relations (CER) (ASEAN Secretariat 2003). To start with, closer economic cooperation between ASEAN and the United States began at the APEC Summit in Los Cobos, Mexico, on 26 October 2002. At the time, the United States proposed the establishment of the Enterprise for ASEAN Initiative (EAI), "which aims to build a network of FTAs between the United States and individual ASEAN countries" (ASEAN Secretariat 2003: 6). The deal was made possible due to the close economic relations between the two parties. The United States has been ASEAN's major trading partner, accounting for about 15.8 percent of ASEAN's total trade with the world in 2001 or about US$108.4 billion.[19] Meanwhile, U.S. imports from ASEAN accounted for about 17 percent in 2001, although ASEAN accounts for only 5–7 percent of total U.S. trade with the rest of the world. Moreover, the institutionalization of the free trade agreement between the two parties was significant because it was the first time the United States had ever conducted a bilateral FTA pact with any Asian country. The first stage of the agreement will involve a free trade arrangement between the United States and Singapore, which will not be implemented until 2004 since the U.S. government is still drafting the agreement and has to present it to Congress. Prior to the signing of the U.S.-Singapore Bilateral Free Trade Agreement (BFTA), the former U.S. Trade Representative, Robert Zoellick, stipulated that there is only one major problem that has to be resolved, namely the free transfer of capital.[20] The deal to implement an FTA with Singapore is hoped to be a blueprint for similar bilateral economic cooperations with other Southeast Asian countries.

An important discussion between ASEAN and India also took place at the Eighth ASEAN Summit in Cambodia. This was the first ASEAN-India Summit to be held where both parties agreed to broaden and deepen the economic linkages between each other (ASEAN Secretariat 2003: 4). However, the first consultation between the Economic Ministers of ASEAN and India actually took place a month earlier in Bandar Seri Begawan, Brunei Darussalam, on 15 September 2002. Previously, the Indian government had initially announced its desire to reduce its peak tariff rates to the East Asia tariff levels within a three year period. Subsequently, a Joint Study on AFTA-India Linkages for the Enhancement of Trade and Investment was conducted, which recommended that the formation of an India-AFTA Regional Trade and Investment Area (RTIA) was feasible.[21] One of the reasons for the creation of an India-AFTA RTIA was the increase of trade linkages between the two parties. Between 1993 until 2001, for example, two-way trade between the two parties doubled from US$2.9 billion to US$9.9 billion. At the moment, both parties have an ASEAN-India Economic Linkages Task Force (AIELTF), which is preparing a Framework Agreement to Enhance ASEAN-India Economic Cooperation for future consideration during the ASEAN-Indian Economic Cooperation.

A month prior to the opening of the Eighth ASEAN Summit, a Joint Ministerial Declaration on the AFTA-CER Closer Economic Partnership (CEP) was also signed in Brunei Darussalam, on 14 September 2002. This is expected to increase the two way trade between the involved countries by up to US$40 billion by 2010. Moreover, it is also hoped that the CEP framework will be incorporated into the AFTA framework so that greater economic cooperation will be made possible between ASEAN countries and the CER group. Initially, the AFTA-CER linkage was developed in 1995. However, it was only at the Fifth AEM-CER Consultation in Chiang Mai, Thailand, in October 2000 that Economic Ministers from both regions agreed to the formation of the High Level Task Force to conduct a feasibility study on the formation of the AFTA-CER Free Trade Area and other relevant issues surrounding closer integration between ASEAN and CER countries.[22] Subsequently, the AFTA-CER CEP Implementation and Co-ordination Group (ACCICG) identified seven areas of economic cooperation, including (1) the protection for intellectual property; (2) standards and quality assessment; (3) trade in services; (4) the implementation of the CEPT scheme; (5) the development of small and medium enterprises; (6) industrial cooperation; and (7) E-ASEAN[23] (ASEAN Secretariat 2003: 4–5).

Apart from those developments, ASEAN countries are also attempting to strengthen their own regional integration. On 8 October 2003, in Bali, for example, ASEAN member countries agreed to expand ASEAN cooperation by establishing an ASEAN Community (AC) by 2020. The Declaration of ASEAN Concord II will reinforce three elements of cooperation, namely political and security cooperation, economic cooperation, and sociocultural cooperation, which were all included in the 1976 Declaration of ASEAN Concord I.[24]

ASEAN's main objective in forming an AC was to ensure lasting peace, stability, and prosperity in the Southeast Asian region. Moreover, ASEAN leaders also agreed to form the ASEAN Security Community (ASC), the ASEAN Economic Community (AEC), and the ASEAN Sociocultural Community (ASCC) as frameworks to help achieve the objective of a dynamic, cohesive, resilient, and integrated ASEAN Community. Recently, as a result of increasing global economic competition, during the thirty-eighth AEM held in Kuala Lumpur in August 2006, ASEAN member countries announced the acceleration of AEC to 2015, five years earlier than originally planned (Global Justice Update 2006). Subsequently, during the twelfth ASEAN Summit in Cebu in January 2007, ASEAN leaders also pledged to accelerate the overall timeframe of AC to 2015. A spokesman from the ASEAN Secretariat declared that ASEAN has subscribed to the notion of democratic peace whereby member countries rely on democratic peace to promote regional peace and stability.[25] Despite this, ASEAN Secretariat officials and regional leaders refused to admit that the AC would lead to the creation of a military bloc or a political union. The former Head of External Relations of the ASEAN Secretariat, Sundram Pushpanathan, for example, assured that an AC would not become a *Fortress of ASEAN*.[26] Similarly, the Prime Minister of Malaysia, Dr. Mahathir, also confirmed that the AC would never become an ASEAN Union.[27] However, given the slow progress of ASEAN in the past, the Indonesian President, Megawati, stated that the signing of the Declaration of ASEAN Concord II was "a watershed in the history of ASEAN."[28]

The announcement from ASEAN leaders to establish AEC, in particular, deserves special attention as it connotes the deepening of economic integration in the region. Initially, ASEAN Economic Ministers have commissioned a leading consulting firm, McKinsey and Co., and an ASEAN High Level Task Force (AHLTF) to provide some general frameworks and ideas needed to make the AEC into realization (Soesastro 2005: 3–4).[29] Several elements of recommendations from McKinsey and AHLTF were later adopted by the ASEAN Economic Ministers (Soesastro 2005: 4). Among others, ASEAN was committed to: (1) institute new mechanisms and to strengthen the implementation of the existing regional economic integration initiatives (such as the ASEAN Free Trade Area [AFTA] and the ASEAN Investment Area [AIA]); (2) address the development divide between the ASEAN-6 and the CLMV countries by incorporating technical and development cooperation in ASEAN economic integration initiatives; (3) realize an integrated economic community through the implementation of liberalization and cooperation measures; (4) accelerate the integration of the eleven identified priority sectors. For some scholars in the Southeast Asian region, such as Hew (2003), the establishment of an AEC is necessary given the increasingly competitive globalized environment. The growing markets of China and India are perceived as increasing threats to the overall economic competitiveness of the ASEAN region. From this perspective, as Hew further argues, the AEC would allow ASEAN to revitalize and remain competitive *vis-à-vis* the rising challenges of globalization.

All these developments suggest that "international policy is changing rapidly[,] and it will continue to develop as negotiations proceed on various bilateral, regional and multilateral fronts" (Lloyd 2002: 12). However, it remains to be seen whether states involved in these schemes will be able to implement the agreements fully. Before retiring, the former ASEAN Secretary General, Rudolfo Severino, expressed his frustration over some ASEAN countries' reluctance to make significant changes to their nationalistic FEP, which consequently stalled many ASEAN's economic integration initiatives.[30] The challenges that ASEAN has to confront today are not merely to maintain the current regional integration initiatives amongmember countries, but also to conduct greater cooperation with its Northeast Asian, West Asian, and other non-Asian counterparts. Despite greater complementarity within the economic relationships between these regions, Southeast Asian countries are faced with the challenge of setting aside their national economic interests for the sake of regional economic integration. The bilateral FTA between China and ASEAN, for example, will be overshadowed by the strained relationship that has existed between some ASEAN member countries and China in the past. It is by no means clear that this agreement will signal an end to ASEAN member countries' suspicion of China. Nevertheless, greater integration between Southeast Asian countries and their Northeast Asian counterparts is inevitable because of the greater benefits to be accrued from such arrangements. In fact, the scope of many RIA initiatives between the two regions will most likely expand in the future.

Indonesian State and Non-state Actors' Perceptions of the Creation of AFTA

Since the inception of the ASEAN Preferential Trading Arrangement (ASEAN-PTA) in 1977, Indonesia has always demonstrated a rather ambiguous attitude toward ASEAN regional economic integration initiatives. As mentioned in Chapter 5, Indonesia always wanted better control over its own economy before agreeing to greater levels of economic cooperation with its neighboring states (Kartadjoemena 1977: 71). This attitude persisted even when Indonesia undertook trade liberalization measures during the early 1990s. In a subsequent analysis of Indonesian FEP, Anwar (1994) confirmed the ambiguity in Indonesian attitudes toward ASEAN regional economic integration initiatives. Specifically, in the area of economic cooperation, Indonesia has been rather pessimistic about relying on ASEAN for several reasons, all of which are still valid when examining the perceptions of Indonesian state and non-state actors of the creation of AFTA. Firstly, in the early period of economic cooperation, Indonesia was a relatively poor country in comparison to its neighboring partners. Indonesian economists at the time were convinced that it was necessary for Indonesia to conduct a protectionist economic policy in order to achieve an appropriate level of economic development. Secondly, Indonesia preferred to protect its infant industries and conducted trade mostly with non-ASEAN member countries, mainly Japan and the United States. Thirdly, the majority of Indonesian entrepreneurs were reluctant to enter the ASEAN regional market since Indonesia itself was already a large nation composed of over 100 million people during the 1980s. Fourthly, Indonesia had always regarded regional economic cooperation projects as a way for richer ASEAN countries, particularly Singapore, to exploit the large Indonesian market. Finally, Indonesians also recognized the highly competitive nature of the ASEAN market. As a result, many Indonesians were pessimistic about the Association's proposed regional economic integration mechanisms. Therefore, many state and non-state actors during the New Order period thought that the country should not focus on ASEAN economic cooperation.

On the whole, however, the majority of the Indonesian population has been unaware of the development of ASEAN economic integration initiatives. This is both because of the minimal attempt made to disseminate information on ASEAN's development to the public, and the public's lack of interest toward the issue of foreign affairs in general. At the same time, only a few members of the governmental elite, particularly during the New Order period, were aware of the development of ASEAN. Decisions on ASEAN were largely the concern of President Suharto, the army, staff at the Ministry of Foreign Affairs (MFA), and a small academic circle, especially the Centre for Strategic and International Studies (CSIS). The overall perception of the political elite toward their country's involvement in ASEAN was relatively positive. However, it is also important to note that, as Leifer (1983: 153) observes, "Indonesia was caught between aspiration and achievement" in ASEAN and its regional economic integration initiatives. On the one hand, Indonesia's involvement in the Association was regarded as important owing to ASEAN's potential to establish an extensive economic relationship between Southeast Asian countries. On the other hand, many Indonesians have also been frustrated over their country's inability to influence other ASEAN member states' foreign economic policy (FEP). It has been widely acknowledged that the Indonesian political elite can be nationalistic, particularly in discussions over Indonesia's position in ASEAN. National aspirations concerning regional entitlements exist owing to the sheer size of the country in terms of land mass and population. The military has also continued to express nationalistic pride over Indonesia's past heroic struggle against the imperialist powers. However, Indonesia still cannot exert much influence over other member states' behavior, including within the economic field.

The perceptions held by Indonesian domestic constituents toward AFTA in the past have been largely centered around the policymakers. There has been limited analysis of the perceptions of the wider Indonesians public, such as domestic non-governmental organizations (NGOs) and civil society organizations (CSOs), of the creation of AFTA. Generally, during the New Order administration, non-state actors did not participate in the FEP decision-making process. The only interest groups capable of influencing the policies of the Indonesian government were members of the academic community and the business community. During the process of the creation of AFTA, for example, the Indonesian Chambers of Commerce and Industry (KADIN—*Kamar Dagang dan Industri Indonesia*) was the only interest group large enough to present the views of the Indonesian business community on the formation of AFTA. However, in general, the attitude of KADIN toward the formation of AFTA remained passive due to the heavy centralization of the FEP-making process. At the same time, the views of other interest groups in the country were largely ignored. The New Order's heavy centralization of power and the ability of the state apparatus to repress or to neutralize dissident opinions have raised some doubts over the ability of Indonesian NGOs or CSOs to influence the country's overall direction (Eldridge 1995: 5). There are also many Indonesian NGOs or CSOs that serve the government by acting as a channel for social and political participation (Budiman 1988). As a result, the support shown toward the creation of AFTA at the time primarily represented the economic interests of those in power.

Therefore, in general, the majority of Indonesians remained somewhat indifferent toward ASEAN (Anwar 1994: 200) and AFTA. One of the major reasons for this indifference was because the Association was still largely considered an intergovernmental organization. Many actions conducted within the ASEAN framework were perceived to come largely from the wishes or perceptions of the government elite concerning the direction that should be pursued by the Association. Indonesian leaders were also concerned about enhancing Indonesia's influence over other ASEAN member countries. It was clear that Indonesia's leadership in the region was somewhat imaginary. Indonesia, despite its vast geographical size and large population, has kept a rather low profile with regard to foreign policy in ASEAN and has not been able to provide a sense of direction to the Association. Apart from heavy bureaucratization in the initial implementation of AFTA, Indonesian support toward this scheme was also limited because of a lack in appropriate information being disseminated to the public.

Conclusion

This chapter has provided a detailed analysis on the development of AFTA, ASEAN's regional economic integration initiatives beyond the Southeast Asian region, and Indonesian state and non-state actors' perceptions toward the creation of the AFTA scheme. Despite the indifferent attitude amongIndonesians toward ASEAN regional economic integration in the past, the introduction of AFTA in 1992 signaled a significant improvement within ASEAN regional economic integration. AFTA was considered a milestone in ASEAN cooperation due to its capacity to act as a catalyst for a greater cooperation or, perhaps, integration in the region. It is one of the most ambitious regional projects that ASEAN has proposed to date. However, just as previous ASEAN regional economic integration initiatives (i.e., ASEAN-PTA, AIP, AIC, and AIJV) failed owing to the divergent national economic interests amongASEAN member countries, it remains questionable whether AFTA will survive. The economic crisis of 1997, in particular, was a major setback to the progress of AFTA. The economic crisis did not only paralyze some ASEAN countries' economies, but also fragmented the political and social structures of these countries. At the onset of the economic crisis, some Southeast Asian countries wanted to postpone the implementation of AFTA. In contrast, however, ASEAN decided that the schedule of AFTA should instead be accelerated to 1 January 2002, from the initially agreed date of 1 January 2003.[31]

The acceleration of the AFTA schedule was the only logical and rational thing to do for ASEAN, although this move was against popular opinion (Severino 1999). The acceleration of AFTA was hoped, *inter alia*, to bring back a supportive investment climate in member countries as well as to provide a positive sign to the world economy of ASEAN's intention to remain open economically. Further initiatives were also conducted to improve economic relations with non-ASEAN countries, which were evident in the discussions over the future possibility of the APT as well as other bilateral negotiations with the United States, India, and the CER countries. All these developments suggest that policymakers in the Southeast Asian region are increasingly interested in expanding current ASEAN economic cooperation beyond AFTA. However, it is too early to suggest that the scope of ASEAN's activities will be expanded into the APT framework in the near future. The Indonesia government, for example, supported the development of APT, but refused to elaborate further on the way in which cooperation within the APT framework can be expanded. Cooperation with non-ASEAN countries, in Jakarta's point of view, should always be treated cautiously.

Notes

1. As quoted in Means (1995: 149). However, Means also notes that analysts came to rather diverse conclusions about the impacts of NAFTA on Southeast Asian exports. A Canadian study, for instance, forecast that the trade-diversion effects would be less than 0.5 percent of all East Asian exports to the United States. A similar study conducted by the East-West Centre in Honolulu also claimed that the trade-diversion effect would affect less than 1 percent of ASEAN's total exports, which may vary for individual countries.

2. Initial discussions regarding the implementation of economic cooperation initiatives in ASEAN began at the Fourth AMM in 1971. As mentioned in Chapter 5, it was General Romulo, the President of the Philippines, who initiated closer economic cooperation amongASEAN member countries. General Romulo's view was later supported through an ASEAN-United Nations Development Program (UNDP) project that involved 41 international experts assisting ASEAN to conduct closer economic cooperation. This two year long project finally resulted in the *Kansu Report*, which became the major

backbone for ASEAN cooperation in industrial development, agriculture and forestry, transport, finance, monetary, and insurance services. The Kansu Report also suggested that the creation of a Common Market was overly optimistic, and that member states of ASEAN should foster its infant industries through the use of ISI policies (Soesastro 2000: 204).

3. The conflict between Indonesia and Singapore resulted in the latter's insistence on having only a 1 percent stake in Indonesia's Urea Project. Another dispute also prevailed between Indonesia and the Philippines over the production of superphospate. To date, only the Urea projects in Indonesia and Malaysia have continued, which is largely due to the fact that the allocated plants in both countries were commercial long before the AIP scheme was initiated.

4. Due to such problems, the AIC scheme was later replaced with the Brand-to-Brand Complementation (BBC) scheme, which allowed ASEAN member countries to provide incentives for automotive multinationals to relocate their production to lower cost countries within the Association. To date, the BBC scheme remains the most successful amongall ASEAN's economic cooperation initiatives prior to AFTA.

5. However, it is important to note that concessions under the CEPT scheme should not be less favourable to the PTA concessions, which existed as of 31 December 1992. Moreover, all products covered under the ASEAN-PTA scheme, but are not transferred to the CEPT scheme, will continue to enjoy the existing Margin of Preference (MoP), or the ASEAN-PTA's main mechanism, as of 31 December 1992.

6. Apart from all manufactured goods, CEPT also covers capital goods and processed agricultural products. The CEPT, however, does not cover unprocessed agricultural products, including agricultural raw materials and all agricultural products that involve minimal change from original products. Further details on the implementation of AFTA and the CEPT scheme can be obtained from the *AFTA Reader*, published by the ASEAN Secretariat (1993).

7. This, however, varies for new ASEAN members whereby Vietnam would have to comply with this agreement by 2006, Laos and Myanmar by 2008, and Cambodia by 2010.

8. This requirement, however, may be waived under certain circumstances. Consultation between the involved parties is normally carried out to settle such differences.

9. According to Imada et al. (1991: 4), for example, in the absence of Singapore, the total of intra-ASEAN trade only amounted to 5 percent. However, Plummer (1997: 206) also adds that it is difficult for a regional grouping to meet the normal determinant of a 50 percent intra-trade level. To date, it is only the EU that has exceeded that mark, although this level was reached through forty years of cooperation. Even the U.S. led economic integration, NAFTA, has only been able to achieve a 33 percent intra-trade level.

10. See also appendix 6 for details concerning ASEAN's five major trading partners as of 2001.

11. For further details on the content of the ASEAN Sixth Summit, especially on the Hanoi Plan of Action and Statement of Bold Measures, refer to the ASEAN Secretariat (1999).

12. For further details on the Framework Agreement on the AIA visit the ASEAN Secretariat official web site (accessed 2003) at http://www.aseansec.org/2280.htm.

13. The EAEC was originally known as the East Asian Economic Group (EAEG). Initially, the EAEG was developed to pool the pan-Asian sentiments toward the Western members of APEC. EAEC, however, was developed as a compromise solution placed within APEC (Öjendal 2001: 168).

14. The exception to this is the Tumen River Area Development Program (TRADP), which is primarily concerned with large-scale transport and energy infrastructure projects (Dent 2002c: 71).

15. The Sunshine Policy was first introduced by the South Korean President, Kim Dae Jung, in order to underline the peaceful management of the division of the Korean Peninsula. Previous South Korean governments had sought the containment of North Korea. This policy envisions greater interactions between South Korean and North Korea through the funnelling of economic assistance and diplomatic favours from South Korea to North Korea. For further information regarding the Sunshine Policy visit the *Korean Times* (2003) official web site at http://www.korea.net.

16. For further analysis of the ASEAN-China Framework Agreement on Comprehensive Economic Cooperation, visit the ASEAN Secretariat (2002c) official web site at http://www.aseansec.org/8thsummit/8thsummit_china.htm.

17. This scheme, however, does not apply to some sensitive agricultural and fisheries products, nor to petrochemical and petroleum goods.

18. For details concerning Japan's major trading partners as of 2001 see Appendix 7. The data in Appendix 7 shows that, recently, Singapore and Thailand were ranked seventh and ninth respectively among the top ten major destinations for Japanese exports, while Indonesian and Malaysia were ranked fourth and eighth respectively.

19. For details concerning the U.S.' major trading partners as of 2001 refer to appendix 7.

20. As reported by the Business Day official web site (2002). For further details visit www.bday.co.za/bday/content/direct/1,3523,1228609–6078–0,00.html.

21. A report concerning the ASEAN-India Economic Linkage can be found in the ASEAN Secretariat's (2002d) press release, or visit the ASEAN Secretariat official web site at http://www.aseansec.org/12315.htm.

22. As reported in the ASEAN Secretariat (2000b) official web site at http://www.aseansec.org.

23. E-ASEAN is an attempt "link up ASEAN members by internet and electronic means so ASEAN becomes one cyberspace" (Tay and Estanislao 2000: 19).

24. Details of the Declaration of ASEAN Concord II are available at the ASEAN Secretariat official web site (accessed 2004) at http://www.aseansec.org/15159.htm.

25. As quoted in Luard (2003).

26. As quoted in Parameswaran (2003). S. Pushpanathan is currently the Principal Director of Bureau for Economic Integration and Finance at the ASEAN Secretariat.

27. As quoted by the Jakarta Post (2003) or visit the Jakarta Post official web site at http://www.thejakartapost.com/detailweekly.asp?fileid=20031008.@01.

28. As quoted by the *BBC News* (2003b), or visit *the BBC News* official web site at http://news.bbc.co.uk/1/hi/world/asia-pacific/3167120.stm.

29. In its recommendations, McKinsey's ASEAN Competitiveness Study, which was carried out for nine months, from May 2002 until February 2003, recommended ASEAN to undertake bold liberalization measures in a number of prioritised sectors. In addition, it was recommended that ASEAN should undertake four initiatives within those prioritised sectors, including: (1) the elimination of non-tariff barriers (custom efficiency, harmonization of procedures, and the removal of duplication in testing and licensing procedures); (2) to enhance tariff reforms (eliminating intra-regional tariffs to reduce the amount of paperwork and speed-up custom clearance); (3) to create a level playing field for capital (eliminating restrictions on cross-border investments); and (4) to improve

regional collaboration (achieving single market through targeting cooperation in several important areas, such as the flow of skilled labours across the region and technical assistance for newer member countries) (Schwarz and Villinger 2004). Meanwhile, the AHLTF gave three key recommendations as a first step toward realising the AEC, which include: (1) to strengthen the current economic cooperation initiatives, including economic cooperation for trade in goods, trade in services, investments, and intellectual property rights (IPRs); (2) the introduction of new initiatives and measures in integrating the economies of ASEAN. A key element in the second set of recommendation is the introduction of eleven priority sectors, including wood-based products, automotive (Indonesia), rubber-based products, textiles and apparels (Malaysia), fisheries, agro-based products (Myanmar), electronics (Philippines), healthcare, E-ASEAN (Singapore), air travel, and tourism (Thailand) (Vietnam was given the responsibility as the co-ordinator of the logistic sector in 2006); and (3) the institutional strengthening of ASEAN economic initiatives, which includes reaffirming ASEAN Economic Ministers (AEM) as co-ordinators of all ASEAN economic integration initiatives as well as resolving issues of policy. For further details of the Recommendation of the High-Level Task Force on ASEAN Economic Integration, visit the official web site of the ASEAN Secretariat (accessed 16 November 2005), at http://www.aseansec.org/hltf.htm.

30. As quoted by the *ABC News International* (2002), or visit the *ABC News International* official web site at www.abcnews.go.com.

31. As reported in the ASEAN Secretariat (1998a) official web site at http://www.aseansec.org/1619.htm

Chapter 6

Contemporary Indonesian Perceptions of AFTA

One of the main issues highlighted in New Regionalism Approach (NRA) is the spontaneous nature of regionalization, which emphasizes the role of domestic actors in the regionalism process (Hettne 1999; Schulz et al. 2001a). The present chapter deals with this issue, and provides a detailed analysis of empirical data findings which demonstrates the symbiotic nature of the relationship between Indonesian nationalism and ASEAN regional economic integration. In a more specific manner, this chapter provides an analysis of the perceptions held by Indonesian state and non-state actors toward their country's involvement in AFTA. Apart from being the result of intergovernmental agreement, regionalism may also be perceived as the outcome of the demands made by various domestic interest groups whose participation in the policy-making process has been increasing throughout the world (Grossman and Helpman 2002: 1). Therefore, this analysis of the contemporary perceptions of Indonesian state and non-state actors of AFTA will include the views held by governmental officials, non-governmental agencies (i.e., business associations and various non-governmental organizations [NGOs]), and selected foreign embassies in Jakarta.

As with previous chapters, the area of discussion in this chapter is divided into several parts in order to facilitate our analysis on the contemporary Indonesian perceptions of ASEAN regionalism, with specific reference to AFTA. The first area of discussion involves the identification of some background factors that influence the contemporary perceptions of Indonesian state and non-state actors of ASEAN's regional economic integration initiatives. Specific focus on this area of discussion is to analyze Indonesian state and non-state actors' perceptions of ASEAN's regional economic integration schemes prior to the economic crisis of 1997. Meanwhile, the second area of discussion in this chapter is based on the conceptual framework laid out in Chapter 3, which include: first, ASEAN regionalism and Indonesia's economic development; second, ASEAN regionalism and Indonesian nationalism; third, ASEAN regionalism and Indonesia's international autonomy, bargaining power, and the ability to contain the negative forces of globalization; and, fourth, the process of dissemination regarding ASEAN and AFTA. Finally, the third area of discussion of this chapter is an overall analysis of the perceptions of Indonesian state and non-state actors of the current implementation of AFTA.

The Contemporary Attitude of Indonesians toward AFTA

The perceptions of Indonesian state and non-state actors of AFTA in recent years have been changing. The emergence of the regional economic crisis in 1997, in particular, has played a major role in changing their attitudes toward ASEAN regional economic integration schemes. This change of attitude was actually stimulated by the economic crisis in that there was a consensus among Indonesian policymakers that enhanced regional economic integration in the Southeast Asian region would provide a fundamental mechanism to alleviate the economic crisis. As a result, the Indonesian government welcomed ASEAN's initiative to accelerate the AFTA schedule as envisioned in the Statement on Bold Measures.[1] This statement reflected the realization of ASEAN leaders that the economic crisis would have disastrous effects on the business dynamics and the economies of ASEAN member countries. It is for this reason that the member countries of ASEAN agreed to initiate some concrete measures to minimize the negative effects of the economic crisis.[2] Although AFTA in itself was not able "to address the regional upheaval and was certainly not designed to deal with such events" (Narine 2002: 186), ASEAN leaders were convinced that the acceleration of AFTA would stimulate economic growth and renewed business confidence, which, in turn, would speed up the process of economic recovery in the region. As it stood, Indonesia managed to place as many as 6,346 items (88.43 percent) on to AFTA's inclusion list in 2000, and 6,461 items (90.04 percent) in 2001 (Depperindag 2000: 27), which reflected Indonesia's genuine commitment toward AFTA.

Apart from a need to alleviate the economic crisis, Indonesian state and non-state actors were also inclined to strengthen ASEAN economic regionalism through AFTA for the overall benefits accrued from regional integration strategy (RIS), which have already been analyzed in Chapter 3. The field research also reveals that, because of their nation's commitment to AFTA, Indonesian state and non-state actors were convinced that the country could move closer to achieving its objectives of sustained economic development and the maintenance of national unity. With its capacity to promote economic growth and competitiveness, AFTA will have positive knock-on effects on the overall economic development of Indonesia, leading to prosperity. This nationwide prosperity will help the Indonesian government to minimize the threat of national disintegration presently posed by several ethno-nations (i.e., Aceh, Papua, etc.), which has become a serious post-crisis phenomenon in Indonesia. Moreover, the Indonesian government will also be able to increase its autonomy and bargaining power in the international arena through its full commitment in the ASEAN regional economic integration schemes. In the age of an increasing drive toward multilateralism, pressure groups (i.e., the business community, the academic community, NGOs and Civil Society Organizations [CSOs]) in Indonesia are demanding that their government should play an active role in the international arena.

Greater prosperity throughout the Southeast Asian region will also increase the prestige and power of other ASEAN member countries. Such conditions, in turn, will give ASEAN member countries greater autonomy and bargaining power when dealing with major powers (i.e., the United States and the EU) in many multilateral negotiations. In the long-term, this RIS is also hoped to contribute to the promotion of Indonesian culture and identity at both regional and international levels. Therefore, the need to minimize the negative impacts of the economic crisis and other important incentives outlined above have acted as stimulants to promote the speeding up of the AFTA schedule.

However, the Indonesian government's commitment toward the implementation and the schedule acceleration of AFTA drew some criticisms from various sources in Indonesia. Indonesian domestic pressure groups (i.e., business associations, NGOs, CSOs), for example, were very skeptical of Indonesia's entrance into the AFTA scheme. A year prior to the implementation of the AFTA scheme in January 2002, for example, the Indonesian Chambers of Commerce and Industry (KADIN—*Kamar Dagang dan Industri Indonesia*) expressed its concern about AFTA and made an official demand that the Indonesian government should delay Indonesia's entry into the scheme until 2005.[3] Almost a year after its implementation, the Indonesian government was still receiving stiff criticism over its commitment to AFTA. In the face of possible increases in fuel, power, and telephone prices in early 2003, for example, various Indonesian labor organizations and members of the Indonesian Entrepreneurs Association (APINDO—*Asosiasi Pengusaha Indonesia*) maintained that the Indonesian government's commitment to AFTA was proof that the government was more concerned about the country's global position than the welfare of its people (Guerin 2003). The anti-AFTA elements in Indonesia contended that the government should be more concerned about domestic problems rather than giving priority to regional trade liberalization issues.

Equally important in analyzing contemporary Indonesian attitudes toward AFTA was the introduction of the Regional Autonomy Laws (OtDa—*Otonomi Daerah*), which challenged the AFTA scheme. In 1999, the Habibie administration issued Act No. 22/1999, which is a regional government law,[4] and Act No. 25/1999,[5] which is concerned with the fiscal balance between central and regional governments. Both regulations were officially implemented in January 2001. As analyzed in Chapter 3, these two Acts were aimed at decentralizing the heavily centralized system employed by the New Order regime.[6] More comprehensively, Act No. 22 was used to make a fundamental shift in government functions from the central to the regional level, while Act No. 25 was employed in conjunction with the former Act to focus upon the fiscal relations between the central and regional governments (Silver et al. 2001: 346). These two acts have generated great concern, particularly over the issue of ethnonationalism. In KADIN's view, for example, the OtDa will complicate the investment climate in Indonesia as a result of several new provincial tax collection laws that could hinder business transactions.[7] Following the implementation of these regulations, many provincial governments have issued numerous provincial laws which have greatly bureaucratized the relationship between officials and the business sector. The Indonesian government, on the other hand, argues that such changes are a natural result of political transition in Indonesia, and should be considered *reform euphoria*.[8] Nevertheless, in the short run, diverging investment laws across the country do create a substantial challenge to the central government's commitment to AFTA.

ASEAN Regionalism and Indonesia's Economic Development

One main motive behind the Indonesian government's support for a regional integration strategy (RIS) is the achievement of sustained economic development. Although attitudes toward ASEAN have been generally positive, the majority of respondents interviewed remained cautious about ASEAN's current project, AFTA, and Indonesia's involvement in the scheme. The majority of respondents were convinced that Indonesia was not ready to get involved in the AFTA scheme due to the economic crisis of 1997. This was the prevalent view among the majority of respondents who took a convergence standpoint. However, those in the maximalist camp argued that Indonesia was ready to enter the AFTA scheme, and felt that this scheme would help Indonesia to escape from the current economic crisis, apart from other benefits that will be analyzed in the following sections (i.e., strengthening Indonesian nationalism, increasing bargaining power, international autonomy, and the ability to resist the negative forces of globalization). Minimalists, on the other hand, rejected this idea and argued that Indonesia should focus on its domestic economic problems before any further commitment to ASEAN and its AFTA scheme. Some representatives from Indonesian NGOs and CSOs, for example, believed that certain trade liberalization measures, such as AFTA, may be detrimental to the well-being of many Indonesians. Accordingly, rather than as a means to promote sustained economic development, regionalism was viewed as detrimental to Indonesia's domestic economy. Nevertheless, the symbiotic nature of the relationship between regionalism and nationalism in the context of ASEAN and Indonesia was demonstrated by the fact that the majority of respondents fell within the maximalist and convergence categories.

Maximalist

Those within the maximalist camp viewed ASEAN and Indonesia's commitment to ASEAN and its AFTA scheme as positive. Maximalist respondents believed that ASEAN regionalism should be strengthened because, among other things, it contributes to the achievement of sustained economic development in member countries. On the whole, the majority of government officials and representatives from the ASEAN Secretariat and foreign embassies were convinced that ASEAN and its AFTA scheme are crucial to sustaining Indonesia's sustained economic development. To start with, all the governmental officials from the eleven central governmental institutions and two provincial government institutions interviewed had no hesitation in expressing their support of strengthening regionalism in Southeast Asia.[9] ASEAN, in the eyes of most governmental officials, is still regarded as the main pillar of Indonesian foreign policy. Indonesia is expected to continue to enhance its activities at the regional level. One official from the Ministry of Foreign Affairs (MFA)[10] affirmed how important it was for Indonesia to conduct a *good neighboring* policy toward other ASEAN member countries. By prioritizing ASEAN, the objectives of regional stability, harmony, and prosperity can be achieved. This, in turn, creates the necessary space for Indonesia to focus on its progression beyond its current status as a developing country. Therefore, it is seen to be in the national interests of Indonesia to co-operate closely with other ASEAN member countries. This line of argument was shared by officials at various different governmental institutions. Some officials, such as those from the Ministry of Industry and Trade (Depperindag—*Departemen Perindustrian dan Perdagangan*)[11] and the Ministry of Finance (MoF),[12] even expressed personal support for Indonesia's involvement in ASEAN regional cooperation.

The majority of government officials interviewed also expressed a maximalist attitude toward the development of AFTA and Indonesia's participation in this scheme. Officials at the MFA and the Depperindag, for example, have been leading supporters of AFTA, and regard this scheme as representative of Indonesia's national interests at the regional level. The same officials also believed that there is a general consensus among policymakers that Indonesia would be left behind if participation in AFTA was discarded. Moreover, it was also hoped that AFTA would help alleviate Indonesia's internal economic problems, particularly those associated with good corporate governance, lack of skilled workers, and so on. AFTA has essentially aimed to increase the level of efficiency and competitiveness in the region, which means that Indonesia is obliged to solve its own internal problems immediately. Criticism concerning AFTA to date mostly came from local entrepreneurs. The official respondents, however, thought that it was very unlikely that the government would ever get a positive response about trade liberalization from local entrepreneurs. A recent report issued by the Depperindag reveals that 46 percent of commodities exported to the ASEAN market are ready to compete within AFTA.[13] As far as the Depperindag officials were concerned, many Indonesian industries are ready to compete in AFTA. In fact, by 2001 Indonesia was able to comply with AFTA's requirements by putting nearly 90 percent of the items included in the inclusion list.

Other governmental officials at other institutions, such as the Central Bank of Indonesia (BI)[14] and MoF, were also enthusiastic about AFTA. These institutions were acting in compliance with AFTA. The BI, alongside the MFA and the

Depperindag, is regarded as one of the main pillars of AFTA. This is in spite of the fact that the AFTA scheme is solely concerned with the eradication of tariffs among member countries, which is irrelevant to the BI's main activities. Nevertheless, according to the respondents at the BI, AFTA was a stepping-stone for Indonesia toward competing in the international market. The BI itself had been active in preparing Indonesia to enter AFTA in monetary terms. Past arrangements with other Southeast Asian Central Banks have been sustained to support the realization of AFTA, such as the ASEAN Swap Arrangement and the Bilateral Swap Arrangement (BSA).[15] The Southeast Asian Central Banks (SEACEN)[16] has also extended its monetary cooperation in the form of the ASEAN Surveillance Coordinating Unit (ASCU), which has had the objectives of strengthening the implementation of AFTA and acting as a buffer to prevent future crises. However, officials at the MoF were more optimistic about the progress of AFTA and criticized the Depperindag for its rather conservative measures to liberalize the Indonesian market. The respondents argued that the Depperindag had often implemented policies to protect various Indonesian industries, such as those evident in the steel, clove, and sugar industries. Officials from the MoF felt that AFTA should be taken very seriously, and the ministry regarded the scheme as a positive contribution to the economic development of the country. On the whole, therefore, respondents from both institutions believed Indonesia was ready to enter AFTA.

Other respondents who held a maximalist standpoint were representatives from the ASEAN Secretariat[17] and from various foreign embassies. To start with, as the best informed and most closely involved in the Association's activities, the representatives of the ASEAN Secretariat were by far the biggest supporters of ASEAN's regionalism attempts. The most prevalent concern expressed by the representatives of the Secretariat concerned the limitations imposed on the Secretariat's operations. Since its conception, the Secretariat has been criticized by the academic circle and the general public about its ineffectiveness in realizing the aspirations of Southeast Asian people. In their defense, however, the respondents argued that the public was unaware that the main functions of the Secretariat were limited to initiating, monitoring, and implementing the policies decided on by the member governments. The Secretariat, therefore, only works for ASEAN member governments and is incapable of setting up its own policies without prior consultation with all ASEAN member governments. These limitations persist despite attempts to upgrade the position of Secretary General to a Ministerial level in 1992. Although most integration schemes are normally tied into member countries' political interests, the Secretariat has arguably been successful in maintaining the progress of regional integration in Southeast Asia.

Meanwhile, the representatives of ASEAN and non-ASEAN foreign embassies also gave their views about Indonesia's participation in ASEAN and AFTA and their country's experiences in dealing with regionalism. To start with, the representatives of both the Royal Embassy of Thailand[18] and the Embassy of Brunei Darussalam[19] also expressed their government's enthusiasm toward the strengthening of regionalism in Southeast Asia.[20] The Ambassador of Thailand, in particular, stressed that support for regionalism is prevalent among both state and non-state actors in Thailand. His country's contributions to ASEAN have been significant since the Association's conception. Aside from being one of the founding fathers and the birthplace of ASEAN, Thailand has been active in proposing a number of schemes to enhance regional integration measures. The former Thai Prime Minister, Anand Panyarachun, for example, initiated AFTA in the early 1990s. ASEAN has also influenced the majority of foreign policies in Thailand since the Association's creation in 1967. Although relationships with neighboring countries have generally been good, Thailand's Prime Minister, Thaksin Shinawatra, endorsed a foreign policy that will allow Thailand to take a more proactive role at the regional level.[21] Although trade relationships have been positive between Thailand and Indonesia,[22] the respondent expressed his concern regarding a number of issues that may create problems in the immediate future if not properly handled by the Indonesian authorities. Among some of the most pressing issues are the complex bureaucracy of local authorities, security issues, and the question of Indonesia's leadership, which has been waning in ASEAN since the economic crisis began.

As with Thailand and Indonesia, Brunei Darussalam also place ASEAN at the cornerstone of its foreign policy. Brunei's contribution to regionalism in Southeast Asia is large. Apart from hosting a number of important ASEAN meetings and other activities, Brunei is also one of the major coordinators for ASEAN's dialogue partners, such as ASEAN-New Zealand (1985–1988), ASEAN-Canada (1988–1991), and so on, all of which reflect Brunei's commitment toward regional cooperation in Southeast Asia.[23] The representative of the Brunei Embassy in Jakarta felt that both his government and the Indonesian government saw the increasing regionalism in Southeast Asia as positive. The respondent also seemed to suggest that both his government and the Indonesian government have been very committed to ASEAN and its AFTA scheme. Since the economic crisis in 1997, for example, there has been an acceleration in economic integration, apparent in the context of AFTA and in the increased number of joint investments among ASEAN entrepreneurs. In 2001 alone, many entrepreneurs from both Indonesia and Brunei expressed their interest in conducting joint investments in agribusiness. Despite this, the representative of the Brunei Embassy also noted that some problems still existed between Brunei and its ASEAN counterparts. Brunei is a relatively small country that relies on oil as its main source of income. As a result, there was a limited amount of space and few natural resources available for foreign investment to take place in Brunei. Meanwhile, the majority of Brunei's economy was comprised of small and medium size enterprises (SMEs), which cannot compete with the many multinationals that operate in other ASEAN countries. Consequently, economic initiatives between Brunei and its ASEAN counterparts remain modest.

Similar to other respondents in this category, the representatives of the U.S. Embassy,[24] the German Embassy,[25] and the British Embassy[26] also regarded the

Southeast Asian regionalism process as positive. The United States, in particular, saw the growing Southeast Asian market as having potential for foreign investments. The U.S. automotive industry, for example, is deeply interested in the
Southeast Asian region. According to the representative from the U.S. Embassy,
the three largest U.S. automotive companies, Chrysler, Ford, and General Motors, have recently been in the region to conduct feasibility studies for investment, acknowledging that the Southeast Asian region is important to U.S. economic interests. In a speech made by the former U.S. Trade Representative,
Charlene Bershefsky, at the U.S. Ambassadors Tour Annual Dinner in Washington D.C. in 2000, it was clear that the United States regarded the US-ASEAN
relationship as mutually beneficial. The Southeast Asian region has recently
been the recipient of nearly US$42 billion of American investment, while the
United States is the central market for exports from the region with a value ex-
ceeding US$80 billion in goods and services in 1999 alone. It is, therefore, only
logical for the United States to continue to support strengthening regionalism in
the Southeast Asian region.

At the same time, both Great Britain and Germany also agreed with their
American counterpart, but provided a rather more idealistic explanation for the
logic of regionalism in Southeast Asia. They felt that regionalism clearly reflects
the needs of member countries to forge a relationship. In this context, ASEAN
has been successful and has been able to play a major role in enhancing the interest of its member countries in the international fora. The German government
encouraged the strengthening of the regionalism process in Southeast Asia, and
argued that the benefits of an integrated region will exceed the benefits that individual states might have in managing alone. The British Embassy official, on
the other hand, argued more from the point of view of economics to explain his
government support toward regionalism in Southeast Asia. As with the United
States, Britain has substantial investments in the region. In Indonesia alone, the
UK is the second largest foreign investor after Japan, with total investments
amounting to US$50 billion in 2000. The British government was, therefore,
very committed to the agreement made within ASEM. There has been recent
concern about the growing economic uncertainty in the region, particularly in
Indonesia. It was felt that the move toward regionalism has somehow been
halted since the economic crisis began, and most countries in the region have
been more concerned with domestic rather than regional issues. Despite this, the
respondent remained optimistic about the future of regionalism in Southeast
Asia, although could not guarantee any deepening regional integration in the
region.

In terms of AFTA, officials from the ASEAN Secretariat and ASEAN foreign embassies believed that the implementation of AFTA and Indonesia would
benefit substantially from its commitment in the AFTA scheme. Although since
the economic crisis began member governments have been engrossed with domestic problems, relationship among them remain relatively stable. Commitment to the AFTA's schedule shows that the economic crisis has not damaged
the relationships between member countries. In addition, it was felt that there

was little to suggest that the progress of CEPT had been disrupted by the recent economic crisis. The only disruption caused to CEPT came from certain members' insistence on protecting some of their industries, such as the Malaysian automotive industry. Despite this, it was felt that AFTA, as of 2001, was still on track, which proved that the economic crisis had been the major catalyst in the ASEAN regionalization process. Similar views were also expressed by the representatives of non-ASEAN foreign embassies.[27] The U.S. representative, in particular, applauded the progress of regionalism in Southeast Asia and the Indonesian government's efforts to maintain its position in AFTA despite the economic crisis. The only concern expressed by the majority of non-ASEAN foreign embassy representatives was about Indonesia's passivity in the Association in recent years. This was seen to have affected the regionalization process in Southeast Asia and also the relationships between member countries. Indonesia did not seem to have either the financial capacity or the time to assume leadership in the region in the short-term, as most resources were allocated to manage domestic problems, such as eradicating poverty, corruption, threat of national disintegration.

Minimalist

Minimalist respondents did not feel that ASEAN regionalism contributes much to Indonesian economic development. As a result, they opposed regionalism, or at least the concept of open regionalism to which ASEAN subscribes, and argued that the Indonesian government should focus more on domestic problems. Those who opposed the concept of regionalism were generally the representatives of Indonesian NGOs and CSOs. Pressure groups, such as the Urban Poor Consortium (UPC),[28] the National Front for Indonesian Labor Struggle (FNPBI—*Front Nasional Perjuangan Buruh Indonesia*),[29] the Association of Indonesian Muslim Intellectuals (ICMI—*Ikatan Cendikiawan Muslim Indonesia*),[30] and the International NGO Forum on Indonesian Development (INFID),[31] believed that regionalism had never contributed significantly to Indonesia's economic development. For the representatives from both UPC and FNPBI, for example, Indonesia needed to concentrate on its internal problems before embarking upon regional or international adventures. They felt that Indonesia's current problems extend beyond that of the economic crisis. One of Indonesia's persistent problems has been the poor quality of its human resources, which has been exacerbated since the economic crisis began in 1997. Indonesia's ability to compete with its ASEAN counterparts has been undermined partly because the human resource problem has not been adequately addressed. The world economy normally regards developing countries, such as Indonesia, as a good place for foreign investments owing to its abundance of cheap labor. The minimalist respondents, however, strongly criticized the government's decision to use cheap labor as a tool in marketing campaigns to attract foreign investment. Southeast Asian countries such as Malaysia and the Philippines are still able to attract foreign investment despite higher labor costs in total production costs (roughly around 20 percent in comparison to Indonesia's 5–8 percent). Moreover, the minimalist respondents also believed that Indonesia should reconsider its position in ASEAN, to prevent the country becoming a *consumer market* (major importer) in the Association's economic cooperation schemes. However, others in the minimalist group paid more attention to trade liberalization at the global level. For ICMI, ASEAN was not particularly significant for Indonesia, aside from creating regional stability and security. It was felt that ASEAN countries have traditionally conducted trade with other non-ASEAN countries. Therefore, regionalism was not excessively important at the present time. The idea of regionalism had somehow changed in recent years as countries have become more open to the world market. A closed form of regionalism, such as trade bloc, was seen by the ICMI to be preferable since Indonesia was not yet capable of competing in the world market.

The same representatives of Indonesian NGOs and CSOs also held a minimalist standpoint toward the development of AFTA. Reasons for opposition varied according to the different concerns of each individual pressure group. On the whole, however, there were four major reasons why they resisted AFTA. Firstly, the majority of Indonesian NGOs and CSOs were pessimistic about AFTA since ASEAN economies are still highly competitive among one another. Apart from that, it was felt that many ASEAN countries were overly preoccupied with their national interests, such as in the agricultural sector, which is still considered a sensitive area in need of protection by most member countries. As a result, it was felt that ASEAN still lacked economic openness in comparison to other regional organizations. It was thought, therefore, highly unlikely that the Indonesian economy would be positively impacted by the implementation of AFTA. Secondly, even if AFTA did influence the economic activities of member countries, the impact of the scheme would be limited in comparison to policies pursued by other multilateral bodies, such as the WTO. A third problem was seen to lie in the Association's reluctance to allow the active participation of civil society groups in the decision-making process. To date, as pointed out earlier by respondents in the maximalist camp, issues such as labor, the environment, human rights, and democracy have hardly been discussed by the Association. ASEAN is criticized by most representatives of Indonesian NGOs and CSOs for having placed too much emphasis on trade-related issues in AFTA. They also argued that concentration on trade alone would only benefit a small proportion of the ASEAN community. The Association should widen the focus of its cooperation schemes, particularly those related to issues such as development, the environment, and so on. Finally, although some information regarding ASEAN-related activities was indeed available, it was felt that the amount of information passed on to the general public was limited, highly technical and expensive to obtain.

As regards Indonesia's participation in AFTA, the majority of respondents in the minimalist camp also noted that the economic situation in Indonesia during the post-1997 economic crisis was not conducive to the country's involvement in AFTA. Apart from being a consumer market (major importer) for other ASEAN countries, there was also a shortage of skilled human resources in Indonesia, which would make the country less competitive to other ASEAN countries. If the government insisted on pursuing its position in the scheme, the majority of respondents predicted that Indonesia would become a consumer market (i.e., major importers) for other ASEAN countries. Another problem was seen to be the shortage of Indonesian skilled human resources, which could not compete with other ASEAN countries. It was reported in 2001 that 76 percent of the Indonesian workforce had attended only primary education (through to sixth grade) and did not possess the technological training or knowledge for the numerous positions open (Gross 2001: 1). As an agrarian country, about 50 percent of the Indonesian labor force consists mainly of farmers.

Despite this, the Indonesian agricultural industry, such as rice production, has not prospered as well as those in neighboring countries, such as Thailand. Food shortages are very common these days while the prices of agricultural products have been very expensive. Moreover, ASEAN was also criticized for its inability to cope with the concerns of the Indonesian people. The Indonesian government has been concentrating on national economic recovery and, at the same time, neglecting its commitment to AFTA. The government was criticized for not being more aggressive at the regional level. Some minimalists were also concerned about the Indonesian political elite and their influence on government decisions in ASEAN and AFTA. The economic interests of the political elite were thought to influence the Indonesian government's pursuit of protectionist measures, such as that being imposed on agriculture industry, in AFTA. If this is indeed the case, the scheme may turn out to be useless.

Convergence

A Convergence standpoint was generally held among a handful of government officials, members of Indonesian business associations, the academic community, and representatives of some Indonesian NGOs and CSOs. All respondents within the convergence category held a generally pragmatic attitude toward Indonesia's commitment to ASEAN and its AFTA scheme. Support for ASEAN regionalism would prevail as long as ASEAN and its AFTA scheme contributed toward the achievement of sustained economic development in Indonesia. In general, however, the majority of respondents within the convergence category believed that Indonesia's commitment to ASEAN and AFTA would improve the country's economic development.

To start with, government officials from the Ministry of Co-operative, Small and Medium Enterprises (MoC-SMEs),[32] the Investment Coordinating Board (BKPM—*Badan Koordinasi Penanaman Modal*),[33] the Custom and Excise Office,[34] the National Logistic Agency (BULOG—*Badan Usaha Logis-*

tik)[35] expressed their enthusiasm about ASEAN regionalism. They were convinced that the strengthening of ASEAN regionalism would have a tremendous effect on Indonesia's sustained economic development. Despite this, the same government officials were quite cautious about commenting about AFTA and their country's involvement in the scheme. With regard to AFTA, respondents from these four institutions were concerned about the competitive nature of ASEAN economies, the speedy implementation of AFTA, and the potentially exploitative nature of trade liberalization in general. Moreover, the same officials were also concerned about the lack of information regarding AFTA and Indonesia's readiness to join in the scheme. At the same time, Indonesia's readiness to join AFTA was generally felt to depend on the country's immediate, internal problems. With regard to the development of AFTA, respondents disagreed about competitiveness among ASEAN economies. The BULOG representative was also concerned about the impact of AFTA and AFTA's timeframe on the agricultural sector. The respondent believed that both the content and the schedule of the AFTA agreement should be re-studied. At present, it appears that most countries are being forced to speedily expand their inclusion list. If this approach continues, it was felt that it would benefit only the countries in the region that were fully equipped to face trade liberalization measures, such as Singapore. Despite this, officials from the four government institutions above felt that AFTA has the potential to promote economic development in the country due to its capacity to create efficiency and to attract foreign investment.

Meanwhile, out of the four representatives of business associations interviewed, only the representative from the Association for the Advancement of Small Business (PUPUK—*Perkumpulan Untuk Peningkatan Usaha Kecil*) showed reservation toward ASEAN.[36] For the majority of these representatives, such as those from the Indonesian Chambers of Commerce and Industry (KADIN—*Kamar Dagang dan Industri Indonesia*),[37] the Indonesian Entrepreneurs Association (APINDO—*Asosiasi Pengusaha Indonesia*),[38] and the Indonesian Society of Small and Medium Scale Entrepreneurs (KUKMI—*Kerukunan Usahawan Kecil dan Menengah Indonesia*),[39] ASEAN remains the main focus in the Indonesian economy. The Head of KADIN, for example, continuously reiterated how important it was to *be ASEAN and to think ASEAN*.[40] According to the respondent, globalization has been the rhetoric of most major Western powers which have been implementing protectionist measures to serve their own national interests. In response, it was felt that the Indonesian government should take a more active role in pushing other ASEAN countries to counter unbalances created by the West. For the majority of the representatives from Indonesian business associations, the Southeast Asian region was still better off with than without ASEAN.

Enthusiasm toward ASEAN was equally reflected toward AFTA. Such support was even present among members of KADIN who had previously been major critics of AFTA. KADIN had persistently asked the government to delay Indonesia's entry into the scheme for several reasons.[41] Firstly, KADIN argued that most Indonesian entrepreneurs were not prepared to join AFTA. Secondly,

KADIN also insisted that the weak security and poor economic situation in the country would compromise the implementation of AFTA. Thirdly, there was also a growing consensus among members of KADIN that Indonesia, as the largest ASEAN market, would be a competing ground for both domestic and foreign entrepreneurs. It would not be in the interests of many domestic interest groups to allow the demise of local SMEs. The representatives of KADIN also felt that there was miscommunication between the Indonesian media and KADIN. KADIN had asked the government to delay the AFTA schedule only in certain sectors, such as the retail sector, from the originally agreed 2002 to 2005. In regard to the retail sector, members of KADIN disagreed with government officials who insisted that the binding nature of the AFTA agreement should be respected. In contrast, KADIN argued that it has never asked the government to pull back fully from AFTA as such an action would have a detrimental effect on Indonesia's position at the global level. A binding agreement or commitment cannot be broken, but it can be delayed. Within many international agreements there is the recognition of a nation's right to defend its own national interests first, and this also applies to AFTA. In the view of the respondent, the United States has often been reluctant to open up its agricultural sector in the WTO since such this would undermine its own national interest. The Indonesian economy is far smaller than the American economy, but still has its own national interests and should be able to defend them. The recent wave of large retail TNCs entering the country has not created favorable conditions for local retailers.

As for the remaining industrial sectors, KADIN believed that Indonesia would be ready for AFTA. This also applies to other ASEAN member countries, even to those that have been severely hit by the economic crisis. Thailand, for instance, has been very supportive toward AFTA by opening its agricultural sector, which has been liberalized since 1995. In recent years, Thailand has become one of the major exporters of rice and sugar to other ASEAN countries. IMF prescriptions have meant that many Southeast Asian economies have remained open. Indonesia will also adopt such an approach despite domestic concerns over the country's involvement in AFTA. Since the signing of the first Letter of Intent (LoI) with the IMF on 31 October 1997, Indonesia has been forced to open up even its traditionally protected agricultural sector. Although this has a detrimental effect on domestic prices, the Indonesian government and major interest groups will remain committed to the IMF's prescriptions. This, in turn, should have a positive result on the country's commitment to AFTA.

However, other Indonesian business associations did not share KADIN's views. For example, the representative from APINDO was convinced that Indonesia would be negatively affected if it continued with its commitment to AFTA. The respondent also argued that Indonesia, even long before the economic crisis, could not compete with other ASEAN countries or at the global level. Indonesia's export growth in wood products and apparels, for example, had decreased by about 21 percent and 11 percent respectively between 1989 and 1996.[42] It was thus deemed unrealistic for Indonesia to become involved in any regional trade liberalization measures. The respondent felt that Indonesia was behind in terms of good corporate governance, competitive technical skills, and the flexibility needed to achieve efficiency. Moreover, PUPUK was also concerned about the increasing tendency for large TNCs to decentralize their production and distribution activities which, in turn, might have a very damaging effect on local Indonesian entrepreneurs. The remaining respondents in the business community generally regarded the development of AFTA as positive, although they thought that the government should take a very cautious approach toward further economic liberalization in the country. They also stressed that the government would face difficulties in gaining support from the Indonesian business community if planning was not in their interests.

As with the representatives of Indonesian business associations, members of the academic community in Indonesia also expressed their support for ASEAN regionalism. In the view of Dr. Hadi Soesastro from the CSIS, the existence of ASEAN remained important for Indonesia.[43] In the last thirty-five years, ASEAN's contribution to the region's development has been significant, particularly as a major stabilizing force in Southeast Asia. Because Southeast Asia was more stable, countries in the region were able to focus on their own development. His associate at the CSIS, Dr. Cornelis Luhulima, also felt that Indonesia had always supported regionalism in Southeast Asia.[44] The former President Suharto was possibly one of the first people to coin the term an *integrated Southeast Asia*. The New Order government's pragmatic approach toward ASEAN was primarily due to senior military officers' preoccupation with preserving sovereignty and nationalism. Furthermore, Dr. Dewi Anwar was even more optimistic about Southeast Asian regionalism, and implied that her ideal would be to have an ASEAN Community in the near future, although she admitted that such an ideal may be somewhat unrealistic.[45]

Despite the prevalence of positive views about ASEAN, some members of the academic community also retained certain skepticisms, particularly on the issue of ASEAN's capacity to find economic complementarity among its members. As a supporter of a macro-regionalism at the Asia-Pacific level, Prof. Lepi Tarmidi argued that the search for economic complementarity was more feasible at the APEC level than at the ASEAN level.[46] Most ASEAN member countries have traditionally been trade partners with APEC's non-ASEAN members and he felt that it was logical for Indonesia to focus more upon the development of APEC than on ASEAN. The original six ASEAN members were initially skeptical about entering the APEC forum, but later changed their minds owing to the non-binding nature of the agreement, which offered ASEAN countries the chance to pull back from APEC. For Dr. Bustanul Arifin, on the other hand, it was not a question of which regional grouping Indonesia should belong to.[47] He felt that specific attention should be given to enhanced cooperation outside the economic field, since economic cooperation had largely failed to generate any substantial improvements for member countries.

Members of the academic community also gave varying responses regarding the development of AFTA and Indonesia's participation in the scheme. With regard to the development of AFTA, nearly all respondents agreed that it had been very positive, although some held a convergent standpoint on the issue. The majority of members of the academic community believed that AFTA had made a positive contribution toward the development of ASEAN member countries. One of the most important contributions highlighted was AFTA's capacity to provide a much needed stepping-stone for member countries to compete in the world market. AFTA was, after all, intended to transform the conservative, protectionist, and inward-looking economic policies of member countries. The majority of respondents from the academic community also agreed that it was not the intention of ASEAN member countries to conduct trade liberalization at the regional level *per se*. AFTA would make ASEAN member countries more confident that they will eventually become one of the major economic powers in Asia, if not in the world. Despite this, the majority of respondents also agreed that the issues of nationalism and sovereignty still limit the development of AFTA. Dr. Soesastro, in particular, criticized member countries' excessive persistence in protecting their own national interests. He felt that Malaysia, for instance, had continued to take protectionist measures to defend the national interests of its automotive industry. For the benefit of its two national cars, Proton and Perodua, the Malaysian government has postponed the liberalization of its automotive industry until 1 January 2005. As of February 2004, tariffs imposed on the Malaysian automotive industry were between 42 and 300 percent. The Malaysian government planned to cut these tariff rates to 20 percent only, instead of the 5 percent imposed in other ASEAN countries (Shari 2003). Generally, therefore, it was felt that ASEAN countries remained closed.

Although the majority of members of the academic community viewed the existence of ASEAN as positive, many of them also showed reservation about the development of AFTA and Indonesia's participation in the scheme. In the view of Dr. Anwar, for example, many people were unhappy with the government's decision to implement AFTA. Indonesia was simply not ready to enter the AFTA scheme as a result of the economic crisis. It was, therefore, rather unrealistic to ask many Indonesian domestic industries to participate in AFTA since they needed time to recover. In the worst case scenario, Indonesia would be flooded with foreign goods if the government maintained its policy on AFTA. On the whole, Dr. Anwar believed that AFTA would be difficult to implement in Indonesia. Even if the country had not been hit by the economic crisis, Indonesia had a long tradition of protectionism in the region. It could even be argued that there is no reason for Indonesia to participate in AFTA when the country itself already constitutes a large market. The amount of investment conducted by Indonesian entrepreneurs in other ASEAN countries was limited. In 2003 alone, for example, the Board of Investment of Thailand (BOIT) only noted one foreign investment from Indonesia.[48] It was felt to be difficult to persuade Indonesians that AFTA would be beneficial to the national economy.

Moreover, it would also be difficult to convince Indonesians that trade liberalization at the ASEAN level would provide a training ground for competition in the world market. Moreover, Prof. Tarmidi also added that the economic crisis will create problems for member countries which fail to reach the agreed targets. As of February 2000, for example, there were about 53,229 items listed into the inclusion list. However, the crisis will undermine AFTA targets since developing member countries will find it difficult to follow the developed countries in liberating their economies.

On the whole, however, the majority members of the academic community believed that Indonesia was definitely ready to join AFTA, although the scheme should be treated cautiously. For Dr. Soesastro, Dr. Luhulima, and Prof. Tarimidi, Indonesia was far more ready than its ASEAN counterparts, such as Malaysia and Thailand, to join the AFTA scheme. The Indonesian market was liberalized in 1995, when the AFTA arrangement was still in its infancy. Dr. Soesastro also added that, prior to 2002, nearly 60 percent of Indonesian traded items had already reached a 0–5 percent tariff level. The respondent felt optimist that the remaining 30 percent of traded items would reach a tariff level of below 10 percent by the time AFTA was implemented. Generally, therefore, Indonesia's tariff levels are relatively low, although there are some exceptions, such as those in the automotive, chemical, iron, and steel industries, where tariff rates are still above 50 percent.[49] In addition, Dr. Luhulima also postulated that lowering the Indonesian tariff rates to 0–5 percent would have little impact on the overall domestic economy as the average tariff rate of Indonesia at the time of the interview (2001) was 8 percent. He even criticized some Indonesian business associations, particularly KADIN, for insisting that the government should postpone the AFTA schedule to 2005. Instead of pulling back from AFTA, he felt it would be better to differentiate between the industrial sectors that were ready, such as garment and electronics, and those that were not ready, such as agriculture sector, to join AFTA.[50] Meanwhile, although Prof. Tarmidi remained skeptical that AFTA would be implemented fully by 2002, he was convinced that the Indonesian market was by far one of the most liberated markets in the region. Many of the liberalization measures in the country have been in line with the country's commitment to the WTO and other multilateral agreements. Moreover, owing to the recent chaotic domestic economic conditions, he felt that Indonesia was bound to liberalize further, and the level of trade would increase following trade liberalization, thus increasing the growth potential of the country.

Apart from members of various Indonesian business associations and members of the academic community, there were also some representatives of Indonesian NGOs and CSOs who held a convergence standpoint on the issue. Indonesian NGOs and CSOs, such as the Pesticide Action Network Indonesia (PANI),[51] the Federation of the Indonesian Workers Union (FSPSI—*Federasi Serikat Pekerja Seluruh Indonesia*),[52] Indonesian Consumer Organization (YLKI),[53] the Leadership for Environment and Development (LEAD),[54] the Uni—Social Democrat (UNISOSDEM),[55] and Information and Civic Studies (KLIK—*Kajian Layanan Informasi untuk Kedaulatan Rakyat*),[56] generally support the concept of regionalism in Southeast Asia as long as it serves Indonesia's national interests. At the same time, however, the representatives from these NGOs and CSOs also felt rather indifferent about ASEAN. Regional issues, after all, have not been on the agenda of many Indonesian NGOs and CSOs. Among these NGOs and CSOs, only PANI that showed genuine interest about both national and regional issues.[57] For the remaining NGO and CSO workers, the main reason for overlooking regional issues was the limited amount of information disseminated on Southeast Asian regionalism issues by both the ASEAN Secretariat and the government. Another reason has been that NGOs and CSOs did not see ASEAN as a potential threat to the national development of the country. The majority of NGOs and CSOs interviewed were convinced that larger international institutions, such as the WTO and the IMF, pose a greater threat to the preservation of national sovereignty and the national interests of the country.

Unlike PANI, other NGOs and CSOs that fall within convergence category were largely uninformed about the development of ASEAN, in spite of their knowledge of the history of ASEAN. As the Head of the Federation of the Indonesian Workers Union (FSPSI) postulated, Indonesia is presently experiencing acute internal problems, which makes it impossible for local NGOs and CSOs, including FSPSI, to focus on Indonesia's foreign policy or ASEAN. Despite this, they were still interested in the development of ASEAN, although most information concerning this issue had come mainly from the media. FSPSI was mainly concerned with possible trade liberalization measures both at regional and international levels, which would have significant impacts on the well-being of domestic workers. Meanwhile, the representatives from YLKI, LEAD, UNISOSDEM, and KLIK maintained that negotiations between governments and pressure groups were easier to conduct at the ASEAN level than at the macro-regional level, such as APEC. Experts at the macro-regional level mainly consist of those trained in developed countries whose opinions often neglect the main concerns of local consumer protection groups. Negotiations with other consumer protection groups at the ASEAN level are more effective since problems encountered among groups in the region would have more similarities than those encountered at the broader Asia-Pacific level. Despite this, all the maximalist respondents interviewed criticized the government for its lack of interest in involving local NGOs and CSOs in dealing with regional problems. This has been evident, *inter alia*, in the lack of attempts made by the government to properly disseminate information regarding ASEAN-related matters to local NGOs and CSOs.

The representatives from civil society organizations also supported the development of AFTA and Indonesia's participation in the scheme. In the view of representative of PANI, for example, AFTA was preferable to other multilateral trade liberalization measures, such as those of the WTO. In 1996, PANI and other similar pressure groups in Southeast Asia conducted a preliminary study on the feasibility of AFTA. Although the study showed positive results, PAN has recently raised concern over the proposed decrease in Indonesia's tariff levels on agricultural products when AFTA is implemented. At the same time, the country is also expected to reduce its import tariffs on rice to zero percent. Despite this, AFTA was seen to be inevitable, and, as a result, PANI has made significant efforts to study the scheme further. Despite their support toward AFTA, some NGOs and CSOs that fall within the convergence category also expressed concerns over the items in AFTA's inclusion list and over the public reaction toward the government's decision to accelerate the schedule of the scheme. The representatives from UNISOSDEM, FSPSI, and the Indonesian Human Rights Group (Komnas-HAM—*Komisi Nasional untuk Hak-Hak Asasi Manusia*),[58] for example, believed items included in the scheme's list should be added on step-by-step. It was felt, therefore, that there should be more meetings among ASEAN member governments' officials in order to increase the efficiency of AFTA. In addition, they also criticized decisions made within the AFTA framework as highly illogical. Southeast Asian leaders, for example, had been very reluctant to discuss any important issues apart from trade, such as labor and the environment. By neglecting these important issues, it was expected that the implementation of AFTA would likely face stiff opposition from many domestic forces.

ASEAN Regionalism and Indonesian Nationalism

The question of Indonesian nationalism versus ASEAN regionalism has been the central analysis of this book. The importance of this question lies in whether Indonesian nationalism acts as an impediment to the development of ASEAN regionalism. Those respondents categorized as maximalists contended that Indonesian nationalism can be strengthened through the country's commitment in ASEAN. On the other hand, Indonesian minimalists maintained the opposite, and argued that Indonesian nationalism is gradually weakening today as a result of increased trade liberalization. All respondents within the convergence category held a rather pragmatic view on the subject, and insisted that emphasis should be placed on the concept of *logical nationalism,* in which regionalism is perceived as an enhancement of Indonesian national interests, rather than *romantic nationalism.* On the whole, however, the relationship between nationalism and regionalism was once again proven to be symbiotic since the majority of respondents could be placed within the maximalist and convergence camps.

Maximalist

The respondents within the maximalist camp believed mainly that ASEAN regionalism is crucial to the well-being of Indonesian nationalism. In addition, ASEAN regionalism was thought to be useful in helping the Indonesian government eradicate its many domestic problems, particularly the threat of national disintegration. The maximalist camp consisted mainly of two representatives from Indonesian government institutions, officials from the ASEAN Secretariat and representatives from various foreign embassies. The majority of these respondents supported the argument that Indonesian nationalism would be strengthened through further commitment to the ASEAN regionalization process. Among governmental officials, only officials at the Ministry of Foreign Affairs (MFA) and the Ministry of Finance (MoF) expressed a maximalist attitude on the issue of the relationship between Indonesian nationalism and ASEAN regionalism. The official respondent from the MoF argued that Indonesia has so far been committed to the process of regionalization in Southeast Asia and the Indonesian government has given no indication that it might take any drastic moves that may jeopardize its commitment in AFTA. Many Indonesians have begun to realize that ASEAN and its AFTA scheme will serve Indonesia's overall national interests at the domestic and global levels. At the domestic level, Indonesia's participation in AFTA will help Indonesia achieve sustained economic development, which is a necessary ingredient of national stability and unity. At the international level, Indonesia's participation in AFTA will give the country a much needed stepping-stone toward wider multilateral trade agreements, such as those within WTO frameworks.

An official from the MFA also believed that, to a large extent, the majority of Indonesians still perceive the tariff elimination measures within the AFTA agreement as positive. The official respondent interviewed, for example, convinced that AFTA would contribute significantly to the economic development of Indonesia. The more prosperous Indonesia, the more likely that the Indonesian government would be able to eradicate many domestic problems, particularly those associated with the threat of national disintegration. The rise of ethnonationalism in Indonesia has been associated with unequal economic distribution throughout the country. Therefore, AFTA has become part of Indonesia's national interests. Another encouraging aspect of AFTA has been ASEAN countries' attempts to overcome the problem of economic competition. The small markets of Singapore and Brunei, for example, are becoming increasingly dependent on their neighbors as sources of natural resources. Even a large country such as Indonesia has become increasingly dependent on Thailand for rice imports. This is a starting point from which ASEAN's initiatives for further regionalism can be taken up. Another way to increase the levels of intra-trade is to focus upon the development of finished goods production rather than on raw materials. A number of Southeast Asian countries have initiated such projects in the past but failed to sustain them as a result of their incapacity to produce and to sell high quality products. This issue remains a challenge for the participants of AFTA. Indonesians are now increasingly aware of the positive outcomes that regional trade liberalization will bring to the country. It is, therefore, unlikely that nationalism will present a major stumbling block to the progress of regionalism.

Meanwhile, the representatives of the ASEAN Secretariat and foreign embassies also gave their perceptions about Indonesian nationalism and ASEAN regionalism. Most representatives of the ASEAN Secretariat and foreign embassies convinced that Indonesia has still followed through on its commitment at the regional level. There is no significant evidence to suggest that Indonesia will be withdrawing from any arrangements made at the ASEAN level. The representatives of the ASEAN Secretariat in particular noted that even in the past Indonesia has never actually withdrawn from ASEAN's regionalism initiatives. The failure of past projects has led to an agenda of compromise that will accommodate the interests of all member countries. It is important to point out that ASEAN is still relatively young and is learning to accommodate the differences between its members. The respondents expected that the Association would come up with new and fresh ideas to promote further integration. As regards the AFTA agenda, Indonesia is still one of the most open countries in the region. By the end of 2000, for example, Indonesia was ranked third among AFTA participants, behind only Thailand and Malaysia for the number of items listed for inclusion under the CEPT scheme.[59] In addition, the respondents also thought that the Indonesian public is becoming increasingly aware that their country's commitment to ASEAN and AFTA will help the Indonesian government manage the many domestic problems that have emerged since the economic crisis in 1997. The threat of national disintegration, for example, has been mounting since Suharto stepped down from presidency in 1998. Uneven economic prosperity throughout Indonesia could be better dealt with if Indonesia remained focused on its foreign economic policy (FEP), particularly on AFTA.

Moreover, the representatives of the U.S. embassy also added that the Indonesian government is still able to balance its interests at the regional level. It was felt, therefore, inappropriate to refer to nationalistic sentiments among Indonesian citizens against ASEAN. The respondent also added that the most negative reactions were directed toward international institutions, such as the IMF, the World Bank, and developed countries, such as Australia, Britain and the United States. The respondent referred to the number of demonstrations held in front of the U.S. and the British embassies since the start of the economic crisis. The representatives of the Thai and the Brunei Embassy also held a maximalist standpoint on the issue. It was argued by both respondents that most people in the Southeast Asian region have probably realized that they no longer live in isolation. Collective attempts to cope with the challenges of globalization are therefore inevitable. To that end, the Thai government proposed a flexible engagement system in 1998, which will enable each member state to deal solely with its own problems. Consultation at the regional level will only be conducted if the troubled member government is unable to cope with the problems on hand. The notion of nationalism and regionalism should, therefore, be balanced out, depending on each individual country's need at that time. Despite this, both respondents convinced that ASEAN has been able to maintain member countries' sovereignty and national unity. In light of possible threat of disintegration Indonesia, for example, the Thai government, as noted in Chapter 3, was committed to support Indonesia's national unity. The representative of the Brunei Embassy similarly insisted that nationalism has not caused problems in the development of ASEAN. On the contrary, most ASEAN countries realize the necessity of regionalism initiatives to handle regional problems.

Minimalist

Those in the minimalist camp did not believe that ASEAN regionalism has contributed much to the preservation of Indonesian nationalism. Many respondents in the convergence category felt that ASEAN's continued pursuit of open regionalism has threatened Indonesian culture and identity. The majority of respondents within the minimalist camp consisted mainly of representatives from Indonesian NGOs and CSOs. One prominent nationalist figure during the research interview was Adi Sasono, the Head of ICMI. Sasono convinced that nationalism has been a quite significant force in Indonesia in recent years. As mentioned in Chapter 5, Sasono was once regarded as the nationalistic figure who introduced the *People's Economy* (*Ekonomi Kerakyatan*) system when he held the post of Minister of Co-operatives and SMEs during the Habibie administration. The people's economy system was regarded as highly nationalistic as it did not favor the development of large conglomerates, which were mainly composed of ethnic Chinese Indonesians and foreigners. At the time it was feared that such a policy would hinder the development of foreign investment in the country. On the contrary, the Indonesian economy in fact improved when the policy was implemented. The Indonesian economy is mainly composed of many SMEs, although their contribution was only about 14 percent of the total national GDP in 2001.[60] Unemployment was at a high of 20 percent at the time, and the poverty level reached 39 percent in 1999. The People's Economy system was introduced at that time to balance the economy by making it more efficient and preventing monopolization of the distribution and production processes. Sasono, therefore, rejected the nationalist tag attached to his policy. The policy worked reasonably well and created a significant change in the economy. By the time Habibie was removed from office in September 1999, the inflation level was down to about 10 percent, from an initial 77 percent, while the poverty level was slashed to about 14 percent.

Despite this, Sasono still regarded nationalism as a significant force in Indonesia and Indonesia does not necessarily benefit from ASEAN's attempt to promote open regionalism. Open regionalism in Southeast Asia has prompted the Indonesian government to open up its market, which has allowed transnational corporations (TNCs) to take charge of the Indonesian economy. Not only is Indonesia now flooded with foreign goods, Indonesians are increasingly influenced by foreign cultures. Therefore, it was hardly surprising to find nationalist sentiments in Indonesia, particularly since TNCs have begun to threaten Indonesian national identity. The respondent also mentioned the conflict between

IBRA, Guthrie Ltd., and Indonesian local farmers as another example of the negative relationship between nationalism and regionalism. Nationalist sentiments against multinational companies normally occur when companies threaten the livelihood of local people. Although IBRA insisted that such nationalist sentiments were provoked by members of the local company involved, the respondent was convinced that nationalism among local people still exists although it may not be virulently expressed. On the whole, Indonesia is experiencing problems of governmental mismanagement, which are caused mainly by the lack of strong leadership. The current government's foreign policy has been very vague in comparison to those of the Old Order and the New Order governments. It is very unfortunate that Indonesia lacked a foreign policy focus at the start of the economic crisis.

Other respondent categorized within the minimalist camp was the representative of the National Student League for Democracy (LMND—*Liga Mahasiswa Nasional untuk Demokrasi*).[61] The respondent believed that Indonesian nationalism and ASEAN regionalism have been used rhetorically by certain group of people to protect their economic interests. As with the Head of ICMI, the representative of LMND also argued that ASEAN regionalism is nothing more than a trade block that makes up the current capitalist system. Indonesian nationalism and the creation of ASEAN and its AFTA scheme have not only represented the economic interests of certain groups,[62] but they have also been transformed in order to accommodate the interests of developed countries and large TNCs. The economic crisis has played a major role in eroding Indonesian nationalism and sovereignty as Indonesia was forced by international actors and institutions to remain economically open. During the early stage of the economic crisis, the government itself was unable to turn to its closest allies in ASEAN, as they too were facing domestic problems. It is, therefore, reasonable to suggest that Indonesian nationalist sentiments have abated and do not pose any immediate impediment to the progress of ASEAN's regionalization process. The representative of LMND also pointed out that the work of ASEAN has been limited to talks and discussions only. Therefore, even if Indonesia has insisted on conducting a strong protectionist policy, it remains very unlikely that the progress of AFTA will be halted. As with the concept of nationalism itself, the concept of regionalism is regarded by many in the pressure groups as having an urban bias and being full of rhetoric.

Convergence

The majority of respondents interviewed held a convergence standpoint, arguing that the ASEAN regionalization process can be perceived as an extension of Indonesian national interests at the regional level. Many respondents in this category believed that most Indonesians subscribed to a more logical concept of nationalism. In this context, Indonesians today were not necessarily inward-looking, but more aware of regional and international issues. This has been a common view among the representatives from most governmental institutions, business associations, members of the academic community, and Indonesian NGOs and CSOs. For Indonesian government officials, ASEAN is considered important to the Indonesian government owing to the Association's ability to, among other things, maintain regional harmony and security. In addition, a large proportion of government officials also believed that regionalism is necessary to oppose the challenge of the globalization. Some respondents also held a very pragmatic approach toward the issue, claiming that Indonesia should reassess the benefits of entering into multilateral arrangements, including ASEAN. However, the same pragmatists also argued that ASEAN is the only multilateral organization that Indonesia should belong to, at least at the present time. It was further argued that through its presence in ASEAN, Indonesia is better able to preserve its national sovereignty. The representative of the Investment Coordinating Board (BKPM), for example, stressed that it is impossible for each ASEAN country to struggle on its own in an era of globalization. Similarly, the representatives from the Ministry of Co-operative, Small and Medium Enterprises (MoC-SMEs) also added how important it was to control nationalism because it might hinder Indonesia's own development.

During the post-crisis period, two issues were controversial in relation to the debate over the rise of nationalistic sentiment in Indonesia. The first issue was the Indonesian Banking Restructuring Agency's (IBRA)[63] dealings in the sale of Indonesian assets to a Malaysian palm oil company, Kumpulan Guthrie Ltd.[64] The deal struck between the two parties involved a palm oil plantation, which covered about 265,777 hectares of land across several Indonesian provinces[65] and was previously owned by one of the largest Indonesian conglomerate groups, Salim Group. Initially, the Salim Group promised local farmers that they would acquire control of over 70 percent of the land in the near future. However, the agreement between the local farmers and the Salim Group soon became invalid when IBRA took over the plantations and the Salim Group was forced to deal directly with the new owner. The sale of this asset provoked major debates among Indonesian politicians. Key nationalist figures argued that the sale ignored the interests of local farmers. More importantly, they were also concerned that Malaysia would become the major palm oil producer if the asset was handed over to the Malaysians.[66] Apart from that, the agreement also violated a 1999 forestry law, which restricts a company's control to only 20,000 hectares of land in one province, or a total of 100,000 hectares throughout the country. Nationalist sentiments were not only prevalent in the capital, but also among provincial government officials and local farmers. In Riau, for example, members of the provincial parliament played the nationalist card by threatening the security of potential foreign investors. However, some supporters of Kumpulan Guthrie in the Indonesian government argued that the cancellation of the sale agreement would be a major blow to Indonesia's efforts to regain the confidence of foreign investors, which had been fading since the economic crisis began.

The IBRA was indeed facing a dilemma, torn between the concerns of the provincial governments and local farmers and the importance of protecting Indonesia's international credibility. By March 2001, however, the IBRA decided to go ahead with the agreement and sold the disputed asset to Kumpulan Guthrie for a total of US$368 million. Kumpulan Guthrie has made a token gesture to local interests by allowing local farmers to control 10 percent of its land within a three to five year timeframe, along with a further 20 percent of public shareholding. Although the deal raised anger among some Indonesian domestic constituents, an IBRA official interviewed argued that nationalistic sentiments had been stirred up by certain individuals who were interested in acquiring shares in the disputed asset. Moreover, he also argued that there was a possibility that members of the Salim Group were also involved in stirring up public anger in an attempt to repossess their old assets. Although the Indonesian government prohibits such actions, members of the Salim Group were potentially able to repossess their old assets by setting up a *shadow company*[67] that claimed to have no affiliation to the Group. Moreover, the respondent also believed that the Salim Group had paid the local farmers to protest against foreign control of the disputed land, which created an impression that nationalistic sentiments were rising.[68] The IBRA official was not convinced that there had been any strong nationalistic upsurge against foreign investment in the country. According to him, concern over the issue of nationalism was exaggerated and was not necessarily a factor that would halt the progress of AFTA.

A more recent rise in nationalistic sentiment in the country is evident in the case of the implementation of the Regional Autonomy Laws (OtDa—*Otonomi Daerah*). Although the majority of government officials held a convergent standpoint on the relationship between nationalism and regionalism, some respondents also contended that the implementation of the OtDa brought new challenges to the concept of Indonesian nationalism. Although the Indonesian government has recently been putting efforts into revising the content of the OtDa, many sections of Indonesian society maintain that the Indonesian government is not yet ready to handle the possibly chaotic implementation of the OtDa. One main problem highlighted is that the OtDa would trigger conflict between the central and the provincial governments. Furthermore, there are only a handful of provinces that would be able to prosper economically once the law is implemented. A study by the Depperindag (2000: 40) has revealed that there are only five provinces that will benefit from the implementation of the OtDa, which include Riau, Papua, East Kalimantan, Aceh, and South Sumatra, all of which are resource rich provinces. Others, including Jakarta, could face bankruptcy once the OtDa is implemented. Moreover, the Indonesian business community was concerned about the 1,006 different bureaucratic provincial regulations (PERDA—*Peraturan Daerah*) that will cause problems to Indonesian domestic trade and international competitiveness.[69] Provincial governments have clearly become accustomed to the centralized system employed by the New Order government. The sudden implementation of OtDa has given them greater authority over their own region. However, perceptions among officials at the provincial governments have been varied since the OtDa was implemented.

Among governmental institutions, the Ministry of Home Affairs (MHA) and the Directorate General of Central and Local and Fiscal Balance (DPOD—*Dewan Perimbangan Otonomi Daerah*)[70] have been two of the most active government institutions in overseeing the implementation of the Regional Autonomy Laws (OtDa—*Otonomi Daerah*). The author, however, was only able to conduct interview with a representative from the DPOD since it proved difficult to meet with officials from the MHA. The questions set for the respondent were largely designed to stimulate discussion on the implementation of the OtDa and their impact on AFTA. Although the respondent held a convergent stance on the issue of nationalism *vis-à-vis* regionalism, he believed that the immediate public interpretation of the OtDa has been highly ethnonationalistic. However, in the eyes of the Indonesian government, this public response is to be expected and is part of the process of further democratization in the country. The central government has conducted many dialogues with its provincial counterparts to reach an understanding between the involved parties. The respondent also added that, to date, most provincial constituents mainly support the general concept of OtDa. Despite this, the respondent argued that the implementation of the OtDa will have a major impact on the ASEAN regionalism process, particularly in the short-term. One main problem that was highlighted was the lack of human resources to cope with the demand generated by the OtDa. With the implementation of these laws, individual provincial laws will create inefficiency within AFTA, particularly those laws related to provincial investment. Attempts to anticipate such problems, however, have been made by the central government. For example, revisions have been made regarding the sixty-eight problematic provincial regulations that might produce a negative impact on the investment climate throughout Indonesian provinces. The former Minister of Home Affairs, Hari Sabarno, announced that many of these laws should be pulled back from operation.[71]

Officials at other governmental institutions also held a similar position regarding the implementation of the OtDa and the progress of AFTA. Officials at both National Development Planning Board (BAPPENAS—*Badan Perencanaan Pembangunan Nasional*)[72] and the Custom and Excise Office, for example, believed that Indonesia has extensive immediate problems with the implementation of the OtDa, particularly regarding the rise of ethnonationalism, which will have substantial effects on the progress of AFTA. The officials from BAPPENAS pinpointed the central government's inability to provide a concrete plan to handle both the OtDa and AFTA. The problem does not exist only between the central and the provincial governments, but also among officials in the capital. The Directorate General of the Custom and Excise Office asserted that the implementation of the OtDa is chaotic at the moment and its impact on regionalism would be significant. Indonesian provinces will not be allowed to develop equally after the implementation of the OtDa. Another problem with the implementation of the OtDa is the lack of appropriate facilities in some of the provinces, which will produce diverse outcomes among provinces when AFTA is implemented. The failure to address these issues properly will greatly impact on Indonesia's involvement in many regional cooperation schemes.

One provincial government institution interviewed, the Depperindag of East Java, however, provided a contrasting point of view.[73] The officials there argued that the introduction of the OtDa would be a positive contribution toward the progress of AFTA. Many local districts were disinterested in dealing with foreign investments prior to the implementation of the OtDa. The introduction of this law has promoted a sense of openness by allowing provincial entrepreneurs to deal directly with foreign investors.[74] Recently, the Depperindag office in East Java has also taken the initiative to promote openness within its region by allowing one of its district areas, Malang, to conduct a trade relationship with Johor of Malaysia. Such initiatives, however, pose another problem for the provincial government. Various districts throughout East Java have been competing against each other to attract foreign investments. It was suggested by the officials interviewed that there is a need to synergize the policies pursued in these districts. Generally, therefore, according to the officials interviewed, the implementation and the acceleration of AFTA will not be beneficial for individual Indonesian provinces for the time being. The various districts need to synergize all their policies prior to concentrating on foreign investments.

As with officials from various Indonesian governmental institutions, members of KADIN interviewed took an equally pragmatic approach on the relationship between nationalism and regionalism. Within KADIN, for example, members expressed different opinions about the subject. For KADIN's Head of ASEAN Committee, for instance, the government has acted in an excessive manner to promote Indonesian nationalism. The result of such conduct has been detrimental to the Indonesian economy. The respondent cited one example of such conduct, which was the government's indecision in solving the conflict between entrepreneurs and workers. The absence of adequate labor laws has intensified labor movements since the economic crisis. Indonesian workers often express their dissatisfaction through demonstrations that disrupt productivity and efficiency in the workplace. Subsequently, the representative from KADIN suggested that the government should have been more consistent and decisive in handling the widespread labor movements that may have slowed down the progress of the Indonesian economy. The government, moreover, has taken protectionist measures regarding international trade, which has hampered the national economy. Some sectors, such as industry and trading, communications, and energy, are still closed to foreign investments. Inefficiency in these industries has emerged as a result of the lack of competition. On the whole, therefore, Indonesia has not prospered well under its protectionist policy.[75] On the whole, therefore, Indonesia has not prospered well under a protectionist policy. The concept of Indonesian nationalism, therefore, must be changed, and should not be based on romantic notions, but on rationality. Moreover, the Head of KADIN also stated his concern over the impact of the rise of ethnonationalism, which was resulted from the introduction of OtDa, toward AFTA. KADIN's early hypothesis suggests that AFTA would be affected substantially by the introduction of OtDa because various provincial governments might impose divergent investment and trade laws toward foreign products and entities. To that end, KADIN has formed a monitoring team, Regional Autonomy Watch (KPPOD— *Komite Pemantauan Pelaksanaan Otonomi Daerah*), that will oversee the implementation of the OtDa and their impacts on AFTA.[76]

As with most government officials, the majority of respondents in the academic community can also be placed within the convergence camp with regard to their attitudes toward the relationship between Indonesian nationalism and ASEAN regionalism. For both Dr. Dewi Anwar and Dr. Cornelis Luhulima, Indonesians are ambivalent about nationalism. On one hand, Indonesia has been fully integrated into the capitalist system, despite the rhetoric that Indonesian society is based on socialist principles.[77] Up until the present day, it has been common for leaders to preach about the importance of Indonesian nationalism. However, Indonesians are also influenced by consumerism and by external conditions. More importantly, Suharto's role in making AFTA possible should be noted. Although most of his advisers and other ASEAN countries were skeptical about it, the Indonesian leader was convinced that regional trade liberalization was the way to face globalization. On the other hand, national pride is still important to most Indonesians. Some Indonesian policymakers, for example, still believed that Indonesia could stand on its own feet, without assistance from other countries. In recent years, however, there have been some changes to the context of Indonesian nationalism as a result of the recent wave of democratization in the country. The majority of Indonesians are no longer inward looking in their attitude toward regionalism, although they may continue to resist pressure from the West. This is not to suggest that Indonesia is xenophobic toward the West, and Indonesians are becoming more aware of their regional consciousness. Nowadays most Indonesians base their nationalism on rational ideas (or pragmatic self interest) rather than on romantic notions.

Others in the academic community, such as Dr. Hadi Soesastro and Dr. Bustanul Arifin, asserted that regionalism is one possible way to maintain Indonesian sovereignty *vis-à-vis* globalization. Despite this, members of the academic community also criticized ASEAN member governments' inability to utilize the Association fully. Most countries in the region are still overly concerned with preserving their national sovereignties. Protectionist policies, such as those in the Indonesian agricultural sector and the Malaysian automotive sector already mentioned, remain major stumbling blocks toward further trade liberalization in the region. In many ways, therefore, ASEAN still remains ineffectual. Member countries have always aspired to participate in international events, but are incapable owing to the lack of proper organization in the Association. However, it is also important to note that the majority of ASEAN countries are more concerned about the threat of globalization than regionalism. To that end, the majority of the people in the region have acknowledged the importance of an efficient regional organization that is able to represent their interests at the international level. Northeast Asian countries have been asked to join ASEAN member countries to form a greater East Asian grouping. However, most members of the academic community were rather pessimistic about the progress of APT since ASEAN is still trying to adapt to the inclusion of its other new members.

There are divergent perspectives on the emergence of ethnonationalism as a result of the implementation of the OtDa. On the one hand, the implementation of the OtDa will create more bureaucracy at the provincial level, which will affect the investment climate in the country. However, respondents in the academic community who held such opinions regarded the emergence of ethnonationalism as a short-term euphoria resulting from the democratization process. Moreover, the misinterpretation of the OtDa might also result in the issuance of many bureaucratic laws which are not conducive to the national investment climate. Therefore, the implementation of the OtDa and the emergence of ethnonationalism will remain a major challenge for the central government. On the positive side, however, the implementation of the OtDa will enable all provinces to handle their own affairs, although most provincial regulations should be in line with central government ones. For Prof. Lepi Tarmidi, however, it was an exaggeration to suggest that the OtDa would have any substantial impacts on the implementation of AFTA. Even long before the OtDa was introduced, many areas in Indonesia, such as Riau and Batam, were already involved in various Growth Triangle (GT) initiatives. This indicates that some of these provinces already have the necessary experience to deal with regional trade liberalization. However, it is also important to note that only a limited number of Indonesian provinces have been involved in the GT initiatives.

ASEAN Regionalism and Indonesia's Autonomy, Bargaining Power, and Ability to Contain the Negative Forces of Globalization

Three related factors that encourage state and non-state actors to support an RIS are the likelihood that an RIS will increase a country's international autonomy, thereby boosting its bargaining power and helping to contain the negative forces of globalization. Respondents from the maximalist camp argued that ASEAN has helped to increase Indonesia's international autonomy and bargaining power in the international arena. More importantly, ASEAN was perceived as a tool to contain the negative forces of globalization. Minimalist respondents, on the other hand, maintained that ASEAN has had little impact on Indonesia's international autonomy, bargaining power, and has not acted as a buffer against globalization. Most minimalist respondents argued that events in Indonesia are still largely influenced by international conditions. Consequently, minimalist respondents remained skeptical about whether ASEAN could bring about the aforementioned benefits of regionalism. Finally, those within the convergence category maintained that ASEAN's influence on Indonesia's international autonomy, bargaining power, and its ability to contain the negative forces of globalization has only been obvious since the economic crisis of 1997. The significant number of respondents within the maximalist category affirmed the symbiotic nature of ASEAN regionalism and Indonesian nationalism.

Maximalist

Those within the maximalist camp believed that ASEAN has greatly contributed to Indonesia's autonomy and bargaining power in the international arena. Apart from that, maximalist respondents also felt that Indonesia would be better able to resist the negative forces of globalization through ASEAN. The most respondents within the maximalist category were officials from governmental institutions, representatives from Indonesian business associations, members of the academic community, and representatives from the ASEAN Secretariat and foreign embassies. Officials from Indonesian government institutions, such as those from the Ministry of Foreign Affairs (MFA), Ministry of Industry and Trade (Depperindag), the Investment Coordinating Board (BKPM), and the National Logistic Agency (BULOG), and all representatives from Indonesian business associations, particularly the Indonesian Chamber of Commerce and Industry (KADIN), thought that ASEAN was as a useful platform from which to promote Indonesia's international autonomy and bargaining power. They felt that ASEAN's contribution to Indonesia's international autonomy and bargaining power was clearly demonstrated in Indonesia's involvement in the WTO and in trade disputes with other regional groupings, such as the EU and NAFTA. The dispute between ASEAN, the EU, and NAFTA over the agricultural sector is a case in point. Subsequently, member countries of the EU and NAFTA imposed as much as 24 percent tariffs for agricultural products originating from ASEAN countries, while imposing lower tariff rates at around 1 percent for agricultural products from Africa, the Caribbean, and the Pacific (ACP) group. ASEAN, according to an MFA official, greatly benefits Indonesia because it can increase the country's bargaining power with the EU and NAFTA member countries. The Head of BULOG[78] shared a similar point of view and pointed out that Indonesia would find it easier to cope with the high agricultural tariffs imposed by most member countries of OECD (Organization for Economic Cooperation and Development) through collective action taken at the regional level.

All Indonesian government officials interviewed also believed that multilateral trade bodies, such as the WTO, only represent the national interests of developed countries. All government officials and the representatives of the business associations also argued that although there may be differences in the interests of ASEAN member countries, on the whole, ASEAN countries usually raised similar concerns during multilateral trade negotiations. The significance of ASEAN had become more apparent since joining of three new member countries, Lao, Cambodia, and Burma, and with the possible expansion of ASEAN into ASEAN plus Three (APT). Many Indonesian government officials thought that any further enlargement of the Association was positive as it would increase Indonesia's international autonomy, bargaining power, and act as a buffer against globalization.

Some members of the academic community shared similar views to those expressed by government officials and representatives of Indonesian business associations. In AFTA-related matters, in particular, members of academics, such as Dr. Hadi Soesastro, Dr. Cornelis Luhulima, and Dr. Bustanul Arifin, believed that the scheme had made a positive contribution toward the development of ASEAN member countries. One of the most important contributions highlighted was AFTA's capacity to provide a much needed stepping-stone for member countries to compete in the world market. AFTA was, after all, intended to transform the conservative, protectionist, and inward-looking economic policies of member countries. The majority of respondents also agreed that it was not the intention of ASEAN member countries to conduct trade liberalization at the regional level *per se.* AFTA makes ASEAN member countries more confident that they will eventually become one of the major economic powers in Asia, if not in the world. Consequently, ASEAN member countries, through their commitment to AFTA, will be able to increase their international autonomy, bargaining power, and their ability to contain the negative forces of globalization.

Meanwhile, representatives from the ASEAN Secretariat and foreign embassies believed that ASEAN has helped to increase the international autonomy and bargaining power of its member countries. In the absence of ASEAN, member countries would find it even more difficult to cope with the great challenges posed by the process of globalization. It was for this very reason that the representatives from the ASEAN Secretariat, Thai Embassy and Brunei Embassy were positive about ASEAN enlargement and the strengthening of APT. Meanwhile, representatives from non-ASEAN foreign embassies believed that ASEAN member countries' bargaining power and international autonomy have been weakened since the economic crisis in 1997. However, representatives of the ASEAN Secretariat and all foreign embassies interviewed felt that ASEAN member countries also realized that deeper regionalism in Southeast Asia was important as a mechanism not only to escape from the current economic crisis, but also to maintain or increase their bargaining power and international autonomy. The United States, in particular, hoped that ASEAN would proceed with deeper economic integration, not only among ASEAN member countries, but also with Australia and New Zealand. The representative of the U.S. Embassy thought that such integration would not only increase solidarity among these economies, but would also boost economy and trade, thus enabling member countries to achieve their respective objectives.

Minimalist

Unlike those in the maximalist camp, respondents in the minimalist camp argued that ASEAN's contributions to Indonesian international autonomy and bargaining power have been minimal. Apart from that, ASEAN's insistent pursuit of open regionalism has limited Indonesia's ability to resist the negative forces of globalization. The majority of minimalist respondents were representatives from Indonesian NGOs and CSOs. Most of them were convinced that the contribution of ASEAN toward increasing Indonesia's international autonomy and bargaining power has been minimal. Moreover, they also added that ASEAN has been ineffective in resisting the negative forces of globalization. According to a representative from the Indonesian Consumer Group (YLKI), although globalization is an importance force that must be discussed and dealt with, the Indonesian government and most Indonesian citizens remained unaware of the issue and the negative impacts that might ensue. To date, neither the ASEAN Secretariat nor the Indonesian government had provided enough information on the way in which positive globalism and regional governance could be implemented while resisting all the negative forces of globalization.

Moreover, a representative of the National Student League for Democracy (LMND) also felt that regionalism in Southeast Asia represented regional capitalism that supported, instead of opposing, global capitalism. In reality, as with international trade in general, regionalism was only a trade agreement between the rich and the poor. As a result, ASEAN regionalism has not improved the fate of many Indonesian poor people. Indonesian labors, for example, have been fully exploited by transnational corporations (TNCs). When Indonesian labors rose to challenge these international entities, they simply moved to other locations in other ASEAN countries. ASEAN, as a regional grouping, has been unable to regulate this irresponsible behavior from TNCs. Therefore, this was felt to indicate that ASEAN's contributions to increasing Indonesia's international autonomy, bargaining power, and in resisting the negative forces of globalization have been minimal. Many representatives from Indonesian NGOs and CSOs felt that ASEAN should be more vocal in negotiations at a multilateral level so that its contributions can be felt among the poor.

Convergence

There were only two respondents that could be placed within the convergence category, both of whom were members of the academic community. Both respondents believed that ASEAN had helped to increase Indonesia's international autonomy, bargaining power, and ability to resist the negative forces of globalism only since the economic crisis in 1997. In the view of Dr. Anwar and Prof. Tarmidi, the impact of the economic crisis toward the development of ASEAN regionalism has been significant. On the one hand, the economic crisis had weakened the relationship among ASEAN member countries. There were several reasons for this. Firstly, ASEAN was never equipped to deal or to cope with the economic crisis. It would have been somewhat illogical for member countries to seek assistance from the Association when the economic crisis hit the region. Instead, all countries hit by the economic crisis automatically sought assistance from institutions outside ASEAN. Thailand and Indonesia, for example, agreed to loan packages from the IMF in August and October 1997. It was for this reason that ASEAN became irrelevant during the crisis. Secondly, member countries, particularly Indonesia, became engrossed with domestic problems, such as social unrest and the increasing threat of national disintegration, which meant that time and energy spent on regional economic cooperation was limited. Thirdly, there were complications in the relationship between member countries during the economic crisis. Countries that were not hit by the economic crisis were under an obligation to help the troubled ones. If assistance did not come from richer countries, relationships became strained. This has been evident in the relationship between Indonesia and Singapore in recent years. Nonetheless, precisely because of the crisis, and precisely because ASEAN was helpless during the crisis, there has been a realization that something has to be done to improve the situation. The crisis has thus become a catalyst in promoting greater regional cooperation among member countries, which, subsequently, helped to increase member country's international autonomy and bargaining power in the future.

Despite this, Dr. Anwar also added that ASEAN's enlargement process has actually weakened the grouping's international autonomy and bargaining position. Dr. Anwar did not agree with the admittance to the Association of new member countries, particularly Myanmar. Initially, ASEAN member countries expected Myanmar to be an observer before getting full membership into the Association, but for strategic and economic reasons, Myanmar was accepted as a full member. ASEAN leaders feared that an economic gap between ASEAN and Myanmar would exist if the latter was not accepted as a member of the Association. However, Dr. Anwar argued that Myanmar should have learnt how the Association works and, most importantly, should have dealt with their own domestic problems before joining. He felt, therefore, that the admittance of Myanmar into the Association had led to a deterioration in the level of Indonesia's international autonomy and its bargaining position in the international arena.

Other Relevant Issues: Dissemination of Information Regarding ASEAN and AFTA

Another issue analyzed in this book is the dissemination of information regarding ASEAN and AFTA-related issues to the general public by both the Indonesian government and the ASEAN Secretariat. Resistance to ASEAN and its

AFTA scheme often resulted from the lack of information, rather than nationalism, provided to the general public. Most knowledge regarding ASEAN and its development has been generated from either educational institutions or from publications provided for the general public. The field research reveals, however, that only a minority of the Indonesians interviewed have been able to access a significant amount of information regarding ASEAN and AFTA. It has been suggested that documents and newsletters regarding the development of ASEAN have not been widely available to the public, with the exception of ASEAN's annual report (Anwar 1994: 249). The majority of recipients have been members of the academic community and important economic actors. More importantly, the field research also reveals that the information passed on to governmental officials has not been equally distributed. This is the result of a lack of synergy between top and low level government officials on how to implement some of ASEAN's policies. Since the economic crisis emerged in 1997, however, the media has been taking a more active role in disseminating information regarding ASEAN, particularly since the implementation of AFTA. The dissemination of information is indeed crucial for the future of ASEAN regionalism as it promotes greater consciousness about regional issues and problems among Southeast Asians. If inadequate dissemination persists, especially from the top level, it is likely that ASEAN will continue to be an exclusive club for government officials at the ministerial level.

Maximalist

Those in the maximalist category generally believed that both the Indonesian government and the ASEAN Secretariat have provided sufficient information to the general public. The majority of respondents placed within the maximalist camp were made up of some officials from governmental institutions and the representatives from the ASEAN Secretariat and foreign embassies in Jakarta. Responses regarding the aforementioned issue varied among government officials, depending on the institution in which the respondents worked. Officials who worked at the government institutions that deal directly with ASEAN-related issues, such as the Ministry of Foreign Affairs (MFA), the Department of Industry and Trade (Depperindag), the Custom and Excise Office, and the Ministry of Co-operative, Small and Medium Enterprises (MoC-SMEs), stated that they had been making substantial efforts to disseminate information to the public. Information was generally available through newsletters or publications, or the official web site of all the ministries that dealt with ASEAN-related activities. Normally, all top-level officials at the ministerial level were required to obtain information on ASEAN-related issues. Subsequently, the information had to be disseminated to their subordinates. In some governmental institutions, particularly the MFA, there is a Sub-Directorate of ASEAN Socialization and an AFTA unit that have the responsibility of disseminating ASEAN-related information to the general public, including the academic community and the private sector. In addition, the representatives of these government institutions also claimed to have conducted various workshops providing substantial amounts of information to the public, which were normally coordinated with the cooperation of the ASEAN Secretariat. On the 21 March 2001, for example, the Indonesian government and the ASEAN Secretariat launched the CEPT Outreach Program to publicize the CEPT program to the business community.[79] It was hoped that this program would enable the business community to reap the full benefits from AFTA. Moreover, government institutions such as the Depperindag also granted local companies consultations outside formal conferences and seminars.

The respondents who believed that both the Indonesian government and the ASEAN Secretariat had provided enough information to the public also pinpointed several problems in the information dissemination process. Government officials reported that the majority of Indonesian entrepreneurs had not been interested in becoming involved in many ASEAN activities. The CEPT Outreach Program held in Jakarta, for example, attracted only four local companies, in comparison with the one hundred Japanese companies, and a substantial number of government officials and representatives from various foreign embassies and the ASEAN Secretariat. The majority of entrepreneurs was reluctant to attend many ASEAN activities, and preferred to send their representatives instead. This caused problems of miscommunication between government officials and leaders of local companies. Even when a meeting was attended by leaders of local companies, any information then disseminated to their employees had been very limited. The underlying problem is that the majority of Indonesian entrepreneurs have failed to comprehend the benefits that they may reap from AFTA. Aside from the fact that Indonesia itself is already a large market, the majority of Indonesian enterprises also tend to conduct business with companies from non-ASEAN countries.

Meanwhile, officials of the ASEAN Secretariat and foreign embassies in Indonesia were optimistic about the dissemination process of the Secretariat and the Indonesian government. The only exception was the representative of the Brunei Embassy, who felt that both ASEAN and its member governments had been reluctant to provide comprehensive information on ASEAN to the public. However, the respondent thought that both sides, the authority and the public, were equally responsible for the failure of the dissemination program. The majority of the public had not paid much attention to the development of ASEAN, which could either be due to the Association's lack of progress or the fact it has done little for Southeast Asians in recent years. One important tool in the dissemination process is the media. Up until recently, however, the media has failed to deliver much information, which is partly due to censorship and the public's lack of interest in the subject.

For the ASEAN Secretariat, however, problems with regard to dissemination were mainly the fault of the government. The Secretariat claimed to have consistently communicated its policies to the public. This process normally stopped at the governmental level. ASEAN is an inter-governmental organization that has adopted a non-interference system. Individual governments, there-fore, have the right to either publicize or not to publicize ASEAN's policies to the public. The Secretariat normally passes information on to each member country's AFTA Unit. The Secretariat has refused to take responsibility for the way in which these Units might then disseminate such information at the na-tional level. Moreover, the Secretariat also claimed that it had attempted to en-courage the involvement of NGOs and CSOs in the past; particularly among ASEAN affiliated NGOs. In many cases, however, NGOs and CSOs were often reluctant to make any substantial contribution to issues proposed by the Secre-tariat. Therefore, it is perhaps unfair to point the finger of blame at the Secre-tariat alone.

The remaining foreign embassies in Indonesia, on the other hand, main-tained that the information provided by the Secretariat had been well dissemi-nated to the general public. AFTA-related issues, for example, were said to have been aired frequently by the local media in recent years. The representative of the U.S. Embassy, in particular, was convinced that Indonesians were fully aware that their country is a major player in the region and were thus interested in hearing about ASEAN and AFTA. It was also claimed that the media was active in passing information to the public. In fact, ASEAN and AFTA-related issues appeared more frequently in the local media than, for example, multilat-eral trade issues. Other respondents in this category also felt that although the information provided had been sufficient, it was also important to inform non-ASEAN embassies on the most recent activities of the Association. To that end, the relationship between foreign embassies and the Secretariat should be ex-panded. During the field research, for example, the representative of the British Embassy was unsure of his government's view on many questions posed by the author, which suggests that there is limited interaction between the Secretariat and non-ASEAN foreign embassies.

Minimalist

Unlike respondents in the maximalist camp, those in the minimalist camp believed that both the Indonesian government and the ASEAN Secretariat have provided limited information to the general public. The majority of government officials interviewed held a minimalist standpoint on the issue. One of the most profound problems was that ASEAN-related information has also not been well disseminated among government officials. At the time when the interviews were conducted, the majority of government officials stated that both ASEAN and AFTA issues were still very abstract to them. Decision-making processes on both issues have been mainly the concern of policymakers at the MFA, and per-haps the Depperindag for AFTA-related matters. Another problem was the lack of synergy among governmental institutions regarding ASEAN's various initia-tives on regional integration. Some governmental officials also noted that even officials at the top ministerial level had been indifferent about ASEAN and AFTA, since many of the intergovernmental forums conducted at the regional level had been a place for informal talks and discussions only as opposed to an opportunity to concentrate on the real issues and problems that had to be tackled. Government representatives sent to these meetings have been forced by their superiors to attend. Some respondents also pointed out that the dissemination process in ASEAN and AFTA had only touched those who were directly involved, such as the private sector and a small number of interest groups. The same respondents, however, also questioned the usefulness of disseminating ASEAN and AFTA information to all layers of Indonesian society since most people were still only concerned about issues that directly affected them.

Concern regarding the dissemination of ASEAN-related information was also prevalent among members of the business community. Although some Indonesian business associations realized that both the ASEAN Secretariat and Indonesian government had tried to disseminate information on ASEAN and AFTA-related issues, they felt that such activities should be expanded. Aside from regular workshops and seminars on AFTA, there had been little in the way of public relations work to promote AFTA to the general public. This is important because it would not only increase people's awareness of AFTA, but it would also increase their level of consciousness about regionalism and Indonesian foreign policy in general. The usual claim has been that problems of dissemination arise not only from the authority responsible, but also from the lack of interest shown by the general public. The business community opposed such a statement, stating that public interest could be generated if the subject was intensely promoted. To date, both the ASEAN Secretariat and the government had only disseminated general facts about ASEAN-related activities, but had not elaborated on the importance of involvement in their activities. Most business associations also complained that the information provided by the government was extremely technical. Finally, the business community also thought that the government should make fundamental changes to minimize bureaucracy so that information regarding ASEAN and AFTA could be more appropriately disseminated. Moreover, the majority of respondents interviewed in the business community category also agreed that SMEs were major constituents that had been left behind by ASEAN and AFTA.[80] Most SMEs claimed that neither government officials nor the ASEAN Secretariat had ever contacted them or invited them to participate in any regional activities. Some companies categorized as medium-sized enterprises acknowledged the existence of ASEAN and AFTA, and some even expressed interest in becoming more fully involved in the scheme. However, most of them stated that information from governmental institutions had not only been very technical, but also expensive to obtain. Therefore, for the private sector, the problem lay not only in the lack of interest expressed by the general public, but also the willingness of the government and the ASEAN Secretariat to promote their activities.

As the major recipients of ASEAN information, the perspectives of pressure groups were the most important ones. As with respondents in other categories, the majority of people interviewed in the NGO and CSO category also held a minimalist standpoint on the subject. The problem in the relationship between ASEAN and local NGOs and CSOs was twofold. On the one hand, it is true that many local NGOs and CSOs have not been provided with appropriate information regarding ASEAN and its activities. As a result, the majority of local NGOs and CSOs were uninformed about the development of the Association. Although some NGOs and CSOs also admitted that both the ASEAN Secretariat and the Indonesian government had provided significant information regarding ASEAN and AFTA, both institutions had focused the dissemination on certain actors, mainly economic actors and members of the academic community. Most of the representatives of pressure groups also realized that ASEAN had been quite active in promoting regionalism in Southeast Asia, but thought that the Association should expand its activities to encourage greater participation from NGOs and CSOs. Most representatives claimed that they had never been contacted by the ASEAN Secretariat or been invited to any of the Association's activities. Even those who had dealt with the Association in the past stated that the Association had been slow to respond to their enquiries. Yet societies in the region are changing and are demanding a more democratic form of practice. To date, ASEAN and its member governments have been ignoring such demands.

On the other hand, some NGOs and CSOs, such as the Urban Poor Consortium (UPC), the Front National for the Indonesian Labor Struggle (FNPBI), the National Student League for Democracy (LMND), the Indonesian Friends of the Earth (WALHI—*Wahana Lingkungan Hidup*),[81] and Indonesian Consumer Group (YLKI), also admitted that the majority of people had not paid any attention to the development of ASEAN, including the AFTA scheme. Most NGOs and CSOs thought that AFTA did not pose an immediate threat to the Indonesian people. There was greater concern about other multilateral governing bodies, such as the IMF, WTO, and the World Bank. The same NGOs and CSOs also argued that since the creation of ASEAN, the Association has brought only poverty, not prosperity, to Southeast Asians. For most people, ASEAN and AFTA are tools used by a group of rich people to serve their economic interests. However, ASEAN and AFTA should also be seen as agents of public decision. Therefore, a regional network that provides sufficient information to the public regarding the development of ASEAN and AFTA should be established. The field research also revealed that there is an interest in building an ASEAN-wide network to accommodate the interests of people at the grass-roots level in the region. Unfortunately, bureaucracy at both the governmental and the regional level has limited the opportunity for such networks.

Convergence

Those within the convergence category felt that the Indonesian government and the ASEAN Secretariat have provided sufficient information to the public.

However, they also believed that ASEAN's process of information dissemination should be expanded to include a wider range of domestic constituents, particularly small and medium size enterprises (SMEs), NGOs, and CSOs. Respondents within the convergence camp were mainly composed of members of the academic community. Members of the academic community realized that, in the past, ASEAN has provided limited information to the public. Recently, however, there have been substantial changes in the way in which the Association disseminates information regarding its activities to the public. One major drawback of ASEAN has been that the Association is an exclusive forum for member countries' foreign ministers. Some members of the academic community also pointed out that many things within the Association have been kept secret and confidential, alongside a strong tradition of bureaucracy. This has been part of the non-interference system practiced by ASEAN. Many people have acknowledged that ASEAN was formed this way to accommodate the interests of member countries' foreign ministers (Wanandi 2000: 31; Soesastro 2000: 189). In the last few years, there have been suggestions that the Association's existing organizational structure should be replaced. One suggestion has been to create a *Council of Ministers*, which would invite the Economic Ministers of all member countries to work together with Foreign Ministers, thus limiting the monopoly of ASEAN Foreign Ministers over activities within the Association. Another suggestion has been to elevate the position of national leaders in the decision making process. To date, these suggestions have either been ignored or rejected.

At the same time, however, members of the academic community also stated that most of the dissemination process would have to come from the top level. It is, therefore, important for policymakers to prioritize the involvement of the general public. From the field research, the author found that there were some mixed ideas on whether the present structure of ASEAN allows for the involvement of people at the grass-roots level. A member of the academic community, Dr. Cornelis Luhulima, asserted that Indonesian foreign policy was better implemented during the New Order period. The strongly autocratic methods of the regime enabled the government to create a more effective foreign policy than the present government, and also forced a consensus of view among various government institutions. Most members of the academic community, however, thought otherwise, arguing that such an autocratic method limits the involvement of people at the grass-roots level. ASEAN has tried to boost the involvement of Southeast Asian CSOs and NGOs by conducting various meetings between the Secretariat and people's representatives at the grass-roots level. The recent ASEAN People's Summit, which was held in Batam in 2000, was an example of community building at the regional level. There has been some recognition among top level governmental officials of the importance of involving non-state actors in regional activities. As a result, members of the academic community perceived ASEAN's process of dissemination of information should be expanded to include these pressure groups.

Conclusion

The chapter has provided an illustration in the way in which the contemporary relationship between nationalism and regionalism can be regarded as symbiotic. More specifically, it has shed a light on the contemporary perceptions of the recent development of ASEAN and its main economic integration mechanism, AFTA. Although to a large extent there have been few changes in the way Indonesian state and non-state actors perceive ASEAN and AFTA since the initiation of AFTA in 1992, it is clear that the majority of Indonesians are increasingly more aware of regional issues. The emergence of the regional economic crisis in 1997, in particular, acted as a catalyst to bring about greater awareness among Indonesians about regionalism. There is no doubt that both the media and the emergence of new information technologies are also responsible for increasing public awareness of regional issue. This new development signals greater challenges for ASEAN in the immediate future. The Association, among other things, will be expected to interact better with its people. This is particularly applicable to recent ASEAN attempts to promote AFTA. Although there were quite divergent views on the development of AFTA, the majority of Indonesian state and non-state actors interviewed believed that this scheme would bring improve economic condition in the country.

Nevertheless, there was still doubt regarding Indonesia's readiness to implement the AFTA scheme. The regional economic crisis was most often cited by the majority of the respondents as the major problem for Indonesia in implementing the AFTA scheme. However, the most pressing problem that caused resistance toward AFTA was the lack of proper information disseminated to the public. It is for this reason that the new challenge for ASEAN is not only to become more interactive with its people, but also to become more transparent and accountable. Thus, the activities of ASEAN must be expanded to accommodate the increasing numbers of CSOs and NGOs throughout the region. This should be seen as a new mechanism to minimize any possible public misunderstanding of the scheme. ASEAN must take into account that Indonesians, as with the citizens of other ASEAN countries, no longer perceive regionalism as a threat to their daily lives, but as means to serve their country's national interests. To sum up, therefore, the success of ASEAN's current and future projects will be determined by the Association's capacity to become less bureaucratic, and more transparent and accountable to its people.

Notes

1. Specific details concerning the Statement on Bold Measures can be obtained from the ASEAN Secretariat (1998b) official web site at http://www.aseansec.org/8756.htm.

2. Apart from the acceleration of the AFTA schedule, the 1998 Statement on Bold Measures also postulates other mechanisms that are useful to economic recovery, which include short-term measures to enhance the investment climate (i.e., an agreement between each ASEAN country to extend additional special privileges to qualified ASEAN and non-ASEAN investors, which was to be effective for applications made between 1 January 1999 and 31 December 2000) and the establishment of the ASEAN Industrial Cooperation (AICO) scheme.

3. As reported in *Kompas* (2001a).

4. Also known as the Provincial Government Act (UUPD—*Undang-Undang Peraturan Daerah*).

5. Also known as the Financial Balance between Central and Provincial Governments Act (UUPKPD—*Undang-Undang Perimbangan Keuangan Pusat dan Daerah*).

6. The New Order regime's policy of centralization has often been criticized on the grounds that it increased socio-economic inequalities between regions by transferring wealth from resource-rich provinces to Jakarta (Tadjoeddin et al. 2001: 283). One of the New Order's main reasons for pursuing such a policy was that the existence of the Indonesian state has been challenged throughout history by various ethnonationalist movements. During the Old Order and the New Order periods, both governments used centralization to limit and control such separatist movements.

7. As reported in *Kompas* (2001b), or visit the *Kompas* official web site at www.kompas.com/business/news/0102/10.htm.

8. As postulated by Mr. Kadjatmiko, who at the time held the position of the Director of Balancing Fund of the Directorate General of the Fiscal Balance Committee of Provincial Autonomy (DPOD—*Dewan Perimbangan Otonomi Daerah*), during an interview conducted on the 10 August 2001. The DPOD is a branch of the Ministry of Finance (MoF) that deals solely with the financial aspects of provincial autonomy. Reform euphoria refers to the condition in which the majority of the population demands greater democratization in all aspects of domestic politics. In contemporary Indonesia, such euphoria resulted from the economic crisis and the resignation of Suharto as President, which led to demands for further democratization and greater autonomy among Indonesian provinces.

9. Each governmental institution has one ASEAN Unit that functions as a tool to synchronize the policies issued both at the regional and domestic levels. The ASEAN Unit at the Ministry of Foreign Affairs (MFA), for example, deals with the general issue of ASEAN cooperation, while similar units at the Ministry of Trade and Industry (Depperindag) and the Ministry of Finance (MoF) deal with, respectively, trade and finance related matters within ASEAN cooperation. There is also an AFTA Unit in the MFA, which deals specifically with AFTA-related matters. The only governmental institutions interviewed that do not have an ASEAN Unit are the State Logistic Agency (Bulog) and the Indonesian Bank Restructuring Agency (IBRA). This is because such governmental institutions focus solely on domestic issues. Despite this, officials at both BULOG and IBRA were able to participate in the research interview as a result of the recently expanded scope of their activities. BULOG, for instance, has consistently expressed its concerns over the possibility of trade liberalization measures in the agricultural sector, both at the regional or the international level. Similarly, the scope of IBRA's activities has indirectly gone beyond the national level. The sale of troubled Indonesian banks and their assets has recently attracted the interest of many conglomerates from neighboring countries, particularly from Malaysia.

10. An interview was conducted on the 13 December 2000 in Jakarta. The interview was conducted with a representative of the Sub-Directorate of Commodity and Natural Resources who wished to remain anonymous.

11. An interview was conducted on the 19 February 2001 with Ketut Suwarko, Head of the Sub-Division of ASEAN Regional Cooperation, in Jakarta.

12. An interview was conducted on the 3 March 2001 with Dr. Bambang Marsoem, Head of International and Regional Economic Cooperation, and his assistant, Solehudin Masyar, in Jakarta.

13. As reported in *Kompas* (2001d: 13). The article also reveals that the high rate competitive sectors include the metal, machine, and electronic industries. Meanwhile, the low rate competitive sectors are the chemical, agricultural, and forestry industries.

14. An interview was conducted with two officials from the International Trade Co-operation Division and two officials from the International Economic and Institution Studies of BI on the 20 February 2001, in Jakarta. All respondents wished to remain anonymous.

15. The ASEAN Swap Arrangement scheme actually began in 1978 following the signing of the Memorandum of Understanding (MoU) among Southeast Asian countries' Central Banks. The scheme aims to provide short-term liquidity reserves for ASEAN members who have difficulties with their balance of payment, as well as to increase the level of monetary cooperation among member countries. Following the economic crisis of 1997, the ASEAN Swap Arrangement facility was increased from an initial US$200 million to US$ 1billion. While the founding fathers of ASEAN and Brunei contributed a total of US$900 million, or US$150 million each, the new members of ASEAN contributed US$50 million, US$28 million, US$17 million, and US$5 million respectively. The ASEAN Swap Arrangement scheme was later extended into the BSA scheme, which was initiated following the ASEAN Finance Deputy Ministers Meeting (AFDM) with their three Northeast Asian counterparts, Japan, South Korea, and China (a follow-up meeting of the Chiang Mai Initiative of 2000). The BSA aims to provide short-term support in the form of swap arrangements between ASEAN countries and their three Northeast Asian partners.

16. SEACEN was formed into a legal entity in 1982, and is composed of eight central banks from both ASEAN and non-ASEAN member countries (Bank Indonesia, Bank Negara Malaysia, Central Bank of Myanmar, Nepal Rastra Bank, Bangko Sentral ng Pilipinas, Monetary Authority of Singapore, Central Bank of Sri Lanka, and Bank of Thailand). In recent years membership was expanded to include the Central Bank of China, Taipei, and the Bank of Mongolia. The headquarter of the SEACEN Research and Training Centre is located in Kuala Lumpur, Malaysia.

17. An interview was conducted on the 7 December 2000 with the officials at the Bureau of Trade, Industry and Services, in Jakarta who wished to remain anonymous.

18. An interview was conducted on the 17 October 2000 with Somphand Kokilanon, the Ambassador of Thailand for the Republic of Indonesia, in Jakarta.

19. An interview was conducted on the 21 August 2001, in Jakarta, with a respondent who wished to remain anonymous.

20. Attempts to conduct interviews with the representatives from other ASEAN countries' embassies were made but were rejected on the grounds of the sensitivity of the issues discussed. Meanwhile, other non-ASEAN countries' embassies were also approached, including the Embassy of Japan and the Delegation of the European Commission in Jakarta, but both declined to give interviews.

21. As reported by the Thailand Ministry of Foreign Affairs (2001), or visit the Thailand Ministry of Foreign Affairs official web site at http://www.mfa.go.th.

22. The level of FDI that comes from Thailand to Indonesia has been relatively high. In 2000 alone, for instance, thirty-eight Thai projects were approved by the Indonesian government with a total investment value of US$2.3. billion, which ranked Thailand as the fifteenth largest investor in Indonesia (BKPM 2000). In the following year, or 2001, the total value of Thailand's investment in Indonesia increased to US$3 billion, which came from only three projects (BKPM 2002). On the other hand, however, the Board of Investment of Thailand (BOIT) reported that there was only one Indonesian project approved by the Thai government, amounting to US$28.6 million. For detailed data regarding foreign investment in Thailand, visit the BOIT official web site (accessed 2003) at http://www.boi.go.th/english/tid/data/BOI_statistics_fi.html.

23. The representative of the Embassy of Brunei, however, refused to comment on the question of Indonesia's involvement in ASEAN due to the sensitivity of the subject.

24. An interview was conducted on the 11 October 2000 with David C. DiGiovanna, the Economic Officer of the U.S. Embassy, in Jakarta.

25. An interview was conducted on the 30 November 2000 with Alex Stedtfelt, the First Economic Officer of the German Embassy, in Jakarta

26. An interview was conducted on the 23 March 2000, in Jakarta, with a representative of the British Embassy who wished to remain anonymous.

27. The representative of the British Embassy, however, claimed that his government did not have any specific points of view regarding Indonesia's involvement in AFTA, although his government had been very keen about the development of AFTA to date.

28. An interview was conducted on the 9 October 2000 with Wardah Hafidz, the Head of UPC, in Jakarta.

29. An interview was conducted on the 23 November 2000 with Dita Indah Sari, the Head of the FNPBI, in Jakarta

30. An interview was conducted on the 2 February 2001 with Adi Sasono, the Head of ICMI. Previously, Adi Sasono held the position of Minister of Co-operative, Small and Medium Enterprises during the Habibie administration.

31. An interview was conducted on 18 January 2001 with Boni Setiawan, an INFID activist, in Jakarta. Setiawan is currently the Executive Director of the Institute for Global Justice (IGJ).

32. An interview was conducted on the 16 November 2000 with Dr. Noer Soetrisno, Special Staff for Production Division, in Jakarta.

33. An interview was conducted on the 18 December 2000 with Darmawan Jayusman, Director of International Promotion Division, in Jakarta.

34. An interview was conducted on the 9 August 2001 with Dr. Permana Agung, the Directorate General of Custom and Excise, in Jakarta.

35. An interview was conducted on the 14 August 2001with Widjanarko Puspoyo, the former Head of BULOG, in Jakarta.

36. The interview with the representative of PUPUK was conducted on the 3 September 2001 with the Executive Director, Alam Putra, in Surabaya, East Java.

37. KADIN was formed on the 24 September 1968, to work in partnership with the Indonesian government and other national development institutions. It was also intended to function as a forum for Indonesian state-owned enterprises, co-operatives, and private businesses. KADIN was officially acknowledged by the government under Presidential Decree No. 1/1987, and was legalized under Law No. 1/1987 (Kompas 2004: 44). It is important to note that most Indonesian business associations are also members of

KADIN, which is the largest and the most influential business association in Indonesia. Therefore, the views of KADIN, to some extent, represent the general view of the majority of Indonesian business associations. Two research interviews were carried out with the representatives of KADIN, one with the Head of the ASEAN Committee Section, Iman TAufik, on the 26 November 2000, and the other with the Head of KADIN, Aburizal Bakrie, on the 23 August 2001. Both interviews took place in Jakarta. Aburizal Bakrie is currently serving as the Minister for People's Welfare under the Susilo Bambang Yudhoyono administration. During the early phase of Yudhoyono administration, Bakrie also served as the Coordinating Minister of Economics.

38. An interview was conducted on the 19 October 2000 with Djimanto, the Vice-President of APINDO, in Jakarta.

39. An interview was conducted on the 25 August 2001 with Dr. Mohammad Syargawi, the Vice-President of KUKMI, in Jakarta

40. KADIN is a member of the ASEAN Chamber of Commerce and Industry (ASEAN-CCI). It was decided during a meeting attended by forty-nine members of the ASEAN-CCI Committee in Bangkok, in December 1995, that the permanent ASEAN-CCI Secretariat should be established in Jakarta. Subsequently, the Indonesian Head of KADIN, Aburizal Bakrie, took over the ASEAN-CCI presidency from 1996–1997 (Kompas 2004: 44).

41. As reported in *Kompas* (2001a).

42. This data was also confirmed by Aswicahyono and Pangestu (2000: 471–2) in their analysis of Indonesia's exports and levels of competitiveness.

43. An interview was conducted on the 6 December 2000 in Jakarta. Dr. Hadi Soesastro was the Executive Director of the CSIS at the time of the interview.

44. An interview was conducted on the 21 August 2001 in Jakarta. Dr. Cornelis Luhulima was a Senior Researcher at the CSIS at the time of the interview.

45. An interview was conducted on 24 January 2001 in Jakarta. Dr. Dewi Fortuna Anwar was the former Assistant Minister for Foreign Affairs during the Habibie Administration. At the time of the interview, she held the position of the Executive Director for Research at the Habibie Centre, Research Associate at the Indonesian Institute for Sciences (LIPI—*Lembaga Ilmu Pengetahuan Indonesia*), and a Senior Researcher at the Centre for Information and Development Studies (CIDES).

46. An interview was conducted on the 5 March 2001 in Jakarta. Prof. Lepi Tarmidi was a Senior Lecturer of Economics and the Director of APEC Study Centre at the University of Indonesia at the time of the interview.

47. An interview was conducted on the 7 September 2001 in Jakarta. Dr. Bustanul Arifin was the Director of the Institute for the Development of Economics and Finance (INDEF) at the time of the interview.

48. As reported in the BOIT official web site at http://www.boi.go.th.

49. Indonesia's automotive industry has the highest tariff rates to date. Reports by the Asian Automotive Business Review (2000), for instance, indicated that import tariffs for passenger cars could reach as much as 65 percent plus 30 percent luxury tax. Prior to 1999, the tariff rate for the same item was 200 percent, plus 35 percent luxury tax.

50. According to the respondents from the BKPM, the Indonesian government, until now, classified foreign investment into three categories, which were open, semi-open, and closed. The classification depends upon the capacity of the industry to compete with foreign competitors. Industries categorized as closed, such as agriculture and communication industries, are normally in their infancy level, while those categorized as open, such as textile and garment, are capable of competing with foreign competitors.

51. PANI was originally formed following a meeting of various civil society groups in Penang, Malaysia, in 1982, under the auspices of the International Organization of Consumers Union (IOCU). The meeting was held to discuss concern over the irrational use of pesticides. To date, the group is committed to protect the health and safety of the people and the environment from pesticides and genetic engineering. The interview with the Director of PANI, Reza Tjahyadi, was conducted through electronic mail. The information sent to the author was received on 8 February 2001.

52. FSPSI has been traditionally known as the government's supported trade union. Despite the recent rise in the number of trade unions, FSPSI claims to have the largest membership in Indonesia. Yacob Nuwa Wea, who at the time held the position of the Head of FSPSI, was interviewed on the 20 January 2001 in Jakarta. He is currently the State Minister of Manpower and Transmigration under the Megawati administration.

53. An interview was conducted on the 9 September 2001 with Indah Sukmaningsih, the Director of YLKI, in Jakarta.

54. An interview was conducted on 25 August 2001 with M. Kismadi, the National Program Director of LEAD, in Jakarta

55. An interview was conducted on the 25 September 2001 in Jakarta with Bambang Warih Koesoema, the Executive Director of UNISOSDEM.

56. An interview was conducted on the 20 July 2001with the Head of KLIK, Yasir Alimi, in Hull, UK.

57. The activities of PAN Indonesia cover the whole Asia-Pacific region. In 1988, for example, PAN Indonesia, along with similar organizations in other Southeast Asian countries, formed the Southeast Asian Sustainable Network. Subsequently, in 1996, the group also became a board member of the Southeast Asian Council on Food Security and Fair Trade, which was formed in Quezon City, Philippines. In general PAN Indonesia has traditionally supported the notion of regionalism in Southeast Asia.

58. An interview was conducted on the 10 August 2002 with Dr. Charles Himawan, a member of the Board of Directors of the KOMNAS-HAM. He is also a faculty member of the Department of Economics at the University of Indonesia.

59. Data for the CEPT Product List for the year 2000 is provided in Chapter 5, Table 5.2.

60. In 2001 alone, there were 40,195,516 SMEs, which accounted for about 99.9 percent of total enterprises in Indonesia. Detail statistics of Indonesian SMEs can be obtained from the official web site of the Ministry of Co-operative-Small and Medium Enterprises (MoC-SMEs) (2001) at http://www.depkop.go.id.

61. An interview was conducted on the 20 December 2000 with Reindhardt Sirait, in Jakarta. Sirait was an activist of LMND at the time of the interview.

62. The military's involvement in Indonesian daily economic life was often cited as a case in point. The Indonesian military has often used nationalistic themes for the purpose of securing their economic interests in the country. The involvement of the Indonesian military in business has been prevalent since the early 1970s, through the formation of the *Kartika Eka Paksi Foundation*. To date, the foundation owns a total of twenty-six firms and seven joint ventures (Langit 2002), most of which support the welfare of military personnel and their families.

63. Two interviews were conducted with the representatives from the IBRA, the first was with Noegroho Soetardjo, Head of Agency Planning and Secretariat Division, on 7 March 2001, and the second was with Swasti Sawitri, an Economic officer of the IBRA Jakarta Branch, on the 31 July 2001. Both interviews took place in Jakarta.

64. The IBRA is a special government agency that was established in 1998 and is responsible for the rehabilitation of the Indonesian banking sector after the economic crisis.

The main activities of IBRA are to control assets previously owned by the troubled private sector and to sell those assets within the mandated timeframe of 2004. Although the IBRA preferred to sell these assets to other Indonesian entrepreneurs, the economic crisis made it impossible for other Indonesian conglomerate groups to purchase these assets. As a result, many of the troubled assets were subsequently offered to foreign investors.

65. The largest palm oil plantation was in Riau, North Sumatra.

66. Malaysia and Indonesia are the world's two largest palm oil producers, with Malaysia accounting for about half of the global output and Indonesia about 30 percent.

67. According to the IBRA official interviewed, the term "shadow company" here means a new company established by the owners of troubled assets in order to repossess their old assets. They have conducted such an action through their associates or affiliates who claim to have no connection with the owner of the troubled asset.

68. Despite such claims, the respondent failed to produce any hard evidence to indicate malpractice in either the bidding process or the supposed bribery conducted by the Salim Group.

69. As reported in *Kompas* (2001c), or visit the *Kompas* official web site at http://www.kompas.com.

70. An interview was conducted on the 10 August 2001 with Kadjatmiko, the Secretary of the Directorate General of DPOD, in Jakarta.

71. As reported by the Support for Decentralization Measures (SfDM) (2002: 3).

72. An interview was conducted on the 20 August 2001 with an official at the Bureau of Balance of Payment and International Relations who wished to remain anonymous.

73. An interview was conducted with officials of the Government of East Java Province, Industry and Trade Office on 2 September 2001 in Surabaya, East Java. All respondents in this government institution wished to remain anonymous.

74. However, it is important to note that under Governmental Decree No. 25/05/2000 all forms of cooperation conducted between provincial governments and foreign institutions shall not contradict similar agreements made by the central government.

75. The Indonesian daily newspaper, *Kompas* (2004: 40), for example, reported that, due to the absence of competition, communication costs in Indonesia have remained one of the highest in Southeast Asia. The International telephone rate in Indonesia reached as much as US$2.5 per minute in comparison to Singapore and Malaysia, both of which had international telephone rates below US$1 per minute.

76. The formation of the KPPOD was initiated during the national discussion on Saving the Regional Autonomy, which was conducted on 7 December 2000. Various civil society groups and academic think-tanks agreed to form an independent institution that is responsible for monitoring the implementation of the regional autonomy law. Further information regarding the KPPOD can be found at the Committee's official web site at http://www.kppod.org.

77. Indonesian society has been regarded as socialist owing to the emphasis on cooperation and collective behavior. The concept of *gotong royong* (mutual assistance), which refers to a collectivist organization of the economy that is based on the principle of family, was apparent even before the independence period.

78. The interview was conducted on the 14 August 2001 with Widjanarko Puspoyo, the Head of BULOG, in Jakarta.

79. The first round of the CEPT Outreach Program was held in Manila, Ho Chi Minh City, Kuala Lumpur, and Singapore on 26 March, 30 March, 4 April, and 6 April 2001 respectively.

80. The degree of evidence was demonstrated when the representative from the Indonesian Society of Small and Medium Scale Enterprises (KUKMI) even asked the interviewer to explain details concerning the implementation of AFTA. More interestingly, however, was the fact that even KUKMI, which shares office space with the Depperindag, claimed to have obtained little information regarding AFTA from the government.

81. Interview was conducted with Longgena Ginting, an activist of WALHI, on 4 March 2001, in Jakarta.

Chapter 7

Conclusion

The main objective of this book has been to analyze the dynamic relationship between nationalism and regionalism. As demonstrated throughout the book, nationalism and regionalism stand in a symbiotic relationship to one another. Therefore, the relationship between the two variables is not necessarily contentious, and it can be mutually reinforcing. This analysis hopes to contribute to the ongoing debate within the New Regionalism Approach (NRA), most of which has focused on an analysis of the regional-global nexus. In contrast, this book has provided a domestic focus on the pursuance of a regional integration strategy (RIS). Thus, as with some of the current analyzes of the relationship between nationalism and trade liberalization (Crane 1999; Shulman 2000; Helleiner 2002; Pickel 2003), this book also argues that, in light of the increasing trend toward globalization and regionalism, nationalists today must change or adjust their strategy in order to achieve their objectives of: (1) sustained economic development; (2) national unity; (3) the state's autonomy in international fora; (4) the promotion of national identity; (5) the formation of regional collective action to contain the negative forces of globalism and to achieve regional governance through positive globalism and regionalism; and (6) the elevation of the nation-state's bargaining power at the international level.

Therefore, in this concluding chapter, the author aims to recapitulate on the analysis of the relationship between Indonesian nationalism and ASEAN regionalism. The results of the case study analysis suggest a shifting paradigm in the attitude of Indonesian state and non-state actors toward ASEAN and its activities in recent years, albeit not a drastic one. The shift is from a traditional nationalistic approach, which reflects an inward-looking attitude, to a more liberal approach toward the concept of ASEAN regionalism. In this context, regionalism is no longer perceived as a threat that undermines the sovereignty of a nation, but is perceived as an enhancement of Indonesian national interests. Essentially, the new form of Indonesian nationalism today is not necessarily dogmatic, or based on a romanticized notion of nationhood. This shift suggests that Indonesians are increasingly aware of regional issues and want ASEAN to expand its activities and to include a wider range of participants within society. The primary analysis of this chapter, therefore, will examine NRA and the findings of this study to explain the relationship between Indonesian nationalism and ASEAN regionalism.

NRA and the Research Findings: Explaining the Relationship between Indonesian Nationalism and ASEAN Regionalism

NRA analysis has traditionally placed regionalism in the framework of a regional-global nexus. As mentioned in Chapter 3, however, NRA's emphasis on the multidimensionality, heterogeneity, flexibility, and the fluidity of regionalism implies that the domestic domain is as important as regional and global aspects to explain the emergence and the development of regionalism. Unlike previous theoretical approaches, such as neo-realism, that used state interest as the single criterion to explain regionalism (Gilpin 2001), NRA stresses that "geographical, historical, cultural and economic variables—as well as patterns of conflict/security and other criteria-all create patterns of interaction and produce conceptions of "regionness" (Schulz et al. 2001b: 252). As a result, NRA analysis does not consider the state to be the main determinant of regionalism, but also other actors, including market actors and civil society. However, up until now, NRA analysis has paid too much attention to *regional* non-state actors, while neglecting *domestic* actors that contribute as much as those regional actors in promoting regionalism. In contrast, this book has analyzed the contribution of the domestic state, market and civil-society actors to explain the rise of regionalism. More specifically, it has provided an analysis of the *perception* of domestic actors toward the pattern of regionalism that exists in their region. This issue is crucial because domestic actors are the people who are directly affected by policies issued by the states involved in a regional grouping.

One main aspect that has to be addressed in analyzing the local-regional nexus is the concept of nationalism, which is one of the most potent ideologies in modern history, and as such is capable of undermining the process of regionalism. Traditionally, nationalists' major concern about their country's involvement in a regional grouping is the loss of sovereignty that may ensue. The prevalent assumption among nationalists in the past was that regionalism involves a series of compromises made among different states and, thus, does not *fully* represent the national interests of the country. Moreover, nationalists in the past have also criticized the supposed benefits derived from the formation of a regional grouping (Hatsuse 1999: 105), much of which have gone to the powerful and wealthy, and not to the weak and the poor. As a result, therefore, a strained relationship between nationalists and the advocates of regionalism grew.

It is, however, too naïve to suggest that the same relationship exists between nationalism and regionalism today. The proliferation of regionalism in the late twentieth century and early twenty-first century is different from the regionalism that grew during the first wave in the 1950s and 1960s, the purpose of which was to achieve harmony, prosperity, and peace. In recent years, however, some scholars, particularly Shulman (2000), have demonstrated how a modern RIS is underpinned by several rationales that might also appeal to nationalists. As highlighted in Chapter 3, the primary rationales behind an RIS are sustained domestic economic development, the promotion of national unity, the enhancement of a state's autonomy in international fora, the promotion of national identity, collateral action against global capitalist movements, and the improvement of members states' bargaining power at the international level. These motives are not only prevalent among members of the majority nation within a nation-state, but also members of the minority nations that may or may not seek independence from the former. Thus, nationalists today are not necessarily hostile to the idea of RIS.

It is, therefore, clear that the relationship between nationalism and regionalism does not always have to be in conflict, as has previously been suggested. Yet it is important to point out that this is still a tentative hypothetical assumption. There is great variation in the type and the shape of regional groupings throughout the world and such theorization may only be applicable to certain regional groupings. This book has utilized the case study of the relationship between Indonesian nationalism and ASEAN regionalism. The aforementioned theory appears suitable for an analysis of the relationship between the two concepts in the geographical area concerned. The case study of the contemporary relationship between Indonesian nationalism and ASEAN regionalism shows that the two variables are not mutually exclusive, even when nationalistic sentiments are continuously stimulated by internal (i.e., threat of national disintegration) and external (i.e., regional economic crisis) forces. In the past, particularly during the New Order period, Indonesia's aspirations within ASEAN were not fulfilled (Leifer 1983: 153), which led to a sense of frustration on the part of the political elites who sought to influence the course of action taken by other ASEAN member states. In reality, therefore, Indonesia was incapable of extending its influence in ASEAN and on its member countries' foreign policy. Although today nationalism is still an important element in an analysis of Indonesians attitudes toward ASEAN, contemporary Indonesian perspectives on the Association are somewhat different to those in the past. There is no doubt that the majority of Indonesian state and non-state actors still feel indifferent about ASEAN and AFTA. However, the Association is still expected to continue to exist and to improve its current cooperation initiatives.

On the whole, most respondents interviewed during the field research can be placed within the convergence category. The majority of Indonesians (at least among the policymakers and those who are influential in the decision-making processes), therefore, can be referred to as *new nationalists*, which is based on the notion of logical nationalism rather than romantic nationalism. Indonesian nationalism at the end of the twentieth and the beginning of the twenty-first centuries is no longer protectionist and inward-looking. In foreign economic policy (FEP), for example, new nationalism (logical nationalism) in Indonesia is demonstrated through the country's continued support for ASEAN and its activities. However, it is important to note that Indonesian state and non-state actors' support of the Association will remain only as long as it serves member countries' national interests. The majority of respondents were also positive about

ASEAN's continued existence and its contribution toward increasing Indonesia's bargaining power, international autonomy, and ability to resist the negative forces of globalization. Many Indonesian state and non-state actors still perceived ASEAN as an effective bargaining tool in many multilateral trade negotiations. Therefore, the majority of Indonesian state and non-state actors did not perceive Indonesian nationalism as an impediment to the ASEAN regionalization process.

To start with, the case study analysis reveals that one of the most important motives for Indonesian domestic constituents to support ASEAN is the Association's perceived ability to generate sustained economic development. Indonesian state and non-state actors generally support the idea of ASEAN regionalism. Indonesian domestic constituents, both state and non-state actors, continuously maintain the importance of ASEAN as the main pillar of Indonesian foreign policy. Support for ASEAN prevails generally as a result of the Association's capacity to generate stable and harmonious relationships among member countries. A more stable and harmonious ASEAN region provides member countries more space to focus on their economic development. However, there are also those who believe that ASEAN has contributed little toward Indonesia's economic development, a view commonly held by a small number of Indonesian NGOs and CSOs. In their view, ASEAN provided little assistance to Indonesia during the economic crisis. Moreover, many representatives of Indonesian NGOs and CSOs thought that the Indonesian government should put more priority on the solving of domestic problems before embarking upon regional or international adventures, precisely because of the need to recover from the economic crisis.

Although the existence of ASEAN has generally been perceived as positive by the majority of Indonesian state and non-state actors, the Association's main project to date, AFTA, has failed to establish similar support. From the case study analysis, there are five main criticisms commonly leveled at AFTA. Firstly, unlike ASEAN, which has been useful in promoting Indonesia's good name, regional harmony, acting as a buffer against external attacks and subversion, as a vehicle for autonomous regional order, as an international bargaining tool, and a means of enhancing Indonesia's international stature, AFTA has been perceived as a threat that will undermine the development of the Indonesian economy, particularly small and medium enterprises (SMEs). Secondly, a large number of Indonesian non-state actors, particularly members of the academic community and larger economic actors, remain convinced that the current state of the Indonesian domestic economy is not conducive to the implementation of AFTA. Apart from an acute internal economic problem, the implementation of the regional autonomy law (OtDa) is perceived as having a significant impact on the way in which AFTA is implemented in Indonesia. Thirdly, many Indonesians also believe that AFTA will become like other ASEAN economic cooperation initiatives in the past. For many Indonesians, AFTA is viewed mainly as a platform for talks and discussions among ASEAN foreign policymakers. One reason for this is that ASEAN countries have continued to pursue protectionist policies, as a result of their relative resource wealth. Moreover, the majority of Indonesian policymakers are concerned about the competitive nature of ASEAN member economies, which makes the objective of regional economic integration difficult to achieve. In the immediate future, at least, Indonesia, like the majority of ASEAN economies, will remain dependent on trade with non-ASEAN countries. Fourthly, the majority of Indonesians remain convinced that the implementation of AFTA will only benefit large economic actors. Despite being adversely affected by the economic crisis, Indonesian large economic actors have been able to re-accumulate sufficient capital and resources to compete in the AFTA scheme. Fifthly, however, in comparison to the multilateral economic arrangements (i.e., under the auspices of the WTO), there is a widespread conviction among Indonesians state and non-state actors that AFTA does not pose an *immediate* threat to the national economic development of Indonesia.

In general, therefore, AFTA has not generated much support because it has been perceived as a mechanism that will undermine Indonesia's economic development and as a tool to lessen the country's sovereignty. Although it is true that the signing of AFTA in 1992 was an indication of a shift from the traditional approach of economic nationalism to liberal reform in Southeast Asia (Stubbs 2000c: 298), it would be inaccurate to suggest that Indonesia lost control over foreign goods that came into the country when the scheme was first implemented in 2002. Many Indonesians, as mentioned above, are more cautious about multilateral trade agreements made at the global level rather than regional level. Indonesian government officials also affirmed that Indonesia would remain committed to AFTA trade liberalization measures. Even those representing domestic businesses and industries, such as the Indonesian Chambers of Commerce and Industry (KADIN) and other smaller business associations, were convinced that the majority of Indonesia's domestic industries are ready for AFTA. Moreover, the case study analysis also reveals that members of the academic community remain convinced that the *degree of openness* among ASEAN countries today is still varied. The impact that AFTA may have on ASEAN economies are still uncertain. It is difficult to analyze the development of AFTA as it is still in its early stages. Another serious issue to be addressed is whether or not ASEAN member governments will actually be able to implement full trade liberalization in the region.

Apart from the achievement of sustained economic development, ASEAN also serves Indonesian nationalism and autonomy in the international arena. Although national pride is still important to most Indonesians, they are also influenced by consumerism and by external conditions. As a result, the context of Indonesian nationalism has changed somewhat, especially as a result of the recent wave of democratization in the country. The majority of Indonesians subscribe increasingly to the notion of *logical nationalism*, rather than *romantic nationalism*, the emphasis of which is on a more outward approach to international affairs and a more pragmatic approach to Indonesian foreign policy. As a result, many Indonesians, including the majority of Indonesian government officials, representatives of Indonesian business associations, members of the academic community, and representatives of Indonesian NGOs and CSOs, are no longer inward-looking in their attitude toward regionalism. Indeed, the majority of Indonesians now feel that Indonesia's participation in ASEAN and its AFTA scheme is important because it will help Indonesia achieve sustained economic development and thus ensure domestic stability and unity. Moreover, the increasing threat of national disintegration in Indonesia is also thought to be better handled with the collective support from other ASEAN member countries. Support expressed by some ASEAN member governments, such as Singapore and Thailand, assures Indonesia of its neighbors' commitment in supporting Indonesia's territorial integrity.

ASEAN is also useful to Indonesia because it can help increase Indonesia's bargaining power in the international arena and resist the negative forces of globalization. Many Indonesian domestic constituents are aware that they cannot resist the negative forces of globalization alone. Not only is Indonesia now flooded with foreign goods, many Indonesian domestic constituents also feel that the Indonesian government is fighting a losing battle in its international trade negotiations. ASEAN's contributions to Indonesia's international autonomy and bargaining power have been clearly demonstrated during the many trade disputes between the WTO and other regional groupings, particularly the EU and NAFTA. Although ASEAN member countries may have different interests, they have, on the whole, raised similar concerns during many multilateral negotiations. Moreover, the significance of ASEAN as a bargaining tool has grown since the joining of three new member countries, Lao, Cambodia, and Burma, and with the possible expansion of ASEAN into ASEAN plus Three (APT). The majority of Indonesian government officials, representatives of business associations, and members of the academic community are convinced that the expansion of the ASEAN membership and the possible creation of APT will increase Indonesia's bargaining power. This, in turn, will provide greater power for Indonesia to help it resist the negative forces of globalization.

The case study analysis has also shed a light on the problem of information dissemination, and the way in which the lack of adequate dissemination has resulted in limited support for AFTA from Indonesian state and non-state actors. While it is clear that the Association and its member governments have generally provided limited, highly technical and expensive information to the general public, it is also true that the Indonesian public at any rate has shown a lack of interest about Indonesian FEP in ASEAN. This lack of interest was visible even throughout the post-crisis period, when the majority of Indonesians were more concerned about the escalating domestic problems. The ASEAN Secretariat has always insisted that the Association has placed importance on the dissemination process. The problem generally occurs at the governmental level, where ministers tend to be cautious about disseminating information to the public. Positive attempts have been made to promote the Association's activities to the general public through various workshops and seminars, such as the ASEAN People's Assembly and the CEPT Outreach Program. Nonetheless, public attendance at such events has been minimal, suggesting that the majority of Indonesians remain passive about ASEAN and its activities.

Therefore, the majority of Indonesian state and non-state actors interviewed during the field research identified two major areas in ASEAN that need to be improved, including the organizational structure of the Association and the process of information dissemination. Firstly, the traditional image of ASEAN as an exclusive club for governmental officials, particularly Foreign Ministers, is resented by the majority of Indonesians, who also deplore the high levels of bureaucracy that exist within the Association. As a result, ASEAN and its member governments are accused of having neglected the demands made by smaller domestic non-state actors. New approaches to minimize the problem of exclusivity, such as the inclusion of either other state ministers or national leaders in the decision-making process, were simply rejected by member governments of ASEAN. In any case, such proposals would do little to promote a bottom-up approach within the Association. Therefore, new efforts to minimize the problem of exclusivity should focus on the incorporation of non-state actors in the decision-making process. Secondly, ASEAN must intensify the process of disseminating information regarding its activities to the public. While most of the Indonesian public are aware of the existence of ASEAN, the Association only provides limited, if not highly technical and expensive, information regarding its activities to the public. Another worrying aspect is the fact that information has been disseminated unevenly among different economic actors. For example, information on AFTA related matters has only been disseminated to large economic actors. This presents a major problem for the majority of Indonesian economic actors, most of whom are SMEs. Officials at various governmental institutions have also expressed their concern about the uneven nature of ASEAN's information dissemination process. Information on ASEAN related matters has so far been monopolized by the Ministry of Foreign Affairs (MFA), and to certain extent, the Ministry of Trade and Industry (Depperindag), particularly on issues surrounding the implementation of AFTA.

Therefore, this book has made a number of important points to the ongoing debate within NRA analysis and other analyzes of the relationship between nationalism and regionalism. Firstly, it is important to note that a regional grouping should be structured to accommodate the interests of a wider range of domestic participants. To this end, a regional organization must encourage the involvement of non-state actors in many of its projects or activities. Secondly, although the field research findings show some hostility toward an RIS from certain domestic actors, this does not suggest that nationalism and regionalism stand in conflict. The hostility prevalent among some non-state actors in a country toward an RIS does not so much result from an inward-looking nationalist attitude or the divergence in the interests of regional actors (i.e., government officials) and local actors (i.e., the business community and NGOs/CSOs), but results rather from a lack of information about and the inadequate promotion of regional activities, provided by the state to non-state actors. However, it is also important to note that the intensive promotion of regional activities is no a guarantee that support for an RIS will be generated within the public domain. However, the provision of adequate information would at least provide the public with a suitable basis upon which to form their opinions.

Indonesian Nationalism and ASEAN Regionalism: From Nation-State to Region-State?

The evolution of a nation-state into a region-state would, indeed, involve a long and difficult process to endure. To date, there is no regional grouping in the world capable of transforming itself into a perfect region-state, not even the most advanced regional grouping in the world, the EU. The rejection of the Europeans toward the making of the European-wide constitution in 2005 exemplifies the difficulty to push the transformation from a nation-state into a region-state. In the context of ASEAN, this regional grouping is still relatively young, and would have to endure similar difficulties to that encountered by the EU if it was to transform itself into a region-state. Although most of the key ASEAN member countries are relatively more open and more interconnected to each other these days, it remains unlikely that countries in the region will be fully able to surrender part of their sovereignty to a larger regional institution. Although citizens in ASEAN countries are increasingly facing similar problems and challenges, such as human rights abuses, environmental problems, etc., key policymakers in these countries are still reluctant to provide ASEAN with greater space to respond to those problems. Instead, regional collective actions have been carried out only at the time when these problems emerged.

Another element that undermines ASEAN's evolution process into a region-state, as has been pointed out many times in this book, is the limited participation of the general public in the decision-making process of ASEAN. This tendency has made ASEAN incapable of producing policies directly relevant to the people of Southeast Asia. Some regional integration observers, such as Chandra (2005) and Vatikiotis (2005), have consistently insisted that the people of the region should come first in any of the regional integration initiatives undertaken by ASEAN. The recent attempt by ASEAN policymakers and intellectuals to introduce an ASEAN Charter is a case in point. To date, the draft of this Charter has been prepared by a group of individuals representing former foreign ministers of ASEAN member countries as well as those representing the academic circles. For Vatikiotis, however, if ASEAN was to draw from the European experience in setting up a region-wide constitution, similar attempt by Southeast Asian nations is doomed to failure. One has to bear in mind that the architects of the European Charter failed to emphasize the actual needs and concerns of Europeans. In other words, the people must be consulted on what should be incorporated into a Charter. The same principle should also be applied in the making of an ASEAN Charter.

On the other hand, it is also important to stress that the strengthening of ASEAN regionalism would be a positive approach that could ensure further economic, political, and social equality in this region. At the moment, it is still possible that the strengthening of regionalism in Southeast Asia (i.e through the establishment of an ASEAN Community) would enable the emergence of a stronger regional institution than that of the ASEAN Secretariat. However, this new, and stronger, regional institution should have clearer objectives for promoting "positive regionalism," based on openness, transparency, and democracy. Another important aspect to take into consideration is the popularity of an eventual new regional institution among the Southeast Asian people. It is, therefore, clear that the strengthening of ASEAN could only be a more relevant regional grouping if it was able to be more transparent and inclusive. Without all these aforementioned efforts, it would be unlikely that the process of transformation from a nation-state into a region-state would take place in this region.

Conclusion

Regionalism and nationalism are two major concepts that influence international relations today. There is little doubt that the current wave of regionalism and the continued existence of nationalism imply that a complementary relationship has developed between the two. It is, therefore, important to re-emphasize in the concluding remarks of this book that nationalism and regionalism stand in a symbiotic relationship to one another. This book hopefully provides a significant contribution to new understandings of these concepts. More importantly, it is hoped that this book provides new directions within NRA with which to explain the rise and the development of regionalism today. The case study on the relationship between Indonesian nationalism and ASEAN regionalism has shed some light on the complementary relationship between the two concepts. Throughout its existence, ASEAN has experienced both major achievements and setbacks. The regionalism agenda has been expanded to cover a wide range of issues, such as politics, security, economics and social cooperation. Although the majority of Indonesian domestic state and non-state actors still feel quite indifferent about the Association, its existence is still considered useful, particularly as a vehicle to promote their country's interests at the domestic (i.e., promotion of unity), regional (i.e., promotion and expansion of national culture and identity and the formation of regional collective action against the negative forces of globalization), and international levels (i.e., promotion of the state's autonomy and the elevation of bargaining power). The Southeast Asian region is arguably better off with than without ASEAN.

Despite this, it is inevitable that the future of regionalism in Southeast Asia will depend upon ASEAN's ability to promote greater transparency and openness in many of its activities. ASEAN has been strongly criticized for, among other things, its highly complex organizational and bureaucratic structure, which limits the greater participation of a wider range of domestic actors. In recent years, the failure of ASEAN to address the economic crisis has also damaged the reputation of the Association. As a result, the relevance of ASEAN has been brought into question. While the Association is still faced with the challenge of becoming more democratic in its activities, the pursuit of further regional economic integration is underway with the introduction of AFTA. However, perspectives on this particular scheme are varied among different domestic actors in each ASEAN country. In Indonesia, for example, both state and non-state actors expressed concern that regional trade liberalization would further exacerbate the already acute national economic situation.

While skepticism prevails, it is, however, inappropriate to suggest that ASEAN is no longer relevant. It is hoped that in the immediate future the Association will introduce significant changes to deal with the aforementioned problems. One important step that would improve understanding of ASEAN and its activities would be the improved dissemination of proper information to all layers of society. It is also important to emphasize that the indifferent attitude prevalent among Indonesians toward ASEAN is not so much an offshoot of nationalistic sentiments, but more a result of the lack of adequate information regarding the Association and its activities. The Association should, therefore, increase its public relations exercises to promote itself to the general public. This will be very important, not only to encourage public awareness of ASEAN and its activities, but also to increase Indonesians' knowledge and understanding of their immediate neighbors. In the more democratic country that Indonesia is today, domestic actors will continue to demand a more open and transparent ASEAN.

APPENDIX 1

List of ASEAN Affiliated NGOs, as of May 2004

No	Name of ASEAN Affiliated NGOs	Headquarters
1	ASEAN Inter Parliamentary Organization (AIPO)	Indonesia
2	ASEAN Port Authorities Association (APAA)	Philippines
3	ASEAN Bankers Association (ABA)	Singapore
4	ASEAN Paediatric Federation (APF)	Singapore
5	ASEAN Federation of Accountants (AFA)	Philippines
6	ASEAN Council of Japan Alumni	Indonesia
7	ASEAN Law Association (ALA)	Singapore and Malaysia
8	ASEAN Confederation of Employers (ACE)	Philippines
9	ASEAN University Sports Council (AUSC)	Malaysia
10	ASEAN Federation of Furniture Manufacturers (AFFMA)	Indonesia
11	ASEAN Association of Radiologist (AAR)	Philippines
12	ASEAN Handicraft Promotion and Development Association (AHHPADA)	Thailand
13	ASEAN Valuers Association (AVA)	Malaysia
14	ASEAN Insurance Council (AIC)	Indonesia
15	ASEAN Football Federation (AFF)	Indonesia
16	ASEAN Federation for Psychiatric	Philippines
17	ASEAN Federation of Electrical Engineering Contractors (AFEEC)	Philippines
18	ASEAN Confederation of Women's Organization (ACWO)	Singapore
19	ASEAN Orthopaedic Association (AOA)	Singapore
20	ASEAN Neurosurgical Society (ANS)	Indonesia
21	ASEAN Constructors Federation (ACF)	Singapore
22	ASEAN Federation of Mining Association (AFMA)	Indonesia
23	ASEAN Council of Teachers (ACT)	Philippines
24	AASEAN Fisheries Federation (AFF)	Indonesia
25	ASEAN Federation of Forwarders Association (AFFA)	Indonesia
26	ASEAN Non-Governmental Organization for the Prevention of Drugs and Substance Abuse	Malaysia
27	ASEAN Association of Medical Laboratory Technologists (AAMLT)	Indonesia
28	ASEAN Law Student Association (ALSA)	Indonesia
29	ASEAN Vegetable Oil Club (AVOC)	Malaysia
30	ASEAN Business Forum (ABF)	Singapore
31	ASEAN Federation of Land Surveying and Geomatics (ASEAN FLAG)	**Malaysia**
32	ASEAN Intellectual Property Association (AIPA)	**Singapore**
33	ASEAN Federation of Heart Foundation (AFHF)	**Indonesia**
34	ASEAN Thalassaemia Society (ATS)	**Indonesia**
35	ASEAN NGO Coalition on Ageing	**Thailand**
36	ASEAN Oleochemical Manufacturers	**Malaysia**
37	ASEAN Federation of Flying Club (AFFC)	**Malaysia**
38	**ASEAN Forestry Students Association (AFSA)**	**Indonesia**

Continued on next page

Appendix 1—Continued

No	Name of ASEAN Affiliated NGOs	Headquarters
39	ASEAN Chess Confederation (ACC)	Singapore
40	ASEAN Cosmetic Association (ACA)	Singapore
41	ASEAN Academics of Science, Engineering and Technology (ASEAN CASE)	Malaysia
42	Confederation of ASEAN Journalist (CAJ)	
43	Committee for ASEAN Youth Cooperation	Malaysia
44	Federation of ASEAN Consulting Engineers (FACE)	Malaysia
45	Federation of ASEAN Shippers Council (FASC)	
46	Federation of ASEAN Shipowners Association (FASA)	Singapore
47	Federation of ASEAN Newspaper Publisher (FANP)	
48	Federation of ASEAN Economic Association (FAEA)	Indonesia
49	Federation of ASEAN Public Relation Organizations (FAPRO)	Singapore
50	ASEAN Co-operative Organization (ACO)	Indonesia
51	ASEAN Association for Planning and Housing (AAFH)	Philippines
52	ASEAN Chambers of Commerce and Industry (ASEAN CCI)	Malaysia
53	ASEAN Federation of Engineering Organization	
54	ASEAN Standard Trade Industry	
55	Medical Association of Southeast Asian Nations (MASEAN)	Singapore
56	Music industry Association (MIA)	Singapore
57	Confederation of ASEAN Societies of Anaesthesiologists	
58	Rheumatism Association of ASEAN (RAA)	Indonesia
59	Southeast Asia Association of Seismology and Earthquake Engineering (SEASEE)	Philippines
60	Veterans Confederation of ASEAN Countries (VECONAC)	**Philippines**
61	Southeast Asia Regional Institute for Community and Education (SEARICE)	**Thailand**
62	ASEAN Tours and Travel Association (ATTA)	
63	ASEAN Motion Picture Producers Association (AMPPA)	
64	ASEAN Council of Museum (ACM)	
65	ASEAN Council of Petroleum Cooperation (ACPC)	
66	ASEAN College of Surgeons (ACS)	
67	ASEAN Cardiologists Federation (ACF)	
68	ASEAN Consumer Protection Agency (ACPA)	
69	ASEAN Federation of Jurists (AFJ)	
70	ASEAN Trade Union Council (ATUC)	
71	ASEAN Federation of Women (AFW)	
72	**ASEAN Banking Council (ABC)**	

Source: Nishikawa (1983: 48); ASEAN Secretariat official website (accessed 2004)

APPENDIX 2

The Level of Tariff Barriers Since the Collapse of Bipolarity in Late 1980s

	Year	Simple mean tariff % (1)	Standard deviation tariff rates % (2)	Weigh- ted mean tariff % (3)	Share of lines with internati onal peaks % (4)	Share of lines with specific tariffs % (5)
EU	1988	3.3	5.6	3.6	3.6	13.8
	1998	3.5	5.0	2.7	2.3	12.6
Australia	1991	8.0	12.9	7.4	15.5	1.1
	1999	5.7	7.3	3.8	12.2	0.7
North America						
Canada	1989	7.7	7.0	6.5	14.2	2.5
United States	1989	5.7	6.7	4.1	8.0	13.0
	1999	4.3	11.4	2.8	6.3	8.3
Mexico	1991	13.2	4.3	11.9	18.9	0.0
	1999	10.1	9.4	14.7	24.5	0.0
Latin America						
Argentina	1992	12.2	7.7	12.7	31.0	0.0
	1999	11.0	8.3	10.7	39.5	0.0
Brazil	1989	42.4	17.2	32.0	92.4	0.2
	1999	13.6	7.8	12.6	54.0	0.0
Chile	1992	11.0	0.5	11.0	0.0	0.0
	1999	10.0	0.5	9.9	0.0	0.0
Colombia	1991	5.7	8.2	6.4	1.6	0.0
	1999	11.8	6.2	10.7	22.9	0.0
East Asia						
China	1992	41.3	30.8	32.6	78.4	0.0
	1998	16.8	11.1	15.7	43.4	0.4
Taiwan	1989	12.3	9.5	9.9	16.7	0.5
	1999	8.8	9.4	5.2	10.6	2.1
Japan	1988	5.9	8.0	3.3	8.6	11.5
	1999	4.8	7.3	2.3	7.6	2.6
Korea, Rep.	1988	18.8	8.1	13.8	72.8	10.2
	1999	8.7	5.9	5.9	4.8	0.8
S.E. Asia						
Indonesia	1989	21.9	19.7	13.2	50.5	0.3
	1999	**10.9**	**14.1**	**6.2**	**26.9**	**0.1**

Continued on next page

Appendix 2—Continued

	Year	Simple mean tariff % (1)	Standard deviation tariff rates % (2)	Weighted mean tariff % (3)	Share of lines with international peaks % (4)	Share of lines with specific tariffs % (5)
S.E. Asia						
Malaysia	1988	20.6	19.9	13.8	54.0	6.2
	1997	7.1	31.0	4.9	15.9	0.4
Philippines	1988	28.0	14.2	22.5	77.2	0.1
	1999	10.0	8.8	6.7	24.1	0.0
Singapore	1989	0.5	2.2	0.5	0.1	1.1
	1995	0.0	0.0	0.0	0.0	0.2
Thailand	1989	38.5	19.6	33.0	72.8	21.9
	1995	21.6	15.4	15.0	57.6	1.8
Vietnam	1994	12.7	17.8	18.6	32.4	1.0
	1999	15.1	17.7	17.3	37.3	0.6

Notes:
1. Simple mean tariff is the un-weighted average of the effectively applied rates for all products subject to tariffs.
2. Standard deviation of tariff rates measures the average dispersion of tariff rates around the simple mean.
3. Weighted mean tariff is the average of effectively applied rates weighted by the product import shares corresponding to each partner country.
4. International peaks are tariff rates that exceed 15 percent.
5. Specific tariffs are tariffs that are set on a per unit basis or that combine ad-valorem and per unit rates.

Source: World Bank (2001: 336–9)

APPENDIX 3

List of Respondents

Government Institutions

Departemen Koperasi, Perusahaan Kecil dan Menengah Republik Indonesia (DEPKOP-UKM)/Ministry of Co-operative, Small and Medium Enterprises (MoC-SMEs)
Production Division
Jl. H.R. Rasuna Said, Kav. 3-5, Jakarta 12940
Respondent: Dr. Noer Soetrisna
16 November 2000

Departemen Luar Negeri (DEPLU)/Ministry of Foreign Affairs
Department of ASEAN Cooperation
Jl. Taman Pejambon No. 6, Fl. 11, Jakarta
Respondent: anonymous
13 December 2000

Badan Koordinasi Penanaman modal (BKPM)/Investment Co-ordinating Board
International Promotion Division
Jl. Gatot Subroto No. 44, Jakarta 12190
Respondent: Darmawan Jayusman
18 December 2000

Departemen Perdagangan dan Industry (DEPPERINDAG)/Ministry of Trade and Industry
Sub-Directorate of ASEAN Cooperation
Respondent: Ketut Suwarko
Jl. Ridwan Rais 5, Jakarta
19 February 2001

Central Bank of Indonesia
International Trade Cooperation Division and International Economic and Institution
Studies Division
Jl. M. H. Thamrin 2, Jakarta10010
Respondent: anonymous
20 February 2001

Departemen Keuangan (DEPKEU)/Ministry of Finance
International and Regional Economic Cooperation
Secretariat General Bureau of Foreign Cooperation
Jl. Lapangan Banteng Timur No. 2-4, Jakarta 10710
Respondents: Dr. Bambang S. Marsoem and Solehudin Masjar
21 February 2001

Badan Penyehatan Perbankan Nasional (BPPN)/Indonesian Banking Restructuring
Agency (IBRA)
Central Office

Agency Planning and Secretariat Division
Wisma Bank Danamon, 30th floor, Jl. Jendral Sudirman, Kav. 45-46, Jakarta 12930
Respondent: Noegroho D. Soetardjo
7 March 2001

Indonesian Banking Restructuring Agency (IBRA), Jakarta Branch
Gedung Atrium Grd. 1-7, Jl. Senen Raya 135, Jakarta 10410
Respondent: Swasti Sawitri
31 July 2001

Direktorat Jendral Bea dan Cukai Republik Indonesia/Custom and Excise Republic Indonesia (DGCE)
Directorate General
Jl. A. Yani, Gedung A, Lt. 1, Jakarta 13230, Kotak Pos 108, Jkt 1002
Respondent: Dr. Permana Agung
9 August 2001

Dewan Perimbangan Otonomi Daerah (DPOD)/Board of Provincial Autonomy
Directorate General of Central and Local Fiscal Balance
Ministry of Finance of the Republic of Indonesia
Jl. Dr. Wahidin No. 1, Jkt 10710
Respondent: Kadjatmiko
10 August 2001

Badan Usaha Logistik (BULOG)/State Logistic Agency
Secretariat Bulog, Jl. Gatoto Subroto No. 49, Jak-Sel 12950, P.O. Box 2346
Respondents: Widjanarko Puspoyo
14 August 2001

Badan Perencanaan Pembangunan Nasional (BAPPENAS)/National Development Planning Board
Bureau of Balance of Payment and International Relations
Jl. Taman Suropati No. 2, Jakarta 10310
Respondent: anonymous
20 August 2001

Government of East Java Province, Industry and Trade Office
Jl. Siwalankerto II/42, Surabaya 60236
Respondents: Liri L. Ildham and Drs. Didi Teguh Wiyono
2 September 2001

Business Associations

Asosiasi Pengusaha Indonesia (APINDO)/Association of Indonesian Entrepreneurs
Jl. Cikini 1 No. 3B, Jakarta 10330
Respondent: Djimanto
19 October 2000

Kamar Dagang dan Industri Indonesia (KADIN)/Indonesian Chambers of Commerce and Industry
Sub-Committee of ASEAN
Jl. Bendungan Hilir Raya 60, Jakarta 10210
Respondent: Iman Taufik
26 November 2000

Kamar Dagang dan Industri Indonesia (KADIN)/Indonesian Chambers of Commerce and Industry
Wisma Bakrie 7th floor, Jl. HR. Rasuna Said Kav. B1, Jakarta 12910
Respondent: Aburizal Bakrie
23 August 2001

Kerukunan Usahawan Kecil dan Menengah Indonesia (KUKMI)/Indonesian Society of Small and Medium Scale Entrepreneurs
Secretariat General, Jl. Cikini IV No. 15, Jakarta 10330
Respondent: Dr. Ir. Mohammad Syargawi
25 August 2002

Perkumpulan untuk Peningkatan Usaha Kecil (PUPUK)/Association for the Advancement of Small Business
Jl. Ketintang Madya No. 111, Surabaya 60231
Respondent: R. Alam Surya Putra
3 September 2001

Academic Community

Centre for Strategic and International Studies (CSIS)
Jl. Tanah Abang III, No. 23-27, Jakarta Pusat
Respondent: Dr. Hadi Soesastro
6 December 2000

Habibie Centre
Jl. Kemang Raya Selatan No. 98, Jakarta Selatan 12560
Respondent : Dr. Dewi Fortuna Anwar
24 January 2001

APEC Centre, University of Indonesia
Jl. Salemba Raya No. 4, Jakarta
Respondent: Prof. Lepi Tarmidi
5 March 2001

Centre for Strategic and International Studies (CSIS)
Jl. Tanah Abang III, No. 23-27, Jakarta Pusat
Respondent: Dr. C. P. F. Luhulima
21 August 2001

Institute for Development of Economics and Finance (INDEF)
Jl. Wijayakarta II No. A-4, Kuningan Barat, Jakarta 12710

Respondent: Dr. Bustanul Arifin
7 September 2001

Pressure Groups

Urban Poor Consortium (UPC)
Billy Moon H 1 No.7, Jakarta
Respondent: Wardah Hafidz
9 October 2000

Front Nasional Perjuangan Buruh Indonesia (FNPBI)/Front National for the Indonesian
Labour Struggle
Jl. Tebet Timur IIIK, No. 2, Jakarta Selatan
Respondent: Dita Indah Sari
13 November 2000

Liga Mahasiswa Nasional untuk Demokrasi (LMND)/National Student League for Democracy
Jl. Danau Towuti Blok G1/31, Bendungan Hilir, Jakarta
Respondent: Reindhard Sirait
20 December 2000

International Financial Development (INFID)
Jl. Mampang Prapatan XI/23. Jkt 12790
Respondent: Boni Setiawan
18 January 2001

Federasi Serikat Pekerja Seluruh Indonesia (FSPSI)/Federation of Indonesian Workers
Union
Jl. Raya Pasar Minggu KM 17, No. 9, Jakarta
20 January 2001

Ikatan Cendikiawan Muslim Indonesia (ICMI)/Association of Indonesian Muslim Intellectuals
Jl. Haji Agus Salim No. 117
Respondent: Adi Sasono
2 February 2001

Pesticide Action Network Indonesia (PANI)
Respondent: Reza Tjahjadi
8 February 2001 (electronic mail)

Wahana Lingkungan Hidup (WALHI)/Friends of the Earth
Jl. Tegal Parang Utara No. 14, Jakarta 12790
Respondent: Longgena Ginting
4 March 2001

Kajian Layanan Informasi untuk Kedaulatan Rakyat (KLIK)/Information and Civic Studies

Yogyakarta
25 July 2001 (in Hull)

Komisi Nasional Hak-Hak Asasi Manusia (KOMNAS-HAM)/Indonesian National
Commission on Human Rights
Jl. Latuharhari No. 4B, Menteng, Jakarta Pusat
Respondent: Dr. Charles Himawan
10 August 2001

Leadership for Environment and Development (LEAD)
Jl. Tebet Raya No. 88, Jakarta
Respondent: M. S. Kismadi
25 August 2001

Yayasan Lembaga Konsumen Indonesia (YLKI)/Indonesian Consumers Organization
Jl. Pancoran Barat VII/1, Duren Tiga, Jakarta 12760
Respondent : Indah Sukmaningsih
9 September 2001

Uni Sosial Demokrat (UNISOSDEM)/Uni Social Democrat
Jl. Berdikari Kav. 2, Palmerah, Kebayoran Lama, Jakarta
Respondent : Bambang Warih Kusuma
25 September 2001

ASEAN Secretariat and Foreign Embassies

U.S. Embassy
Jl. Merdeka Selatan 4-5, Jakarta 10110
Respondent: David C. DiGiovanna
11 October 2000

Royal Thai Embassy
74, Jl. Imam Bonjol, Jakarta Pusat 10310
Respondent: H.E. Mr. Somphand Kokilanon
17 October 2000

ASEAN Secretariat
Bureau of Trade, Industry and Services
Jl. Sisingamangaraja, 70A, Jakarta 12110, Indonesia
Respondents: anonymous
7 December 2000

German Embassy
Jl. MH. Thamrin No.1, Jakarta, 10310
Respondent: Alexander Stedtfeld
30 November 2000

British Embassy
Jl. M.H. Thamrin No. 75, Jakarta Pusat 10310

Respondent: anonymous
25 March 2001

Brunei Embassy
Wisma GKBI Lt. 19, Suite 1901, Jl. Jendral Sudirman No. 28, Jakarta 10210
Respondent: anonymous
21 August 2001

APPENDIX 4

The ASEAN Declaration

(Bangkok Declaration)

Bangkok, 8 August 1967

The Presidium Minister for Political Affairs/Minister for Foreign Affairs of Indonesia, the Deputy Prime Minister of Malaysia, the Secretary of Foreign Affairs of the Philippines, the Minister for Foreign Affairs of Singapore and the Minister of Foreign Affairs of Thailand:

MINDFUL of the existence of mutual interests and common problems among countries of South-East Asia and convinced of the need to strengthen further the existing bonds of regional solidarity and cooperation;

DESIRING to establish a firm foundation for common action to promote regional cooperation in South-East Asia in the spirit of equality and partnership and thereby contribute toward peace, progress and prosperity in the region;

CONSCIOUS that in an increasingly interdependent world, the cherished ideals of peace, freedom, social justice and economic well-being are best attained by fostering good understanding, good neighbourliness and meaningful cooperation among the countries of the region already bound together by ties of history and culture;

CONSIDERING that the countries of South East Asia share a primary responsibility for strengthening the economic and social stability of the region and ensuring their peaceful and progressive national development, and that they are determined to ensure their stability and security from external interference in any form or manifestation in order to preserve their national identities in accordance with the ideals and aspirations of their peoples;

AFFIRMING that all foreign bases are temporary and remain only with the expressed concurrence of the countries concerned and are not intended to be used directly or indirectly to subvert the national independence and freedom of States in the area or prejudice the orderly processes of their national development;

DO HEREBY DECLARE:

FIRST, the establishment of an Association for Regional Cooperation among the countries of South-East Asia to be known as the Association of South-East Asian Nations (ASEAN)

SECOND, that the aims and purposes of the Association shall be:

1. To accelerate the economic growth, social progress and cultural development in the region through joint endeavors in the spirit of equality and partnership in order to strengthen the foundation for a prosperous and peaceful community of Southeast Asian nations;

2. To promote regional peace and stability through abiding respect for justice and the rule of law in the relationship among countries of the region and adherence to the principles of the United Nations Charter;

3. To promote active collaboration and mutual assistance on matters of common interest in the economic, social, cultural, technical, scientific and administrative fields;

4. To provide assistance toe ach other in the form of training and research facilities in the educational, professional, technical and administrative spheres;

5. To collaborate more effectively for the greater utilization of their agriculture and industries, the expansion of their trade, including the study of the problems of international commodity trade, the improvement of their transportation and communications facilities and the raising of the living standards of their peoples;

6. To promote South-East Asian studies;

7. To maintain close and beneficial cooperation with existing international and regional organization with similar aims and purposes, and explore all avenues for even closer cooperation among themselves

THIRD, that to carry out these aims and purposes, the following machinery shall be established:

(a) Annual Meeting of Foreign Ministers, which shall be by rotation and referred to as ASEAN Ministerial Meeting. Special Meetings of Foreign Ministers may be convened as required.

(b) A standing committee, under the chairmanship of the Foreign Minister of the host country or his representative and having as its members the accredited Ambassadors of the other member countries, to carry on the work of the Association in between Meetings of Foreign Ministers.

(c) Ad-Hoc Committees and Permanent Committees of specialists and officials on specific subjects.

(d) A national Secretariat in each member country to carry out the work of the Association on behalf of that country and to service the Annual or Special Meetings of Foreign Ministers, the Standing Committee and such other committees as may hereafter be established.

FOURTH, that the Association is open for participation to all States in the South-East Asian Region subscribing to the aforementioned aims, principles and purposes.

FIFTH, that the Association represents the collective will of the nations of South-East Asia to bind themselves together in friendship and cooperation and, through joint efforts and sacrifices, secure for their peoples and for posterity the blessings of peace, freedom and prosperity.

DONE in Bangkok on the Eighth Day of August in the Year One Thousand Nine Hundred and Sixty-Seven.

For the Republic of Indonesia :

ADAM MALIK
Presidium Minister for Political
Minister for Foreign Affairs

For the Republic of Singapore :

S. RAJARATNAM
Minister of Foreign Affairs

For Malaysia :

TUN ABDUL RAZAK
Deputy Prime Minister,
Minister of Defence and
Minister of National Development

For the Kingdom of Thailand :

THANAT KHOMAN
Minister of Foreign Affairs

For the Republic of the Philippines :

NARCISO RAMOS
Secretary of Foreign Affairs

Source: ASEAN Secretariat official website (accessed 2002) at http://www.aseansec.org

APPENDIX 5

The Building of a Just, Democratic, Transparent, and Accountable ASEAN Community for the People of Southeast Asia

Statement of recommendations/ proposals from Southeast Asian civil-society organizations and non-governmental organizations to the ASEAN policymakers presented at the Roundtable Discussion on 'Building the ASEAN Community: Prospects and Challenges', 4th August 2005, Jakarta, Indonesia

In light of the plans initiated by the Association of Southeast Asian Nations (ASEAN) to create the ASEAN Community by 2020, we, the representatives of civil-society organizations and non-governmental organizations throughout Southeast Asia, would like to present our recommendations to the making of the ASEAN Community to the policymakers at the ASEAN Secretariat and ASEAN member states.

First, reiterating the essence of the 1967 Bangkok Declaration highlighting the prime motivation for the creation of ASEAN in ensuring peace, stability, and prosperity in the Southeast Asian region, it is imperative that the current and future deepening of regional integration under ASEAN's auspices should reflect those aforementioned objectives.

Second, recognizing the necessity of a more democratic ASEAN and the increasing importance of civil-society groups in Southeast Asia, it is also imperative that ASEAN, as well as its current activities and its future integration schemes, particularly the ASEAN Community, should be more transparent, accountable, and, more importantly, pro-people.

Third, conscious of possible negative impacts that the process of globalization may bring, ASEAN member states should enhance its unitary stance to contain the negative forces of globalization.

Fourth, acknowledging the general unawareness regarding ASEAN among Southeast Asian people and, at the same time, the importance of ASEAN regionalism for the people of Southeast Asia, it is more relevant for ASEAN and its member states to concentrate upon the deepening of regionalism in the Southeast Asian region before embarking upon greater East-Asia or East-Asia-Oceania/Pacific regionalism.

Fifth, despite our support toward further regionalism in Southeast Asia, ASEAN and its member states should also take into account the economic, social, and political differences of all ASEAN member countries when making future decisions regarding enhanced regionalism in Southeast Asia.

Based on those aforementioned considerations, our recommendations/proposals with regard to the building of the ASEAN Community are as follows:

(1) There should be efforts to transform ASEAN into an institution that highly values democracy, transparency, and accountability *vis-à-vis* the people of Southeast Asia;

(2) There should be efforts to enhance the participation of civil-society groups in ASEAN's decision making process;

(3) ASEAN member states should consider to provide a stronger role to the ASEAN Secretariat and its Secretary-General, who will be chosen by and be directly responsible to the people Southeast Asia;

(4) ASEAN Secretariat should be more open, active, and responsive *vis-à-vis* the public;

(5) ASEAN and its member states should also reassess the relevance of the *non-interference* principle, as this principle often hinders regional integration in Southeast Asia, and also brings suffering to the weaks and poor;

(6) The ASEAN Inter-Parliamentary Organization (AIPO) should be given a wider role in the regionalization process, and consideration should be made to transform AIPO from a merely organization into a real parliamentary system, whose thoughts, decisions, and voice should represent the interests of Southeast Asian people;

(7) Trade and economic liberalization should not be the sole benchmark of regionalism in Southeast Asia;

(8) There should be further efforts to promote the regionalization process from *within* and *below* in order to ensure that the building of the ASEAN Community reflects the demands made by all of Southeast Asian people.

(9) ASEAN and the member states should make further efforts to improve and widen their socialization programs regarding ASEAN's current and future regionalization attempts;

(10) ASEAN should make efforts to act as a unitary and effective bargaining block in the international fora so that its usefulness can be observed and supported by the people of Southeast Asia. However, ASEAN and its member states should still bear in mind points (1) and (2) which ensures that decision-making processes regarding the SEA region are open, transparent and accountable.

(11) In light of the emergence of bilateral free trade agreements (BFTAs) and/or bilateral economic partnership agreements (BEPA) that have been pursued by many Southeast Asian member-states, ASEAN member countries should realize that ASEAN, as a larger regional grouping, could be better equipped to deal with non-ASEAN member countries or other regional grouping. ASEAN should also consider punishing member countries that unilaterally pursue this BFTA/BEPA strategy as it undermines ASEAN cohesion as a whole.

(12) ASEAN should focus on ASEAN regionalism prior to pursue with wider East-Asian regionalism initiatives. This is imperative given the relatively weak and slow regionalization process in the Southeast Asian region. The pursuance of wider East Asian (or East-Asia-Oceania/Pacific) regionalism would only undermine the notion of democracy, openness, transparency, accountability, and effectiveness of ASEAN regionalism efforts;

We, the signatories of this statement, hereby believe that the building of the ASEAN Community would be far more relevant for the people of Southeast Asia if ASEAN and its member states take the aforementioned recommendations into account. We express our support for the building of a democratic, open, transparent, accountable, and prosperous ASEAN Community

Jakarta, 4th August 2005

Signed and endorsed by:
1. Institute for Global Justice (IGJ), Jakarta, Indonesia

2. Working Group on Public Sector Forum (WGPSR), Jakarta, Indonesia
3. Center for Orang Asli Concerns (COAC), Subang Jaya, Malaysia
4. Youth Coordination Centre International (YCCI), Bangkok, Thailand
5. Alternative ASEAN Network on Burma, Bangkok, Thailand
6. Third World Network (TWN), Penang, Malaysia
7. Sustainability Watch Network, Quezon City, the Philippines
8. Asian Secretariat for the Development of Human Resources in Rural Areas (AsiaDHRRA), Quezon City, the Philippines
9. Southeast Asian Council for Food Security and Trade (SEACON), Selangor, Malaysia
10. Education and Research Association for Consumer (ERA Consumer), Selangor, Malaysia
11. Vietnam Research Team on Cross-Border Migration in Greater Mekong Sub-Region (GMS)
12. Mekong Migration Network (MMN), Ho Chi Minh City, Vietnam
13. United Islamic Centre of East Timor (UNICET), Dili, Timor Leste
14. Documentation for Action Groups in Asia (DAGA), Hong Kong SAR
15. Commune Council Support Project, Phnom Penh, Cambodia
16. Center for Pesantren and Democracy Studies (CEPDES), Jakarta, Indonesia

Contact detail:
Bonnie Setiawan, Executive Director, The Institute for Global Justice (IGJ), Jl. Diponegoro No. 9, Menteng, Jakarta Pusat 10310, Tel: (021) 3193-1153, Fax: (021) 391-3956, email: igj@globaljust.org

APPENDIX 6

ASEAN-5 Major Trading Partners (2001)*

Indonesia's Major Trading Partners			
Exports		**Imports**	
Japan	13,530	Japan	7,046
United States	9,916	Singapore	3,773
Singapore	7,081	South Korea	3,608
South Korea	4,068	China	3,120
China	3,535	United States	2,750
Taiwan	2,294	Australia	1,830
Malaysia	2,038	Malaysia	1,719
Germany	1,948	Saudi Arabia	1,550
UK	1,560	Thailand	1,502
Hong Kong	1,356	Germany	1,461

Malaysia's Major Trading Partners			
Exports		**Imports**	
United States	17,816	Japan	14,211
Singapore	14,913	United States	11,839
Japan	11,770	Singapore	9,293
Hong Kong	4,063	Taiwan	4,193
Netherlands	4,060	China	3,804
China	3,821	South Korea	2,958
Thailand	3,360	China	2,139
Taiwan	3,263	Germany	2,743
South Korea	2,963	Indonesia	2,241
UK	2,310	Hong Kong	1,892

Philippines' Major Trading Partners			
Exports		**Imports**	
United States	8,994	Japan	6,098
Japan	5,054	United States	4,993
Netherlands	2,976	South Korea	1,950
Singapore	2,308	Singapore	1,793
Taiwan	2,127	Taiwan	1,607
Hong Kong	1,580	Hong Kong	1,259
Thailand	1,358	China	953
Germany	1,323	Thailand	897
Malaysia	1,112	Saudi Arabia	887
Korea	1,044	Indonesia	760

Singapore's Major Trading Partners			
Exports		**Imports**	
Malaysia	21,122	Malaysia	20,094
United States	18,755	United States	19,159
Hong Kong	10,820	Japan	**16,091**
Japan	**9,341**	**China**	**7,195**

Continued on next page

Appendix 6—Continued

Singapore's Major Trading Partners			
Exports		**Imports**	
Taiwan	6,264	Thailand	5,159
China	5,329	Taiwan	4,932
Thailand	5,304	Saudi Arabia	4,229
South Korea	4,688	Germany	3,835
Germany	4,297	South Korea	3,823
Netherlands	4,035	Hong Kong	2,765

Thailand's Major Trading Partners			
Exports		**Imports**	
United States	13,246	Japan	13,881
Japan	9,964	United States	7,198
Singapore	5,287	China	3,711
Hong Kong	3,298	Malaysia	3,078
China	2,863	Singapore	2,854
Malaysia	2,722	Taiwan	2,599
UK	2,328	Germany	2,562
Netherlands	2,028	South Korea	2,121
Germany	1,568	United Arab Emirates	1,529
Belgium	**1,417**	**Australia**	**1,310**

Note: *Millions of US$
Source: IMF (2002)

APPENDIX 7

United States and Japan Major Trading Partners (2001)*

United States Major Trading Partners			
Exports		**Imports**	
Canada	405,760	Canada	220,138
Japan	57,639	Japan	129,708
UK	40,798	China	109,392
Germany	30,114	Germany	60,492
South Korea	22,197	UK	42,367
France	20,125	South Korea	36,491
Netherlands	19,525	Taiwan	34,779
China	19,235	France	30,984
Taiwan	18,152	Italy	24,954
Singapore	17,692	Malaysia	23,072
Japan's Major Trading Partners			
Exports		**Imports**	
United States	122,701	United States	63,713
China	30,948	China	57,780
South Korea	25,292	South Korea	17,221
Taiwan	24,256	Indonesia	14,883
Hong Kong	23,252	Australia	14,385
Germany	16,562	Taiwan	14,180
Singapore	14,713	United Arab Emirates	12,850
UK	12,146	Malaysia	12,824
Thailand	11,837	Thailand	10,353
Netherlands	**11,489**	**Saudi Arabia**	**12,316**

Note: *Million US$
Source: IMF (2002)

Selected Bibliography

ABC News International. "China-S.E. Asia Sign Trade Pact." *ABC News*, November 4, 2002. http://www.abcnews.go.com/ (accessed 4 November, 2002)

Abidin, M. Z. "ASEAN and its Inter-Regional Economic Links." In *ASEAN Beyond the Regional Crisis: Challenges and Initiatives*, edited by M. Tan, 243–73. Singapore: ISEAS, 2001.

Abrash, A. "Indonesia after Suharto." *Foreign Policy in Focus* 3, No. 34, (November 1998).

Abu-Lughod, J. *Before European Hegemony: The World System AD 1250–1350*, Oxford: Oxford University Press, 1989.

Acharya, A. "Regionalism and the Emerging World Order: Sovereignty, Autonomy, Identity." In *New Regionalism in the Global Political Economy*, edited by S. Breslin *et al.*, 20–32. London: Routledge, 2002.

Adler, E., and M. Barnett. "Security Communities in Theoretical Perspective". In *Security Communities*, edited by E. Adler and M. Barnett, 3–28. Cambridge: Cambridge University Press, 1998

Agung, I. A. A. G. *Twenty Years Indonesian Foreign Policy: 1945–1965*. The Hague: Mouton & Co, 1973.

Akrasanee, N. "ASEAN in the Past 33 Years: Lessons for Economic Co-operation." In *A New ASEAN in a New* Millennium, edited by S. S. C. Tay, *et al.*, 35–42. Jakarta and Singapore: CSIS and ISEAS, 2000.

Alatas, A. "'ASEAN Plus Three' Equals Peace Plus Prosperity," Paper presented at the Regional Outlook Forum, January, Singapore, 2001.

Allen, G. C., and A. G. Donnithorne. *Western Enterprise in Indonesia and Malaya*. London: George Allen and Unwin Ltd, 1957.

Alm, J., R. Aten, and R. Bahl, "Can Indonesia Decentralize Successfully? Plans, Problems, and Prospects." *Bulletin of Indonesian Economic Studies* 37, No. 1 (2001): 83–102.

Alvstam, C. G. "East Asia: Regionalization Still Waiting to Happen?" In *Regionalization in a Globalizing World: A Comparative Perspective on Forms, Actors, and Processes*, edited by S. Schulz, *et al.*, 173–97. London: Zed Books, 2001.

Amnesty International. "Indonesia: ASEAN Regional Forum Members Must Address Mounting Violations in Aceh." *Amnesty International*, News Service No. 88, May 17, 2001. http://web.amnesty.org (accessed January 25 2002).

Andaya, L. Y. "Ethnonation, Nation-State, and Regionalism in Southeast Asia." Paper presented at the Proceedings of the International Symposium Southeast Asia: Global Area Studies for the 21st Century, Center for Southeast Asian Studies, Kyoto University, October 1997.

Anderson, B. *Imagined Communities*. London: Verso/New Left Books, 1983.

Anderson, K., and R. Blackhurst. "Introduction and Summary." In *Regional Integration and the Global Trading System*, edited by K. Anderson and R. Blackhurst, 1–15. Hertfordshire, UK: Harvester Wheatsheaf, 1993.

Anoruo, E., and Y. Ahmad. "Openness and Economic Growth: Evidence from Selected ASEAN Countries." *The Indian Economic Journal* 47, No. 3 (1999): 110–17.

Anwar, D. F. "Megawati's Search for an Effective Foreign Policy." In *Governance in Indonesia: Challenges Facing the Megawati Presidency*, edited by H. Soesastro, *et al.*, 70–90. Singapore: ISEAS, 2003.

———. "Indonesia's Transition to Democracy: Challenges and Prospects." Paper presented at the Conference of Rethinking Indonesia: A Conference on Contemporary Indonesia, Melbourne University, Australia, March 2001a.

———. "ASEAN Enlargement: Political, Security, and Institutional Perspectives." In *ASEAN Enlargement: Impacts and Implications*, edited by M. Tan and C. L. Gates, 26–44. Singapore: ISEAS, 2001b.

———. "Indonesian Foreign Policy in 2000." *Habibie Centre*. 2000. www.habibie.net/2001/Indonesia/archives/paperspeech/dfa/ritp2000.rtf (accessed March 11 2001).

———. *Indonesia in ASEAN: Foreign Policy and Regionalism*. Singapore: ISEAS, 1994.

———. *Indonesia and the Security of Southeast Asia*. Jakarta: CSIS, 1992.

Arndt, H. W. *The Indonesian Economy: Selected Papers*. Singapore: Chopmen Publisher, 1984.

Arrighi, G. *The Long Twentieth Century: Money, Power, and the Origins of Our Times*. London: Verso, 1994.

ASEAN Institute of Strategic and International Studies. *ASEAN People's Assembly 2000 Handbook*. Batam, Indonesia: ASEAN-ISIS, 2000.

ASEAN Secretariat. *Towards a Single Economic Space*. Jakarta: ASEAN Secretariat, 2003.

———. *Southeast Asia: A Free Trade Area*. Jakarta: ASEAN Secretariat, 2002a.

———. "ASEAN Leaders Sign Landmark Tourism Agreement." *ASEAN Secretariat Press Release*, November 4, 2002b. http://www.aseansec.org (accessed March 20, 2003).

———. "ASEAN-China Framework Agreement on Comprehensive Economic Co-operation." 2002c. http://www.aseansec.org/ (accessed January 26, 2003)

———. "The First ASEAN Economic Ministers and the Minister of India Consultation." 2002d. http://www/aseansec.org/ (accessed January 26, 2003).

———. "Joint Statement of ASEAN + 3in Support of Sovereignty, Territorial Integrity and National Unity of Indonesia." 2000a. http://www.aseansec.org/ (accessed November 18, 2001).

———. "The 12th Meeting of the AFTA Council, Manila, Philippines, 6 October 1998." 1998a. http://www.aseansec.org/ (accessed January 26, 2003).

———. "Statement on Bold Measures, ASEAN Secretariat." December 16, 1998b, http://www.aseansec.org/ (accessed January 26 2003).

———. "ASEAN Affiliated NGOs, as of 3 May 2004." http://www.aseansec.org/ (accessed September 10, 2005).

———. "Declaration of ASEAN Concord II, 7 October 2003." http://www.aseansec.org/ (accessed February 5, 2004).

———. "Economic Statistics." http://www.aseansec.org/ (accessed November 12, 2003).

———. "Framework Agreement on the ASEAN Investment Area." http://www.aseansec.org/ (accessed May 12, 2003).

———. "Treaty of Amity and Cooperation in Southeast Asia, Indonesia 24 February 1976." http://www.aseansec.org/ (accessed May 10 2003).

———. "Framework Agreement on Enhancing ASEAN Economic Co-operation." http://www.aseansec.org/ (accessed March 19, 2003).

————. "Framework for the AFTA-CER Closer Economic Partnership." http://www.aseansec.org/ (accessed January 26, 2003).

————. "ASEAN Trade Data." http://202.154.12.3/trade/publicview.asp (accessed December 12, 2002).

————. "The ASEAN Declaration (Bangkok Declaration), Bangkok 8 August 1967." http://www.aseansec.org/ (accessed October 3, 2002).

————. "Overview: Association of Southeast Asian Nations." http://www.aseansec. org/ (accessed July 19, 2002).

————. *AFTA Readers, Volume 1, Questions and Answers of the CEPT and AFTA.* Jakarta: ASEAN Secretariat, 1993.

ASEAN Tourism Forum. "ATF Objectives, ASEAN Tourism Forum." 2003. http://www.atf2003.com/ (accessed January 18, 2003).

Asia-Europe Meeting. "Asia-Europe Meeting: Background." http://asem.inter.net.th/ (accessed February 8, 2003).

Asian Automotive Business Review. "The Four ASEAN Nations Struggle to Develop their Automotive Industries While At the Same Time Try To Liberalize Them." *Asian Automotive Business Review* 11, No. 2 (2000): 26–31.

Asia Recovery Information Center. "ASEAN + 3 Bond Market Initiative." http://aric.adb.org/ (accessed January 21, 2004).

Asian Development Bank. *Asian Development Outlook 2002.* Manila, Philippines: ADB, 2002.

————. *Key Indicators of Developing Asian and Pacific Countries 2001, Vol. 23.* Manila: Asian Development Bank, 2001.

————. *Asian Development Outlook 1999.* Manila: the Asian Development Bank and Oxford University Press, 1999.

Asiaweek. "Thoughts of Adi Sasono." December 18, 1998. http://www.asiaweek.com (accessed April 15, 2001).

Aswicahyono, H., and M. Pangestu. "Indonesia's Recovery: Exports and Regaining Competitiveness." *The Developing Economies* 38, No. 4 (2000): 454–89.

Axline, W. A., ed. *The Political Economy of Regional Co-operation: Comparative Case Studies.* London: Pinter Publisher, 1994.

————. "Underdevelopment, Dependence, and Integration: The Politics of Regionalism in the Third World." *International Organization* 31, No. 1 (1977): 83–105.

Bajo, C. S. *The Political Economy of Regionalism: Business Actors in MERCOSUR: In the Petrochemical and Steel Sectors.* Maastricht, the Netherlands: Shaker Media, 2001.

Baker, M. "Downer Backs Jakarta's Aceh Action." *The Age.* June 19, 2003. http://www.theage.com.au/ (accessed June 19, 2003).

Balaam, D. N., and M. Veseth. *Introduction to International Political Economy.* New Jersey: Prentice-Hall, Inc, 1996.

Balassa, B. *The Theory of Economic Integration.* London: George Allen and Unwin Ltd, 1961.

Baldwin, R. E. *A Domino Theory of Regionalism.* National Bureau of Economic Research Working Paper No. 4465. Cambridge, MA: NBER, 1993.

————. *The Political Economy of U.S. Import Policy.* Cambridge, MA: MIT Press, 1985.

Bandoro, B. "SBY's Leadership for Indonesia and the World." *The Jakarta Post.* May 23, 2005. http://www.thejakartapost.com (accessed September 26, 2005).

Banega, C., B. Hettne, and F. Söderbaum. "The New Regionalism in South America." In *Regionalization in a Globalizing World: A Comparative Perspective on Forms, Actors, and Processes,* edited by M. Schulz et al., 234–49. London: Zed Books, 2001.

Bappenas:National Development Planning Agency. *Indonesian Economy in the Year 2003: Prospects and Policies.* Jakarta: Bappenas, 2003.

Barry, D., and R. C. Keith. "Introduction: Changing Perspectives on Regionalism and Multilateralism." In *Regionalism, Multilateralism and the Politics of Global Trade,* edited by D. Barry and R. C. Keith, 3–22. Vancouver: University of British Columbia Press, 1999.

Bastian, J. "Trade Diplomacy and Regional Integration." Paper presented at the World Bank Workshop, London Schools of Economic, London, July 1996.

Baylis, J. "International Security in the Post-Cold War Era." In *The Globalization of World Politics: An Introduction to International Relations,* edited by J. Baylis and S. Smith, 193–211. Oxford: Oxford University Press, 1997.

Bayoumi, T. and B. Eichengreen. "Operationalizing the Theory of Optimum Currency Areas." In *Market Integration, Regionalism and the Global Economy,* edited by R. E. Baldwin *et al.,* 187–227. Cambridge: Cambridge University Press, 1999.

BBC News. "Liberian Foes Clinch Peace Deal." August 19, 2003a. http://news.bbc. co.uk/ (accessed August 19, 2003).

———. "ASEAN Leaders Agree Trade Plan." October 7, 2003b. http://news.bbc.co.uk (accessed October 7, 2003).

———. "ASEAN Reticent Over East Timor." May 21, 2002. http://news.bbc.co.uk/ (accessed May 21, 2002).

———. "Global Migration Reaches Record High." November 2, 2000. http://news.bbc.co.uk/ (accessed November 2, 2000).

———. "IMF to Indonesia's Rescue." June 25, 1998. http://news.bbc.co.uk/ (accessed September 7, 2001).

Bello, W., "ASEAN's Fateful Choice: 'Enlargement' or to 'Deepen'?" *Focus on the Global South.* 1997. http://www.focusweb.org (accessed October 19, 2001).

Bende-Nabende, A. *Globalization, FDI, Regional Integration, and Sustainable Development: Theory, Evidence and Policy.* Hants, UK: Ashgate Publishing Ltd, 2002.

Bereciartu, G. J., *Decline of the Nation-States.* Nevada: University of Nevada Press, 1994.

Bershefsky, C. "America and ASEAN: Shared Vision, Shared Destiny." Keynote address at the U.S. Ambassadors Tour Annual Dinner, Washington, DC, June 15, 2000.

Bhagwati, J. "U.S. Trade Policy: The Infatuation of Free Trade Areas." In *The Dangerous Drift to Preferential Trade Agreements,* edited by J. Bhagwati and A. O. Krueger, 1–18. Washington, DC: AEI Press, 1995a.

———. "Regionalism and Multilateralism: An Overview." In *New Dimensions in Regional Integration,* edited by J. De Melo and A. Panagariya, 22–51. Cambridge: Cambridge University Press, 1995b.

———. *The World Trading System at Risk.* Princeton, NJ: Princeton University Press, 1991.

Bhalla, A. S., and P. Bhalla. *Regional Blocs: Building Blocks or Stumbling Blocks.* New York: St. Martin's Press Inc, 1997.

Billig, M. *Banal Nationalism.* London: Sage Publications, 1995.

Birch, A. H. *Nationalism and National Integration.* London: Unwin Hyman, 1989.

BKPM:Investment Co-ordinating Board. "Press Release 2nd February 2003." 2003. http://www.bkpm.go.id (accessed May 13, 2003).

———. "Foreign Investment Ranked by the Country of Origin: 2001." 2002. http://www.bkpm.go.id/ (accessed 4 March 4, 2003).

———. "The President of the Republic of Indonesia Presidential Decree No. 96/2000 Concerning Business Fields Closed and Open to Investment Under Certain Conditions." 2000a. http://www.bkpm.go.id (accessed January 11, 2001).

———. *Statistics on Investment: Up to July 31, 2000.* Jakarta: State Ministry of Investment and State Owned Enterprises, 2000b.

———. "BKPM." http://www.bkpm.go.id/ (accessed May 25, 2004).

Blanchard, O,, and L. Katz. "Regional Evolutions." *Brooking Papers on Economic Activity* 1 (1992): 1–75.

Board of Investment of Thailand. "Foreign Investment from Major Countries." http://www.boi.go.th/english (accessed January 17, 2003).

Bøås, M. "The Trade-Environment Nexus and the Potential of Regional Trade Institutions." In *New Regionalism in the Global Political Economy*, edited by S. Breslin, 48–65. London: Routledge, 2002.

Bond, E. "Multilateralism versus Regionalism: Tariff Co-operation and Inter-Regional Transport Costs." In *Regionalism and Globalization: Theory and Practice*, edited by S. Lahiri, 16–38. London: Routledge, 2001.

Booth, A. *The Indonesian Economy in the Nineteenth and Twentieth Centuries: A History of Missed Opportunities.* London: Macmillan Press Ltd. and St. Martin Press, Inc, 1998.

———. "Introduction." In *The Oil Boom and After: Indonesian Economic Policy and Performance in the Soeharto Era*, edited by A. Booth, 1–38. New York: Oxford University Press, 1992.

———. "Survey of Recent Developments." *Bulletin of Indonesian Economic Studies* 24, No. 1 (1988): 3–36.

Bowie, A., and D. Unger. *The Politics of Open Economies: Indonesia, Malaysia, the Philippines, and Thailand.* Cambridge: Cambridge University Press, 1997.

Bowles, P. "Regionalism and Development After (?) the Global Financial Crisis." In *New Regionalism in the Global Political Economy*, edited by S. Breslin et al., 81–103. London: Routledge, 2002.

———. "Regionalism and Development after the Global Financial Crisis." *New Political Economy* 5, No. 3 (2000): 433–55.

———. "ASEAN, AFTA, and the 'New Regionalism.'" *Pacific Affairs* 70, No. 2 (1997): 219–33.

Bowles, P., and B. Maclean. "Understanding Trade Bloc Formation: The Case of the ASEAN Free Trade Area." *Review of International Political Economy* 3, No. 2 (1996): 319–48.

Breslin, S., and R. Higgot. "Studying Regionalism: Learning From the Old, Constructing the New." *New Political Economy* 5, No. 3 (2000): 333–52.

Breslin, S., R. Higgot, and B. Rosamond "Regions in Comparative Perspective." In *New Regionalism in the Global Political Economy*, edited by S. Breslin, 1–19. London: Routledge, 2002.

Breuilly, J. *Nationalism and the State.* Chicago: Chicago University Press, 1985.

Brewer, A. *Marxist Theory of Imperialism: A Critical Survey.* London: Routledge, 1990.

Brotodiningrat, S. D. M. "Speech by Ambassador Soemadi D. M. Brotodiningrat at the Asia Society Luncheon, Los Angeles, 13 January 2005." *Embassy of Indonesia in the United States.* 2005. http://www.embassyofIndonesia.org/ (accessed September 26, 2005).

Budiman, A. "Democratization is Possible." *Inside Indonesia* 17 (1988): 2–4.

Bunnel, F. P. "Guided Democracy Foreign Policy 1960–1965." *Indonesia (Cornell Modern Indonesia Project, Ithaca)*, 2 (October 1966): 37–76.

Business ASEAN Newsletter (2003). "ASEAN Business Leaders Urged to Promote a Single Market." 4, No. 2. (June 2003): 1(N).

Business Day. "First U.S., Asia Free Trade Pact Near." November 19, 2002. www.bday.co.za/bday/ (accessed November 19, 2002).

Business Online. "Australia, Indonesia, Sign Trade, Investment Framework." September 29, 2005. http://www.thebusinessonline.com (accessed February 8, 2003).

Business Traveler Asia Pacific. "A Beach for a Backyard." October, 1997, 60–67(N).

Cai, K. G. "Is a Free Trade Zone Emerging in Northeast Asia in the Wake of the Asian Financial Crisis?" *Pacific Affairs* 4, No. 1 (2001): 7–24.

Caporaso, J. "International Relations Theory and Multilateralism: The Search for Foundations." *International Organization* 46, No. 3 (1992): 599–632.

Carr, E. H. *Nationalism and After.* London: Macmillan, 1945.

Caves, R. "Economic Models of Political Choice: Canada's Tariff Structure." *Canadian Journal of Economics* 9, No. 2 (1976): 278–73.

Challis, R. *Shadow of a Revolution: Indonesia and the Generals.* Glouchestershire: Sutton Publishing Ltd, 2001.

Chalmers, I. "Introduction." In *The Politics of Economic Development in Indonesia,* edited by I. Chalmers and V. R. Hadiz, 1–35. London and New York: Routledge, 1997.

Chalmers, I., and V. R. Hadiz. "The Rise of Statist-Nationalism." In *The Politics of Economic Development in Indonesia,* edited by I. Chalmers and V. R. Hadiz, 71–90. London and New York: Routledge, 1997.

Chandra, A. C. "Southeast Asian Civil Society and ASEAN Charter: The Way Forward." Paper presented at the ASEAN Trade Union-NGOs Dialogue on ASEAN Economic Integration: Defining the Stakes for the ASEAN Working People, organized by the Friedrich Ebert Stiftung (FES), Singapore, September 2006.

———. "The Role of Civil Society in the Building of an ASEAN Community." *The Jakarta Post,* 10 August 10, 2005, 6(N).

Chang, T. C., and K. Raguraman. "Singapore Tourism: Capital Ambitions and Regional Connections." In *Interconnected Worlds: Tourism in Southeast Asia,* edited by P. Teo, et al., Pp. 47–63. Oxford: Elsevier Science Ltd., 2001.

Charrier, P. "ASEAN's Inheritance: The Regionalization of Southeast Asia, 1941–61." *The Pacific Review* 14, No. 3 (2001): 313–38.

Chase-Dunn, C. *Global Formation: Structures of the World Economy.* Oxford: Blackwell Publisher, 1989.

Chavez, J. J., and A. C. Chandra. *Dilemmas of Competition and Community-Building: Developing Civil Society Response to Regional Trade and Economic Integration.* Manila: SEACA, 2008.

Chirathivat, S., C. Paschusanond, and P. Wongboonsin. "ASEAN Prospects for Regional Integration and the Implications for the ASEAN Legislative and Institutional Framework." *ASEAN Economic Bulletin* 16, No. 1 (1999): 28–52.

Christie, C. J. *A Modern History of Southeast Asia: Decolonization, Nationalism, and Separatism.* New York: Tauris Academic Studies, 1996.

Chng, M. K. "ASEAN Economic Co-operation: The Current Status." *Southeast Asian Affairs,* (1985): 31–53.

Chung, Sang-Ho. "A Move Towards an East Asian Community and Its Future Outlook." *The Journal of East Asian Affairs* 5, No. 2 (2001): 396–420.

Clinton, B. "Building a New Pacific Community." Paper presented at Waseda University, Tokyo, Japan, July 1993.

Cobban, A. *The Nation State and National Self Determination.* London: Collins, 1969.

Cohen, B. J. "The Political Economy of Currency Regions." In *The Political Economy of*

Regionalism, edited by E. D. Mansfield, et al., 50–76. New York: Columbia University Press, 1997.

Coleman, W. D., and G. R. D. Underhill. "Introduction: Domestic Politics, Regional Economic Co-operation, and Global Economic Integration." In *Regionalism and Global Economic Integration: Europe, Asia, and the Americas*, edited by W. D. Coleman, et al., 1–16. London: Routledge, 1998.

Connor, W. "A Nation is a Nation, is a State, is an Ethnic Group, is a . . . ." *Ethnic and Racial Studies* 1, No. 4 (1978): 379–88.

Cox, R. W. *Approaches to World Order*. Cambridge: Cambridge University Press, 1996.

———. *Production, Power, and World Order: Social forces in the Making of History*. New York: Columbia University Press, 1987.

Cox, R. W., with T. J. Sinclair. *Approaches to World Order*. Cambridge: Cambridge University Press, 1996.

Crane, G. T. "Economic Nationalism: Bringing the Nation Back In." *Millennium: Journal of International Studies* 27, No. 1 (1998): 55–75.

De Melo, J., and A. Panagariya, eds. *New Dimensions in Regional Integration*. Cambridge: Cambridge University Press, 1993.

De Melo, J., A. Panagariya, and D. Rodrik. "The New Regionalism: A Country Perspective." In *New Dimensions in Regional Integration*, edited by J. De Melo and A. Panagariya, 159–92. Cambridge: Cambridge University Press, 1993.

Denoon, D. B. H., and E. Colbert. "Challenges for the Association of Southeast Asian Nations (ASEAN)." *Pacific Affairs* 71, No. 4 (1998): 505–23.

Dent, C. M. *The Foreign Economic Policies of Singapore, South Korea, and Taiwan*. Cheltenham, UK: Edward Elgar Publishing Ltd, 2002a.

———. "Introduction: Northeast Asia—A Region in Search of Regionalism." In *Northeast Asian Regionalism: Learning from the European Experience*, edited by C. M. Dent and D. W. F. Huang, 1–33. London: Routledge Curzon, 2002b.

———. "The International Political Economy of Northeast Asian Economic Integration." In *Northeast Asian Regionalism: Learning from the European Experience*, edited by C. M. Dent and W. F. Huang, 65–95. London: Routledge Curzon, 2002c.

———. "The Eurasian Economic Axis: Its Present and Prospective Significance for East Asia." *The Journal of Asian Studies*, 60, No. 3 (2001a): 731–59.

———. "ASEM and the 'Cinderella Complex' of EU-East Asia Economic Relations." *Pacific Affairs*, 74, No. 1 (2001b): 25–52.

———. *The European Economy: The Global Context*. London: Routledge, 1997.

Depperindag:Ministry of Industry and Trade. *Kesiapan Daerah Dalam Menyongsong Era Perdagangan Bebas ASEAN (Provincial Readiness to Face the ASEAN Free Trade Era)*. Jakarta: Directorate Regional Co-operation and Directorate General of Industrial Co-operation and International Trade, Depperindag, 2000.

Dessler, D. "What's at Stake in the Agent-Structure Debate?" *International Organization* 43, No. 3 (1989): 441–73.

Dicken, P. *Global Shift: The Internationalization of Economic Activity*. London: Paul Chapman Publishing Ltd, 1992.

Djiwandono, J. S. "Role of the IMF in Indonesia's Financial Crisis." In *Governance in Indonesia: Challenges Facing the Megawati Presidency*, edited by H. Soesastro, et al., 196–228. Singapore: ISEAS, 2003.

Djojohadikusumo, S. "The Government's Program on Industries." *Ekonomi dan Keuangan Indonesia* 7, No. 1 (1954): 702–36,

Dobson, W. "Business Network in East Asia: Diversity and Evolution." In *Business,*

Markets and Government in the Asia Pacific, edited by Rong-I Wu and Yun-Peng Chu, 24–47. London: Routledge, 1998.

Dos Santos, T. "The Structure of Dependence." *American Economic Review* 60, No. 2 (1970): 231–36.

Dougherty, J. E., and R. L. Pfaltzgraff Jr. *Contending Theories of International Relations: A Comprehensive Survey*. New York: Harper Collins Publishers, Inc, 1990.

Down to Earth. "IMF Withholds Funds Again." No. 11, December 2000–January 2001. http://dte.gn.apc.org/Au11.htm (accessed March 11, 2002).

Dutta, M. "The Asia-Pacific Community: Some Comments." In *Asia-Pacific Economies: Promises and Challenges*, edited by M. Dutta, 93–100. Greenwich, CT: JAI Press, 1987.

Economist Intelligence Unit. *Country Forecast: Indonesia, May*. London: Economist Intelligence Unit, 2005a.

———. *Country Report: Indonesia, January*. London: Economist Intelligence Unit, 2005b.

———. *Country Profile 2005: Indonesia*, London: Economist Intelligence Unit, 2005c.

——— *Indonesia: Country Report, June 2003*. London: Economist Intelligence Unit, 2003.

Edmonds, C., and J. Verbiest. *The Role of Preferential Trading Arrangements in Asia*. ERD Policy Brief Series, Economic and Research Department, No. 8. Manila: ADB, 2002.

Edwards, M. *NGOs Rights and Responsibilities: A New Deal for Global Governance*. London: The Foreign Policy Centre and NCVO, 2000.

Edwards, S. "Openness, Productivity and Growth: What Do We Really Know?" *Economic Journal* 108, No. 447 (1998): 383–98.

El-Agraa, Ali M. *Economic Integration Worldwide*, London: Macmillan, 1997.

———. *The Economics of the European Community*. Hertfordshire, UK: Harvester Wheatsheaf, 1994.

———, ed. *International Economic Integration*. London: Macmillan Ltd, 1988.

Eldridge, P. J. *Non-Government Organizations and Democratic Participation in Indonesia*. Oxford: Oxford University Press, 1995.

Ethier, W. J. "Regional Regionalism." In *Regionalism and Globalization*, edited by S. Lahiri, 3–15. London: Routledge, 2001.

European Commission. *Unity, Solidarity, Diversity for Europe, Its People and Its Territory*. 2001. http://europa.eu.int/ (accessed May 28, 2002).

European Union On-Line. "Enlargement: Basic Arguments." http://europa.eu.int/ (accessed March 7, 2003).

———. "The EU's Relations with Cambodia." http://europa.eu.int/ (accessed March 5, 2003).

———. "The EU's Relations with East Timor." http://europa.eu.int/ (accessed 5 March 5, 2003).

———. "The History of the European Union." http://europa.eu.int/ (accessed September 13, 2002).

Evans, P. B., H. K. Jacobson, and R. D. Putnam, eds. *Double-Edged Diplomacy: International Bargaining and Domestic Politics*. Los Angeles and London: University of California Press, 1993.

Falk, R. *Predatory Globalization: A Critique*. Cambridge: Polity Press, 1999.

Farrands, C. "Society, Modernity, and Social Change: Approaches to Nationalism and Identity." In *Identities in International Relations*, edited by J. Krause and N. Renwick, 1–21. London: Macmillan Press Ltd, 1996.

Fawcett, L., and A. Hurrell. *Regionalism in World Politics: Regional Organization and International Order*. New York: Oxford University Press, 1995.

Feridhanusetyawan, T. "Escaping the Debt Trap." In *Governance in Indonesia: Challenges Facing the Megawati Presidency*, edited by H. Soesastro, et al., 229–68. Singapore: ISEAS, 2003.

Fifield, R. H. *National and Regional Interests in ASEAN: Competition and Co-operation in International Politics*. Occasional Paper No. 57. Singapore: ISEAS, 1979.

Filho, L. C. *New Regionalism and Latin America: The Case of Mercosul*. London: Institute of Latin American Studies, University of London, 1999.

Finch, M. H. J. "The Latin American Free Trade Association." In *International Economic Integration*, edited by A. M. El-Agraa, 237–56. London: Macmillan Ltd., 1988.

Fore, K. "Beyond AFTA Where Does Northeast Asia Fits In?" *International Herald Tribune*, January 31, 2002. http://www.iht.com/ (accessed 31 January 2002).

Frankel, J. A. *National Interest*. London: Pall Mall Press Ltd, 1970.

Frankel, J. A., and D. Romer. "Does Trade Cause Growth?" *American Economic Review* 89, No. 3 (1999): 379–99.

Freeman, M. "ASEAN Investment Area: Progress and Challenges." In *ASEAN beyond the Regional Crisis: Challenges and Initiatives*, edited by M. Than, 80–125. Singapore: ISEAS, 2001.

Free Trade Area of the Americas. "Overview of the FTAA Process." http://www.ftaa-alca.org/View_e.asp (accessed February 4, 2003).

Freund, C. "Different Paths to Free Trade: The Gains from Regionalism." *Quarterly Journal of Economics* 115, No. 4 (2000): 1317–41.

Fukuyama, F. "The End of History?" *The National Interest*, 16 (Summer 1989): 3–18.

Fund for Peace. "Perspectives from Asia on Military Intervention." Washington, DC: The Fund for Peace, 2002.

Galtung, J. "A Structural Theory of Imperialism." *Journal of Peace Research* 8, No. 1 (1971): 81–117.

Gamble, A., and A. Payne. *Regionalism and World Order*. London: Macmillan Press Ltd, 1996.

Geertz, C. *Old Societies and New States: The Quest for Modernity in Asia and Africa*. New York: Free Press, 1963.

Gellner, E. *Thought and Change*. Oxford: Weidenfeld and Nicolson, 1964.

Genberg, H., and F. N. De Simone "Regional Integration Arrangements and Macroeconomic Discipline." In *Regional Integration and the Global Trading System*, edited by K. Anderson and R. Blackhurst, 167–95. Hertfordshire: Harvester Wheatsheaf, 1993.

General Agreement on Tariffs and Trade. "The Text of the General Agreement on Tariffs and Trade." Geneva: GATT, 1947. http://www.wto.org (accessed August 8, 2001).

Gershman, J. "Fighting Terrorism, Undermining Democracy in Indonesia." *Foreign Policy in Focus*, September, 2001. http://www/fpif/org (accessed December 30, 2001).

Ghosh, B. N. *Dependency Theory Revisited*. Aldershot, UK: Ashgate, 2001.

Giddens, A. *Central Problems in Social and Political Theory*. Berkeley: University of California Press, 1979.

Gill, S. "Knowledge, Politics, and Neo-Liberal Political Economy." In *Political Economy and the Changing Global Order*, edited by R. Stubbs and G. R. D. Underhill, 48–59. Ontario: Oxford University Press, 2000.

Gilpin, R. *Global Political Economy: Understanding the International Economic Order*. Princeton, NJ: Princeton University Press, 2001.

————. *The Political Economy of International Relations*. Princeton, NJ: Princeton University Press, 1987.

————. *U.S. Power and the Multinational Corporations*. New York: Basic Books, 1975.

Glassburner, B. "The Economy and Economic Policy: General and Historical." In *The Economy of Indonesia: Selected Readings*, edited by B. Glassburner, 1–15. Ithaca and London: Cornell University Press, 1971.

Global Justice Update. "ASEAN Sepakat untuk Percepat Integrasi Ekonomi Hingga Lima Tahun (ASEAN Agrees to Accelerate Economic Integration until Five Years)." *Global Justice Update* 4, No. 69–70: 1–31 [August, 2006].

Goff, P. M. "Invisible Borders: Economic Liberalization and National Identity." *International Studies Quarterly* 44, No. 4 (2000): 533–62.

Gordenker, L., and T. G. Weiss. "Pluralizing Global Governance: Analytical Approaches and Dimensions." In *NGOs, the UN, and Global Governance*, edited by T. G. Weiss and L. Gordenker, 17–47. London: Lynne Riener Publishers, 1996.

Gordon, B. K. *Towards Disengagement in Asia*. Englewood Cliffs, NJ: Prentice-Hall, 1969.

————. *The Dimensions of Conflict in Southeast Asia*. Englewood Cliffs, NJ: Prentice-Hall, Spectrum Books, 1966.

Gowa, J. *Allies, Adversaries, and International Trade*. Princeton, NJ: Princeton University Press, 1994.

Gray, M. "Foreign Direct Investment and Recovery in Indonesia: Recent Events and their Impacts." *Institute of Public Affairs* 14, No. 2 (2002). http://www.kaltimprimacoal.co.id/ (accessed February 11, 2003).

Greenfield, L. *Nationalism: Five Roads to Modernity*. Cambridge, MA: Harvard University Press, 1992.

Grether, J., and M. Olarreaga. *Preferential and Non-Preferential Trade Flows in World Trade*. Staff Working Paper ERAD-98–10, Economic Research and Analysis Division. Geneva: WTO, 1998.

Grieco, J. M. "Anarchy and the Limits of Co-operation: A Realist Critique of Newest Liberal Institutionalism." *International Organization*, 42, No. 3 (1988): 485–507.

Gross, A. *Human Resources Issues in Southeast Asia*. Washington, DC: Pacific Bridge Inc., 2001.

Grossman, G. M., and E. Helpman. *Interest Groups and Trade Policy*. Princeton, NJ: Princeton University Press, 2002.

————. "Protection for Sale." *American Economic Review*, 84, No. 4 (1994): 833–51.

Grugel, T., and W. Hout. *Regionalism across the North-South Divide: State Strategies and Globalization*. London: Routledge, 1999.

Grundy-Warr, C., and M. Perry. "Tourism in an Inter-State Borderland: The Case of the Indonesian-Singapore Co-operation." In *Interconnected Worlds: Tourism in Southeast Asia*, edited by P. Teo, et al., 64–83. Oxford: Elsevier Science Ltd., 2001.

Guerin, B. (2003), "Indonesia Unwilling Player in Global FTA Game." *Asia Times Online*. January 11, 2003. http://www.atimes.com/ (accessed January 11, 2003).

Guerreri, P., and P. C. Padoan. *The Political Economy of European Integration: States, Markets and Institutions*. New York: Harvester Wheatsheaf, 1989.

Gundlach, E. *Openness and Economic Growth in Developing Countries*. Kiel Institute World Economics Working Paper No. 749. Kiel, Germany: Kiel Institute, 1996.

Haarløv, J. *Regional Cooperation in Southern Africa: Central Elements of the SADCC Venture*. CDR Research Report No. 14. Copenhagen: Centre for Development Research, 1988.

Haas, E. "The Study of Regional Integration: Reflection on the Joy and Anguish of Pre-theorizing." *International Organization* 24 (1970): 607–646.

———. *Beyond the Nation-State*. Stanford, CA: Stanford University Press, 1964.

———. *The Uniting of Europe*. Stanford, CA: Stanford University Press, 1958.

Haggard, S. "The Political Economy of Regionalism in Asia and the Americas." In *The Political Economy of Regionalism*, edited by E.D. Mansfield and H.V. Milner, 20–49. New York: Columbia University Press, 1997.

———. *Developing Nations and the Politics of Global Integration*. Washington, DC: The Brooking Institutions, 1995.

Hall, C. M. "Tourism and Political Relationship in Southeast Asia." In *Interconnected Worlds: Tourism in Southeast Asia*, edited by P. Teo et al., 13–26. Oxford: Elsevier Science Ltd., 2001.

Hall, C. M., and S. Page. "Introduction: Tourism in South and Southeast Asia—Region and Context." In *Tourism in South and Southeast Asia*, edited by C. M. Hall and S. Page, 3–28. Oxford and Woburn, MA: Butterworth-Heinemann, 2000.

Hallet, A. H., and C. P. Braga. *The New Regionalism and the Threat of Protectionism*. Policy Research Working Paper No. 1349. Washington, DC: The World Bank, 1994.

Halliday, F. "Nationalism." In *The Globalization of World Politics: An Introduction to International Relations*, edited by J. Baylis and S. Smith, 359–73. Oxford: Oxford University Press, 1997.

———. *Rethinking International Relations*. London: Macmillan Press Ltd, 1994.

Harvie, C., and H. Lee. "New Regionalism in East Asia: How Does it Relate to the East Asian Economic Development Model?" *ASEAN Economic Bulletin* 19, No. 2 (2002): 123–40.

Hatsuse, R. "Regionalism in East Asia and the Asia-Pacific." In *Globalism, Regionalism, and Nationalism: Asia in Search of its Role in the 21st Century*, edited by Y. Yamamoto, 105–25. Oxford: Blackwell, 1999.

Hawley, J. P. "Interests, State Foreign Economic Policy, and the World System: The Case of the U.S. Capital Control Programs, 1961–1974." *Sage International Yearbook of Foreign Policy Studies* 8 (1983): 223–54.

Hechter, M. *Containing Nationalism*. Oxford and New York: Oxford University Press, 2000.

Hechter, M., and M. Levy. "The Comparative Analysis of Ethnoregional Movements." *Ethnic and Racial Studies* 2, No. 3 (1979): 262–74.

Heilperin, M. *Studies in Economic Nationalism*. Geneva: Publications de L'Institute Universitaire de Hautes Etudes Internationales, No. 35, 1960.

Heinrich, J., and D. E. Konan. "Prospects for FDI in AFTA." *ASEAN Economic Bulletin* 18, No. 2 (2001): 141–159.

Helleiner, E. H. "Economic Nationalism as a Challenge to Economic Liberalism? A Lessons from the 19th Century." *International Studies Quarterly* 46, No. 3 (2002): 307–29.

Helleiner, G. K. "Protectionism and the Developing Countries." In *Protectionism and World Welfare*, edited by D. Salvatore, 396–418. Cambridge: Cambridge University Press, 1993.

Henderson, C. *Asia Falling: Making Sense of the Asian Crisis and its Aftermath*. New York: Business Week Books and McGraw-Hill Co, 1998.

Henwood, D. "Does Globalization Matter?" *In These Times*, March 31, 1997, 14–6.

Hernandez, C. G. "Introduction and Summary: ASEAN People's Assembly 2003." In *Towards an ASEAN Community of Caring Societies*, edited by ASEAN Institute of

Strategic and International Studies (ASEAN-ISIS) and Institute for Strategic and Development Studies (ISDS), 1–9. Manila: ISDS, 2003.

Hettne, B. "Regionalism, Security and Development: A Comparative Perspective." In *Comparing Regionalism: Implications for Global Development*, edited by B. Hettne et al., 1–53. Basingstoke, Hampshire, UK and New York: Palgrave, 2001.

———. "Globalization and the New Regionalism: The Second Great Transformation." In *Globalism and the New Regionalism*, edited by B. Hettne et al., 1–24. London: Macmillan Press Ltd, 1999.

———, ed. *International Political Economy: Understanding Global Disorder*. London: Zed Books, 1995.

———. *The New Regionalism: Implications for Global Development and International Security*. Helsinki: United Nations University/World Institute for Development Economic Research (UNU /WIDER), 1994.

Hettne, B., A. Inotai, and O. Sunkel, eds. *Comparing Regionalisms: Implications for Global Development*. Basingstoke, Hampshire, UK and New York: Palgrave, 2001.

———, eds. *National Perspectives on the New Regionalism in the North*. London: Macmillan Press Ltd, 2000a.

———, eds. *National Perspectives on the New Regionalism in the South*. London: Macmillan Press Ltd, 2000b.

———, eds. *The New Regionalism and the Future of Security and Development*. London: Macmillan Press Ltd, 2000c.

———, eds. *Globalism and the New Regionalism*. London: Macmillan Press Ltd, 1999.

Hettne, B., and F. Söderbaum. "Theorizing the Rise of Regionness." *New Political Economy* 5, No. 3 (2000): 457–73.

Hew, Denis. *Towards an ASEAN Economic Community by 2020: Vision or Reality? Viewpoint*. Singapore: Institute of Southeast Asian Studies (ISEAS), 2003.

Hewitt, T., H. Johnson, and D. Wield, eds. *Industrialization and Development*. Oxford and Milton Keynes, UK: Oxford University Press and the Open University, 1997.

Heywood, A. *Key Concepts in Politics*. Hampshire, UK: Palgrave, 2000.

Higgot, R. "Regionalism in the Asia-Pacific: Two Steps Forward, One Step Back." In *Political Economy and the Changing Global Order*, edited by R. Stubbs and G. R. D. Underhill, 254–63. Ontario: Oxford University Press, 2000.

———. "ASEM: Toward the Institutionalization of the East Asia-Europe Relationship." In *Regionalism, Multilateralism, and the Politics of Global Trade*, edited by D. Barry and R. C. Keith, 194–210. Vancouver: University of British Columbia Press, 1999.

Hill, H. *The Indonesian Economy*. Cambridge: Cambridge University Press, 2000.

———, ed. *Indonesia's New Order: The Dynamics of Socio-Economic Transformation*. Honolulu: The University of Hawaii Press, 1994.

———. "Manufacturing Industry." In *The Oil Boom and After: Indonesian Economic Policy and Performance in the Soeharto Era*, edited by A. Booth, 204–57. New York: Oxford University Press, 1990.

Hirst, P., and G. Thompson. *Globalization in Question*. Oxford: Blackwell, 1996.

Hitiris, T. *European Community Economics*. Hertfordshire, UK: Harvester Wheatsheaf, 1991.

Hobbes, T. *Leviathan*, edited by C. B. Macpherson. London: Penguin Books, 1968.

Hobden, S., and R. W. Jones. "World System Theory." In *The Globalization of World Politics: An Introduction to International Relations*, edited by J. Baylis and S. Smith, 125–46. Oxford: Oxford University Press, 1999.

Hobsbawn, E. J. *Nations and Nationalism Since 1780: Program, Myth, Reality.* Cambridge: Cambridge University Press, 1990.

————. "Introduction: Inventing Traditions." In *The Invention of Traditions,* edited by E. J. Hobsbawn and T. Ranger, 1–14. Cambridge: Cambridge University Press, 1983.

Hobson, J. *Imperialism: A Study.* Ann Arbor: University of Michigan Press, 1965.

Hocking, B., and M. Smith. *Beyond Foreign Economic Policy: the United States, the Single European Market and the Changing World Order.* London: Pinter Publication, 1997.

Hoekman, B., and M. Leidy. "Holes and Loopholes in Integration Agreements: History and Prospects." In *Regional Integration and the Global Trading System,* edited by K. Anderson and R. Blackhurst, 218–45. New York, NY and London: Harvester Wheatsheaf, 1993.

Hoffmann, S. "Obstinate or Obsolete? The Fate of the Nation-State and the Case of Western Europe." *Daedalus* 95 (Summer 1966): 862–915.

Hoogvelt, A. *Globalization and the Postcolonial World: The New Political Economy of Development.* London: Macmillan, 1997.

Horrowitz, D. *Ethnic Groups in Conflict.* Berkeley: University of California Press, 1985.

Horsman, M., and A. Marshall. *After the Nation-State: Citizens, Tribalism and the New World Disorder.* London: Harper Collins Publishers, 1995.

Howard, M. *The Lessons of History.* Oxford: Oxford University Press, 1991.

Hroch, M. "From National Movement to the Fully Formed Nation: The Nation-building Process in Europe." In *Mapping the Nation,* edited by G. Balakrishnan, 78–97. New York and London: Verso, 1996.

Hurrell, A. "Regionalism in Theoretical Perspectives." In *Regionalism in World Politics: Regional Organization and International Order,* edited by L. Fawcett and A. Hurrell, 37–73. Oxford: Oxford University Press, 1995.

Hutchinson, J., and A. D. Smith. *Nationalism.* Oxford and New York: Oxford University Press, 1994.

Hveem, H. "Explaining the Regional Phenomenon in an Era of Globalization." In *Political Economy and the Changing Global Order,* edited by R. Stubbs and G. R. D. Underhill, 70–81. Ontario: Oxford University Press, 2000.

————. "Political Regionalism: Master or Servant of Economic Internationalization?" In *Globalism and the New Regionalism,* edited by B. Hettne et al., 85–115. London: Macmillan Press Ltd, 1999.

Ikenberry, G. J., D. A. Lake, and M. Mastanduno, eds. "Introduction: Approaches to Explaining American Foreign Economic Policy." In *The State and American Foreign Economic Policy,* edited by G. J. Ikenberry et al., 1–14. Cambridge, MA: Cornell University Press, 1988.

Imada, P., M. Montes, and S. Naya. *A Free Trade Area: Implications for ASEAN.* Singapore: ISEAS, 1991.

Indonesian Ministry of Foreign Affairs. "Indonesia's Foreign Policy." June 17, 2003. http://www.deplu.go.id/ (accessed December 13, 2003).

International Monetary Fund. "IMF Completes Eighth Review of Indonesia Program, Approves US$469 Million Disbursement." *IMF News Brief,* March 28, 2003. http://www.imf.org/ (Accessed August 30, 2003).

————. *Direction of Trade Statistics Yearbook.* Washington, DC: IMF, Real Sector Division, Statistic Department, 2002.

————. "Letters of Intent: Memorandum of Economic and Financial Policies: Medium Term Strategy and Policies for 1999/2000 and 2000." *IMF.* 2000. http://www.imf.org/ (accessed April 23, 2002).

Interprovincial Trade in Canada. *Interprovincial Trade in Canada 1988–1996*. Ottawa: The Division, 1998.

Isaak, R. A. *International Political Economy: Managing World Economic Change*. New Jersey: Prentice Hall, Inc, 1991.

Islamic Republic News Agency. "ASEAN Must Help Bring Peace to Aceh," 28 May 28, 2003. http://www.irna.com/en/ (accessed May 28, 2003).

Jakarta Post. "Susilo in Control, but Tougher Challenges Ahead." 20 October 2005, 1.

———. "Bali Concord II Sets as ASEAN New Course," October 8, 2003. http://www.thejakartapost.com/ (accessed October 8, 2003).

Jalata, A. "Ethno-nationalism and the Global 'Modernizing' Project." *Nations and Nationalism* 7, No. 3 (2001): 385–405.

Jelin, Elizabeth. *Dialogues, Understanding and Misunderstanding: Social Movements in MERCOSUR*. Oxford: Blackwell Publishers, 1999.

Johnson, G., and K. Scholes. *Exploring Corporate Strategy: Text and Cases*. Harlow, UK: Pearson Education Limited, 2002.

Johnson, H. G. *Economic Nationalism in Old and New States*. Chicago: University of Chicago Press, 1967.

Jovanovich, M. N. *International Economic Integration: Limits and Prospects*. London: Routledge, 1998.

———. *International Economic Integration*, London: Routledge, 1992.

Kartadjoemena, H. S. *The Politics of External Economic Relations: Indonesia's Options*. Singapore: ISEAS, 1977.

———. "Regional Cooperation in Southeast Asia: An Indonesian View." In *Performance and Perspectives of the Indonesian Economy*, edited by M. A. Anwar, 199–250. Tokyo: Institute of Developing Economies, 1976.

Katsumata, H. "Reconstruction of Diplomatic Norms in Southeast Asia: The Case for Strict Adherence to the 'ASEAN Way.'" *Contemporary Southeast Asia* 25, No. 1 (2003): 104–21.

Katzenstein, P. J. "Regionalism and Asia." *New Political Economy* 5, No. 3 (2000): 353–68.

———. *The Culture of National Security: Norms and identity in World Politics*. New York: Columbia University Press, 1996.

———. "Introduction: Domestic and International Forces and Strategies of Foreign Economic Policy." In *Between Power and Plenty: Foreign Economic Policies of Advanced Industrial States*, edited by P. J. Katzenstein, 3–22. Wisconsin: Wisconsin University Press, 1978a.

———. "Conclusion: Domestic Structures and Strategies of Foreign Economic Policy." In *Between Power and Plenty: Foreign Economic Policies of Advanced Industrial States*, edited by P. J. Katzenstein, 295–336. Wisconsin: Wisconsin University Press, 1978b.

———. "International Relations and Domestic Structures: Foreign Economic Policies of Advanced Industrial States." *International Organization* 30, No. 1 (1976): 1–45.

Keating, M., and J. Loughlin. *The Political Economy of Regionalism*. London: Frank Cass & Co., Ltd, 1997.

Kedourie, E. *Nationalism*. London: Praeger, 1960.

Kegley, C. W. "The Neoidealist Moment in International Studies? Realist Myths and the New International Realities." *International Studies Quarterly*, 37, No. 2 (1993): 131–46.

Kemp, M. C., and H. Wan. "An Elementary Proposition Concerning the Formation of Custom Unions." *Journal of International Economics* 6 (1976): 95–7.

Kenen, P. "The Theory of Optimum Currency Areas: An Eclectic View." In *Monetary Problems of the International Economy*, edited by A. Swoboda and R. Mundell, 41–60. Chicago: University of Chicago Press, 1969.

Keohane, R. O. *After Hegemony: Co-operation and Discord in the World Political Economy*. Princeton, NJ: Princeton University Press, 1984,

Keohane, R. O. and J. S. Nye. *Power and Interdependence*. Boston: Little Brown, 1977.

Kindleberger, C. *The World in Depression: 1929–1939*. Berkeley, CA: University of California Press, 1973.

Koffman, J. "How to Define Economic Nationalism? A Critical Review of Some Old and New Standpoints." In *Economic Nationalism in East-Central Europe and South America*, edited by H. Szlajfer, 17–54. Geneva: Librairie Droz, 1990.

Kohen, B. J. "The Political Economy of Currency Regions." In *The Political Economy of Regionalism*, edited by E. D. Mansfield and H. V. Milner, 50–76. New York: Columbia University Press, 1997.

Kohn, H. *The Idea of Nationalism: The Study of Its Origins and Backgrounds*, New York, NY: Macmillan Company, 1944.

Koht, H. "The Dawn of Nationalism in Europe." *The American Historical Review* 52, No. 2 (1947): 265–80.

Kompas. "Merombak KADIN, Menyelamatkan Sektor Riil (Changing KADIN, Saving the Real Sector)." February 21, 2004, 40(N).

———. "KADIN Minta AFTA Ditunda Hingga Tahun 2005 (KADIN Asks AFTA to be Postponed until 2005)." February, 2001a.

———. "KADIN Bentuk Tim Pemantau Otonomi Daerah (KADIN Forms a Provincial Autonomy Monitoring Team)." February 5, 2001b. http://www.kompas.com (accessed February 6, 2001).

———. "1.006 PERDA Beratkan Dunia Usaha (1,006 Provincial Regulations are Burdensome to Businesses)." 6 September, 2001c. http://www.kompas.com/ (accessed September 6, 2001).

———. "46 Persen Produk Industri Siap Bersaing di AFTA (46 Percent of Industrial Product are Ready to Compete in AFTA)." 22 August, 2001d, 13(N).

Kooistra, M. *Indonesia: Regional Conflicts and State Terrors*. London: Minority Rights Group International, 2001.

Korean Times. "Sunshine Policy at a Glance." May 23, 2003. http://www.korea.net/ (Accessed December 9, 2003).

Krasner, S. D. *International Regimes*. Ithaca, NY: Cornell University Press, 1983.

———. *Defending the National Interest: Raw Materials Investments and U.S. Foreign Policy*. Princeton: Princeton University Press, 1979.

Krueger, A. O. "Rules of Origin as Protectionist Devices." NBER Working Paper No. 4352. Washington, DC: NBER, 1993.

Krugman, P. *What Do We Need to Know About the International Monetary System*. Princeton, NJ: InternationalFinance Section, Essays in International Finance No. 190, 1993.

Lähteenmäki, K., and J. Käkönen "Regionalization and its Impact on the Theory of International Relations." In *Globalism and the New Regionalism*, edited by B. Hettne, 203–27. London: Macmillan Press Ltd, 1999.

Langhamer, R., and V. Hiemenz. *Regional Integration among Developing Countries*. UNDP-World Bank Trade Expansion Program, Occasional Paper No. 7. Washington, DC: World Bank, 1991.

Langit, R. "Indonesia's Military: Business As Usual." *Asia Times Online*, August 16, 2002. http://www.atimes.com/ (accessed August 16, 2002).

Lapid, Y., and F. Kratochwil. "Revisiting the 'National': Toward an Identity Agenda in Neorealism." In *The Return of Culture and Identity in IR Theory*, edited by Y. Lapid and F. Kratochwil, 105–28. London: Lynne Rienner Publishers, Inc, 1996.

Laux, J. K. "The Return to Europe: The Future Political Economy of Eastern Europe." In *Political Economy and the Changing Global Order*, edited by R. Stubbs and G. R. D. Underhill, 264–73. Oxford: Oxford University Press, 2000.

Lawrence, R. *Regionalism, Multilateralism, and Deeper Integration*. Washington, DC: Brooking Institution, 1995.

Lay, C. *Nasionalisme Etnisitas: Pertaruhan Sebuah Wacana Kebangsaan (Ethnicity Nationalism: Gambling on the Nationality Discourse)*. Jakarta: Institut Dian/Interfidei, 2001.

Legge, J. D. *Sukarno: A Political Biography*. London: Penguin, 1975.

Leifer, M. "The Changing Temper of Indonesian Nationalism." In *Asian Nationalism*, edited by M. Leifer, 153–69. London: Routledge, 2000.

———. *Indonesia's Foreign Policy*. London: George Allen and Unwin, 1983.

Lenin, V. I. *Imperialism, the Highest Stage of Capitalism: A Popular Outline*. Moscow: Progress Publishers, 1966.

———. *Critical Remarks on the National Question*. Moscow: Foreign Language Publishing House, 1951.

Leong, S. "The East Asian Economic Caucus (EAEC): 'Formalized' Regionalism Being Denied." In *National Perspectives on the New Regionalism in the South*, edited by B. Hettne et al., 57–107. London: Macmillan Press Ltd, 2000.

Levy-Faur, D. "Economic Nationalism: From Friedrich List to Robert Reich." *Review of International Studies* 23, No. 3 (1997a): 359–70.

———. "Friedrich List and the Political Economy of the Nation-State." *Review of International Political Economy* 4, No. 1 (1997b): 154–78.

Lim, Chong Yah. *Southeast Asia: The Long Road Ahead*. Singapore: World Scientific Publishing Co. Pte. Ltd, 2001.

Lim, L. H. "A Triangle Love Affair? Tourism in the Indonesia-Malaysia-Singapore Growth Triangle." Unpublished Honor Thesis, Department of Geography, National University of Singapore, 1999.

Linblad, J. T. "The Importance of Indonesianisasi During the Transition from the 1930s to the 1960s." Paper presented at the conference on Economic Growth and Institutional Change in Indonesia in the 19th and 20th Centuries, Amsterdam, February 25, 2002.

Linnan, D. K. *Indonesian Bankruptcy Policy and Reform: Reconciling Efficiency and Economic Nationalism*. Singapore: ISEAS, 1999.

Lipsey, R. G. "The Theory of Customs Unions: A General Survey." *Economic Journal* 70, No. 279 (September 1960): 496–513.

Lipsey, R. G., and K. A. Chrystal. *Principles of Economics*. Oxford: Oxford University Press, 1999.

List, F. *The National System of Political Economy*. London: Longmans, Green, 1904.

Lloyd, P. J. *New Regionalism and New Bilateralism in the Asia-Pacific*. Singapore: ISEAS, 2002.

Loveard, K. "Trouble is Brewing in Aceh: The Army Mobilizes for Yet More Ethnic Unrest." *Asiaweek*, April 11, 1997. http://www.asiaweek.com (accessed June 2, 2002).

Luard, T. "ASEAN: Changing, but Only Slowly." *BBC News*, October 8, 2003. http://news.bbc.co.uk/ (accessed October 8, 2003).

Lukas, A. "EC-ASEAN in the Context of Inter-regional Co-operation." In *Western*

Europe and Southeast Asia: Co-operation or Competition, edited by G. Schiavone, 104–16. London: Macmillan, 1989.

Machlup, F. *A History of Thought on Economic Integration*. London: Macmillan Ltd, 1977.

Mackie, J. A. C. "The Indonesian Economy, 1950–1963." In *The Economy of Indonesia: Selected Readings*, edited by B. Glassburner, 16–69. Ithaca, NY, and London: Cornell University Press, 1971.

Madjiah, L. E. "East Timor: To Be or Not To Be A Member of ASEAN?" *The Jakarta Post*, June 24, 2003. http://www.thejakartapost.com/ (accessed June 24, 2003).

Magee, S. P., W. A. Brock, and L. Young. *Black Hole Tariffs and Endogenous Policy Theory: Political Economy in General Equilibrium*. New York: Cambridge University Press, 1989.

Makito, Noda. "The Role of Nonstate Actors in Building an ASEAN Community." In *Road to ASEAN-10: Japanese Perspectives on Economic Integration*, edited by S. Sueo, and N. Makito, 167–94. Tokyo: Japan Centre for International Exchange, 1999.

Maneerungsee, W. "South Korea Plans FTA with ASEAN: Study on Free Trade Area Under Way." *Bangkok Post*, September 15, 2002. http://search.bangkokpost.co.th/ (accessed September 15, 2002).

Manning, C. "Indonesia's New Cabinet." *APEC Economies Newsletter* 5, No. 9 (September 2001): 1–2.

Mansfield, E. D. "Effects of International Politics on Regionalism in International Trade." In *Regional Integration and the Global Trading System*, edited by K. Anderson and R. Blackhurst, 199–217. London: Harvester Wheatsheaf, 1993.

Mansfield, E., and R. Bronson. "The Political Economy of Major-Power Trade Flows." In *The Political Economy of Regionalism*, edited by E. Mansfield and H. Milner, 188–208. New York: Columbia University Press, 1997.

Mansfield, E. D., and H. V. Milner. "The Political Economy of Regionalism: An Overview." In *The Political Economy of Regionalism*, edited by E. D. Mansfield and H. V. Milner, 1–19. New York: Columbia University Press, 1997.

Marer, P., and M. Montias. "The Council for Mutual Economic Assistance." In *International Economic Integration*, edited by A. M. El-Agraa, 128–65. London: MacmillanPress Ltd, 1988.

Martin, P. "When Nationalism Meets Continentalism: The Politics of Free Trade in Quebec." In *The Political Economy of Regionalism*, edited by M. Keating and J. Loughlin, 236–61. London: Frank Cass & Co., Ltd., 1997.

Marx, K., and F. Engels. *The Communist Manifesto*. New York: Appleton-Century-Crofts, 1955.

Marxist-Leninist Daily. "The End of the Auto Pact." January issue, 2001. http://www.cpcml.ca/ (accessed March 29, 2001).

Mattli, W. *The Logic of Regional Integration: Europe and Beyond*. Cambridge: Cambridge University Press, 1999.

Mayall, J. *Nationalism and International Society*. Cambridge: Cambridge University Press, 1990.

McGrew, A. G., and P. Lewis *Global Politics: Globalization and the Nation-State*. Cambridge: Polity Press, 1992.

McKinnon, R. "Optimum Currency Area." *American Economic Review* 53, No. 4 (1963): 717–25.

Meadwell, H. "The Politics of Nationalism in Quebec." *World politics* 45, No. 1 (1993): 203–41.

Meadwell, H., and P. Martin. "Economic Integration and the Politics of Independence." *Nations and Nationalism* 2, No. 1 (1996): 67–87.

Means, G. P. "ASEAN Policy Responses to North American and European Trading Arrangements." In *New Challenges for ASEAN: Emerging Policy Issues*, edited by A. Acharya and R. Stubbs, Pp. 146–81. Vancouver: University of British Columbia Press, 1995.

Meier, G. M. *Leading Issues in Economic Development*. Oxford: Oxford University Press, 1984.

Mill, J. S. "Consideration on Representative Government." In *The Dynamics of Nationalism*, edited by L. L. Snyder, Pp. 120–1 (1872). London: D. Van Nostrand Company, Ltd, 1964.

Miller, L. H. *Global Order: Values and Power in International Politics*. Boulder, CO: Westview Press, 1998.

Milner, H. V. "Industries, Governments, and the Creation of Regional Trade Blocs." In *The Political Economy of Regionalism*, edited by E. D. Mansfield and H. V. Milner, 77–106. New York: Columbia University Press, 1997.

Ministry of Co-operative, Small and Medium Enterprises. "Statistik Usaha Kecil Menengah (UKM) (Statistic of SMEs)." 2001. http://www.depkop.go.id/ (accessed 7 January 7, 2002).

Mitrany, David. *A Working Peace*. Chicago: Quadrangle Books, 1966.

Mittelman, J. H. "Rethinking the "New Regionalism" in the Context of Globalization." In *Globalism and the New Regionalism*, edited by Hettne et al., 25–53. London: Macmillan Press Ltd, 1999.

———. "Rethinking the "New Regionalism" in the Context of Globalization." *Global Governance* 2, No. 2 (1996a): 189–213.

———, ed. *Globalization: Critical Reflections*. Boulder, CO: Lynne Rienner, 1996b.

Mizuno, K. "Indonesian Politics and the Issue of Justice in East Timor." In *Governance in Indonesia: Challenges Facing the Megawati Presidency*, edited by H. Soesastro et al., 114–64. Singapore: ISEAS, 2003.

Mols, M. "Co-operation with ASEAN: A Success Story." In *Europe's Global Links: The European Community and Inter-Regional Cooperation*, edited by G. Edwards and E. Regelsberger, 66–83. London: Pinter Publishers, 1990.

Monzano, G. "Is There any Value Added in the ASEAN Surveillance Process?" *ASEAN Economic Bulletin* 18, No. 1 (2001): 94–100.

Moravcsik, A. "Reassessing Legitimacy in the European Union." *Journal of Common Market Studies* 40, No. 4 (2002): 603–24.

———. *The Choice for Europe: Social Purpose and State Power from Messina and Maastricht*. Ithaca, NY: Cornell University Press, 1998.

———. "Preferences and Power in the European Community: A Liberal Intergovernmental Approach." *Journal of Common Market Studies* 31, No. 4 (1993): 473–524.

———. "Negotiating the Single European Act: National Interest and Conventional Statecraft in the European Community." *International Organization*, 45 (1991): 19–56.

Morgenthau, H. J. *Politics among Nations*. New York: Knopf, 1978.

———. "Another 'Great Debate': The National Interest of the United States." *American Political Science Review* 46, No. 4 (1952): 961–88.

Muhaimin, Y. A. *Bisnis dan Politik: Kebijaksanaan Ekonomi Indonesia 1950–1980 (Business and Politic: The Economic Policy of Indonesia 1950–1980)*. Jakarta: LP3ES, 1990.

Mundell, R. "A Theory of Optimal Currency Areas." *American Economic Review* 51, No. 4 (1961): 657–665.

Muni, S. D. "India in SAARC: A Reluctant Policy-Maker." In *National Perspectives on the New Regionalism in the South*, edited by B. Hettne et al., 108–31. London: Macmillan Press Ltd., 2000.

Murphy, C. N., and R. Tooze, eds. *The New International Political Economy*. Boulder, CO: Lynne Rienner, 1991.

Myint, H. *Economic Theory and Underdeveloped Countries*. New York: Oxford University Press, 1971.

Myrdal, G. *Economic Theory and Underdevelopment Regions*. London: Duckworth, 1957.

Nairn, T. *The Break Up of Britain: Crisis and Neo-Nationalism*. London: New Left Books, 1977.

Narine, S. "ASEAN in the Aftermath: The Consequences of the East Asian Economic Crisis." *Global Governance* 8, No. 2 (2002): 179–94.

Narongchai, A. "The Political Economy of ASEAN Economic Co-operation." *TDRI Quarterly Review* 7, No. 3 (1992): 3–11.

The Nation. "Aceh Crisis: Government Agrees to Search for GAM Leaders," May 27, 2003. http://www.nationmultimedia.com/ (accessed May 27, 2003).

National Development Information Service. *Indonesia 1967–1977: Decade of Development*. Jakarta: NDIS, 1977.

National Intelligence Council. "Growing Global Migration and Its Implications for the United States." 2001. http://www.cia.gov/ (accessed July 11, 2002).

Nazir, M. *Metode Penelitian (Research Method)*. Jakarta, Indonesia: Ghalia, 1999.

Nishikawa, J. *ASEAN and The United Nations System*. Regional Study No. 9. New York: United Nations Institute for Training and Research, 1983.

Nugroho. *Indonesia: Facts and Figures*. Jakarta: Central Bureau of Statistics/Badan Pusat Statistik, 1967.

Nye, J. S. *International Regionalism: Readings*. Boston: Little Brown, 1968.

———. "Patterns and Catalysts in Regional Integration." *International Organization* 19 (Autumn 1965): 870–884.

Odén, B. "The Southern Africa Region and the Regional Hegemon." In *National Perspectives on the New Regionalism in the South*, edited by B. Hettne et al., 242–64. London: Macmillan Press Ltd., 2000.

———. "New Regionalism in Southern Africa: Part of or Alternative to the Globalization of the World Economy?" In *Globalism and the New Regionalism*, edited by B. Hettne et al., 155–80. London: Macmillan Press Ltd, 1999.

Ohlin, B. G. *Interregional and International Trade*. Cambridge, MA: Harvard University Press, 1933.

Ohmae, K. *The End of the Nation-State: The Rise of Regional Economies*. New York: The Free Press, 1995.

———. *The Borderless World*. New York: Fontana, 1990.

Öjendal, J. "Southeast Asia at a Constant Crossroads: An Ambiguous 'New Region'." In *Regionalization in A globalizing World: A Comparative Perspective on Forms, Actors, and Processes*, edited by M. Schulz et al., 147–72. London: Zed Books, 2001.

Okita, S. "Regionalism and the Asia Pacific Development Outlook." In *The Future of the Pacific Rim: Scenarios For Regional Co-operation*, edited by B. K. Bundy, S. D. Burns, and K. V. Weichel, 71–76. Westport, CT: Praeger, 1994.

Oomen, T. K. *Citizenship, Nationality, and Ethnicity: Reconciling Competing Identity*. Cambridge: Polity Press, 1997.

Organization for Economic Co-operation and Development. *The Cost of Reducing CO_2*

Emissions: Evidence from Green. Paper of the Working Party No. 1 of the Economic Policy Committee, Paris: OECD, 1992.

Oxley, A. *The Challenges of Free Trade.* Hertfordshire: Harvester Wheatsheaf, 1990.

Paaw, D. "Economic Progress in Southeast Asia." In *Man, State, and Society in Contemporary Southeast Asia*, edited by R. O. Tilman, 556–84. London: Pall Mall Press, 1969.

Pacific Asia Travel Association. "The Rise of Sub-Regional Tourism—Bloc by Bloc." *PATA Newsletter*, September 3, 1999. http://www.hotelonline.com (accessed February 5, 2001).

Padoan, P. C. "Regional Agreements as Clubs: The European Case." In *The Political Economy of Regionalism*, edited by E. D. Mansfield and H.V. Milner, 107–33. New York: Columbia University Press, 1997.

Palmer, I. *The Indonesian Economy Since 1965: A Case Study of Political Economy.* London: Frank Cass and Company Limited, 1978.

Palmer, N. D. *The New Regionalism in Asia and the Pacific.* Lexington: Lexington Books, 1991.

Panagariya, A., and R. Duttagupta. "The "Gains" From Preferential Trade Liberalization in the CGE Models: Where Do They Come From?" In *Regionalism and Globalization: Theory and Practice*, edited by S. Lahiri, 39–60. London: Routledge, 2001.

Pangestu, M., H. Soesastro, and M. Ahmad "A New Look at Intra-ASEAN Economic Co-operation." *ASEAN Economic Bulletin* 8, No. 3 (March 1992): 344–52.

Panglaykim, J. *Indonesia's Economic and Business Relations with ASEAN and Japan.* Jakarta: CSIS, 1977.

Parameswaran, P. "ASEAN to Adopt Three-Pronged Charter to Speed Up Integration." *Agence France-Presse*, October 2, 2003. http://quickstart.clari.net/ (accessed October 2, 2003).

Parks, J., and H. Elcock. "Why Do Regions Demand Autonomy?" *Regional and Federal Studies* 10, No. 3 (2002): 87–106.

Parsonage, J. "Trans-state Developments in Southeast Asia: Subregional Growth Zones." In *The Political Economy of Southeast Asia: An Introduction*, edited by G. Rodan et al., 248–83. Oxford: Oxford University Press, 1997.

Pauker, G. J. "The Soviet Challenge in Indonesia." *Foreign Affairs* 40, No. 4 (July 1962): 612–26.

Payne, A. "The New Political Economy of Area Studies." *Millennium: Journal of International Studies* 27, No. 2 (1998): 253–73.

Pederson, T. *European Union and the EFTA Countries: Enlargement and Integration.* New York: St. Martin's Press, 1994.

Peng, D. "Invisible Linkages: A Regional Perspective of East Asian Political Economy." *International Studies Quarterly* 46, No. 3 (2002): 423–47.

Pernia, E. M., and P. F. Quising. *Is Economic Openness Good for Regional Development and Poverty Reduction? The Philippines*, ERD Policy Brief Series No. 10. Manila: Economic and Research Department, ADB, 2002.

Perroni, C., and J. Whalley. *The New Regionalism: Trade Liberalization or Insurance?* National Bureau of Economic Research Working Paper No. 4626, Cambridge, MA.: NBER, 1994.

Petri, P. A. "AFTA and the Global Track." *ASEAN Economic Bulletin* 14, No. 2 (1997): 190–200.

Pettman, R. "Globalism and Regionalism: The Cost of Dichotomy." In *Globalism and the New Regionalism*, edited by B. Hettne et al., 181–202. London: Macmillan Press Ltd., 1999.

Phillips, N. "Governance after Financial Crisis: South American Perspectives on the Re-formulation of Regionalism." In *New Regionalism in the Global Political Economy*, edited by S. Breslin et al., 66–80. London: Routledge, 2002.

———. "The Future of the Political Economy of Latin America." In *Political Economy and the Changing Global Order*, edited by R. Stubbs and G. R. D. Underhill, 284–93. Ontario: Oxford University Press, 2000.

Pickel, A. "Explaining, and Explaining with, Economic Nationalism." *Nations and Nationalism* 9, No. 1 (2003): 105–27.

Pincus, J. *Pressure Groups and Politics in Antebellum Tariffs*. New York: Columbia University Press, 1977.

Plummer, M. G. "ASEAN and the Theory of Regional Economic Integration." *ASEAN Economic Bulletin* 14, No. 2 (1997): 202–14.

Pomfret, R. (1998), "Enlargement to Include Formerly Centrally Planned Economies: ASEAN and the EU Compared." Paper presented at the Third Conference East Asia-EU Business, ASEAN-EU Economic Relations, in Como, Italy, April 23–25, 1998.

Porter, T. "The North American Free Trade Agreement." In *Political Economy and the Changing Global Order*, edited by R. Stubbs and G. R. D. Underhill, 245–53. Ontario: Oxford University Press, 2000.

Prebisch, R. *Towards a New Trade Policy for Development*. Report by the Secretariat-General of the United States Conference on Trade and Development, E/CONF 4613, New York: United States Conference on Trade and Development, 1964.

———. "Economic Development of Latin America and its Principal Problems." *Economic Bulletin of Latin America* 7, No. 1 (1962): 223–7.

———. *Economic Survey of Latin America*. United Nations Document No. E/CN.12/164/Rev.1, New York, NY: UN, 1951.

Priyono, B. H. "Konsumerisme (Consumerism)." *Kompas*. March 8, 2003. www.kompas.com/ (accessed September 17, 2003).

Putnam, R. D. "Diplomacy and Domestic Politics: the Logic of Two-Level Games." *International Organization* 43, No. 2 (1988): 427–459.

Ramcharan, R. "ASEAN and Non-Interference: A Principle Maintained." *Contemporary Southeast Asia* 22, No. 1 (2000): 60–87.

Rao, B. *ASEAN Economic Co-operation and ASEAN Free Trade Area: A Primer*. Singapore: Institute for Policy Research, 1996.

Ravenhill, J. *APEC and the Construction of Pacific Rim Regionalism*. Cambridge: Cambridge University Press, 2001.

———. "APEC Adrift: Implications for Economic Regionalism in Asia and the Pacific." *The Pacific Review* 13, No. 22 (2000): 319–33.

———. "Economic Cooperation in Southeast Asia: Changing Incentives." *Asian Survey* 35, No. 9 (1995): 850–66.

Reich, S. "Policy Domain or Public Domain at a Time of Globalization." In *The Market or the Public Domain?: Global Governance and the Asymmetry of Power*, edited by D. Drache, 113–28. London: Routledge, 2001.

Reinhardt, J. M. *Foreign Policy and National Integration: The Case of Indonesia*. Yale University Southeast Asian Studies Monograph Series No. 17. New Haven, CT: Yale University, 1971.

Renan, E. "Qu'est qu'une Nation? (What Is a Nation?)." In *The Dynamics of Nationalism*, edited by L. L. Snyder, 26–29 (1882). London: D. Van Nostrand Company, Ltd, 1964.

Reuters. "EU Drops Arms Embargo on Indonesia." January 17, 2000. http://www.reuters.com (accessed April 22, 2001).

Rigg, J. *Southeast Asia: The Human Landscape of Modernization and Development.* London: Routledge, 1997

Risse-Kappen, T. ed. *Bringing Transnational Relations Back In: Non-State Actors, Domestic Structure, and International Institutions.* Cambridge: Cambridge University Press, 1995.

Rittberger, V., ed. *Regime Theory and International Relations.* Oxford: Clarendon Press, 1993.

Roberts, J. "Yudhoyono's Cabinet Mirrors Conflicts within Indonesia's Ruling Elite." *World Socialits Website.* 2004. http://wsws.org (accessed September 26, 2005).

Robison, R. "Politics and Markets in Indonesia's Post-Oil Era." In *The Political Economy of South-East Asia: An Introduction,* edited by G. Rodan et al., 29–63. Melbourne: Oxford University Press, 1997.

———. "The Politics of 'Asian Values.'" *The Pacific Review* 9, No. 3 (1996): 309–27.

———. *Power and Economy in Suharto's New Order.* Manila: Journal of Contemporary Asian Press, 1990.

———. *Indonesia: The Rise of Capital.* Sidney, Wellington, London, and Winchester, MA: Allen & Unwin Pty., Ltd., Inc, 1986.

Robson, P. "The New Regionalism and Developing Countries." *Journal of Common Market Studies* 31, No. 3 (1993): 329–48.

———. *The Economics of International Integration.* London: Allen and Unwin Ltd, 1987.

Roessingh, M. A. *Ethnonationalism and Political System in Europe.* Amsterdam: Amsterdam Press, 1996.

Rosenau, J. N. *National Interest,* in "International Encyclopedia of Social Sciences." New York: Crowell Collier and Macmillan, 1968.

Royal Institute of International Affairs *Nationalism: A Report.* London: Oxford University Press, 1939.

Ruggie, J. G. *Constructing the World Polity: Essays on International Institutionalization.* New York: Routledge, 1998.

———. *The Antinomies of Interdependence: National Welfare and International Division of Labor.* New York: Columbia University Press, 1983.

Ruland, J. "ASEAN and the Asian Crisis: Theoretical Debate and Practical Consequences for Southeast Asian Regionalism." *The Pacific Review* 13, No. 3 (2000): 421–51.

Rupert, M. *Ideologies of Globalization: Contending Visions of a New World Order.* London: Routledge and RIPE Studies in Global Political Economy, 2000.

Ryan, M. P. *Playing by the Rules: American Trade Power and Diplomacy in the Pacific.* Washington, DC: Georgetown University Press, 1995.

Sadli, M. "Economic Overview." In *Governance in Indonesia: Challenges Facing the Megawati Presidency,* edited by H. Soesastro et al., 182–95. Singapore: ISEAS, 2003.

Sally, R. *States and Firms: Multinational Enterprises in Institutional Competition,* London: Routledge, 1995.

Sang-Ho Chung "A Move toward an East Asian Community and Its Future Outlook." *The Journal of East Asian Affairs* 15, No. 2 (2001): 396–420.

Sasono, A. "Memperkokoh Rakyat Menuju Indonesia Baru (Strengthening the People towards a New Indonesia)," *Sintesis,* No. 29, Year 6, 1999.

Saxonhouse, G. R. "Regionalism and U.S. Trade Policy in Asia." In *The Economics of Preferential Trade Agreements,* edited by J. Bhagwati and A. Panagariya, 108–35. Washington, DC: 1996.

Schiff, M., and A. L. Winters. *Regional Integration as Diplomacy.* World Bank Policy

Research Working Paper, No. 1801, Washington, DC: Development Research Group, World Bank, 1997.

Schirm, S. A. *Globalization and the New Regionalism: Global Markets, Domestic Politics and Regional Co-operation.* Cambridge: Polity Press, 2002.

Schulz, M, F. Söderbaum and J. Öjendal. "Introduction: A Framework for Understanding Regionalization." In *Regionalization in a Globalizing World: A Comparative Perspective on Forms, Actors and Processes,* edited by Schulz et al., 1–21. London: Zed Books, 2001a.

———. "Conclusion." In *Regionalization in a Globalizing World: A Comparative Perspective on Forms, Actors and Processes,* edited by Schulz *et al.*, 250–66. London: Zed Books, 2001b.

———. "Key Issues in the New Regionalism: Comparisons from Asia, Africa and the Middle East." In *Comparing Regionalism: Implications for Global Development,* edited by B. Hettne *et al.*, 234–76. London: Macmillan Ltd, 2001c.

Seers, D. *The Political Economy of Nationalism.* Oxford: Oxford University Press, 1983.

Severino, R. "The Impact of the Economic Crisis on ASEAN a Blessing in Disguise?" Keynote address at the opening of the Seventh ASEAN Editors' Conference, Wisma Antara, Jakarta, April 12, 1999.

Seymond, P. "New Indonesian President Pledges to Encourage Foreign Investment and Private Enterprise." *World Socialist Website.* 1999. http://www.wsws.org/ (accessed November 11, 2001).

Shari, M. "Another Road into Malaysia's Car Market." *Business Week,* February 7, 2003. http://www.businessweek.com/ (accessed February 17, 2004).

Shaw, T. M. "Beyond Any New World Order: The South in the 21st Century." *Third World Quarterly* 15, No. 1 (1994): 139–46.

Shihab, A. "The Indonesian Foreign Policy Outlook." Keynote addressed at the Conference in Observance of the Indonesian National Press Day, the Silver Jubilee of the Confederation of ASEAN Journalists and the 54th Anniversary of IPWI. Jakarta: Indonesian Ministry of Foreign Affairs, February 17, 2000.

Shulman, S. "Nationalist Sources of International Economic Integration." *International Studies Quarterly* 44, No. 3 (2000): 365–90.

Silver, C., I. J. Azis, and L. Schroeder. "Intergovernmental Transfers and Decentralization in Indonesia." *Bulletin of Indonesian Economic Studies* 37, No. 3 (2001): 345–62.

Singapore Ministry of Foreign Affairs. *Transcripts of Remarks by PM Goh Chok Tong to the Media after the 3rd ASEAN Informal Summit.* 1999. http://app9.internet.gov.sg/ (accessed March 12, 2001).

Singer, H. W. "U.S. Foreign Investment in Underdeveloped Areas: The Distribution of Gains between Investing and Borrowing Countries." *American Economic Review* 40, No. 2 (1950): 473–85.

Smith, A. *The Wealth of Nations: An Enquiry Into the Nature and Causes.* London: W. Strahan and T. Cadell, 1776.

Smith, A., R. L. Heilbroner and L. J. Malone, eds. *The Essential Adam Smith.* Oxford: Oxford University Press, 1986.

Smith, A. D. "Theories of Nationalism: Alternative Models of Nation Formation," pp. 1–20, in *Asian Nationalism,* edited by M. Leifer. London: Routledge, 2000.

———. *Nations and Nationalism in a Global Era.* Cambridge: Polity Press, 1995.

Smith, A. L. "Introduction: Abdurrahman Wahid's Economic Agenda: The Views of Leading Decision-Makers and Commentators." In *Gus Dur and the Indonesian Economy,* edited by A. L. Smith, 1–22. Singapore: ISEAS, 2001a.

————. "Indonesia: Transforming the Leviathan." In *Government and Politics in Southeast Asia*, edited by J. Funston, 74–119. Singapore and London: ISEAS and Zed Books Ltd, 2001b.

————. *Strategic Centrality: Indonesia's Changing Role in ASEAN*. Singapore: ISEAS, 2000a.

————. "Indonesia's Foreign Policy under Abdurrahman Wahid: Radical or Status Quo State?" *Contemporary Southeast Asia* 22, No. 3 (2000b): 498–526.

Smith, J. "Global News Stands: The Heartless EU." *Foreign Policy*, 1 March, 2003.

Smith, S. "New Approaches to International Theory." In *The Globalization of World Politics: An Introduction to International Relations*, edited by J. Baylis and S. Smith, 165–90. Oxford: Oxford University Press, 1997.

Snyder, L. L. *The Dynamics of Nationalism*, London: D. Van Nostrand Company, Ltd, 1964.

Soesastro, H. "ASEAN Economic Community: Concept, Costs, and Benefits." In *Roadmap to an ASEAN Economic Community*, edited by D. Hew, 13–30. Singapore: ISEAS, 2005.

————. *Otonomi Daerah dan Free Internal Trade (Regional Autonomy and Free Internal Trade)*. Jakarta: CSIS, 2001.

————. "ASEAN 2030: The Long View." In *A New ASEAN in a New Millennium*, edited by S.S.C. Tay et al., 187–227. Jakarta and Singapore: CSIS and ISEAS, 2000.

————. "Open Regionalism." In *Europe and the Asia-Pacific*, edited by J. Maull et al., 84–96. London: Routledge, 1998.

Sopiee, N. "ASEAN and Regional Security." In *Regional Security in the Third World: Case Studies from Southeast Asia and the Middle East*, edited by M. Ayoob. London: Croom Helm, 1986.

Sraffa, P., and M. H. Dobb. *The Works and Correspondence of David Ricardo Volume I*. Cambridge: University Press for Royal Economic Society, 1951.

Srinivasan, T. N., J. Whalley, and I. Wooton. "Measuring the Effects of Regionalism on Trade and Welfare." In *Regional Integration and the Global Trading System*, edited by K. Anderson and R. Blackhurst, 52–79. Hertfordshire, UK: Harvester Wheatsheaf, 1993.

Strange, S. *The Retreat of the State: The Diffusion of Power in the World Economy*, Cambridge: Cambridge University Press, 1996.

————. *States and Markets*. London: Pinter Publisher, 1994.

Stubbs, R. "Regionalization and Globalization." In *Political Economy and the Changing Global Order*, edited by R. Stubbs and G. R. D. Underhill, 231–34. Oxford: Oxford University Press, 2000a.

————. "Globalization and State Policies." In *Political Economy and the Changing Global Order*, edited by R. Stubbs and G. R. D. Underhill, 297–99. Oxford: Oxford University Press, 2000b.

————. "Signing on to Liberalization: AFTA and the Politics of Regional Economic Cooperation." *Pacific Review* 13, No. 2 (2000c): 297–318.

Sturzo, D. L. *Nationalism and Internationalism*. New York: Roy Publishers, 1946.

Suh, S. "Talking Fast and Loose: The President Often Says Startling Things." *Asiaweek*, February 26, 1999. http://www.asiaweek.com/ (accessed September 17, 2001).

Suharto. *Government Statement Before the Gotong Royong House of Representatives on 16 August 1966*. Jakarta: Department of Information, 1966.

Sulistyowati, R. "President Asks BKPM to Complete Revisions to Investment Laws." *Tempo*, February 27, 2003. http://www.tempo.co.id/ (accessed March 2, 2003).

Sunderlin, W. D., A. Angelse, D. P. Resosudarmo, A. Dermawan, and E. Rianto. "Economic Crisis, Small Farmer Well-Being, and Forest Cover Change in Indonesia." *World Development* 29, No. 5 (2001): 767–82.

Sundrum, R. M. "Indonesia's Rapid Economic Growth: 1968–1981." *Bulletin of Indonesian Economic Studies* 22, No. 3 (1986): 40–69.

Support for Decentralization Measures. "Implementing Obligatory Functions and Minimal Service Standards—The Next Steps." *Decentralization   News*, Issue No. 32, August 2, 2002. http://www.gtzfdm.or.id/ (accessed February 5, 2003).

Suriyamongkol, M. L. *Politics of ASEAN Economic Co-operation: The Case of ASEAN Industrial Projects.* Oxford: Oxford University Press, 1988.

Suryadinata, L. *Elections and Politics in Indonesia.* Singapore: ISEAS, 2002.

Sutter, J. O. "Indonesianisasi: A Historical Survey of the Role of Politics in the Institutions of a Changing Economy from the Second World War to the Eve of General Elections," 1940–1955. Ph.D. dissertation, Ithaca, New York, Cornell University, 1959.

Tadjoeddin, M. Z., W. I. Suharyo, and S. Mishra "Regional Disparity and Vertical Conflict in Indonesia." *Journal of the Asia Pacific Economy* 6, No. 2 (2001): 283–304.

Takeshi, T. "The ASEAN-10 and Regional Political Relations." In *Road to ASEAN-10: Japanese Perspective of Economic Integration,* edited by S. Sueo, et al., 16–36. Tokyo: Japan Centre for International Exchange, 1999.

Tan, F. "Singapore Regrets Breakdown of Peace Pact for Aceh." *Channel News Asia,* May 22, 2003. http://www.channelnewsasia.com/ (accessed May 22, 2003).

Tarling, N. *Nations and States in Southeast Asia.* Cambridge: The Press Syndicate of the University of Cambridge, 1998.

Tavlas, G. S. "The 'New' Theory of Optimum Currency Areas." *The World Economy* 5 (1993): 663–85.

Tay, S. S. C, J. Estanislao, and H. Soeasastro, eds. *A New ASEAN in a New Millennium.* Jakarta and Singapore: CSIS and ISEAS, 2000.

Teo, P., T. C. Chang, and K. C. Ho. *Interconnected Worlds: Tourism in Southeast Asia.* Oxford: Elsevier Science Ltd, 2001.

Thailand Ministry of Foreign Affairs. "Major Foreign Policy Statement." 2001. http://www.mfa.go.th/ (accessed July 24, 2003).

Thee Kian Wie. "Reflections of the New Order "Miracle."" In *Indonesia Today: Challenges of History,* edited by G. Lloyd and S. Smith, 163–80. Singapore: ISEAS, 2001.

Thoha, M. "Pengembangan Ekonomi Kerakyatan: Kekuatan, Kelemahan, Tantangan dan Peluang (The Development of the People"s Economy: The Strength, The Weakness, Challenges and Opportunities)." In *Indonesia Menapak Abad 21 (Indonesia Stepping into the 21st Century),* edited by IPSK and LIPI, 147–71. Jakarta: Millennium Publishers, 2000.

Thomas, K. D., and J. Panglaykim. *Indonesia—The Effect of Past Policies and President Suharto's Plans for the Future.* Sidney: Committee for Economic Development of Australia (CEDA), 1973.

Thompson, K., and R. J. Myers, eds. *Truth and Tragedy: A Tribute to Hans J. Morgenthau.* New Brunswick and London: Transaction Books, 1984.

Time Asia. "Shihab: "Economic" Foreign Policy." 8 November 8, 1999, http://www.time.com/ (accessed January 14, 2001).

Tinbergen, J. *International Economic Integration.* Amsterdam: Elsevier, 1954.

Tivey, L. "States, Nations, and Economies." In *The Nation-State: The Formation of Modern Politics,* edited by L. Tivey, 59–81. Oxford: Martin Robertson, 1981.

Tongzon, J. L. *The Economies of Southeast Asia*. Cheltenham and Northampton, MA: Edward Elgar Publishing Ltd., Inc, 2002.

Tussie, D. *The Less Developed Countries and the World Trading System: A Challenge to the GATT*. London: Francis Pinter, 1987.

Ulack, R., and T. R. Leinbach. "An Opening Review." In *Southeast Asia: Diversity and Development*, edited by T. R. Leinbach et. al. New Jersey: Prentice Hall, Inc., 2000.

Underhill, G. R. D. "Introduction: Conceptualizing the Changing Global Order." In *Political Economy and the Changing Global Order*, R. Stubbs and G. R. D. Underhill, 3–24. Ontario: Oxford University Press, 2000.

———. "Conceptualizing the Changing Global Order." In *Political Economy and the Changing Global Order*, edited by R. Stubbs and G. R. D. Underhill, 17–44. London: Macmillan Press Ltd., 1994.

U.S. Embassy in Jakarta. "Indonesia: Investment Climate Statement." 2000. http://www.usembassyjakarta.org (accessed January 21, 2001).

Vamvakidis, A. "Regional Integration and Economic Growth." *World Bank Economic Review* 12, No. 2 (1998): 251–70.

van Aarle, B. "The Impact of the Single Market on Trade and Foreign Direct Investment in the European Union." *Journal of World Trade* (1996): 121–38.

Van Ruigrok, W., and R. Van Tulder. *The Logic of International Restructuring*, London: Routledge, 1995.

Vatikiotis, M. "People First in Charter of ASEAN." *The Korea Herald*, October 18, 2005. http://www.koreaherald.co.kr/ (accessed September 17, 2006).

———. *Indonesian Politics Under Suharto: Order, Development and Pressure for Change*. London: Routledge, 1994.

Viner, J. *The Custom Union Issues*. New York: Carnegie Endowment For International Peace, 1950.

Waever, O. *Insecurity and Identity Unlimited*. Working Papers No. 14. Copenhagen: Center for Peace and Conflict Research, 1994.

Wall, G. "Conclusion: Southeast Asian Tourism Connections—Status, Challenges and Opportunities." In *Interconnected Worlds: Tourism in Southeast Asia,* edited by P. Teo et al., 312–24. Oxford: Elsevier Science Ltd., 2001.

Wallerstein, I. *Unthinking Social Sciences: The Limits of Nineteenth-Century Paradigms*. Cambridge, MA: Polity Press, 1991.

———. *The Capitalist World Economy*. Cambridge: Cambridge University Press, 1979.

———. "The Rise and Future Demise of the World Capitalist System: Concept for Comparative Analysis." *Comparative Studies in Society and History* 16 (1974): 387–415.

Waltz, K. N. "The Emerging Structure of International Politics." *International Security* 18, No. 2 (1993): 44–79.

———. *The Theory of International Relations*. Reading, MA: Addison-Wesley, 1979.

Wanandi, J. "ASEAN's Past and the Challenges Ahead: Aspects of Politics and Security." In *A New ASEAN in a New Millennium*, edited by S. C. Tay et. al., 25–34. Jakarta and Singapore: CSIS and ISEAS, 2000.

Waslin, M. "Survey of Recent Developments." *Bulletin of Indonesian Economic Studies* 39, No. 1 (2003): 5–26.

Webb, Sara. "ASEAN Ministers to Discuss Boosting Trade, Investment (Update 1)." *Bloomberg*, 27 September 27, 2005. http://www.bloomberg.com (accessed February 19, 2006).

Webber, D. "Two Funerals and a Wedding? The Ups and Downs of Regionalism in East Asia and Asia-Pacific after the Crisis." *The Pacific Review* 14, No. 3 (2001): 339–72.

Weinstein, F. B. *Indonesia's Foreign Policy and the Dilemma of Dependence: Form Sukarno to Soeharto.* Ithaca, NY: Cornell University Press, 1976.

————. "The Uses of Foreign Policy in Indonesia: An Approach to the Analysis of Foreign Policy in the Less Developed Countries." *World Politics* 24, No. 3 (April 1972): 356–81.

Wendt, A. "Constructing International Politics." *International Security* 20, No. 1 (1995): 71–81.

————. "Collective Identity Formation and the International State." *American Political Science Review* 88, No. 2 (1994): 384–96.

————. "Anarchy is What States Make of It: The Social Construction of Power Politics." *International Organization* 46, No. 2 (1992): 391–425.

————. "The Agent-Structure Problem in International Relations Theory." *International Organization* 41, No. 3 (1987): 335–50.

Wescott, R. W. "Types of Cultural Diffusion." In *Across Before Columbus: Evidence of Transoceanic Contacts With the Americas Prior to 1492,* edited by D. Y. Gilmore and S. McElroy. Edgecomb, Maine: The New England Antiquities Research Association (NEARA) Publications, 1998.

Widihandojo, D. S. *The Vulnerable Citizens: Indonesian Chinese and their Identity.* Hong Kong: Documentation for Action Groups in Asia, 2000.

Winters, L. A. "Regionalism for Developing Countries: Assessing the Costs and Benefits." In *Regionalism and Globalization: Theory and Practice,* edited by S. Lahiri, 113–43. London: Routledge, 2001.

————. "Regionalism versus Multilateralism." In *Market Integration, Regionalism, and the Global Economy,* edited by R. E. Baldwin et. al., 7–49. Cambridge, MA: The Press Syndicate of the University of Cambridge and Centre for Economy Policy Research (CEPR), 1999.

Wong, J. "The ASEAN Model of Regional Co-operation." In *Lessons in Development: A Comparative Study of Asia and Latin America,* edited by S. Naya et al., 121–41. San Fransisco: International Center for Economic Growth, 1989.

World Bank. "Overview of World Bank Collaboration with Civil Society," *World Bank.* http://wbln0018.worldbank.org/ (accessed June 13, 2003).

————. *World Development Indicators 2001.* Washington, DC: World Bank, 2001.

————. "Involving Nongovernmental Organizations in Bank-Supported Activities, Operational Directive 14.70." *World Bank.* February, 2000. http://wbln0018.worbank.org/ (accessed July 18, 2002).

————. *The East Asian Miracle—Economic Growth and Public Policy.* New York: Oxford University Press, 1993a.

————. *Indonesia: Sustaining Development.* Jakarta: Country Department III, East Asia and Pacific Regional Office, 25 May, 1993b.

World Trade Organization. "Regionalism: Facts and Figures." 2002. http://www.wto.org/ (accessed May 27, 2003).

————. *Mapping of Regional Trade Agreements: Background Note by the Secretariat.* Geneva: WTO, 2000.

————. "Trading into the Future: The Introduction to the WTO." http://www.wto.org (accessed October 7, 2002).

Yamin, M. *Naskah Persiapan Undang-Undang Dasar 1945 (Manuscript for the Preparation of Basic Constitution of 1945).* Jakarta: Jajasan Prapantja, 1959.

Yergin, D., and J. Stanislaw. *The Commanding Heights: The Battle between Government and the Marketplace that is Remaking the World.* New York: Simon and Schuster, 1998.

Yeung, H. W. C. "The Internationalization of Ethnic Chinese Business Firms from Southeast Asia: Strategies, Processes and Competitive Advantage." *International Journal of Urban and Regional Research* 23, No. 1 (1999): 88–102.

Yew, L. K. *From the Third World to First. The Singapore Story: 1965–2000.* Singapore: Singapore Press Holding/Times Editions, 2000.

Young, O. R. *Global Governance: Drawing Insights from the Environmental Experience.* Occasional Paper, New Hampshire: The Dickey Center, 1995.

Yudhoyono, S. B. "Keynote Address by H. E. DR. Susilo Bambang Yudhoyono, President of the Republic of Indonesia, at a Dinner Tendered by USINDO, Washington DC, 25 May 2005." *The United States-Indonesia Society (USINDO).* 2005a. http://www.usindo.org (accessed September 26, 2005).

———. "On Building the ASEAN Community: The Democratic Aspect." Lecture by H. E. Dr. Susilo Bambang Yudhoyono, President of Indonesia, on the occasion of the 38th anniversary of ASEAN, Jakarta, August 8, 2005b.

Zacher, M. W., and R. A. Matthew. "Liberal International Theory: Common Threads, Divergent Strands." In *Controversies in international Relations Theory: Realism and the Neo-Liberal Challenge*, edited by C. W. Kegley Jr., 117–39. New York: St. Martin Press, 1995.

Zernatto, G. "Nation: The History of a Word." *Review of Politics* 6 (1944): 351–66.

Index

About the Author

Alexander C. Chandra is the Senior Policy Advisor on ASEAN at Oxfam International (OI) (the views expressed in this book do not necessarily represent the views of Oxfam International). He holds a Ph.D. in Southeast Asian Studies from the University of Hull, UK. His primary research interests are in the area of political-economy of Southeast and East Asian regionalism, democratic governance, civil society, and international trade issues. Prior to joining Oxfam International, Chandra was active in Southeast Asian civil society advocacy on ASEAN and "alternative regionalism" in the regional network of Solidarity for Asian People's Advocacies (SAPA) Working Group (WG) on ASEAN, and was serving as one of the SAPA-WG on ASEAN Liaison Persons to ASEAN (Economic and Socio-Cultural Affairs) (2007–2008). He was also a research consultant for some international, Southeast Asian regional, and national non-governmental organization (NGOs), including the Institute for Global Justice, Human Rights Working Group (Indonesia), Southeast Asia Committee for Advocacy (SEACA) (Southeast Asia), Oxfam Hong Kong, and Oxfam America. He has published several single-authored and edited books (*Indonesia and Bilateral Free Trade Agreements* [2005]; *Indonesia and the WTO's Non-Agricultural Market Access* [2005]; *The Economic Impacts of ASEAN-China Free Trade Agreement on the Indonesian Economy* [2006, edited with Daniel Pambudi]; *Checkmate! The US-Indonesia Bilateral Free Trade Agreement* [2007, edited with Herjuno Ndaru]; and *ASEAN @ 40: Civil Society Reflections of Southeast Asian Regionalism* [2008, edited with Jenina Joy Chavez]) and articles in edited books, academic journals, media, monographs (*Dilemmas of Competition and Community-Building: Developing Civil Society Response to Regional Trade and Economic Integration* [2008, with Jenina Joy Chavez]), etc., on ASEAN/East Asian regionalism and international trade issues.

DATE DUE

GAYLORD

PRINTED IN U.S.A.